RELAXcalm

Teaching Teens How to Manage Stress Using Relaxation and Guided Imagery

Jeffrey S. Allen, M.Ed.
and Roger J. Klein, Psy.D.

Publisher's Cataloging-in-Publication (Provided by Quality Books, Inc.)

Allen, Jeffrey S.
    Relax.calm : teaching teens how to manage stress using relaxation and guided imagery / Jeffrey S. Allen and Roger J. Klein.
    p. cm.
    Includes index.
    ISBN-13: 978-0-9636027-9-4
    ISBN-10: 0-9636027-9-9

1. Stress in adolescence — Study and teaching (Secondary) 2. Stress management for teenagers — Study and teaching (Secondary) 3. Relaxation — Study and teaching (Secondary) I. Klein, Roger J. II. Title. III. Title: Relax dot calm.

BF724.3.S86A45 2011   155.5'18
                           QBI11-600040

Illustrated by Matthew Holden & Joel Richter
Cover & book interior design by Joel Richter

Published by Inner Coaching
1108 Western Avenue
Watertown, Wisconsin 53094
(920) 262-0439

The material in this book is provided for educational and informational purposes only, and is not intended to be a substitute for medical advice. A physician or appropriate health care professional should always be consulted for any health or medical condition. The author and publisher disclaim any liability or loss, personal or otherwise, resulting from the use by readers of the methods set forth in this book.

Printed in the United States of America on acid-free paper

First Edition

DEDICATION

We would like to dedicate this book to all of the helping professionals and parents who help young people negotiate the difficult years of adolescence. As the world becomes more complicated, it is comforting to know there are many people willing to do all they can to help teens. We are especially grateful to all of you who are taking the time to read this book and are thankful that you care enough to learn about the power of using relaxation, imagery and positive self-talk in your tool kit of change.

CONTENTS

CONTENTS

CONTENTS

FOREWORD

Over the last 30 years, I have worked with hundreds of children and adolescents, witnessing the negative impact of excessive stress on these young people. I first became familiar with Roger Klein and Jeff Allen's work when I began using their book, *Ready, Set, R.E.L.A.X.*, with individuals and groups. Since then, my relationship with the authors has grown, much to the benefit of my clients. Using Roger and Jeff's program, I have seen a noticeable change in my clients' energy levels, feelings of self worth and coping skills.

While *Ready, Set, R.E.L.A.X.* focuses on younger children, *RELAX. calm* focuses on adolescents and can be used with adults as well. Teenagers can be a difficult population with whom to work. They frequently feel that they lack any real power and turn on themselves to feel like they are in control. The stresses they experience are real and need to be resolved in a positive and uplifting manner. It is here where Roger and Jeff's work shines.

Through the use of engaging scripts, guided imagery, music, relaxation techniques, positive self-talk and more, they give a sense of control and power back to the adolescent. For example, the "Railroad Crossing" script, a personal favorite of mine, offers teens healthy and soothing ways to let go of things that are beyond their control. "Railroad Crossing" teaches teens how to effectively create a positive sensory-based alternative experience. Through the "tool box" of relaxation strategies, teens learn that they are in charge of their thoughts and that they can effectively problem-solve. Through the self-soothing strategies found throughout the scripts in this book, young people discover that they are their own agents of change, making the decisions and choices that ultimately affect who they are and what they will achieve in their life time.

I watched a TV special recently about some of the natural disasters that have occurred around the globe over this past decade.

As I was watching the replay of the coverage of a particularly devastating earthquake, I thought about some of the young people who experience "earthquakes" every day. Life changing events, like family economic challenges, parental discord, or the death of a loved one, throw teenagers off balance and present them with a sense of helplessness that can leave them feeling stressed and powerless.

As I continued to watch the coverage, one of the reporters told a story of a field hospital that was taking care of the most critically injured and vulnerable citizens. Pregnant women, people with infection-ravaged bodies, and people missing limbs were being brought to the hospital where they learned that someone was willing to try and restore some balance to their over-turned lives.

We, too, are willing to help our young adults stand strong, even when they are on shaky ground. *RELAX.calm* provides helping professionals with the tools to teach adolescents self-calming techniques, give them critical components to restore balance to their lives, empower them to make healthy choices and help them develop the confidence in themselves to handle future problems.

There is an added unexpected benefit for the "helper" reading the RELAX scripts to teens. As I read the scripts aloud, I recognize it is not only the adolescent who attains new ways of viewing and experiencing ways to cope with unwanted stress. I, too, feel a calming transformation. I believe you will share this experience as well.

Deanne Ginns-Gruenberg, MA, LPC, RPT-S, BSN
www.selfesteemshop.com

Why Our Youth Need *RELAX.calm*

Abundant research documents that stress diminishes our capacity to listen, understand, comprehend and reorder information — all of which are essential processes for learning.

The fact is, we have been raising a generation of anxiety-ridden youth. In 2009, the fears of 1,033 children grades 2-12 were identified using the American Fear Survey Schedule for Children. The children's greatest fears were terrorist attacks, hurricanes and tornadoes, having to fight in a war, shootings, being kidnapped, being raped and being poor.

Technology has over-exposed children at far too young an age for them to cognitively manage all they hear and see about the above cited events. Media's impact on youth is well documented. More than 170 studies over 28 years demonstrate that media exposure increases the risk for stress and anxiety. Simply watching coverage of natural disasters significantly increased children's fears for months when local storms came their way.

The lives of young people have become so stressful that the American Psychiatric Association is considering a new diagnostic category listed as "Developmental Trauma Disorder." Documentation strongly supports that, even by age 12, children exposed to multiple stressors are frequently given multiple diagnoses simply because the criteria for one diagnosis can be considered the criteria for several diagnoses. Young people's exposure levels to life events traditionally not experienced until adulthood are so commonplace that youth are showing the symptoms of multiple anxiety disorders once attributed only to adults.

Because of technology, we now have very limited control to the amount and kinds of anxiety-producing situations to which young people are exposed. Most agree we now live in a far more volatile, ever changing and uncertain world, all of which is anxiety-producing — even for adults who cope well.

We must equip our youth with ways to better manage the many frightening events to which they are exposed through multiple media sources, as well as in their own communities. *RELAX.calm* is the perfect tool. It is one that is always immediately available, no matter the time or the situation, because it exists within us. It taps into the power we have to control our reactions to fearful and stressful situations through the use of our imagination, self-talk skills, and other internal resources taught by *RELAX.calm*.

Research has clearly documented, for example, that the imagination can alter both the physical and emotional reactions that are associated with stress and anxiety. Virtual imaging is being successfully used to help combat soldiers diminish the symptoms of Post Traumatic Stress Disorder (PTSD).

RELAX.calm provides a wonderful array of strength-based, resilience-building imagery exercises that bring calm and peace. More so, it teaches young people that when bad things are happening, they can change their focus, their view, their "internal dialogue," and get through it all a bit easier. This in turn builds confidence and resilience.

After 45 years of assisting young people who have been exposed to multiple life stress and trauma, the one healing tool I have found to be consistently helpful is using the kinds of sensory activities taught in *RELAX.calm*. These experiential techniques enable young people to view their situations in ways that help them find relief and feel safer and more empowered, despite having difficult challenges.

RELAX.calm ought to be made available to every young person (as well as adults) regardless of the frequency in which they are exposed to stressful situations. It is a wonderfully beneficial way to manage everyday common stressors, as well as those unanticipated or more severe stress inducing incidents we often cannot prevent. When words are not helping, *RELAX.calm* does.

Dr. William Steele, PsyD., MSW
Founder
National Institute of Trauma and Loss in Children
www.starrtraining.org

ACKNOWLEDGEMENTS

We would like to thank the many individuals who have provided their support and expertise in helping us bring *RELAX.calm* to you. We appreciate all of the positive comments the users of *Ready, Set, RELAX* have sent to us through the years. It is gratifying to know that so many children have been helped by the thousands of professionals and parents who use this program. Many of these same individuals have asked for a similar program specifically targeting adolescents. These requests helped motivate us to undertake the current project.

We appreciate the support and encouragement from our families, especially our wives, Nancy Klein and Vicki Allen. Thank you to Kendra Klein for her suggestions and excellent editing of the scripts and Dr. Andrew Pojman for his input. We are also grateful to Julie Larrivee for the time and expertise she brought to proof reading the manuscript. A special thanks to Sheila Larken, MA, LPC, for her contribution to the section on music and teens. Her skill and background in music therapy was invaluable and provides the reader with a better understanding of how to incorporate music as an intervention tool. We thank Dr. William Steele and Deanne Ginns-Gruenberg, MA, LPC, RPT-S for their thoughtful foreword. A very special thank you to Joel Richter whose work on design and layout has provided an inviting format for the reader. The art work inside the book by both Joel Richter and Matt Holden speaks for itself. Others who have assisted us in this project are Jackie Kuhn, OTR, RYT, Caryl Getchell, Barb Erceg, Dr. Jim Silver, Kristin Notaro Allen and Deva Ludwig. Finally, special thanks to you who will be using the tools in *RELAX.calm* to help teens manage their stress and reach their potential.

PART I

Research: Stress and Societal Trends

OVERVIEW

RELAX.calm is a practical handbook for mental heath professionals, teachers, counselors and parents who believe in the importance of empowering adolescents to become a part of their own emotional growth. Specific strategies for helping teens equip themselves with self-soothing techniques and problem resolving response sets will be outlined and explained in depth. This book is intended not only for professionals and parents, but also the adolescent who is looking for ways to reduce the painful feelings that can result from being anxious and stressed. Teens who are interested in improving their athletic, musical or school performance will also benefit from these techniques.

Chapters 1 through 3 in Part I and the *RELAX.calm* Facilitator's Guide section of Part II was written by Dr. Roger Klein, who has over 40 years of experience working with adolescents. Dr. Klein's work as a high school teacher, coach, school psychologist and clinical psychologist, along with having parented two teens, has provided a unique window of understanding and insight into how to help adolescents. Dr. Klein also wrote the progressive muscle relaxation scripts and test preparation scripts. All of the remaining scripts in Part II were written by Jeff Allen, M.A.. Jeff's years of experience as a teacher and writer help bring to life scripts that enable teens to connect with or develop healthy assets essential for emotional growth.

Chapter 1 provides an explanation as to why so many of our teens are suffering from the crippling effects of stress. The stress of their lives leads many of them to seek relief through substances and risky behaviors while others suffer from more internalizing disorders like anxiety and depression.

Chapter 2 outlines a variety of easily used relaxation techniques including muscle relaxation, imagery and music. The role of positive self-talk techniques is also explored.

Chapter 3 provides a framework for using the intervention techniques discussed in a variety of settings including home, school and clinic. Several detailed case histories are also discussed.

RELAX.calm—**Facilitator's Guide** explains how to use the *RELAX. calm* scripts as a treatment intervention or self-help tool.

INTRODUCTION

Today's adolescents worry more than most adults might suspect. Those of us in the "trenches" working with children and adolescents know that, although many young people do receive some type of adult professional help,[1] many are not receiving enough psychotherapy and many others are going undiagnosed. The traditional individual therapy approach cannot adequately deal with the large number of youth suffering from stress-related problems. Typically, only the most severe cases receive attention. The majority of teens who feel anxious or stressed are suffering through the experience the best they can. Others begin to use substances to find relief. Helping professionals understand the importance of aiding teens in developing techniques to help them deal with the stress in their lives. Stress presents as specific psycho-physiologic patterns occurring in children and teens, including anxiety, headaches, sleep-disturbance and attention problems.[2,3] It is also a contributing factor for depression and substance abuse.

Stress is exacerbated when we feel no outlet for frustration and no sense of control. *RELAX.calm* (pronounced relax-dot-calm), gives teens a sense of control over stress by giving them a "tool box" of relaxation skills, such as guided imagery, muscle relaxation, and positive self-talk, that help them self-soothe. Teens come to realize with practice that they can release tension rather than allow it to increase.

We developed the *RELAX.calm* program as an intervention and prevention tool to help enhance the physical and emotional well-being of adolescents. The program can also be used as an adjunct treatment for a variety of emotional

RELAX.calm **offers teens a toolbox of self-soothing relaxation skills including guided imagery, muscle relaxation and positive self-talk.**

problems along with traditional psychotherapy. *RELAX.calm* can be used by therapists, physicians, educators and parents in many different therapeutic settings, in schools, and at home.

As the following chapters discuss, the effectiveness of using relaxation strategies incorporating muscle relaxation, music, imagery and positive self-talk has been demonstrated in a broad range of scientific studies. For example, relaxation techniques have been shown to improve students' self-management skills, decrease state anxiety, increase social interaction skills, improve self-concept, increase attentiveness, reduce test anxiety, raise test scores and achievement, and establish a self-belief that they can be in control of their problems.[4,5,6,7] In addition, numerous studies have shown the benefit of using these techniques to hasten healing from illness or injury and to manage anxiety related to particular treatments for illness.[8] Those of us who use these techniques in our own practices know that they work. I've used the strategies outlined in *RELAX.calm* successfully with clients of all ages over the past 30 years. What I like most about these techniques is the generalization effect. I've had numerous children and adolescents stay in touch with me by e-mail and continue to report using their relaxation and positive self-talk list years after therapy ended. They feel empowered and have been able to apply the techniques learned in therapy years earlier to new problems and stressors in their lives. The case studies in Chapter 3 are compelling illustrations of the efficacy of using relaxation techniques to address a range of anxiety-related problems in children and adolescents.

In almost all cases, the relaxation techniques found in this book are eagerly learned by young people and easily administered. This valuable treatment and prevention tool is too often overlooked. Our hope is that if you are not using these strategies in your clinical practice, at home or in the classroom that you will give them a try.

Muscle relaxation, music, imagery and positive self-talk reduce test anxiety and raise test scores and achievement, and establish an internal locus of control.

The *RELAX.calm* program is intended to help teens:
- understand the negative effects of stress
- develop an awareness of muscle tension and relaxation
- identify stressors in their lives
- learn skills and techniques that will help them relax and reduce tension

- develop a problem-solving response set of internal dialogue
- develop an appreciation of Baroque and other relaxing music
- develop and practice positive self-talk skills
- connect with their internal resources and strengths
- make good choices
- develop healthy attitudes and values

Research inspired scripts help teens develop healthy internal traits such as honesty, caring attitude, sense of self worth and being goal oriented.

RELAX.calm outlines the use of progressive muscle relaxation, guided imagery and positive self-talk as a way to help adolescents overcome stress and develop a sense of being in control of their lives. After teaching progressive muscle relaxation, the program provides a series of scripts inspired by research that demonstrates that teens who exhibit or possess certain internal traits are more likely to make healthy decisions and deal well with the stresses of life. Examples of these internal traits include things such as honesty, caring attitude, sense of self worth and being goal orientated. *RELAX.calm* helps teens develop these types of internal resources, which in turn can help them seek out and foster a stronger set of external resources. Teens who feel supported, have a sense of empowerment, have boundaries and expectations, and who are involved in school or community activities are more likely to be successful than teens who lack these "building blocks" of success.[9] The more external and internal resources a teen has, the more likely he or she is to make healthy choices.[10,11]

Research in the area of cognitive behavioral psychology demonstrates the importance of positive self-talk in overcoming a host of psychological as well as physiological problems.[12] The Teen Script section of this book offers teens an opportunity to use guided imagery to "see" themselves in their mind's eye being successful, making good choices, feeling supported, feeling empowered, being involved, exhibiting strong values, feeling competent with peers and liking themselves. A variety of other topics are covered and listed on pages 63-65 in the cross reference guide to script themes. The scientific basis and other information about the techniques used in *RELAX.calm* are explained in more detail in Chapter 2.

STRESS AND SOCIETAL TRENDS

As early as the 1980s, professionals working with youth related an uneasy sense that children and adolescents had fewer sources of adult support, affirmation and love than in the past.[13] Since that time, the problem has continued to grow. There is evidence that societal changes over the past decades have increased the level of stress felt by a large number of children and adolescents. The following self-reports from students in my therapy practice typify the stresses of early and late adolescence:

> "I'm totally stressed by school and friends and not getting along with my mom…that's why I smoke pot. It settles me down and then I don't have to feel so stressed out." – Bill, grade 9

> "I can't fall asleep and feel totally stressed out. I'm so worried about doing well on the graduation test that it is driving me crazy!" – Ann, grade 12

> "I have a sister who is 10 years old. She has Tourettes Syndrome. She throws things at me, she bites me, she swears at me and then sometimes I'll call her names and my mom yells at me and blames me and I get sent to my room. I feel worried a lot." – Sue grade 8.

> "It was a constant struggle to fall asleep at night. I thought I could self-medicate my problems away by doing drugs, but things just kept on getting

Societal changes over the past decades have increased the level of stress felt by a large number of children and adolescents.

worse and worse until finally I started thinking about suicide." — Mike, college freshman

A look at societal changes from the 1950s through the 1990s helps us understand the difficult challenges our children and teens face. An interesting retrospective study asked adults to rank five spheres of influence on their lives during childhood.[14] The results below list the major influences from greatest (1) to least (5):

Many believe that TV-Media is the number one influence on today's children and adolescents.

1950:	1980:	1990:
1. Home	1. Home	1. Peers
2. School	2. School	2. TV-Media
3. Church	3. Peers	3. School
4. Peers	4. TV-Media	4. Home
5. TV-Media	5. Church	5. Church

Although the study was not continued, many believe that TV-Media is a dominating influence on today's children and adolescents and may well be the number one influence on them. According to a 2010 Kaiser Foundation study, children ages 8 to 10 spend an average of six hours a day during the school year watching television, playing video games and using computers.[15] In the 1960's, television broadcast 27 hours of children's programming a week, much of it shown simultaneously on Saturday morning. By 2005, there were 14 television networks aimed exclusively at children and young adolescents. Each year, child-focused programming expands as marketers continue to seek the increased buying power of children and teens. The Kaiser Family Foundation study found that 71 percent of children ages 8 -13 and teens ages 14–18 have television sets in their bedrooms. Their survey found as children and teens go about their daily lives, the amount of time they spend with entertainment media has risen dramatically, especially among minority youth. According to the study, 8-18 year-olds devoted an average of 7½ hours to using entertainment media across a typical day (more than 53 hours a week). And because they spend so much of that time 'media multitasking' (using more than one medium at a time), they actually manage to pack a total of 10 hours and 45 minutes worth of media content into those 7½ hours. For example, of the 66 percent of teens who own their own cell phones, 46 percent send an average of 118 text messages a day, many of which are sent and read while involved with other media. A 2005 *USA*

Today story featured an article about the excessive amount of time children and teens spend indoors—watching television, playing video games and surfing the Internet.[16] According to the article, the shift to an indoor childhood continues to accelerate with huge declines reported in spontaneous outdoor activities such as bike riding, swimming and touch football. For example, it stated that 27 percent of youth ages 9 to 13 played organized baseball, but only 6 percent play on their own for fun. The dominance of indoor time has taken a toll on exercise patterns and has contributed to a health crisis among both children and teens.[17]

Numerous studies, including longitudinal research, have shown a relationship between children's and teens' exposure to violence and their own violent and aggressive behaviors. Many studies have documented the role of television in fostering violent behaviors among children. Two meta-analyses investigating the relation between violence viewed on television and aggressive behavior in children concluded that exposure to portrayals of violence on television is consistently associated with children's aggressive behaviors.[18,19] Media exposure has also been linked to increased high-risk behaviors, including alcohol and tobacco use and accelerated onset of sexual activity. Newer forms of media have not been adequately studied, but concern is warranted through the logical extension of earlier research on other media forms and the amount of time the average child spends with increasingly sophisticated media.

As children and teens advance in school, academic pressures increase. The difficulty and amount of homework, competition for grades, fear of not being promoted due to "high stakes" state testing programs and peer-pressure are a few of the many situations that can add to an adolescent's level of stress. David Berliner's research points out the flaws in the "No Child Left Behind" policy enacted during George W. Bush's first administration.[20] He argues that the higher the stakes, the less well students tend to perform due to the anxiety produced by these types of tests. Another flaw of the legislation is the goal that all students become proficient readers and be able to read at their grade level. This is an impossible goal for the approximately 17 percent of students who are slow learners with IQ scores between 70 and 85. Such misguided policies contributes to stress-related illnesses.

Both children and adolescents are sometimes over-scheduled with adult run activities. Many have no time to play with peers

The dominance of indoor time—watching television, playing video games and surfing the Internet—has taken a toll on exercise patterns and contributed to a health crisis among children and teens.

Causes of stress common in teens include "high stakes" state testing programs, daily exposure to bad news, family stress, and pressure to grow up fast and engage in adult behaviors.

because they are too busy "practicing." This loss of playtime due to practices and camps has contributed to the loss of neighborhood games. 'Capture the flag,' 'kick the can' and other neighborhood games have all but disappeared. Young teens used to be the organizers of such games. Instead of organizing such games or calling one another to play pick up soccer or baseball, children and teens instant message or text message one another to check the latest practice schedule or compare scores on the latest video game.

Adding to teens' stress levels is the cumulative amount of bad news they are exposed to daily. News of school shootings, war, threats of terror, murder and more bombard them from all directions. An example of the fallout that can occur when teens are overexposed to this type of information is my work with an eighth grade boy, who I will call Bill. He saw me in my private practice to help him overcome his anxiety of an intruder entering his school. This fear developed shortly after a high profile school tragedy that occurred while he was in grade school. Subsequent to that incident, his school began to have 'intruder in the building' drills. Bill, already prone to anxiety due to a history of anxiety disorders in his family, soon developed a phobia and refused to attend school due to his fear that something terrible might happen. His school attendance refusal was successfully treated through relaxation training. An agreement was made with the school to inform him when a drill was going to happen so he could prepare himself using his relaxation techniques. Unfortunately, there was poor communication when he transferred to the high school and a drill occurred without his prior knowledge. He immediately regressed to the school attendance refusal stage, and we had to start treatment once again.

Family stress adds fuel to the fire. Approximately 50 percent of first marriages and 60 percent of second marriages end in divorce.[21] Nationally, one in four families is dealing with a

Tips to Help with Test Anxiety

· Prepare by studying and completing homework
· Attend class and review material regularly
· Study with a friend or parent who can quiz you
· Exercise on a regular basis
· Practice the Learning Scripts on pages 124-139
· Listen and read test instructions carefully
· Focus on slowing your breathing rate
· Scan for tight muscles and relax them
· Stay positive minded and confident
· Use a "mantra" like, "I am prepared and relaxed"

family member with a serious drug or alcohol problem.[22] Nearly 30 percent of children live in homes where the adult partners are violent with one another[23] and about one in four girls and one in six boys are sexually abused by the age of 18.[24]

The pressure to grow up fast and engage in adult behaviors as soon as possible has increased with each decade. David Elkind's book "The Hurried Child" outlines the problems created by this phenomenon. Societal trends and the media place pressure on teens to engage in risky behaviors to prove that they "fit in." According to a report by the Center for Disease Control, 48 percent of high school students have had sexual intercourse and 15 percent of high school students have had four or more sex partners.[25]

Adolescents and Mental Health

Beyond specific stress-related problems, *RELAX.calm* can be used as an adjunct treatment for mental illness. According to the National Institute of Health (NIH), about one in every five children and adolescents suffers from a mental health issue. Other groups estimate more conservatively that one in every 10 has a mental and/or behavioral disorder. The most common disorders among adolescents include depression, anxiety and attention deficit hyperactivity disorder (ADHD). Also included in the NIH study were behavioral problems such as oppositional defiant disorder or conduct disorder; eating disorders such as anorexia nervosa and bulimia; addictive disorders; bipolar disorder; and other disorders commonly seen in childhood and adolescence, such as autism and learning disorders.

10-20 percent of children and adolescents suffer from a mental health issue, with anxiety disorders becoming one of the most common reported illnesses.

Anxiety disorders have become one of the most common mental illnesses reported among children and adolescents. Anxiety disorders represent the primary reason children and adolescents are referred for mental health services, yet many youth with symptoms of these disorders are not being identified.[26] Greater resources and attention are often given to students with disruptive disorders (e.g. hyperactivity, conduct problems and oppositional behavior) than disorders like depression and anxiety that present with internalizing symptoms. To reduce levels of childhood mental illness, interventions need to begin earlier, ideally as prevention prior to the development of significant symptomatology.[27] Anxiety symptoms and disorders have long been recognized as a major mental health problem among adults with a lifetime prevalence rate of 25 percent. Although the exact frequency rate in children

Signs of Stress

Following are symptoms of stress often exhibited by adolescents. Any symptom observed as happening may indicate need for follow up by a parent, teacher, counselor or physician.

· Headaches
· Stomach problems: diarrhea, constipation, nausea, heartburn
· Heart "pounding" or palpitations
· Aches and pains
· Muscle jerks or tics
· Appetite disturbance: loss of appetite or increased eating to comfort oneself
· Sleeping problems: unable to fall asleep, wake up frequently, nightmares
· Complaint of feeling tired
· Shortness of breath
· Grinding teeth
· Stuttering or stammering
· Easily moved to tears or not being able to cry
· Reports feeling anxious, nervous, or tense
· Irritable, short temper, easily angered
· Depressed
· Accident prone
· Feeling overwhelmed and unable to cope
· Nervous laughter, easily startled, jumpy, overly vigilant
· Bored, little or no interest in activities
· Feeling rejected frequently
· Loss of concentration or unable to finish things
· Never or seldom laughs
· Does not have friends
· Poor grades in school, does not finish homework
· Engages in risky behavior
· Substance abuse

and teens is not known, it is likely under-reported and under-diagnosed. Stressful events such as starting school, moving, having learning problems, being teased at school or the loss of a parent through divorce or death are some of the issues that can trigger the onset of an anxiety disorder. However, a specific stressor need not be the precursor to the development of a disorder, as many children and teens are predisposed to anxiety problems due to their physiological and genetic makeup. While children and teens can develop any of the recognized anxiety disorders, some are more common among certain age groups. For example, some tend to be specific to stages of development. Separation anxiety disorder and specific phobias are more common in children age six to nine years old. Generalized anxiety disorder and social anxiety disorder are more common in middle childhood and adolescence, while panic disorder is more typically seen in adolescence. Refer to Appendix A on page 179 for a description of common anxiety disorders. Refer to Appendix E on page 195 for an adaptation of the Holmes-Rahe Life Stress Inventory.

Clinical depression is also on the rise. Depression is one of the most widely studied mental health conditions because of its large burden on individuals, families and society, as well as its links to suicide. Depression is the most widely reported disorder among adolescents. A 2002 longitudinal study of adolescent health indicated over 25 percent of adolescents are affected by at least mild depressive symptoms.[28] The reported prevalence of depression varies, depending on which symptoms and what degree of severity are measured. One of the broadest indicators of depressive symptoms comes from the Youth Risk Behavior Surveillance System (YRBSS). Using a cluster sample of high schools throughout America, students in grades 9-12 were surveyed every two years between 1991 and 2005. The study asks questions such as: *Have you ever felt so sad or hopeless almost every day, for two weeks in a row, that you couldn't do some of your usual activities?* Results from the 2005 YRBSS indicate that 37 percent of female and 20 percent of male high school students reported this level of sadness to the above question. Hispanic students reported higher rates (47 percent of females and 26 percent of males) than their non-Hispanic black and white peers.[29] We know that many teens are not able to access mental health services and depression left untreated has been linked to suicide ideation and attempts. The overall suicide rate for teens has risen 300 percent since the 1950's and currently represents the third leading cause of death in this age group.

An additional concern is the increase in *self-harm*, such as cutting. A recent study found that 15 percent of adolescents reported engaging in self-harm behavior, which is associated with maladjustment, suicide and other health behaviors indicative of risk for negative developmental outcomes.[30]

Substance abuse and experimentation are another prevalent problem among youth. Many report stress as a contributing factor that led to the use of alcohol and/or other drugs. Although substance abuse incidence is widely reported from several

A Depressing Era for Teenagers

These are hard times for teenagers. A study of high school and college students, built on data from psychological surveys in use since 1938, has found that anxiety, depression and other mental-health issues are far more prevalent among youth today than during the Great Depression. A team of researchers analyzed tens of thousands of responses to common psychological surveys, which asked students if they felt sad, dissatisfied, worried, isolated or otherwise mentally troubled. On average, five times as many students in 2007 reported signs of mental illness than did those in 1938. Increases in depression and hypomania—a mixture of anxiety and an unrealistic, manic form of optimism—were particularly acute.

An estimated 8 percent of males and 6 percent of females aged 12-17 had a substance abuse dependence disorder according to a 2006 study.

national surveys using different samples,[31,32] fewer sources assess the prevalence of the more disabling psychiatric diagnosis of substance abuse dependence disorder, in which one's life is controlled by substance use. The 1995 National Survey of Adolescents (NSA) estimated that 8 percent of males and 6 percent of females ages 12-17 had a substance abuse dependence disorder.[33] In 2006, the National Survey on Drug Use and Health (NSDUH) data showed that 8 percent of 12 to 17-year-olds depended on or abused alcohol or illicit drugs. This behavior was slightly higher among female adolescents than male peers (8.4 percent vs 7.9 percent).[34]

> *The link between adolescent mental health and stress has been well documented. There is a need for research-based interventions that are easily understood, administered, and implemented by adolescents themselves. RELAX.calm provides such an intervention and is based on the research and techniques outlined in Chapter 2.*

RELAXATION TECHNIQUES

Stress results when our bodies react in what Selye, the "father" of stress research, called a *general adaptation syndrome.* Selye outlined a syndrome consisting of three stages: an "alarm" reaction, the "resistance" stage and the "exhaustion" stage.[35] In the first stage, the body reacts to the stressor and causes the hypothalamus to produce a biochemical "messenger" that causes the pituitary gland to secrete adreno-corticotrophic hormone (ACTH) into the blood. This hormone causes the secretion of adrenaline and other corticoids, which in turn cause the shrinkage of the thymus and a concomitant influence on heart rate, blood pressure and respiration rate. In the second stage, resistance develops. The third stage, "exhaustion," occurs if there is continuous exposure to the same or similar stressors.

This process was first described as an emergency *fight or flight response* by Dr. Walter Cannon.[36] This reaction was helpful to ancient humans who often needed to prepare for physical action during the hunt or in confrontation with an enemy or other danger. Modern humans continue to have these same physiological responses to stress, however we experience less adaptive benefit, as the majority of our stressors are emotional, not physical. Stress presents as specific psycho-physiologic patterns occurring in children and teens, including anxiety, headaches, sleep-disturbance and attention problems,[37,38] It is also a contributing factor for depression and substance abuse.

Herbert Benson's research indicated a variety of techniques that can be used to "quiet" the aroused sympathetic nervous system.[39]

"Each of us possesses a natural and innate protective mechanism against 'overstress,' which allows us to turn off harmful bodily effects, to counter the effects of the fight-or-flight response. This response against 'overstress' brings on bodily changes that decrease heart rate, lower metabolism, decrease the rate of breathing, and bring the body back into what is probably a healthier balance. This is the Relaxation Response" (Benson, 1975, p. 250).

There are a number of proven techniques that elicit the Relaxation Response - a natural and innate mechanism against "overstress."

Benson suggests that evoking the relaxation response is extremely simple if the following four essential elements are included: 1. A quiet environment; 2. A mental device such as a word or a phrase which should be repeated in a specific fashion over and over again; 3. The adoption of a passive attitude; and 4. A comfortable position.

Currently, there are a number of proven techniques that elicit the Relaxation Response. These include biofeedback, meditation, yoga (see Appendix B p. 185) hypnosis, systematic desensitization, autogenic training, music, imagery, positive self-talk, progressive muscle relaxation (PMR) and behavioral relaxation.

> **A review of the literature of large-group interventions suggests that the most effective of these techniques, when considering cost and ease of implementation, are imagery, positive self-talk, progressive muscle relaxation (PMR), behavioral relaxation and music. These are taught to teens through the *RELAX.calm* program. Details of these techniques are discussed below.**

One of the values of using a multi-method intervention is based on the belief that each person has their own individual style of seeing the world. For some teens, change is accomplished through behavior, which in turn affects cognition and feeling. For others, the key to change is through cognition, which in turn affects feelings and behavior. Some teens may benefit more directly from the use of muscle relaxation while others may benefit more from a cognitive-based success imagery technique.

Imagery

The power of the mind to influence the body is quite remarkable. When people imagine themselves successfully performing a certain behavior, the likelihood for taking part in that behavior increases. It can also be used to replace unwanted images stored from negative or traumatic experiences. Psychologists and others have long noted the mind's ability to mimic internally the possible motions and transformations of objects in the external world.[40] Imagery has been considered a healing tool in virtually all of the world's cultures and is an integral part of many religions. Navajo Indians, for example, practice an elaborate form of imagery that encourages a person to "see" themselves as healthy. Ancient Egyptians and Greeks, including Aristotle and Hippocrates, believed that images release "spirits" in the brain that arouse the heart and other parts of the body. They also thought that a strong image of a disease is enough to cause its symptoms. The power of imagery was noted in the 1700s by philosopher David Hume who wrote:

> "To join incongruous shapes and appearances costs the imagination no more trouble than to conceive the most natural and familiar objects. This creative power of the mind amounts to no more than the faculty of comprehending, transposing, augmenting, or diminishing the material afforded us by the senses and experience."[41]

The study of imagery has long been a part of the science of the mind. During the dominance of Watson and behaviorism, imagery was studied as "conditioned hallucinations." Today, imagery is a well-documented and successful technique used to influence behavior, as well as enhance physical healing[42,43] and motor performance.[44] The National Institute of Health (NIH) reviewed over 300 studies that showed the effectiveness of imagery as a self-regulation technique.[45] More and more of these studies are being completed using children and adolescents as the subjects. Advocates of imagery contend that the imagination is a potent healer that has long been overlooked by practitioners of Western medicine. Although it isn't always curative, imagery can be helpful in many of the problems that people bring to the attention of their primary care physicians. (See *Medical Interest in Muscle Relaxation* on page 39 for more details on relaxation and medical issues.)

Imagery is the most fundamental "language" we have. When we recall events from our past or childhood, we think of pictures,

Imagery is a well-documented and successful technique used to influence behavior, as well as enhance physical healing and motor performance.

sounds and sensations. Past memories are hardly ever remembered through words. Images aren't limited to visual sensing; they can be sounds, tastes, smells or a combination of sensations. A certain smell, for example, may invoke either pleasant or bad memories. Similarly, going to a place where you had a serious accident may instantly create visions of the accident and initiate the flight or fight response. Think, for example, of holding a fresh lemon in your hand. Imagine feeling its slightly rough texture and picture its yellow color. Now imagine cutting it open and seeing some juice squirt out. Smell the lemon's tart aroma. Finally, imagine putting a slice of lemon in your mouth, suck on it and taste the sour flavor as the juices roll over your tongue. More than likely, your body reacted in some way to that image. For example, you may have begun to salivate.

LUANN by Greg Evans

Imagery is the language that the mind uses to communicate with the body. Unfortunately, many of the images and self-talk typical of teens can do more harm than good. In fact, the most common type of imagery is related to worry. The average teen has hundreds of thoughts or images each day. At least half of those thoughts are negative, such as anxiety about completing an assignment or a coming speech, concerns about friends and family, and on and on. A steady dose of worry and other negative images can alter a person's physiology and make her more vulnerable to a variety of ailments, including acne, body pain, headaches and susceptibility to disease and infections.

An important element in helping teens overcome the prevalence of negative self-talk is to teach them how to replace a negative thought with a positive one.

Our thoughts have a direct influence on the way we feel and behave. A person who tends to dwell on sad or negative thoughts is most likely not a very happy person. Likewise, if a student thinks that school is enough to give him a headache, he may, in turn, come home with the headache he pictures each day. This is just another clear example of the power the mind exerts over the body. Important elements in helping teens overcome these negative messages is to teach them how to catch themselves thinking negatively, stop the thought and replace it with a positive thought.

When teens know how to direct and control the images in their heads, they can help their minds and bodies heal. Imagination can be a powerful tool to help combat stress, tension and anxiety. It can also be a vehicle to help achieve goals.

Dr. Charles Garfield has done extensive research on peak performance, both in athletics and in business.[46] He became interested with peak performance in his work with the NASA program, watching astronauts rehearse everything on earth, again and again in a simulated environment before they went to space. He decided to study the characteristics of peak performers. One of the main things his research showed was that almost all world-class athletes and other peak performers use visualization. They see it; they feel it; they experience it before they actually do it. They begin with the end in mind. Mary Lou Retton, the first American gymnast to earn an Olympic gold medal in the "all-around" title with scores of a perfect "10" on the floor exercise and vault, attributed her success to her many hours of performing her routine "in her mind's eye."[47] Her belief and dedication to the power of imagery, according to her own report, contributed greatly to her success.

Experts such as Dale Carnegie, Robert Schuller and Steven Covey have also used imagery to elicit peak performance in individuals. In "Seven Habits of the Most Effective People," Covey suggested that we can use our right brain power of visualization to write affirmations that help us become more congruent with our deeper values in our daily life.[48]

According to Covey, a good affirmation has five basic ingredients:
1. It's personal.
2. It's positive.
3. It's present tense.
4. It's visual.
5. It's emotional.

The scripts in *RELAX.calm* are written with these five principals in mind. Each script instructs the teen to imagine being in a present tense story. The teen is asked to personalize the experience, visualize solving a problem or issue related to the experience, and finally to repeat a positive self-statement in the present tense. Participants are cued to visualize stressful situations in rich detail while remaining calm and resolving the source of the

The scripts in *RELAX.calm* are written using the five principals of a good affirmation: personal, positive, present tense, visual and emotional.

stress. They are asked to see themselves handling the situation with confidence, power and self-control. This helps teach teens the power of their imagination and thoughts and how seeing a solution in their mind can lead them into positive, goal-directed behaviors. It is clear from both research and clinical practice that changes in behavior result from the practice of positive, problem-solving images and self-talk, regardless of the age of the participant.

Visualization can be used in every area of an adolescent's life. Before an athletic or school performance, a classroom presentation, a difficult confrontation or the daily challenge of meeting a goal, one can visualize success clearly, vividly and repeatedly. The ability to use this skill creates an internal "comfort zone." Teens in my clinical practice are always amazed by the effectiveness of visualization in increasing their self confidence and helping them achieve their goals.

Positive Self-Talk

The development of positive self-talk is essential in helping children and teens build a healthy self-concept.

Self-talk is the phrase psychologists use to explain how people direct themselves to relate to the world around them. Self-talk can vary from casual comments to full scale dialogues with ourselves. Research in the field of cognitive behavioral psychology suggests that our emotions follow our thoughts as opposed to our thoughts being governed by our emotions. Therefore what we are saying to ourselves about ourselves is critically important.

Dr. Shad Helmstetter, author and psychologist, refers to positive self-talk as the most powerful force humans have for self-transformation.[49] Like other researchers, he believes that self-talk directly affects our subconscious. Helmstetter uses the analogy of the mind working like a computer. The brain is the hardware and what we say to ourselves is the software. Although we are seldom aware of it, even the most casual admonitions we make to ourselves can make a strong impression on our minds. Some of the power of these impressions is explained by new findings in brain research. Research has found that the brain can not distinguish between a real experience and an imaginary one. When we talk to ourselves, we produce signals in our brain; our bodies respond by producing chemicals that affect our feelings and behavior. This process has been widely documented in the areas of health and stress. When people tell themselves that they are going to get sick, or when they consider themselves types who get sick easily, they are more likely to develop an illness.[50] Likewise, when a student says to themselves that the work is too hard and they will never understand, they are more likely not to do well on their schoolwork or on tests.

The development of positive self-talk is essential in helping children and teens build a healthy self-concept. We usually think of talking as being related to communication, but language specialists have documented the existence of a whole separate track of language called egocentric speech. Egocentric speech refers to the language the child uses to talk to herself, at first out loud and later internally. This self-talk helps to determine the children's reactions and feelings and is pivotal in the formation of self-control, learning, problem solving, and making healthy choices. Children and teens that are successful tend to have developed positive self-statements and have an inner dialogue of encouraging self-talk. Learning to use self-talk positively takes some work, but it can serve as a protective factor against disappointment and the inevitable crises that life brings. Self-regulated, private speech can function as an instructional cue that guides one's thoughts, feelings and behaviors. Self-instructions have an influence on one's appraisal, attention processes and physiological reactions.[51]

The *RELAX.calm* program includes an opportunity for students to repeat a positive self-statement in each script. The purpose of these self-statements is to have the teen develop problem-solving response sets.

Progressive Muscle Relaxation

Progressive muscle relaxation (PMR), developed by Jacobson[52] is still the relaxation technique referred to most often in the literature and likely with the most widespread application. In this technique, the child or adolescent concentrates on progressively relaxing one muscle group after another while comparing the difference between tension and relaxation in each muscle group. The use of PMR is prevalent in the literature as a means of reducing anxiety. Relaxation techniques like PMR have been used to help children and teens become more focused and receptive to subsequent imagery scripts. Lazarus found that the unconscious mind worked more effectively when subjects were relaxed.[53]

According to Chang and Hiebert, PMR at the school level has been used primarily with children diagnosed as hyperactive and/or having learning and academic problems. These authors cite a number of studies which report encouraging results using PMR as

Progressively relaxing one muscle group after another while comparing the difference between tension and relaxation is effective as a means of reducing anxiety.

a behavior-management strategy with hyperactive students.[54]

Porter and Omizo trained two groups of 11 hyperactive boys in relaxation and stretching. Parents of the boys in the second treatment group were requested to encourage them to practice relaxation daily at home, but no evidence was given to indicate that they actually did so. Compared to a control group, both treatment groups improved their scores on the Novicki-Strickland Locus of Control Scale for Children and the Matching Familiar Figures Test.[55]

As early as 1977, Brown found differential treatment effects between a group of hyperactive students receiving only PMR and a group receiving PMR plus "task motivational instructions," in other words, using self-statements that encouraged participation and suggested positive expected outcomes. The combined treatment was significantly more effective than PMR alone in bringing about change on the Davids Rating Scale for Hyperkinesis and Piers-Harris Self-Concept Scale, but no significant differences were noted on three WISC-R subtests. Brown concluded that parental support and cognitive strategies are necessary to augment the effects of PMR.[56]

Reynolds examined the efficacy of cognitive behavioral therapy and relaxation training for the treatment of depression in 30 moderately depressed adolescents who met in small groups for 10 sessions. The cognitive-behavioral and relaxation training groups were superior to the wait-list control group in the reduction of depressive symptoms of both post-test and five-week follow-up assessments.[57] A 2003 study by Goldbeck demonstrated a positive effect using PMR with adolescents with behavioral and emotional problems.[58] In a long term outcome study, PMR was as effective as psychotherapy and pharmacotherapy in reducing anxiety and even more effective than cognitive behavior therapy.[59] Similarly, in a study of depressed child and adolescent psychiatric patients, both groups benefited from as little as one hour a week of relaxation therapy. In that study, self-reported anxiety, as well as anxious behavior and fidgeting, decreased while positive affect was noted to increase.

Muscle-relaxation method melts stress and pounds

Non-dieters in a study at the University of Otago in New Zealand lost an average of 6 pounds in two years simply by practicing progressive muscle relaxation (PMR). Researchers say PMR manages stress to reduce emotional eating.

In a long-term outcome study, PMR was as effective as psychotherapy and pharmacotherapy in reducing anxiety and even more effective than cognitive behavior therapy.

Like imagery, hundreds of well designed studies have concluded that PMR is an effective technique to reduce anxiety and depression, promote both physical and mental well being, and increase learning. *RELAX.calm* uses PMR exercises at the onset to help the teen establish the relaxation response.

Behavioral Relaxation

One does not necessarily have to tense and release muscle groups to achieve deep muscle relaxation. Imagining muscles tense and then consciously releasing tension can achieve the same results. Sometimes termed *behavioral relaxation*, this form of relaxation simply requires the subject to progressively "let go" of the tension in each muscle group rather than first tensing each group and then releasing the tension.[60] A 1998 study compared 18 high school students in a behavioral relaxation group, 20 students in a PMR group, and 17 students in a no-treatment control group.[61] All training was done for Groups 1 and 2 via videotaped instructions of the appropriate relaxation technique. Both groups completed four 20-minute training sessions in two weeks. The day after the last treatments were administered to Groups 1 and 2, all three groups were asked to complete the State-Trait Anxiety Inventory. The findings indicated that the state anxiety scores for Group 1 and Group 2 did not vary significantly from one another, but were both significantly lower than the state anxiety scores for the students in the no-treatment group. These findings indicate that both the behavioral relaxation approach and PMR approach are capable of helping high school students reduce their state anxiety.

Two other studies with high school students as subjects indicated that they are less likely to practice PMR because of the effort it takes to tense muscles.[62] Teens in these two studies both commented that PMR was "hard work." My own experience working with both behavioral relaxation and PMR reinforces these findings. I tend to use PMR with young children and switch to behavioral relaxation with teens. However, it can be helpful to use PMR to introduce teens to self-regulated relaxation. Once a teen shows the ability to become relaxed through PMR, the use of behavioral relaxation should follow.

Both behavioral relaxation and PMR are effective in reducing high school students' anxiety.

Ready, Set, R.E.L.A.X.

Both procedures are combined in a stress management program we designed for elementary school children called *Ready, Set, R.E.L.A.X.*[63] The first part of the program teaches children to use PMR to achieve the relaxation response. After adequate practice with PMR, the children in the original study were able to achieve the relaxation response using behavioral relaxation in the form of stories that incorporated both behavioral relaxation and imagery. The 123 children in the original study out-performed the control group on the Metropolitan Achievement Tests and achieved significantly lower scores on self-report measures of depression and anxiety. In addition, they had a significant increase in their self-report of self-concept as measured by the Piers Harris Self-Concept Scale (see Appendix C on page 186 for details of this study).

Another effective muscle relaxation strategy is called the "fast/slow" technique. This technique is most effective with pre-school and elementary-age children. It requires the child to follow the directions of the facilitator who asks the child to move various body parts as "fast as possible" and then as "slow as possible". Some hyperactive children who rarely move slowly begin to understand the concept of "slow down" when they pair those words with the muscle memory of moving various muscle groups slowly in the fast/slow "game."

A simple, short way to relaxation may be used after a child or teen has mastered progressive or behavioral relaxation. On the count of one, the teen is asked to shift her gaze to the ceiling without moving her neck; on two she is instructed to close her eyes, while continuing to gaze upward, and take a deep breath, and on three, she is cued to let go of the breath, allow her eyes to come to a normal position, bow her head gently forward and release all tension in her muscles while saying the words "calm and relax." While saying "calm and relax" the teen is asked to imagine one hand or the other to begin to feel very light and buoyant, as if a group of helium balloons were attached to the arm. With each slow breath, the suggestion is given that the hand and arm feels lighter and lighter until the hand begins to slowly rise. The higher the arm rises, the deeper the relaxation becomes. The goal is to have the hand reach the level of the teen's face at which time a very deep relaxed state has been achieved. The goal, positive image or phrase is then repeated out loud or with the "inner voice." This exercise is

The children in *Ready, Set, R.E.L.A.X.* study out-performed the control group on the Metropolitan Achievement Tests and achieved lower scores on self-report measures of depression and anxiety.

most effective with teens who have been practicing progressive or behavioral relaxation and are having success reaching a relaxation response. You can give the suggestion to lift one hand or the other slightly if the arm is not rising on its own.

Medical Interest in Muscle Relaxation

The medical community has become increasingly interested in mind-body therapies as the cost of health care increases. Relaxation therapy is inexpensive, easily learned and highly effective in the adjunct treatment of a host of medical conditions. The use of muscle relaxation coupled with imagery has been used for years in the medical treatment of adults. Kabat-Zinn and his colleagues demonstrated the effectiveness of meditation coupled with relaxation in the treatment of panic disorder and reduction of chronic pain.[64] Using the relaxation response, Benson showed significant reduction in blood pressure with patients being treated for hypertension.[65]

Numerous studies have shown positive gains in treating virtually any medical condition when relaxation techniques are used.

One study compared patients being prepared for cardiac surgery by education only or by being taught the relaxation response. The relaxation response group experienced significantly greater reductions in tension and anger than the education only group. Numerous other studies have shown the positive gains in virtually any medical condition when relaxation techniques are used.[66] From the treatment of cancer to the treatment of migraines, relaxation therapy is a proven technique.

The literature supports the same treatment strategies be employed with children as well as adolescents. For example, numerous studies have shown the effectiveness of using progressive muscle relaxation in helping children reduce the intensity and frequency of migraine headaches.[67,68] Kohen teaches muscle relaxation and mental imagery (RMI) exercises to children and adolescents as an adjunct in the management of asthma. Clinical experience indicated that children who learn RMI rate their asthma as significantly reduced in severity, miss fewer days of school and make fewer visits to emergency rooms.[69] Relaxation training improved blood glucose control in non-insulin-dependent children and adolescents suffering from diabetes mellitus.[70]

Morrow and Hickok state that progressive muscle relaxation training is effective in preventing, as well as decreasing, the frequency of post chemotherapy nausea and vomiting.[71] Carroll

& Seers used progressive muscle relaxation along with guided imagery to significantly reduce children's self-report of cancer pain.[72] Relaxation training has been used to successfully treat school phobia,[73] as well as childhood depression.[74]

In a comprehensive literature review, Powers concluded that cognitive behavioral therapy coupled with relaxation is a "well-established treatment" for procedure-related pain in children and adolescents. Treatment includes breathing exercises and other forms of muscle relaxation and distraction, imagery and other forms of cognitive coping skills, filmed modeling, reinforcement/incentive, behavioral rehearsal, and active coaching by a psychologist, parent, and/or medical staff member.[75] Nancy Klein's book *Healing Images For Children: Teaching Relaxation and Guided Imagery to Children Facing Cancer and Other Serious Illnesses*[76] (www.innercoaching.com) is an excellent example of combining many of the same techniques mentioned by Powers.

Music

Therapeutic use of music has been used throughout human history. Shamanistic rituals used music as early as Paleolithic times.[77] Greeks were among the first to investigate therapeutics and practice preventive treatments using music; Plato, Homer, and Aristotle all believed that music was an instrument affecting both the body and soul.[78] According to some scholars, the Bible gives evidence of the Hebrews using music to treat illnesses. French monasteries used music in medieval times to minister to the sick.[79,80] During the sixteenth and seventeenth century, music was used to treat depression or effect behavior change.[81] Following the ideas of Pythagoras, the classical music era composers built a "sacred canon" of specific harmonies, intervals and proportions into their music. Such ideas were specifically used by the composers of Baroque music. Thus, Baroque music was believed to affect the listener by aligning, harmonizing and synchronizing mind and body to more harmonious patterns.[82]

Sedative music, such as Baroque, has been found to be effective in stress reduction as measured by physiological changes such as galvanic skin response, heart rate, pulse rate and blood pressure; respiration rate; electromyogram (a test that is used to record the electrical activity of muscles); and electroencephalogram (which measures and records the electrical activity of your brain).[83,84,85,86,87,88] Research has shown music to have a positive effect on the relaxation response and in stress reduction. It was found to reduce state and trait anxiety, ease stress, decrease anxiety, increase relaxation levels[89] and ease the discomfort of children who are hospitalized.[90]

The musical elements of tone, vibration, rhythm and harmony have effects on the body, mind, and emotions that science is only now beginning to understand. A 2004 meta-analysis study reviewed the results of 11 different studies on the effects of music on adolescents.[91] After exclusion of an extreme positive outlying value, the analysis revealed that music therapy has a medium to large positive effect (ES = .61) on clinically relevant outcomes that were statistically highly significant ($p < .001$) and statistically homogeneous. No evidence of a publication bias was identified. Effects tended to be greater for behavioral and developmental disorders than for emotional disorders; greater for eclectic, psychodynamic, and humanistic approaches than for behavioral models; and greater for behavioral and developmental outcomes than for social skills and self-concept.

Kibler is one of few researchers to measure the interactive effects of music and progressive relaxation. He assessed the effects of music (MU), progressive muscle relaxation (PMR), and music and progressive muscle relaxation together, on stress reduction as measured by change in peripheral skin temperature response prior to the intervention technique(s) and immediately subsequent to it. The effect of combining the PMR and MU treatments appeared to have an increased relaxing effect, although it was not significantly higher than the MU or PMR groups alone.[92]

Reynolds compared the efficacy of five relaxation-training procedures, four of which employed Electromyography (EMG) auditing feedback: 1. Biofeedback only (BFL), 2. Autogenic training phrases (ATP), 3. Music (MU), 4. Autogenic training phrases and music (ATP & MU), and 5. a control group. The purpose of the study was to develop self-regulation of a "cultivated low arousal state" as a countermeasure to tensed muscular reaction to stressful imagery. After eight training sessions, the MU and ATP & MU groups achieved highly significant differences when compared with the control group. The ATP & MU group attained the lowest post-baseline arousal level as measured by the EMG.[93]

Wesecky suggests that the reactivity for rhythm and melodies must be located within a primitive region of the hierarchical structure of the brain because even severely retarded children

Music has a positive effect on the relaxation response and in stress reduction.

respond to music. He demonstrated that music therapy could bring about at least a temporary cessation of the stereotyped movements in children with Rett syndrome.[94] Cratty found improvement in self-help skills of retarded children after using relaxation exercises accompanied by sedative music.[95]

With the advent of "New Age" music in the late 1970s and early 1980s, along with compositions designed to induce relaxation versus excitation states, music therapists expanded their repertoires of musical selections to induce effective changes.[96] Smith and Joyce provided evidence that classical music is more effective than New Age music in effecting the relaxation response.[97]

Music in the life of an adolescent

Music has a great deal of significance in the lives of most adolescents. Teens progress through many developmental tasks including identity formation, increasing independence, expansion of relationships with friends and romantic interests, loyalty to the peer group, and changes in relationship to authority. Popular music accompanies most teens on their journey toward independence and autonomy and is a major part of their lives. Starting in middle school and increasing through the end of high school, teens turn to music listening, whether it is in the foreground or background, for a wide variety of uses. In the book *"Media Violence and Children"* there is discussion of the effects of music on children and adolescents.[98] The author states that because of the efficacy of music, it tends to be the medium of choice when adolescents want to be in a certain mood, when they seek reinforcement for a mood, and when they feel lonely or seek distraction from their troubles. Research shows that males are more likely than females to use music as a tool to increase their energy level and seek stimulation ("get pumped up") while females tend to utilize music to improve mood when feeling sad or somber.[99]

Teens listen to music for pleasure, to share social times with friends, to accompany "peak" experiences of life, and to navigate the turmoil, vulnerabilities, conflicts and achievements of life. For many teens, music provides something of a "soundtrack" during an emotional, ever-changing and often stressful life stage. While most teens choose to listen to music because they like it and not for learning purposes, music listening can provide validation for one's feelings and promote self-reflection and self-understanding. The music they choose can help them to learn more about their

Popular music accompanies most teens on their journey toward independence and autonomy and is a major part of their lives.

emotions and can also facilitate social interaction. Music addresses many issues that are central to the adolescent developmental stage with a direct manner that is not easily attained from adults, and it serves as an essential function in the lives of most adolescents.

There are many ways for children and teens to be *actively* involved in music such as playing, singing, dancing, musical theater, composition or song writing. Organized musical groups such as band or choir can provide musical instruction, social interaction, cooperation in a group setting, self-efficacy and general pleasure. Learning to sing or play an instrument gives a youth skills for self-expression and enjoyment and can be a way to make interpersonal connections with other young people. Making music can also be a positive solitary activity that is a good deal more active than watching TV or playing video games. It is good to learn to enjoy one's own company and playing music can provide one way to do that.

Dancing is another direct relationship with rhythm and music. It provides fun, exercise, socialization, and can have a positive impact on self-esteem. Many dance styles have become popular and are taught in community dance centers around the country including hip-hop, jazz and Irish dance.

Musical skills accompany an individual throughout life, providing opportunities for numerous positive experiences during all life stages. Playing an instrument and singing provide a direct relationship with sound.

Music listening can provide validation for one's feelings and promote self-understanding.

Musical preferences of teens

While pop, rap and rock music are popular with many adolescents, individual taste in music can vary and include various genres. Different types of music affect teens in varying ways. For instance, heavy metal may increase the energy level of a teen who likes that genre, but may cause feelings of anxiety for someone who dislikes it. Research on the effects of music on adolescents has generally shown that musical tastes *reflect* a teen's personality rather than *shape it*. Kids choose music that represents how they already feel about the world and themselves.

There has been a good deal of attention in recent years about how much influence music can have on a teenager's mood and behaviors. Some claim that music lyrics with violent themes, such as some heavy metal and rap, can make a teen behave aggressively. But according to research[100] most heavy metal and rap fans are not particularly troubled or at risk, and are not using drugs, in jail, or failing at school. However, those youths who *are* troubled or at risk tend overwhelmingly to embrace heavy metal and rap. If a child is already at risk for antisocial behaviors, music with aggressive and antisocial themes may reinforce those thoughts and feelings, making the feelings more likely to occur in the future. But if a parent notices a teen becoming totally engulfed in heavy metal or rap culture to the exclusion of other interests accompanied by anti-authoritarian attitudes and actions, the parent needs to begin to address the causes of the young person's strong alienation from mainstream culture.

Musical tastes generally reflect a teen's personality rather than shape it. A teen's favorite music can provide a glimpse into his or her worldview, emotional state, self-concept, struggles and joys.

If an adult wants to understand the world and experiences of a teen, it can be very helpful to listen to the music he or she prefers. A teen's favorite music can provide a glimpse into their worldview, emotional state, self-concept, struggles and joys. Music selections can reflect the wide range of moods and experiences of the teen; they can be a mirror for one's emotions at any given time. A trained music therapist will often ask a teen to select their preferred music in order to share feelings and experiences. In a clinical setting, all types of music are utilized with teens based on individual preferences and the goals of the therapy. Utilizing a teen's preferred music is a good place to "meet them where they're at" and begin to understand their world. Over time, the music therapist often begins to introduce other types of music such as classical, blues, "world" and New Age for interventions such as relaxation and guided imagery, musical improvisation and song writing.

Gabrielle Laden, a sound healing practitioner in Madison, WI who has worked with adolescents for 20 years, likes to use "world music" with teens before delving into European classical music. She finds that world music can take the young person out of the familiar music of youth culture to experience the sound and effects of classical music from other cultures such as Tibetan chants, Japanese Koto, Indian tablas and other traditions. Exposure to various types of music may open the youth to new levels of experience and relationship to music itself and assist in expanding self-discovery. It can be helpful to be exposed to a variety of musical types throughout childhood, in both recorded and "live" forms, in order to create openness to musical experiences, as well as different cultures.

Using music for purposes of relaxation

Many teens will say that they calm down when listening to music they like or that matches their mood. While this can be helpful in validating one's feelings, some types of music may not necessarily facilitate a relaxed state. One study in a state psychiatric hospital found that hard rock and rap music were found to elicit the highest number of inappropriate behaviors with clients who already showed behavioral problems.

Generally, instrumental music is preferable for guided relaxation since there are no lyrics to cause the listener to think about feelings and issues that could keep them in an alert state. Sedative music tends to have a slower beat or no set rhythm. Major modes or an open mode, such as pentatonic, are usually more calming than minor modes which are often associated with sad feelings.

Instrumental music is generally preferred for guided relaxation.

In order to slowly come out of a relaxed state, one can use music with a gentle beat and uplifting tonality. This may assist the individual in coming out of a deeply relaxed state, but maintain calm feelings as they resume activities. Suggestions for music to use with the *RELAX.calm* scripts are listed below.

Suggestions for Music

Pianoscapes (Jones) – Soothing Piano Solos
Pachelbel with Ocean (Liv & Let Liv) – 6 renditions
   of Canon D soundscapes
The Fairy Ring (Rowland) – "New Age" gentle
   rhythms on piano and synthesizer
Ocean Odyssey (Goddard) – Marine Mammal
   recordings with surround sound mix
Music for Accelerated Learning (Halpern)
Relaxation Suite (Halpern)

This music is available for purchase on our web store
   at www.innercoaching.com or by purchase order,
   check, or money order to: Inner Coaching 1108
   Western Avenue, Watertown, Wisconsin 53094.

3

USING RELAX.CALM TECHNIQUES IN SCHOOL AND THERAPEUTIC SETTINGS

School-Based Relaxation Intervention

There is a critical need to teach relaxation skills at all levels of education, as well as in the clinical setting. School psychologists, counselors, social workers, health teachers, physical education teachers and classroom teachers can all implement relaxation training with students. The school setting provides a natural delivery system for a preventative mental health program incorporating relaxation skills. Relaxation training can be helpful for all students, not only those suffering from acute stress-related problems. It has been demonstrated to improve students' self-management skills, decrease state anxiety, increase social interaction skills, improve self-concept, reduce test anxiety, and raise test scores and achievement.[101] Numerous other studies have shown that various measures of anxiety can be lowered and attentiveness can be increased as a result of the use of relaxation procedures or imagery techniques.[102,103,104]

Educators must do everything possible to ensure that children have an opportunity to develop positive attitudes and perceptions of themselves, as attitudes and perceptions of self are formed early in life and remain with us throughout our lives as memory traces and influence our behavior.[105] Children and teens who are given positive messages at home would benefit from reinforcement of those messages at school, while those who receive negative messages at home need exposure to positive messages.

Schools can also provide a system of social support for students. When youth with strong social supports are under even high levels

Relaxation training can help all types of students and can improve self-management skills, decrease state anxiety, increase social interaction skills, improve self-concept, reduce test anxiety, and raise test scores and achievement.

of stress, they exhibit fewer symptoms of anxiety than do youth with less support.[106] Cauce, Comer and Schwartz determined that the long-term effects of a systems-orientated school prevention program were positive.[107] This was an important finding, as prior to this study it was unclear whether preventative efforts had detectable long-term effects, even though their short-term effects were reasonably well established by earlier studies.

The scientific literature supports the idea of a relatively long program as opposed to the introduction of relaxation training in a short time frame. Better relaxation treatment effects were shown when the program was at least six weeks in length. Another important factor in determining success rate is how the program is delivered. Research supports the use of relaxation scripts delivered by people students know. Therefore a program that school personnel themselves could administer should yield optimal results. Within the clinical setting, relaxation as an intervention is more effective after good rapport has been established.

Best results occur with relatively long programs of at least six weeks delivered by school personnel whom students know.

Most research deals with the treatment of an individual or a small group of students. This is especially true when the techniques include a biofeedback component. Perhaps one of the factors that limited research with large groups of students has been the requirement of relatively large blocks of time for teacher training and program implementation. An example of a successful school-wide program is Allen and Klein's implementation of the *Ready, Set, R.E.L.A.X.* program at the elementary school level.[108] The entire school population had the opportunity to be included in the training with minimal time loss from the teaching day. Relaxation scripts were read to the students over the intercom at the same time each day. Details of the program are explained in Appendix C on page 186. For optimal impact, anti-stress practices should be included in every-day school routines.

While many elementary schools use relaxation techniques, most high schools do not. Generally, this is related to the difficulty implementing any school-wide program due to the complexity of a high school class schedule. Successful school-wide programs occur in the elementary school because all of the students are available in a given block of time and students at this age are often more receptive to these techniques due to their general receptiveness to teacher instruction. This is one of the reasons the *Ready, Set, R.E.L.A.X.* program was so successful.

However, programs can be successful at the secondary level even if they are not school-wide. Relaxation techniques at the secondary level are generally introduced and taught to students by health teachers, physical education teachers, counselors, social workers and school psychologists. Classroom teachers who teach focused breathing and a brief one or two minute muscle relaxation exercise can help their students achieve a more relaxed state, increase concentration and participation from the class as a whole. This brief format is easily implemented, as it does not take away from instructional time. High school teachers who use this framework report an overall positive effect and find that the classroom climate is much more conducive to learning.

High school teachers who use a brief relaxation exercise with their class see improved classroom climate for learning.

In addition, studies indicate that adolescents can effectively learn self-relaxation procedures and obtain good results. For example, one study compared the relative efficacy of a therapist-assisted relaxation treatment program with a self-help approach and a self-monitoring condition in the treatment of chronic headaches in adolescents within a school setting.[109] The results indicated that the self-help approach was as effective as the therapist-assisted relaxation condition in reducing the students' headaches. These findings were maintained at a five-month follow-up evaluation. The results suggest that the self-help relaxation procedure is a potential low-cost alternative treatment to a more traditional school-based or therapist-based intervention condition.

Getting Student 'Buy-In'

It is important to lay some groundwork to enlist student cooperation and belief in relaxation techniques in both the school and therapeutic setting. Teens like to have evidence that practicing relaxation techniques are actually beneficial to them. They are able to appreciate the principles and science behind the practice if they are given some direct information and examples.

In my own practice, I always use two specific demonstrations to help my clients understand the power of thoughts. I have also used these successfully in a classroom setting. The first involves a small metal washer (about one inch in diameter) tied to the end of a string about 18 to 24 inches long. You can also simply hook the string to the clip on a pen. Instruct the child or

teen to hold the end of the string between their pointer finger and thumb (emphasize squeezing hard) and holding it in front of their body with their lower arm parallel to the ground and elbow bent at a 90° angle. Then give the following instructions: "Keep your hand and arm perfectly still and simply think about your washer moving left to right across the front of your body. That's right; just think the thought of moving the washer without moving your hand or arm and picture in your mind the washer moving on its own." With this instruction the washer will begin to move in the direction requested. Next use the same instructions and ask that the washer move forward and backward or toward their body and away from their body. Finally ask them to look at you and not to think anything and then give them this instruction. "Now I want you to clear your mind of all thoughts and just listen to my words. Without you even thinking about it, your washer will begin to move in a circle, around and around, in a circle." Repeat this statement several times. Then ask them to look down at the washer; it will be moving in a circle. The movement of the washer occurs because the unconscious is always listening to our thoughts and to others' suggestions. The thought or suggestion of movement triggers the response of small motor muscles in the fingers. This may also be accompanied by imperceptible movement of the arm.

Teens can be shown that practicing relaxation techniques will be beneficial to them through demonstrations that help them understand the power of thoughts.

I follow this activity with the "arm strength" demonstration. Simply ask the client or a student willing to demonstrate to the class to raise one arm or the other straight out from their shoulder to the side of their body (arm parallel to the floor). Then say, "I want to test your arm strength, so I'm going to push down on your wrist with two fingers, and I want you to resist. (push down and then pause.) Now I want you to think the word 'strong' and say 'I am strong' to yourself while I push down on your wrist and you try to keep your arm up. (push down and then pause) Now I want you to think the word 'weak' and say 'I am weak' to yourself while I push down on your wrist and you try to keep your arm up." You can also say to them, "you are weak." With this suggestion, the child or teen finds either a noticeable diminishing of strength or an inability to keep the arm up.

Both of these demonstrations can be used to pique teens' interest and explain the power of our thoughts and words. Our bodies listen to every word we say as result of the action of neuropeptides. Neuropeptides are biochemicals that are called "messenger molecules" because they send chemical messages from the brain to receptor sites on cell membranes throughout the entire body. Like a lock and key mechanism, neuropeptides are the "keys" that open the "locks" on the cell membrane to cause complex and fundamental changes in the cells they lock onto. Thus, neuropeptides are like a molecular language that allows mind, body and emotions to communicate. As a result of neuropeptides, we literally can have a "gut feeling" or a "heavy heart."

Neuropeptides regulate almost all life processes on a cellular level. They are produced primarily in the brain, although almost every tissue in the body produces and exchanges neuropeptides. Scientists have discovered almost 100 different neuropeptides, the first of which were hormones because they are larger molecules. Neuropeptides circulate throughout the body in the blood, lymph and cerebrospinal fluid. Neuropeptides are the reason our body becomes weak when we think of the word "weak," as the memory of what "weak" means is stored within our body neuropeptide memory system.

Therapy Based Relaxation Intervention

School psychologists, counselors and social workers, as well as private clinicians, are in a unique position to implement relaxation techniques in a one-on-one setting. Relaxation techniques are invaluable in the treatment and prevention of a variety of case diagnoses but especially with trauma, depression and anxiety disorders. When treating children or adolescents with these disorders it is important to provide them with tools that they can use to not only "soothe" themselves, but also to help them develop healing positive self-talk statements.

Relaxation techniques are particularly helpful in the treatment of trauma, depression and anxiety disorders.

The first step in therapy is to enlist the client's cooperation and belief in the techniques you will be using to help them heal. To do this I introduce some of the basic tenets of cognitive behavioral therapy (CBT) using the two demonstrations with the washer and string and arm strength detailed in the "Student Buy In" section.

The next step in therapy is to generate a list of positive self-statements, enlisting suggestions from the teen and the parents. I also suggest using statements that are goal behaviors that the teen may not yet be experiencing or believing (e.g. I feel happy, I am worthwhile and important, I always try my best, I listen to my parents, etc.) For good examples of positive self statements check the table of contents in the book, *Ready, Set, R.E.L.A.X.* as well as on pages 5-7 of *RELAX.calm*. Additional positive self statements are listed in Appendix D on page 191 . Part of the teen's homework assignment is to read her list of positive self statements out loud every day.

I then begin to teach them progressive muscle relaxation (PMR) or behavioral relaxation and send them home with either the *Ready, Set, Release* CD or the *Relaxation and Success Imagery* CD (available at www.innercoaching.com) to continue practicing relaxation at home.

Clients have the greatest success when they develop their own positive self-talk recording using their own voice.

The clients who have had the greatest success are those who develop their own positive self-talk recording using their own voice. The script should include a short relaxation exercise followed by a tailor made script. To record the script, bring two tape players to a session, or a tape or CD player and a digital recorder. On one, play relaxing music (see page 45 for suggestions) while on the other, record the client's voice with the background music. Prior to this session, I help my client practice pacing. Most will read their scripts too rapidly and will need practice in order to achieve a slower pace. I also encourage them to use a calm, monotone voice. I play the *Ready, Set, Release* CD or the *Relaxation and Success Imagery* CD to help them model the correct pacing.

Case Studies

The following case studies from my practice present compelling examples of the efficacy of using *RELAX.calm* techniques to treat a variety of anxiety-related problems.

Julie

Julie came to see me at age 19 suffering from depression and drug abuse which led to a suicide attempt. Like others, she found the task of generating a positive self-talk sheet very difficult. Her thoughts about herself had always been negative. Julie had always been her own worst critic. She tended to see her faults and not her strengths. Her parents were good people who were happily married, but very stressed by the behavioral difficulties of Julie's younger brother. Much of their attention and energy was directed toward the brother, as well as Julie's physically handicapped sister. Julie, as the oldest, had taken a great deal of responsibility in caring for her sister. She found leaving home and being on her own as a college freshman very difficult. Although a good athlete and student in high school, she found the rigors of college somewhat overwhelming. She had started smoking pot and drinking alcohol while in her senior year in high school and found herself using daily near the end of her first year in college. She was finding it increasingly difficult to sleep at night and eventually began to think about suicide as an option. She told me that thinking about suicide actually calmed her down and helped her eventually fall to sleep. She found her thoughts continuing to return to the option of suicide. Shortly after she found out that her boyfriend was going out with someone else behind her back, she decided to kill herself. She took an overdose of aspirin, but fortunately was found by her roommate in time to be saved. Julie was a perfect candidate for cognitive behavioral therapy, as she understood immediately the implication of how her thinking contributed to her near death. Julie was also seen by a psychiatrist and started on an antidepressant medication. Several sessions into her treatment she told me that she never knew how good it felt to be relaxed and said, "It feels just like smoking some really good pot." She began using relaxation and listened to the CD, *Relaxation & Success Imagery* (Klein & Klein) daily. Julie posted her positive self-statements on her bedroom door and put them on her MP3 player so that she could listen to them several times a day. Near the end of our tenth session, four months after our first session, she told me that initially she didn't think she would ever really believe the positive things she was saying to herself, but that she indeed believed them now. She discontinued medication after 12 months. I received an e-mail from her two years post treatment. Since treatment she entered a new college and ended up on the Dean's List. She has had some relationship crises, but has been able to stay positive-minded and upbeat. She still has her original positive thought sheet and has added many more and returns to reading them aloud when she finds her mind drifting towards negative thoughts.

Case studies show the efficacy of using *RELAX.calm* techniques to treat a variety of anxiety-related problems

Emily

Emily was 8 years old when I first saw her in my private practice. She was fearful of sleeping in her room and awakened her parents nightly wanting to sleep with them. Bedwetting was also a major problem. Adding to her stress was a learning disability that made school difficult. Emily came from an intact, caring family. There was a history of depression on the maternal side of the family, but there was no presenting pathology in Emily's family. My normal screening using the Parent and Teacher BASC-2 (Behavior Assessment Scale for Children published by

These techniques work with generalized anxiety disorders and obsessive compulsive disorder.

AGS) inventories, the Revised Children's Manifest Anxiety Scale (RCMAS) and Reynolds's Child Depression Inventory supported a diagnosis of anxiety disorder. After spending two sessions with Emily establishing rapport and teaching her the basic principals of cognitive behavioral therapy, I led her through a relaxation exercise using one of the scripts from the *Ready, Set, R.E.L.A.X.* program. She took home a *Ready, Set, Release* CD and practiced relaxation daily. She was instructed to first listen to the CD before she left her room to go to her parent's bedroom. After two weeks of practice she was able to calm herself and was no longer leaving her room. We next addressed the enuresis. A physical exam by her pediatrician was contraindicative of any physical problem causing bedwetting. I showed Emily a picture of the bladder connected to the urethra. I next had her draw her bladder and urethra. I then asked her to draw a line across the bottom of her bladder separating it from the urethra. I asked her to imagine that this line was a gate. I then led her through a progressive relaxation exercise and asked her to picture in her mind her bladder and urethra and then to imagine a gate closing off the urethra. She was then asked to keep a chart of her dry nights so we could track her progress. She continued practicing relaxation daily and each night before bed did a relaxation exercise and in her "mind's eye" imagined a gate closing off her bladder. The frequency of her dry nights increased immediately and within a month she stayed dry nightly. Near the end of her treatment she said, "Dr. Klein, why doesn't everyone learn how to do this?" To her credit she introduced relaxation training to several of her classmates and her teacher.

Bill

In addition to treating clients with generalized anxiety disorders, I have had good success in treating adolescents with obsessive compulsive disorder (OCD) as well. Bill was a 14-year-old who was suffering from OCD. His two primary symptoms were picking the skin from his toe cuticles, as well as licking his lips. Both behaviors were causing physical damage and embarrassment. His lips were raw and bright red and because of the appearance of his feet, he refused to shower with his classmates in school or go to the beach or pool in the summer. He was very motivated to make a change and committed to daily relaxation practice sessions at home using the *Relaxation and Success Imagery* CD. An important aspect of his treatment was to identify his stress triggers. His triggers were primarily due to his tendency to be perfectionist with school and the pressure he felt to fit in with his peers. His parents were motivated as well because they did not want to use medication to help control Bill's anxiety. His treatment was similar to the other two cases. After using the demonstration of the washer and string and arm strength exercises, I led him through some basic breathing exercises. A side benefit of using controlled breathing is that the teen begins to feel that he is in control of his respiration instead of feeling it is out of his control. I always demonstrate to my clients the difference between chest breathing, which occurs when a person is under stress, and stomach breathing (see Chapter 4 for more details). During the next two sessions I worked with Bill on progressive muscle relaxation. He practiced at home on a daily basis and developed a good ability to relax. Once I was confident in his depth of relaxation I began to have him imagine his "triggers" while staying relaxed. This systematic desensitization of his triggers was very successful. In addition, whenever he felt stressed from other events he would repeat his mantra, "calm and relax." At the time of his discharge he was no longer licking or picking and made remarkable gains in self-confidence.

Troy

Recently I've used this same technique of systematic desensitization with a 13-year-old boy who had a storm phobia. Four years previous to our therapy he had witnessed a tornado in the distance. His fear of that tornado hitting his house was very real and cemented the memory of the radio and television storm warnings, the panic and rush of his family calling him inside to the basement, the ominous dark clouds, the thunder and lightening of the rain storm that preceded his sighting of the tornado, and the feeling of the heat and humidity. Subsequent to this storm he began sleeping on the floor as he was afraid to be too close to his bedroom wall in case a tornado would strike in the middle of the night. In addition, he refused to go outside if there was even a severe thunderstorm watch and became nervous on hot and humid days. Whenever traveling in a car he insisted that all the windows be closed because the sound of the wind when the windows were open caused the same intense anxiety responses. In the initial stage of treatment he was very intrigued by the washer and arm strength demonstration and enjoyed the feeling of being relaxed. We developed a list of triggers of his fear and continued to practice

Techniques of systematic desensitization can be applied to most phobic behaviors.

relaxation paired with my description of impending storms beginning with a storm in a neighboring state. He used Inner Coaching's CD *Relaxation & Success Imagery* to practice the same visualizations at home between sessions. I saw him five times over the course of two months. Coincidentally there was a storm warning issued the day of his fifth session. I reframed this warning as a perfect opportunity for him to practice his breathing and relaxation "in vivo." When he came in for his sixth session both he and his mother reported that his fear was completely gone. He was sleeping in his bed, riding in the car with the windows open, and stayed outside to watch the approaching thunder storm that hit shortly after he left his fifth session.

These same techniques can be applied to most phobic behaviors with good success and provide the therapist with a proven way of helping children and teens overcome fears that interfere with what should be a relatively carefree time in their lives.

I've also used these same techniques as an adjunct to treating clients with post-traumatic stress disorder. My primary approach is using the trauma treatment program Structured Sensory Intervention for Traumatized Children, Adolescent and Parents (SITCAP) developed by Dr. William Steele (www.starrtraining.org). Because trauma memories are stored in the body as implicit memories, experiential approaches are essential in helping children and teens process the memories. Using the techniques in the *RELAX.calm* program helps your teen client become empowered by supporting the changes taking place from being a victim to becoming a survivor and then a thriver.

PART II

Scripts

RELAX.CALM — FACILITATOR'S GUIDE

Organization of the *RELAX.calm* scripts

The program scripts are divided into five main themes. You can pick and choose scripts according to the particular goals and needs of the teen(s) with whom you're working.

R. Responsibility: Making good choices for yourself and your relationships.

E. Empowerment: Feeling positive about yourself, competent with peers and feeling supported by others.

L. Learning: Developing skills to acquire and retain knowledge and finding enjoyment in creative pursuits.

A. Attitudes: Developing and practicing the attitudes, values and morals needed to become a healthy person.

X. Expand: Increasing your ability to feel calm and centered.

> **Scripts are organized into themes of Responsibility, Empowerment, Learning, Attitudes and Expanding.**

To address more specific topics within the five main themes use the cross reference grid on pages 63-65, where 17 attributes of healthy adolescent development are identified.

Using Relax.calm

Getting 'buy in': The first step in using the *RELAX.calm* is to enlist participant cooperation and belief in the techniques you will be using by teaching them the power of their own thoughts. Doing the washer and arm strength demonstrations outlined on page 49-50 provides a good start in developing interest in how thoughts can directly relate to behavior.

Progressive Muscle Relaxation: We suggest six to 10 "training" sessions of using the progressive muscle relaxation scripts on pages 68-79, prior to using the scripts in the other sections. If this is not possible, encouraging one daily practice session at home can significantly hasten the training effect. Most teens experiencing anxiety issues are quite motivated to practice these techniques at home because they hope to rid themselves of unwanted feelings of anxiety. Others motivated to practice at home may include teens interested in improving their performance in athletics, music or learning. If you are training a small group or a classroom, identify those who seem to have difficulty achieving a relaxed state. A few individual sessions with a counselor or psychologist can help determine what is causing the difficulty. Some individuals may need to practice one-on-one before being able to relax within a group context. An excellent behavioral relaxation exercise is available on the CD *Relaxation & Success Imagery* by Klein and Klein and can be ordered at www.innercoaching.com.

> Train the participant using progressive muscle relaxation scripts and demonstrate stomach breathing vs. chest breathing.

Breath: Before you begin, demonstrate the difference between chest breathing, which occurs when a person is under stress, and stomach breathing. Correct inhalation and exhalation require fully engaging the diaphragm. When breathing correctly the stomach "inflates" or expands out while inhaling and "deflates" or "caves in" while exhaling. To begin, ask the teen to inhale through their nose and exhale through their mouth. This helps

them focus on the act of breathing. Once they start relaxing, tell them they can breathe in any way that is most comfortable. Most people, as they get relaxed, inhale and exhale through the nose.

Music: Using relaxing music in the background helps anchor the relaxation experience to the music. After a number of training sessions the music alone can elicit the same relaxed state. When introducing a script, begin playing the music, dim the lights if possible and slow down your pace of talking and body language. The more relaxed you are, the easier it is to convey a sense of relaxation in your voice and body language. Allow the music to run one or two minutes before you begin reading and ask the participants to be aware of their breathing. Suggestions for music are listed on page 45.

Relaxation Scripts: The next step is to use a relaxation script so the teen can experience how good it feels to be relaxed. Starting with progressive muscle relaxation scripts beginning on page 68-79 allows the teen to develop some comfort in their ability to relax. The therapist, teacher or parent can read these scripts to the teen or use the *RELAX.calm* CD that is a companion to this program. These scripts can also be downloaded to an iPod or mp3 player at http://www.innercoaching.com. If reading the scripts, give the teen the option of listening with their eyes either open or closed. If they prefer to keep their eyes open, ask them to stare at a certain spot and continue to stare at that spot throughout the script. Some teens with a history of earlier trauma may feel safer with their eyes open. Others may choose to start with their eyes open and, once they feel comfortable, close their eyes. If you are using the exercises in a setting where there may be distracting sounds, give them the suggestion that if they hear sounds while they are relaxing, these sounds will actually help them relax even more. Refer to the relaxation scripts on pages 68-79 if you are reading the beginning relaxation scripts instead of using the *RELAX.calm* CD.

Read scripts at a slow pace with a somewhat monotone voice to give teens time to maintain relaxation and form mental images.

It is important to read the scripts at a slow pace in somewhat of a monotone voice. This pacing is necessary to give teens enough time to maintain relaxation and form mental images while the monotone voice helps promote relaxation. Feel free to change wording or other content in the scripts to fit your intended audience. You will notice that each *RELAX.calm* script begins with the same phrase. The opening is intended to act as an anchor and aid the teen's ability to concentrate on the main body of the script. Both the music and the ability to relax help the teen focus and block out interfering thoughts. If you are uncertain about delivering the scripts, a few practice sessions with a colleague is very helpful. Remember to slow your pace, breath slowly, use a monotone voice, and allow yourself to relax as you read the script.

Follow-up Discussion: For many of the scripts, suggestions are given to the classroom teacher, counselor or therapist for a brief follow-up discussion or activity. The discussion questions and activities can help anchor the positive self statements and overall themes of the scripts.

Using the Scripts—Tips for the Facilitator

1. Dim the lights
2. Play relaxing music (see page 45)
3. Instruct the participant(s) to close their eyes and find a comfortable position. This is most often achieved by dropping their head slightly and placing their hands and arms on their legs. If space permits they may lay on their back with their arms at their sides, with a small pillow placed behind their neck.
4. Begin each script by reading the warm up section with a calm, monotone voice. The more relaxed you are as you read, the easier it is for the participant to relax as they mirror the calmness in your voice.
5. Continue reading the script at an even, slow pace, pausing frequently.
6. You may choose to use the discussion questions and activities provided at the end of the scripts or develop follow up options of your own.
7. Scripts can be repeated or modified to meet a particular interest or circumstance.

When To Use *RELAX.calm*

RELAX.calm scripts can be used almost any time of the day and almost any situation. Here are some examples:

1. To increase concentration
2. To help improve school performance
3. To help calm down after conflict
4. To teach how to use breathing and PMR to achieve the relaxation response
5. To decrease test anxiety
6. To access creativity to enhance writing, music performance, and art
7. To help develop positive self-talk skills
8. To help develop a positive self concept
9. To overcome unwanted habits
10. To help prepare for a restful sleep

We appreciate your interest in using *RELAX.calm* to help adolescents and hope you find it as valuable as we have. We would appreciate your feedback and welcome any questions. Please visit us at http://www.innercoaching.com for more information, to order additional products or to send us your comments. You can also contact us directly at rogerjklein@yahoo.com or kids@ readysetrelax.com.

CROSS REFERENCE OF MAJOR TOPICS

PMR
Progressive Muscle Relaxation (pp 68-79)

	PMR or Behavioral Relaxation	Self Concept	Creativity	Test Preparation	Academics/Learning	Achievement/Involvement	Social Skills/Relationships	Conflict Resolution/Restraint	Problem Solving/Decision Making	Self Improvement	Motivation/Goal Setting/Persistence	Service/Values	Peer Pressure/Bullying	Integrity/Honesty	Personal Health	Nature/Environment	Cooperation/Teamwork
1 - Relaxing Shoulders, Neck & Face	●																
2 - Relaxing Legs & Feet	●																
3 - Relaxing Arms & Hands	●																
4 - Relaxing Lower Body	●																
5 - Relaxing Upper Body	●																
6 - Relaxing the Whole Body	●																
7 - Quick Relaxation Exercise	●																

RESPONSIBILITY
Making good choices for yourself and your relationships. (pp 82-97)

	PMR or Behavioral Relaxation	Self Concept	Creativity	Test Preparation	Academics/Learning	Achievement/Involvement	Social Skills/Relationships	Conflict Resolution/Restraint	Problem Solving/Decision Making	Self Improvement	Motivation/Goal Setting/Persistence	Service/Values	Peer Pressure/Bullying	Integrity/Honesty	Personal Health	Nature/Environment	Cooperation/Teamwork
Forecasting									●		●						
Game of Life											●						
High Expectations											●						
No Repeats							●	●									
Railroad Crossing									●						●		
Smooth Sailing									●					●	●		
Stepping Stones									●		●				●	●	
Tunnel Vision		●							●		●				●		

CROSS REFERENCE OF MAJOR TOPICS

EMPOWERMENT

Feeling positive about yourself and competent with peers. Feeling supported by others. (pp 100-121)

	PMR or Behavioral Relaxation	Self Concept	Creativity	Test Preparation	Academics/Learning	Achievement/Involvement	Social Skills/Relationships	Conflict Resolution/Restraint	Problem Solving/Decision Making	Self Improvement	Motivation/Goal Setting/Persistence	Service/Values	Peer Pressure/Bullying	Integrity/Honesty	Personal Health	Nature/Environment	Cooperation/Teamwork
Amaze Yourself		●								●	●						
Crowd Support		●				●				●	●						
Crystal Clear										●							
Floating By		●					●						●				
Gone Fishing									●								
Into Focus			●										●				
Joy Ride									●				●				
Rain Delay			●						●								
Self Portrait		●														●	
Spring Fever												●				●	
Up in Smoke									●	●						●	

TEST PREPARATION
ACHIEVEMENT TESTS

(pp 124-129)

	PMR or Behavioral Relaxation	Self Concept	Creativity	Test Preparation	Academics/Learning	Achievement/Involvement	Social Skills/Relationships	Conflict Resolution/Restraint	Problem Solving/Decision Making	Self Improvement	Motivation/Goal Setting/Persistence	Service/Values	Peer Pressure/Bullying	Integrity/Honesty	Personal Health	Nature/Environment	Cooperation/Teamwork
General Testing				●													
Achievement - Day 1				●													
Achievement - Day 2				●													
Achievement - Day 3				●													

LEARNING

Developing skills to acquire and retain knowledge.
Finding enjoyment in creative pursuits. (pp 130-139)

	PMR or Behavioral Relaxation	Self Concept	Creativity	Test Preparation	Academics/Learning	Achievement/Involvement	Social Skills/Relationships	Conflict Resolution/Restraint	Problem Solving/Decision Making	Self Improvement	Motivation/Goal Setting/Persistence	Service/Values	Peer Pressure/Bullying	Integrity/Honesty	Personal Health	Nature/Environment	Cooperation/Teamwork
Beached					●											●	
Freeze Frame					●	●											
Snowflake Symphony			●							●							
Star Cruise	●	●															
Welcome Web					●						●		●				

CROSS REFERENCE OF MAJOR TOPICS

ATTITUDES

Developing and practicing the attitudes and values needed to become a complete person. (pp 142-165)

	PMR or Behavioral Relaxation	Self Concept	Creativity	Test Preparation	Academics/Learning	Achievement/Involvement	Social Skills/Relationships	Conflict Resolution/Restraint	Problem Solving/Decision Making	Self Improvement	Motivation/Goal Setting/Persistence	Service/Values	Peer Pressure/Bullying	Integrity/Honesty	Personal Health	Nature/Environment	Cooperation/Teamwork
Bio Bay						●										●	
Extra Extra			●									●					
Heads Up							●						●				
Diversity = Strength							●					●	●				●
Media Madness	●								●			●	●				
Melting Away									●			●				●	
Memories							●			●					●		
Personal Junket									●			●				●	
Scratch the Surface					●		●			●						●	
Three Cheers							●					●		●			
V for Victory							●										●
Vitamin See							●								●		●

X-PAND

Exploring your ability to feel calm and centered. (pp 168-175)

	PMR or Behavioral Relaxation	Self Concept	Creativity	Test Preparation	Academics/Learning	Achievement/Involvement	Social Skills/Relationships	Conflict Resolution/Restraint	Problem Solving/Decision Making	Self Improvement	Motivation/Goal Setting/Persistence	Service/Values	Peer Pressure/Bullying	Integrity/Honesty	Personal Health	Nature/Environment	Cooperation/Teamwork
Elevator Music	●								●								
Pressure Valve	●							●									
Relaxation Angle	●								●								
Taps	●		●		●						●						

Progressive Muscle Relaxation

Learning the relaxation response.

⊘ ◄ ►

Subject:	Progressive Muscle Relaxation
Into Focus:	Students will learn to relax their shoulders, neck and face by tensing and relaxing their muscles.
Phrase:	I am calm and relaxed

PMR 1 — RELAXING SHOULDERS, NECK AND FACE

›› Introduction

Sit comfortably with your eyes closed. Take three long, deep breaths. *(Pause)* Feel yourself relaxing more and more with each breath. Let the rhythm of the music calm you. Feel your muscles relax and your heart and breathing slow. Say to yourself, "**I am calm and relaxed.**"

›› Script

Become aware of your breathing. Inhale through your nose and exhale through your mouth. Slow and relaxed. Feel the air pass through your nose as you inhale and pass over your lips as you exhale. With each breath notice that you become more and more relaxed. Say to yourself, "I am calm and relaxed." Continue to breathe slowly both inhaling and exhaling through your nose.

 Now close your eyes as tight as you can. Squeeze them shut. Feel your face muscles tighten even more by biting down hard. Hold the tension... squeeze hard. Now relax your face. Keep your eyes closed gently. Relax your jaw. Feel the difference between tension and relaxation. Take a deep breath and relax your whole body.

Once again squeeze your eyes closed. Pretend there are lead weights attached to the end of your eyelids pulling them down even farther. Bite down as hard as you can. Feel the tension in your face. Now relax your face. Feel the tension fade away. Now wrinkle your forehead muscles. Scrunch them up and hold the tension while I count to three; one, two, three. Now smooth out your forehead muscles. Smooth and relax. Let go of any tension in your face. As your face relaxes feel the relaxation spread throughout your body.

Tense your shoulders and neck by pulling your shoulders up to your ears. Hold your shoulders in that position. Feel the tension in your back, shoulders and neck. Hold that tension as I count to three; one, two, three. Now let your shoulders drop. Feel the relaxation as you rest your shoulders. Neck relaxed. Shoulders relaxed. Now raise your shoulders up once more. Pull them up right to your ears. Feel the tension in your neck, shoulders, and back. Now drop your shoulders. Relax your neck, shoulders and back. Now, pull your shoulders up one more time. Feel the tension. Hold it while I count to three; one, two, three. Relax your shoulders. Feel your upper back, shoulders and neck relaxing. Take a moment to enjoy this relaxed feeling. *(Pause)* Say to youself, "I feel relaxed and calm."

Now, take a deep breath and as you let it out allow yourself to slowly return to the room. Open your eyes and stretch. Be sure to practice relaxing your face, shoulders and neck tonight when you lay down in bed.

≫ Discussion/Reflection

· Which muscles were the most difficult to relax?

Subject: Progressive Muscle Relaxation

Into Focus: This script teaches you how to relax your hands and arms by tensing and relaxing muscles. Attention will be focused on the awareness of the contrasting feelings of tension and relaxation.

Phrase: "calm" and "relax"

PMR 2 — RELAXING ARMS AND HANDS

» Introduction

Sit comfortably with your eyes closed. Take three long, deep breaths. *(Pause)* Feel yourself relaxing more and more with each breath. Let the rhythm of the music calm you. Feel your muscles relax and your heart rate and breathing slow. Say to yourself, "I am calm and relaxed."

» Script

As you listen to my voice and the music, let all other sounds fade away. Listening, breathing slowly, you are feeling more and more relaxed.

Now pretend you have a warm lump of clay in your right hand. Squeeze it as hard as you can. Make your right hand into a tight fist. Squeeze it closed as hard as you can. Now hold it closed while I count to three; one, two, three. Now relax your right hand and let it go limp. Feel the difference. Feel how good it is for your hand to be relaxed. Smooth out the tension and feel the relaxation. Right hand feeling heavy, relaxed and warm. You may even feel the air current surrounding your limp and relaxed right hand. Now keep your right hand relaxed while we concentrate on your left hand. Pretend you have a warm lump of clay in your left hand. Squeeze it as hard as you can. Make your left hand into a tight fist. Squeeze it closed as hard as you can. Now hold it closed while I count to three; one, two, three. Now relax your left hand and let it go limp. Feel the difference. Feel how good it is for your left hand to be relaxed. Smooth out the tension and feel the relaxation. Left hand feeling heavy, relaxed and warm. You may even feel the air current surrounding your limp and relaxed left hand. As both hands relax you may feel a "tingling" sensation in your finger tips as your blood flows into both hands warming and relaxing them.

Good job! Now relax your whole body while you take a deep breath by breathing in through your nose. Hold that breath for just a moment and then exhale through your mouth. Let the air out slowly, and in your mind say the words **"calm" and "relax."** Breathe slowly and now both inhale and exhale through your nose and let go of any tension. Be aware of this feeling of relaxation. Imagine yourself practicing relaxing your hands tonight while you lay in bed.

Imagine tightening the muscles in your hands and then relaxing those muscles. Relaxing at night can help you fall asleep.

Now, bend your right arm at the elbow, putting your fist near your right shoulder, and tighten all the muscles in your right arm. Make a muscle in your right arm and squeeze it hard. Hold the tension now while I count to three; one, two, three. Relax your arm now and let it go limp as you let your right arm drop to your side. Limp and relaxed. Heavy, relaxed, feel your hands warming. Be aware of the good feeling of relaxation. Relax your arm completely. In your mind say the words **"calm" and "relax."** Now, bend your left arm at the elbow, putting your fist near your left shoulder, and tighten all the muscles in your left arm. Make a muscle in your left arm and squeeze it hard. Hold the tension now while I count to three; one, two, three. Relax your arm now and let it go limp as you let your left arm drop to your side. Limp and relaxed. Heavy, relaxed, feel both hands warming. Be aware of the good feeling of relaxation. Relax your arms completely. In your mind say the words **"calm" and "relax."** Feel your hands warming. Relaxation is the opposite of tension. You can relax by taking a deep breath, saying the words **"calm" and "relax,"** and letting go of all the tension in your muscles. Take a few moments to appreciate the good feeling of relaxation. *(Pause)* Now slowly allow yourself to come back to the room. Open your eyes. Stretch your arms, your legs and your mind.

≫ Discussion/Reflection

- How did it feel when you tensed your muscles?
- What part was hard to do?
- Could you feel the difference between feeling tense and feeling relaxed?

Subject: Progressive Muscle Relaxation

Into Focus: This script will teach you how to relax your legs and feet by tensing and relaxing your muscles.

Phrase: I am calm and relaxed

PMR 3 — RELAXING LEGS AND FEET

» Introduction

Sit comfortably with your eyes closed. Take three long, deep breaths. *(Pause)* Feel yourself relaxing more and more with each breath. Let the rhythm of the music calm you. Feel your muscles relax and your heart rate and breathing slow. Say to yourself, **"I am calm and relaxed."**

» Script

Become aware of your breathing. Inhale through your nose and exhale through your mouth. Slow and relaxed. Feel the air pass through your nose as you inhale and pass over your lips as you exhale. With each breath notice that you become more and more relaxed. Say to yourself, "I am calm and relaxed." Now continue to breathe slowly and both inhale and exhale through your nose.

Stretch your right leg out in front of you and pull your toes on your right foot toward your knee. Your knee should be straight, your foot slightly off the ground, and your toes flexed back toward your knee. Hold that position and feel the tension in your upper leg muscles, your right ankle, foot and toes. Continue to hold this position as I count to three: one, two, three. Good, now relax your right leg, put your foot back on the floor and relax your ankle, foot and toes.

Now let's relax your left leg. Stretch your left leg out in front of you and pull your toes on your left foot toward your knee. Your knee should be straight, your foot slightly off the ground, and your toes flexed back toward your knee. Hold that position and feel the tension in your upper leg muscles, your left ankle, foot and toes. Continue to hold this position as I count to three: one, two, three. Good, now relax your left leg, put your foot back on the floor and relax your ankle, foot and toes.

Now lift both legs and straighten your knees and pull the toes on both feet toward your knees. Tense all the muscles in your legs and ankles. Feel the tension. Now relax your legs and feel the difference. Feel how good it is to relax your legs. Relax your ankles, feet and toes. Relaxation is the opposite of tension. Now push your feet down. Pretend you are stepping into sand and want to bury your feet. Push them down hard and feel the tension in your legs, ankles and feet.

Hold that tension while I count to three: one, two, three. Good, now relax your legs, relax your feet, and relax your toes. Let all your muscles go limp and soft. Say to yourself, "I am calm and relaxed." Feel all the tension drain from your body. Now slowly come back to the room by opening your eyes and stretching. Stretch your arms, legs and your mind.

» Discussion/Reflection

- Did you feel the difference between feeling tense and relaxed?
- What part of your body seemed to relax the fastest?
- When is a good time for you to practice relaxing?

Subject: Progressive Muscle Relaxation

Into Focus: Students will practice relaxing their lower body by tensing and releasing their muscles. Attention will be focused on their awareness on the contrasting feelings of tension and relaxation.

Phrase I am calm and relaxed

PMR 4 — RELAXING LOWER BODY

» Introduction

Sit comfortably with your eyes closed. Take three long, deep breaths. *(Pause)* Feel yourself relaxing more and more with each breath. Let the rhythm of the music calm you. Feel your muscles relax and your heart rate and breathing slow. Say to yourself, "**I am calm and relaxed.**"

» Script

Become aware of your breathing. Inhale through your nose and exhale through your mouth. Slow and relaxed. Feel the air pass through your nose as you inhale and pass over your lips as you exhale. With each breath notice that you become more and more relaxed. Say to yourself, "I am calm and relaxed." Continue to breathe slowly and as you relax begin to both inhale and exhale through your nose.

Think about your toes. Now scrunch them up in your shoes as tight as you can and keep them scrunched up while I count to three; one, two, three. Good, now relax your toes. Let them float in your shoes. Once again, scrunch your toes. *(Pause)* Hold it. Now relax your toes. Now straighten your legs and tense all the muscles in your upper and lower legs by trying to pull your toes toward your knees. Hold this tension while I count to three; one, two, three. Good, now relax your feet, ankles and legs. Put your feet flat on the ground and feel your legs getting heavier and heavier. Relaxation is the opposite of tension. Relax your toes, ankles and legs. Toes relaxed, ankles relaxed, legs feeling heavier and heavier.

Now take another deep breath and hold it. Feel the tension. *(Pause)* Now release it and breathe slowly and easily. With each breath becoming more and more relaxed. Think of being so relaxed that you feel yourself floating down through your chair. Floating, yet heavy; relaxed muscles; clear mind; slow breathing. Now tense the muscles in your hips and stomach. Make your stomach muscles hard. Hold this tense feeling while I count to three; one, two, three. Release the tightness and relax the muscles in your hips and stomach. Stomach relaxed, hips relaxed, legs and feet relaxed, breathing slowing.

Now tense your stomach once more. Make the muscles hard and tense. Hold the tension. Stomach tense and hard… good. Now release the tension. Smooth muscles, relaxed stomach, relaxed hips. Legs and feet relaxed. Toes floating. Breathing slowing. Relaxation is the opposite of tension.

Take a moment to appreciate the good feelings of relaxation. Say to yourself, "I am calm and relaxed." Lower body relaxed and heavy. With each breath, more relaxation. Listen to the music and let any tension float down through your body and out your toes. Now as you do this, slowly allow yourself to come back to the room. Open your eyes. Stretch your arms, your legs and your mind. Practice relaxing your lower body tonight when you are lying in bed. Remember to relax your toes, feet, legs, hips and stomach.

» Discussion/Reflection

- How did it feel when you became relaxed?
- When else could you practice these exercises?
- Why is it good to relax your body?

Subject: Progressive Muscle Relaxation

Into Focus: Students will practice relaxing their body parts by tensing and relaxing their muscles. Attention will be focused on their awareness of the contrasting feelings of tension and relaxation.

Phrase: I am calm and relaxed

PMR 5 — RELAXING WHOLE BODY FROM TOES TO HEAD

≫ Introduction

Sit comfortably with your eyes closed. Take three long, deep breaths. *(Pause)* Feel yourself relaxing more and more with each breath. Let the rhythm of the music calm you. Feel your muscles relax and your heart and breathing slow. Say to yourself, "**I am calm and relaxed.**"

≫ Script

Become aware of your breathing. Inhale through your nose and exhale through your mouth. Slow and relaxed. Feel the air pass through your nose as you inhale and pass over your lips as you exhale. With each breath notice that you become more and more relaxed. Say to yourself, "I am calm and relaxed." Continue to breathe slowly and now both inhale and exhale through your nose. As you breathe out, feel all the tension drain from your lower body. Relax your toes, feet and ankles. Release all the tension from your legs. Feet relaxed, legs relaxed. With each breath notice that you achieve deeper and deeper relaxation. You may also begin to notice your legs getting heavier and heavier. With each breath, heart rate slows and relaxation spreads.

Now, tense your stomach muscles, make them tight and hard. Hold that tension while I count to three; one, two, three. Good, now relax your stomach, smooth out the muscles. Feel your stomach relaxing more and more.

Now make a fist with your right hand. Feel the tension in your right fist and arm as you continue to squeeze. Now relax your hand, release the tension. Let your hand and arm relax. Now squeeze your left hand into a fist. Tense all the muscles in your arm, shoulder and fist. Squeezing and tensing all the muscles of your left hand and arm. Hold the tension. Now release the tension and feel the muscles relax. Relaxing both arms, both hands. Fingers relaxed. Arms beginning to feel heavier and heavier. You may even notice a tingling feeling in your fingers as your hands warm. Arms relaxed and heavy. Lower body and stomach relaxed. Chest relaxed. Now as you relax your arms, pull your shoulders up toward your ears and hold them while I count to three... shoulders up, tension in your back and neck... one, two, three. Drop your shoulders. Relax your neck. Arms and hands relaxed. Breathing slow and easy.

Now take another deep breath, and as you inhale imagine a white light entering your body with the air you inhale. This white light surrounds any tension inside your body. As you exhale, the while light carries the tension out of your body. Body relaxed, arms feeling heavy and relaxed, hands warming. Legs and feet relaxed.

Now tense the muscles in your scalp and forehead by raising your eyebrows as high as you can. Feel the tension in your forehead. Hold it. Now relax your forehead and scalp. Smooth out all the muscles in your face. Eyes relaxed and closed; face relaxed; jaw relaxed.

Now take a deep breath and as you breathe out feel your body become even more relaxed. Let yourself slowly come back to the room. Open your eyes. Stretch your arms, your legs and your mind.

Practice relaxing your whole body at home tonight. A good time to do this is when you are laying in bed getting ready to fall asleep.

» Discussion/Reflection

- Is it getting easier to relax?
- Which muscles relaxed the best?
- When is another time you could practice these exercises?

Subject:	Progressive Muscle Relaxation
Into Focus:	Students will learn to relax their whole body by using the phrase "calm and relax," deep breathing and muscle relaxation.
Phrase:	"calm" and "relax"

PMR 6 — QUICK RELAXATION EXERCISE #1

›› Introduction

Sit comfortably with your eyes closed. Take three long, deep breaths. *(Pause)* Feel yourself relaxing more and more with each breath. Let the rhythm of the music calm you. Feel your muscles relax and your heart and breathing slow. Say to yourself, "I am calm and relaxed."

›› Script

Become aware of your breathing. Inhale through your nose and exhale through your mouth. Slow and relaxed. Feel the air pass through your nose as you inhale and pass over your lips as you exhale. With each breath notice that you become more and more relaxed. Say to yourself, "I am calm and relaxed." Continue breathing slowly and as you relax begin to both inhale and exhale through your nose.

Relax your forehead and facial muscles. Feel the muscles in your neck and shoulders and tell them to relax. As you continue to relax, notice your breathing slowing down. Feel the muscles in your hands and arms and tell them to relax. Let go of all the tension in your face, neck, shoulders, arms and hands. Say to yourself, **"calm" and "relax"** and feel your whole body become even more relaxed. Chest and stomach muscles relaxed. Tell your legs and feet to relax. As you continue to relax say the words, "calm" and "relax" to yourself over and over. "Calm" and "relax." You can use these words any time you feel nervous or tense and your body will respond by becoming relaxed.

Now feel yourself drifting further and further into deep relaxation. You may notice a heavy feeling in your arms and legs. Each breath helps you relax more and more. Enjoy the feeling of relaxation. Practice relaxing any time you feel tense or nervous.

Now, take a deep breath, and as you let it out allow yourself to slowly come back to your room. Open your eyes and stretch. Practice relaxing your whole body tonight at home.

›› Discussion/Reflection

- Explain how your body felt when it was relaxed.
- Was it hard or easy to relax your whole body?
- Would it help you to relax yourself before a test?

Subject:	Progressive Muscle Relaxation
Into Focus:	Students will learn a brief, relaxation exercise that can be used in a variety of settings.
Phrase:	"calm" and "relax"

PMR 7 — QUICK RELAXATION EXERCISE #2

≫ Introduction

Sit comfortably with your eyes closed. Take three long, deep breaths. *(Pause)* Feel yourself relaxing more and more with each breath. Let the rhythm of the music calm you. Feel your muscles relax and your heart and breathing slow. Say to yourself, "I am calm and relaxed."

≫ Script

Become aware of your breathing keeping it slow and relaxed. Breath in through your nose and exhale through your mouth. Notice the air passing through your nostrils as you continue to inhale and the feeling of the air passing over your lips as you exhale. Continue to notice how calm this makes you feel. As you relax begin to both inhale and exhale through your nose. *(Pause)* Each time feel the air coming in and going out. Say in your mind the words **"calm" and "relax."** Now, with your eyes, look up while keeping your neck and head still. Try to look at your eyebrows. Now, take a deep breath and close your eyes. Slowly breathe out and relax your eyes. Say in your mind the words "calm" and "relax." Let go of any tension in your body and allow your whole body to become fully relaxed. Be aware of your body and as you exhale tell any part that is tense to relax completely. Now, take another deep breath and tell your body to relax even more. Breath slowly and enjoy how good it feels to be relaxed. *(Pause)* When you are ready allow yourself to come back to your room. Open your eyes and sit quietly.

Practice this exercise anytime you feel nervous or tense. Remember, just take a deep breath and hold it. Look up to your eyebrows. Close your eyes and slowly breathe out while relaxing your eyes and your whole body. Use this brief relaxation exercise whenever you feel tense or anxious. Practice this exercise at home.

≫ Discussion/Reflection

· Were you able to achieve a feeling of relaxation?
· When could you use this technique?

 **R**esponsibility

Making good choices for yourself and
your relationships.

Empowerment

Feeling positive about yourself and competent
with peers. Feeling supported by others.

 **L**earning

Developing skills to acquire and retain knowledge.
Finding enjoyment in creative pursuits.

 **A**ttitudes

Developing and practicing the attitudes and
values needed to become a complete person.

  **X**-pand

Exploring your ability to feel calm and centered.

Subject:	Responsibility
Into Focus:	Life is unpredictable. But only you can control your reactions to it.
Affirmation:	**I expect success and am able to handle any disappointment.**

FORECASTING

≫ Introduction

Sit comfortably with your eyes closed. Take three long, deep breaths. *(Pause)* Feel yourself relaxing more and more with each breath. Let the rhythm of the music calm you. Feel your muscles relax and your heart rate and breathing slow. Say to yourself, "I am calm and relaxed."

≫ Script

Imagine that you are sleeping in your bed. Your breathing is slow and relaxed. Your body feels heavy, your muscles are loose, you are totally relaxed. Your clock radio alarm comes on like it does every morning. See yourself reach over and hit the snooze button knowing that you have time before you have to get up. As you turn over in bed, you hear a soft voice on the radio. It sounds like a weather forecast. You try to hear it but you can't make out the words. *(Pause)* You doze off and quickly start dreaming. In your dream you see yourself standing in front of a large calendar with a pointer in your hand. You are surrounded by white puffy clouds. You are a weather forecaster on TV and it's time to make your prediction for your day. *(Pause)* You look at the calendar and see that you have a lot to do today. You feel optimistic and excited about the forecast. *(Pause)* Imagine looking into the camera and saying your prediction, "Very busy with a 100% chance of success."

The alarm rings again and the clouds quickly disperse. See yourself reach over and hit the snooze button again. You fall asleep quickly and feel lucky to get back into your dream. The clouds reappear, but this time they are gray. Listen as thunder rumbles in the distance. Despite the forecast you are able to stay calm and relaxed. *(Pause)* Look into the camera and say your prediction, "Bad news with a chance of disappointment."

Your alarm wakes you again. This time you must get up or be late. Imagine sitting up in bed and stretching. Think about your day ahead. Is it busy or stressful or unorganized or unpredictable? *(Pause)* Make a forecast for your day recognizing the clouds that may be forming. *(Long Pause)* Whatever the forecast, you know that you have the skills to stay calm and relaxed.

Take a deep breath and say to yourself three times: **I expect success and am able to handle any disappointment....**

Life is unpredictable and always full of surprises just like the weather. Sometimes it helps to forecast what might be on the horizon to be better prepared to handle a situation. You are confident that you are ready to face the storms and dark skies of life, and know that the sun will always return.

As you breathe slowly return to your room. Open your eyes. Stretch your arms, legs and your mind.

» Discussion/Reflection

· Using description words, talk about your weather forecast for today.

» Fast Fact

A rainbow was visible for 6 hours at Wetherly, Yorkshire (UK) on March 14, 1994. This is rare because most rainbows last only a few minutes.

» Alternate Affirmations

· **I am realistic about my abilities.**
· **I am realistic about my circumstances.**
· **I have the ability to deal with any "forecast" that life brings.**

Subject:	Responsibility
Into Focus:	Do you sometimes wish that growing up was as easy as playing a video game?
Affirmation:	**I set goals and work to achieve them.**

GAME OF LIFE

≫ Introduction

Sit comfortably with your eyes closed. Take three long, deep breaths. *(Pause)* Feel yourself relaxing more and more with each breath. Let the rhythm of the music calm you. Feel your muscles relax and your heart rate and breathing slow. Say to yourself, "I am calm and relaxed."

≫ Script

Imagine yourself in an electronics store. There is a buzz of excitement in the air. Electronic devices of all kinds vie for your attention with their noise and flashing lights. Customers scurry about trying out the hardware. This is a toy store for people of all ages. Listen for the sounds of a video games and let that sound lead you to them. It's time to shop. You are in the market for a video game today. Take some time to try out a few games before you pick the one you want. *(Pause)* Imagine walking to the front of the store with the game you chose and checking out.

When you get home, the first thing you do is put your game into a computer or player and begin to play. You feel quick and alert. You float through level after level. You are making all the right decisions and are beating the odds. *(Pause)* You just conquered the last level and realize that you have won! You feel proud of your accomplishment.*(Pause)*

Now imagine that as you are about to shut the game off, a new game appears. It's called, "Your Future... If You Dare." This wasn't advertised on the box. You wonder what it means. You try to adjust the screen but it remains the same. You decide to take a chance and push the enter button.

The controls now seem to be automatic and move without you touching them. A screen appears entitled, "Me in One Year." Punch in the age you will be in one year and push enter. Look at the screen; there you are one year older. Think about how you would like to be in a year. *(Pause)* How are you different than you are today? *(Pause)* Where are you? *(Pause)* What are you doing? *(Pause)*

You feel relaxed and safe. A screen now appears entitled, "Me in Five Years." Punch in your age in five years and push enter. Look at the screen; there you are five years older. Think about how you would like to be in five years. *(Pause)* How are you different? *(Pause)* Where are you? *(Pause)* What are you doing? *(Pause)*

A screen now appears entitled, "Me in 10 Years." Punch in your age in ten years and push enter. Look at the screen; there you are 10 years older. Think about how you would like to be in 10 years. *(Pause)* How are you different? *(Pause)* Where are you? *(Pause)* What are you doing? *(Pause)*

As you think about this experience say to yourself three times: **I set goals and work to achieve them…**

The screen is now filled with a beautiful kaleidoscope of colors. One changing pattern flows into the next. Enchanting music fills the room. Then one last message is displayed. It says, "GO FOR IT." You have a positive future and you know achieving dreams takes hard work and determination. You are ready to begin and ready to "go for it".

Return to your room. Open your eyes and stretch your arms, legs and mind.

›› Discussion/Reflection

· We know we will look and feel different in the future. What will be different about you in 1, 5, 10 years and beyond?
· Why are short term goals as important as long term goals?
· Do you know anyone who is jeopardizing their future? Can you help them?

›› Resources

Music: *2001 Space Odyssey*

›› Fast Fact

In 1975, Atari Pong became the first video game sold for use in the home.

›› Alternate Affirmations

· **I feel confident about my future.**
· **I plan for the future.**

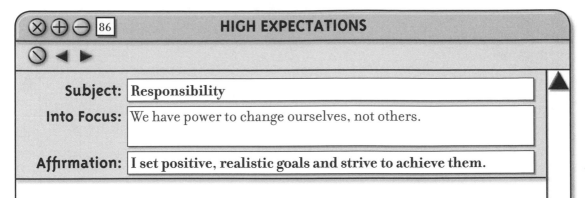

Subject: Responsibility

Into Focus: We have power to change ourselves, not others.

Affirmation: I set positive, realistic goals and strive to achieve them.

HIGH EXPECTATIONS

≫ Introduction

Sit comfortably with your eyes closed. Take three long, deep breaths. *(Pause)* Feel yourself relaxing more and more with each breath. Let the rhythm of the music calm you. Feel your muscles relax and your heart rate and breathing slow. Say to yourself, "I am calm and relaxed."

≫ Script

Imagine yourself in an airplane ready to take off. This is your 1st flight and you are feeling just a bit anxious. Reach over and click on your seatbelt. Put your feet firmly on the floor and lean back. Your plane is about to take off. As the sound of the jet engine gets louder, you reach down and tighten your seat belt. Now as the plane picks up speed your whole body is being pushed back. Feel your back, neck and head press slightly against the soft seat. Grab the arm rests and feel yourself begin to move faster and faster. Look out the window and see only the blur of the runway. The noise increases as the plane begins to pick up more speed. You hold the armrests even tighter as you feel yourself begin to rise into the air. You take several slow relaxing breaths. *(Pause)* The noise of the jet engines begins to fade. You release your grip on the armrests. You open your mouth wide and release the pressure in your ears. Feel your entire body begin to relax. Look out the window and see nothing but blue sky ahead. Look down and see white clouds below. They remind you of an endless carpet of cotton candy. You are now relaxed and excited to see and learn new things. The clouds begin to separate and you see the land below. Brown and green landforms blend together to form a curious quilt of shapes and colors. You now see a great mountain range. Some peaks have caps of snow. The plane is so high up that the mountains are merely bumps on the canvas below.

As you look down, the scenery has changed to a forest. The trees form a giant green sponge. As the sun is absorbed by the trees, a few dots of light begin to sparkle. Soon the streams that wind through the forest glitter like diamonds. As you look, you begin to see a word lighting up below. This word reminds you of a goal that you hope to achieve within the next year. *(Pause)* Picture yourself taking the steps that are needed to achieve this goal. *(Pause)* You are able to accomplish each step by visualizing success. *(Pause)*

Again think of the word or phrase of the goal you wish to achieve. *(Pause)* See the word or phrase representing your goal on the inside of your eyelids. *(Pause)*

Your plane hasn't even landed and you have already had a good trip. You overcame a mild worry about flying. You began to explore the vast and beautiful world we live in. But most importantly, you set a positive goal which, with patience and effort, you can achieve.

The plane is now descending. Lean back and gently hold the arm rests. Take a deep breath. Say to yourself three times: **I set positive, realistic goals and strive to achieve them...** *(Pause)* Return to your room. Open your eyes and think about the goal you set as you stretch your arms, legs and your mind.

ZITS   **by Scott & Borgman**

≫ Discussion/Reflection

· If someone asked you to cite one of your goals in life what would it be?

≫ Activity

On a piece of paper, write down some short term and long term goals for yourself. Date them and put them in your wallet or purse.

≫ Fast Fact

More people are killed annually by donkeys than die in air crashes.

≫ Alternate Affirmations

· **I step back and set goals for myself.**
· **For a large task, I take one step at a time.**

Subject: Responsibility

Into Focus: If they made a movie of your life so far, what would it be? A comedy? A drama? A love story?

Affirmation: I learn from my mistakes.

NO REPEATS

≫ Introduction

Sit comfortably with your eyes closed. Take three long, deep breaths. *(Pause)* Feel yourself relaxing more and more with each breath. Let the rhythm of the music calm you. Feel your muscles relax and your heart rate and breathing slow. Say to yourself, "I am calm and relaxed."

≫ Script

Picture yourself sitting in your room at home. The weekend has just begun but it's raining outside and you have been forced to cancel your outdoor plans. Listen as the raindrops beat down on the roof. The sound catches your interest and you begin to listen to the tap, tap, tap of the falling rain. As time goes on, the sound and rhythm of the rain begins to relax you. *(Pause)* Watch as the raindrops collect on your bedroom window. The raindrops zigzag in little streams racing to the bottom. Pick out a raindrop and watch it as it winds down the windowpane, getting faster and stronger as it mixes with other drops of water. *(Pause)* The glass is fogged up except for the areas the water has streaked down. A dim light comes in making your window a strange, streaky work of art. You are glad that you have an unexpected opportunity to relax.

Breathe slowly, being aware of the flow of air as you breathe. Inhale gently through your nose and exhale through your mouth. You notice that with each breath you become more and more relaxed. Now notice that there is a TV remote control next to you. Pick it up. Lie on your bed and prop your head up with a soft pillow. You are totally relaxed and have low expectations for what will be on TV. Push the power button and punch in your favorite channel. *(Pause)* To your surprise there is a picture of you on the screen. Underneath your picture is a caption entitled, "My Life's Mistakes." Rub your eyes and change channels. As you flip through, every station is the same. You are curious about what this might be and begin to watch the show.

Part One is entitled, "Ways I've Hurt Myself." While maintaining your relaxed state, you see something you have done that was the wrong decision for you. *(Long Pause)*

Part Two is entitled, "Ways I've Hurt Others." Despite this difficult subject, you continue to breathe slowly and evenly. Staying relaxed and calm you see something you have done that had a negative effect on others. *(Long Pause)*

This drama is a little heavy for Saturday morning viewing. Much to your relief, "The End," appears on your TV screen. Hit the power button on the remote. Before the TV turns off, the words "no repeats" flash across the screen. You are determined to not live out these scenes again. You know that you will make better decisions.

Stay calm, breath slowly and repeat to yourself three times: **I learn from my mistakes...** *(Pause)* The rain has stopped, the sun is out and you have great days ahead of you.

Take a deep breath, open your eyes and stretch. Stretch your arms, your legs, and your mind.

≫ Discussion/Reflection

- Do you forgive yourself? Can you forgive others who don't say they are sorry? How do you feel when you tell someone that you are sorry?
- Why is it unrealistic to compare real life to a TV show?
- They say that everyone gets "15 minutes of fame" in their life. What would you want to be known for?

≫ Alternate Affirmations

- **I am accountable for my actions.**
- **I forgive myself and others.**

Subject: Responsibility

Into Focus: Research tells us that we spend a lot of time worrying about things that are beyond our control. On top of that, most of the things we worry about never come to pass.

Affirmation: **I let go when something is beyond my control.**

RAILROAD CROSSING

≫ Introduction

Sit comfortably with your eyes closed. Take three long, deep breaths. *(Pause)* Feel yourself relaxing more and more with each breath. Let the rhythm of the music calm you. Feel your muscles relax and your heart rate and breathing slow. Say to yourself, "I am calm and relaxed."

≫ Script

Imagine that you are out walking. You do not notice anything around you because you are late. You are walking fast, with your head down. Your breathing is quick and shallow. You are in a hurry because you are running behind schedule and you have so much to do. Now you hear a train whistle getting louder and louder. Listen. Soon you see the train on the tracks as it rumbles across your path. Feel the ground vibrate under your feet. You stop a safe distance from the speeding train and worry about falling further behind in your busy day. Your heart is beating faster, your breathing is shallow and you are worried about being late. The dust from the railroad bed forms a small cloud above the ground. The noise is deafening as the railroad cars whiz by. There is a smell of steel and oil in the air.

Then something strange happens. Suddenly, a feeling of calmness comes over you. What can you do but wait for the train to pass? You even laugh at your bad timing. The breeze created by the railroad cars actually feels good on your face. The sun flashes between gaps of the cars in a rhythmic pattern of relaxation. The rumbling ground beneath your feet vibrates and relaxes your toes, feet, ankles, calves, legs, spine, and then, your entire body. The noise is not as noticeable. Your change of attitude has allowed you to notice the different colors of the railroad cars. Some have different markings or pictures on them. You use your imagination to guess what is inside each car. *(Pause)* Look between the cars as they go by, and see green grass on the other side. Focus on the grass. It becomes more and more noticeable. You now feel calm and relaxed. Take a deep breath, and say to yourself three times: **I let go when something is beyond my control...**

Now imagine the red caboose going by. It has the word RELAX in gold letters on its side. The man riding in the caboose tips his cap to you and smiles as if he knows how you are feeling. Step onto the green grass on the other side of the tracks, knowing you can handle unexpected things in your life.

Take a deep breath, and return to your room. Open your eyes, and stretch. *(Pause)* Take a few moments to appreciate the good feelings that come with relaxation.

≫ Discussion/Reflection

- Explain the quote by Sydney Harris, "The time to relax is when you don't have time for it."
- Do you worry about things that are beyond your control?

≫ Alternate Affirmations

- **I manage stress by slowing down and thinking positively.**
- **I organize my time.**

Subject:	Responsibility
Into Focus:	It's easier to "go with the flow," but is it always the right thing to do?
Affirmation:	**I make good decisions.**

SMOOTH SAILING

≫ Introduction

Sit comfortably with your eyes closed. Take three long, deep breaths. *(Pause)* Feel yourself relaxing more and more with each breath. Let the rhythm of the music calm you. Feel your muscles relax and your heart rate and breathing slow. Say to yourself, "I am calm and relaxed."

≫ Script

Imagine that you are walking on an ocean beach. It is a warm, lazy, sunny summer day. You are standing on the wet sand. With your toes, dig into the sand. Curl your toes and feel the sand ooze between them. *(Pause)* Again, dig your toes deep into the wet sand. Curl them and enjoy the cool feeling as the sand oozes between each toe. *(Pause)* Watch as a wave fills the small holes you dug with water. A second wave smoothes them out and erases them completely. You feel relaxed. Bend down and make a handprint in the wet sand. Watch as it fills with water, then disappears. *(Pause)* Walk over to a small pier that is nearby. Hear the boards squeak beneath your feet as you walk to the end of the pier. Sit down and dangle your legs in the cool water. The waves lap against the pier with a soothing, rhythmic sound. This is a great place to relax and catch some good sun. Feel the sun warm your entire body. Look up and enjoy the aerial show by the birds. They soar and dip without moving their wings, coasting on the cool breeze. Their sounds add to the relaxing rhythm. You wish every day could be like this one.

A sailboat enters the picture. Its red, orange and yellow triangular sails add the perfect colors to the landscape. The person sailing is in control of the small boat, making it go in almost any direction. You are mesmerized as you watch the sailor work to steer the craft. Sometimes the sails are full, other times they are slack with no wind in them. Watch as the boat nearly tips over. The sailor quickly rights the vessel, and successfully completes the maneuver. Sometimes the boat darts and glides across the water. Other times it hovers and bounces with the waves. You admire the skill of the sailor and the satisfaction and enjoyment sailing must bring.

In your mind's eye imagine yourself on your own sailboat. Pick colors for your sails. *(Pause)* Put an emblem or picture on the large sail that describes something about yourself that is positive. *(Pause)* Off you go, gliding on the water and riding with the wind. Now move the sails to turn the boat. *(Pause)* Now slow it down. *(Pause)* Then speed it up. *(Pause)* Sailing, like life, is sometimes a challenge and sometimes requires hard work and quick decisions. It is all worth the effort.

It is hard to sail when the wind isn't helping, like trying to swim against the current. It is also hard to go against the crowd and say no to your friends when they are asking you to do something that is against your values or that feels wrong to you. If you feel outnumbered, remember that, like sailing, you cannot direct the wind, but you can adjust your sails and have more control.

When faced with negative peer pressure, think of watching the sailor maneuver in the wind and waves. Set your own course, even if it means going against the current or wind. Only you know what's best for you. Take a deep breath and say to yourself three times: **I make good decisions...**

Take a deep relaxing breath and slowly exhale. As you are exhaling, open your eyes. Stretch your arms, your legs and your mind.

» Discussion/Reflection

- Explain the statement in the story, "You cannot direct the wind, but you can adjust the sails."
- What skills do you have in your life to keep you on the right course?
- Do you ever feel peer pressure in relation to drugs, alcohol or sex?

» Alternate Affirmations

- **I do what is right.**
- **I trust my decisions.**

Subject: Responsibility

Into Focus: Did you know that the Greek word for problem means "push forward"? How do you handle your problems?

Affirmation: I see obstacles and overcome them.

STEPPING STONES

» Introduction

Sit comfortably with your eyes closed. Take three long, deep breaths. *(Pause)* Feel yourself relaxing more and more with each breath. Let the rhythm of the music calm you. Feel your muscles relax and your heart rate and breathing slow. Say to yourself, "I am calm and relaxed."

» Script

Imagine yourself out for a long walk in the woods on a cloudy and chilly day. See yourself rub your hands together to warm them up as you walk briskly forward. Your thoughts swirl like the leaves around you. Your mind is spinning with doubts today. You find that walking is helpful and helps you put things in perspective.

You suddenly notice that you have come to the edge of a stream. You had not expected this interruption and now will need to figure out the best way to cross without getting wet. You notice a rope hanging from one of the tree limbs that stands next to the bank of the stream. If you grab the rope and swing yourself forward you can land on a large rock that is about ten feet from the shore. Leading from the rock is an old tree trunk that has fallen into the water and might allow you to leap from the end of the trunk to another rock that is just a few feet from the other shoreline. You will have to maintain good balance to walk across the tree trunk and have just the right timing to make the final leap.

In your mind's eye you connect the pathway you must take and decide that the hardest part of your journey across will be the first swing across the open water. Despite possible problems with the crossing, you remain confident.

With courage and confidence see yourself swing forward on the rope and let go just at the right moment and land safely and securely on the rock. *(Pause)* Now see yourself balancing on the fallen tree and stepping forward cautiously while maintaining your balance. *(Pause)* Finally, with one last leap you jump from the end of the fallen tree to the rock near the edge of the other side. The final step in solving this problem is the easiest and you jump over the last open water and land on the bank.

You have moved past some of your worries and fears and feel a sense of relief and accomplishment. Take a moment to enjoy this feeling and say to your self three times: **I see obstacles and overcome them.**

Your mind is no longer spinning with doubts and your thoughts are organized and positive. You feel confident that when faced with an unexpected obstacle you have the courage and determination to take the necessary steps for positive change. *(Pause)*

It is time to return to your room. Open your eyes. Stretch your arms, your legs and your mind.

≫ Discussion/Reflection

- Do you believe that in a journey, the first step can sometimes be the hardest? Why?
- Why is it important to visualize and review the steps needed to solve a difficult problem?

≫ Activities

Think of a problem you may have. Privately write a step by step plan to overcome it. Don't forget to pat yourself on the back along the way.

Organize a group to help clean up your local rivers and streams.

≫ Alternate Affirmations

- **Faced with a large task, I take small steps forward**
- **I learn from my mistakes and try again.**

Subject:	Responsibility
Into Focus:	Do you have the vision, focus and confidence for success? Even when things are tough, do you believe there is a "light at the end of the tunnel?"
Affirmation:	Good things lie ahead for me.

TUNNEL VISION

>> Introduction

Sit comfortably with your eyes closed. Take three long, deep breaths. *(Pause)* Feel yourself relaxing more and more with each breath. Let the rhythm of the music calm you. Feel your muscles relax and your heart rate and breathing slow. Say to yourself, "I am calm and relaxed."

>> Script

You just got a new bike and you are anxious to take it out on a long ride. You like this bike and want to take care of it so it will perform well for many years. Push down on one of the tires. It is soft. Take out your air pump and attach the hose to the tire valve. Take a deep breath and push down the handle of the pump. As you exhale, listen as the air hisses into the tube. *(Pause)* Take another deep breath and push the pump handle down to put more air into the tire. *(Pause)* Take one last breath. Push the pump handle hard and slow because the tire is almost full. *(Pause)* When you push your finger on the tire it feels hard. This exercise also leaves you inflated and full of energy.

You check the pressure in the other tire and it feels good. You are ready to ride. Put on your bike helmet and set out on your adventure. The day is calm and clear as you turn off the road and head down the trail reserved just for bikes. The trail is flat and the wind seems to be at your back. You pedal almost effortlessly as you breeze along. *(Pause)*

Follow the trail as it makes its first turn. Your peddling slows as you begin to go up an incline. As you look ahead you notice a steep hill on the path. The muscles in your legs start to burn. The wind now seems to be blowing in your face. Stand up on the pedals and push down with all your might. Breathe deeply and focus on each stroke of the pedals as you move ahead. *(Pause)*

After much effort you reach the top of the hill and now you can slowly adjust your pace. Once again, you move easily along the path. Breathe in and out gently. Notice your heart rate slowing. Feel the muscles in your legs relax.

Now look ahead and see that the bike path enters an old train tunnel. As you approach the entrance you are greeted by a blast of cool, damp air. The cooler air feels comfortable and you stop pedaling and put your foot on the ground. Gaze into the tunnel and see nothing but darkness. You can hear the sound of water dripping inside the tunnel.

The thought enters your mind that if you can't see what's ahead, you should turn around and head back. You stand quietly, focus on slowing your breathing, and let your eyes adjust to the darkness. Before turning around you take one last look into the blackness inside. This time you notice what appears to be a small dot of light in the distance. You are curious as to what's at the other end, so you decide to head toward the light. Because of the darkness you decide it would be safer to proceed by walking with your bike. You step gently, not quite sure of the ground below. The speck of light ahead is a beacon guiding you forward. *(Pause)*

The spot of light slowly grows as does your confidence. You can now faintly see the walls surrounding you and the ground below. Notice the rock formations, the dampness on the walls and the gravel path.

As the light brightens you confidently get back onto your bike and peddle to the end of the tunnel. As you reach the end you are greeted by a burst of daylight. Feel the warmth of the air surrounding you. Take time to enjoy the beautiful scenery that is all around you. Breathe in the fresh air and as you relax say to yourself three times: **Good things lie ahead for me...**

You've biked as far as you planned to today, so you turn around and begin the trip back. This time you know what's ahead and you follow the light at the other end of the tunnel with confidence. You smile knowing your trip back is mostly down hill. You are glad you made the trip. Remember that curiosity, combined with the right amount of courage, can lead you to great things.

Take a deep breath and open your eyes. Stretch your arms and legs and your mind.

≫ Discussion/Reflection

· Name some risks that are worth taking.
· Name some risks that are not worth taking.

≫ Activity

Dust off your bike and go for a ride.

≫ Fast Fact

Since 2000, Google Maps has collected data on over 30,000 miles of designated bike trails in the U.S.

≫ Alternate Affirmations

· **I am persistent.**
· **I am rewarded when I work hard.**

 **R**esponsibility

Making good choices for yourself and
your relationships.

 **E**mpowerment

**Feeling positive about yourself and competent
with peers. Feeling supported by others.**

 **L**earning

Developing skills to acquire and retain knowledge.
Finding enjoyment in creative pursuits.

 Attitudes

Developing and practicing the attitudes and
values needed to become a complete person.

  **X**-pand

Exploring your ability to feel calm and centered.

Subject: Empowerment

Into Focus: Do you ever feel like you are in a rut, thinking and doing the same things everyday? You have the power to change course.

Affirmation: I make positive changes and see things in a new light.

AMAZE YOURSELF

» Introduction

Sit comfortably with your eyes closed. Take three long, deep breaths. *(Pause)* Feel yourself relaxing more and more with each breath. Let the rhythm of the music calm you. Feel your muscles relax and your heart rate and breathing slow. Say to yourself, "I am calm and relaxed."

» Script

Imagine it's morning and you are lying in your bed looking up at the ceiling. You see dust particles dancing in the rays of the morning sun. It's almost time to get up. You are stressing out about all you have to do. You are still tired because you did not sleep very well. Your mind begins to play negative messages and you begin to worry about things that might happen during the day.

Now, in your mind see a maze. At the beginning of the maze is a picture of you getting up every morning. At the end of the maze is a picture of you going to bed each night. Although the maze is complicated, with many twists and turns, your path is always the same. *(Pause)* Now notice an annoying squeaking sound. Look over and see a hamster in a wheel, running full speed but just going around and around. The grinding, high pitched sound gets louder and louder. You take a very deep breath and as you exhale decide to set a new course for yourself. *(Pause)*

Instead of getting up the same way as normal, you decide to get up on the opposite side of the bed. As soon as your feet hit the floor you see things from a different angle. As you get dressed an idea comes to you since you are starting your day from a new perspective. You are going to break out of the maze and change the pattern of your day.

See yourself walking into the bathroom. Pick up a brush or comb. As you are brushing or combing your hair, look into the mirror and make a silly face like one you used to make when you were young and laugh out loud. Reach over and turn on a radio that is in the bathroom. One of your favorite songs is playing. Now see yourself picking up your toothbrush and pretending it is a microphone, imagine that you are lip syncing your favorite song.

You are ready for school. Walk out the door backwards. Take a different route and try to notice new things along the way. You have the strength to change negative thoughts by changing direction. Take a deep breath and say to yourself three times: **When needed, I make positive changes and see things in a new light...**

Take a deep breath and return to your room. Open your eyes and stretch your arms and your legs and your mind

>> Discussion/Reflection

- Do you ever feel you are going around in circles?
- Why is it helpful to sometimes change your pattern of doing things? What are some things that work for you that can help you get out of a rut?

>> Fast Fact

All pet hamsters are descended from a single female wild golden hamster found with a litter of 12 young in Syria in 1930.

>> Alternate Affirmations

- **I make changes when needed.**
- **I have control over who I become.**

⊘ ◀ ▶

Subject: Empowerment

Into Focus: You may use the image of running or biking in a race for this exercise.

Affirmation: When I make an effort, others support me.

CROWD SUPPORT

≫ Introduction

Sit comfortably with your eyes closed. Take three long, deep breaths. *(Pause)* Feel yourself relaxing more and more with each breath. Let the rhythm of the music calm you. Feel your muscles relax and your heart rate and breathing slow. Say to yourself, "I am calm and relaxed."

≫ Script

With your eyes closed imagine that you are having a good dream. As you breathe slowly, enjoy the feeling of complete relaxation and contentment. In your dream you are running in a race for which you have been training for a long time. You are focused and feel strong as you speed on your way. There is a crowd gathered at the finish line.

Listen… you hear the cheers go from a soft murmur *(Pause)* to steady clapping *(Pause)* and finally to a loud roar as you approach the finish line. *(Pause)* The crowd lining both sides of the street waves their arms and hands in the air. You feel the energy and power of their support as you near the end. You do your absolute best, for yourself and for those who have helped you along the way.

Picture yourself now crossing the finish line. You made it! Friends, family and people who care for you surround you to offer congratulations. As you continue to relax repeat, to yourself three times: **When I make an effort, others are there to support me…** Imagine that you wake up from your dream. *(Pause)* You look at the clock and realize it's time to get ready for school. You spring out of bed with an unusual amount of morning energy. Remember that there are people on the sidelines who are rooting for you. Use their support to give you energy along the way.

Take a deep breath, open your eyes and stretch your arms, your legs and your mind.

≫ Discussion/Reflection

- Think of a person in your life who you cheer for and feel good when they succeed.
- In your mind, did you win the race? Does winning always matter?

≫ **Activities**

For one night, replace a passive activity (TV, computer etc.) with an active one (biking, walking, tennis etc.).

Try to make time out for exercise on a regular basis.

≫ **Fast Fact**

The average person walks the equivalent of twice around the world in a lifetime.

≫ **Alternate Affirmations**

· **There are people who want me to succeed.**
· **I thank people who support me.**

FUNKY WINKERBEAN   **by Tom Batiuk**

Subject: Empowerment

Into Focus: Wouldn't it be nice to have a crystal ball to see into your future?

Affirmation: I see a positive future for myself.

CRYSTAL CLEAR

» Introduction

Sit comfortably with your eyes closed. Take three long, deep breaths. *(Pause)* Feel yourself relaxing more and more with each breath. Let the rhythm of the music calm you. Feel your muscles relax and your heart rate and breathing slow. Say to yourself, "I am calm and relaxed."

» Script

Now imagine that you are in a mega shopping mall. There are things happening all around you. The many sounds blend together in a constant beat of excitement. Listen. *(Pause)*

Picture yourself walking by store after store. You can almost tell what each store sells by its particular smell. As you walk by the leather store breathe in and smell the purses, wallets and jackets. *(Pause)* Imagine walking by a store that sells snacks and smelling popcorn and roasted nuts. *(Pause)* Now see yourself in front of an import store. As you breathe in you smell incense and exotic spices. The wonderful smell draws you inside.

You notice colorful baskets, bottles and robes everywhere. Soft chimes add a peaceful sound to the room. A kind elderly man is behind the counter. His hair and beard are long and gray. The wrinkles on his face mark his wisdom. He smiles and softly says you are the one thousandth customer in his store. To celebrate, he hands you a small package. You thank him and head to the escalator which takes you down to the quietest floor of the mall.

You find a place to sit by a fountain. The soft bubbling sound of the fountain relaxes you. Focus on the small package in your hand and slowly open it. *(Pause)* Inside is a small clear glass ball that fits into the palm of your hand. Shake it and it becomes a snow globe. The snow further relaxes you as it bobs and floats, and then gently settles to the bottom. Shake it again. This time, as the snow settles, you see a scene from a time in your life when you were very happy. Remember what you were doing. Recall who else might have been with you—remember where you were and what made this time so happy. Take a moment to enjoy this time and to appreciate the happiness you felt. As you recall this memory you see a picture of it in 3D. Take a moment to visualize this scene and store it in your memory. *(Pause)*

Shake the globe one more time. This time as the snow slowly settles you see a positive scene of your future. Look at it and enjoy it from all sides as you turn the globe in your hand. See yourself feeling confident and happy.

As you continue to relax, say to yourself three times: **I see a positive future for myself...**

You shake the globe again, but realize the magic is gone. You decide to keep the globe to remind you of the positive picture of your future. You realize that you don't need magic to make your dreams come true and begin to plan for a positive future. Return to your room. Open your eyes and stretch your arms, your legs and your mind.

» Discussion/Reflection

- When famous people give advice to young people they almost always say dream big and work hard. Why do they say this?
- Why is it important to reflect on good memories from time to time?
- It is believed that young people will have many different jobs and even careers within their lifetime. How does this affect your thinking for the future?

» Fast Facts

Wendy Suen, a.k.a. Queen Snovari, currently holds the record collection of Mini Glass Snow Globes at 2,050. She has been known to spend more than $4,000 on a single globe.

» Alternate Affirmations

- **I believe my life has a purpose.**
- **I dream today about the future I want to have tomorrow.**

Subject:	Empowerment
Into Focus:	We have power to change our thoughts and reactions.
Affirmation:	**I overcome mean and hurtful rumors.**

FLOATING BY

» Introduction

Sit comfortably with your eyes closed. Take three long, deep breaths. *(Pause)* Feel yourself relaxing more and more with each breath. Let the rhythm of the music calm you. Feel your muscles relax and your heart rate and breathing slow. Say to yourself, "I am calm and relaxed."

» Script

While relaxing, picture yourself sailing to a deserted island in the middle of a lake. Pull your boat on shore. Even though land is visible on all sides, you are still a long way from the nearest shore. Picture yourself walking along the shore and finding a smooth boulder at the water's edge to sit on. Imagine dangling your feet in the cool water. Feel the water wash against the front of your legs. Gently move your legs back and forth. Feel the water wrap around your legs and relax them. You continue to move your legs in a relaxing pattern. Now imagine moving your feet back and forth and feel the water rush between your toes. You continue this movement until your feet, legs and entire body are relaxed. *(Pause)*

An island is a good place for you today because you need time to be alone because you are feeling a little down. You have heard rumors and gossip that you know are not true.

Throw a pebble into the water. The pebble disappears as it enters the still, calm water, but causes a small ring to form on the water's surface. Watch as this small circle becomes wider and wider, and wider and wider. Close your eyes and imagine the ripples from this one pebble extending far out into the lake. You imagine gossip and rumors to be much like the ripple effect of the pebble. Once it gets started it spreads farther and farther until it seems it can't be stopped. However, the ripple effect does get weaker and eventually fades away.

You decide to toss a stone into the water for each hurtful thing that has been said to you. Watch how the ripples spread out and then begin to fade. You already feel the hurt fading away back into smooth water. You decide to return to this image whenever needed.

Walk back to your small boat and get in. There is a light breeze that cools and relaxes you. Hoist the sail, catch the breeze and head for home. You have perfect control of your boat as you skim over the water. You are feeling much better as you inhale the fresh lake breeze.

You are quickly back to shore. Dock your boat and look back at the water. The wind has faded and the water is once again perfectly still. You know deep inside that the ripples of untrue or hurtful things will eventually fade away and disappear. Look down into the glassy water and see a perfect reflection of you. Smile to yourself. As you breath slowly, say to yourself three times: **I overcome mean and hurtful rumors**...

Take a deep breath and return to the room. Open your eyes and stretch knowing that you can skip, float and rise above hurtful and untrue things.

≫ Discussion/Reflection

- Have you been a victim of gossip?
- Have you ever started gossip?
- Why can saying even true things about a person be hurtful and unnecessary?
- Can you stop gossip once it starts? How can you control it?
- Christopher Reeves, who once played Superman and who was later a quadriplegic for many years before he died said, "Your bad days are only good days in disguise." What did he mean?

≫ Activity

Go out and collect flat stones. Find a body of water and skip or toss them in.

≫ Resources

Please Stop Laughing at Me – Jodee Blanco (2003)

≫ Fast Fact

The strongest muscle in the body is the tongue.

≫ Alternate Affirmations

- **I accept things I can not change.**
- **My self esteem helps me ignore gossip.**

Subject:	Empowerment
Into Focus:	This "fish story" is full of surprises.
Affirmation:	I make good decisions under stress.

GONE FISHING

» Introduction

Sit comfortably with your eyes closed. Take three long, deep breaths. *(Pause)* Feel yourself relaxing more and more with each breath. Let the rhythm of the music calm you. Feel your muscles relax and your heart rate and breathing slow. Say to yourself, "I am calm and relaxed."

» Script

Imagine that it is six o'clock in the morning, but you are too excited to be grouchy or tired. You are going fishing!

In your mind's eye, raise your arms and stretch any stiffness from your body. See yourself quickly pack a sandwich, chips and water into a backpack and grab your fishing pole and some bait. Picture yourself walking down a path guarded by tall pine trees. You leave your troubles behind as you walk down the hill to the lake. Enjoy the sweet scent of the flower blossoms along the trail.

It's a beautiful summer day. The early morning fog forms a hazy blanket over the water. Hear the small waves lap the shoreline. Breathe in deeply and smell the fresh lake breeze. Notice a faint smell of fish. This smell tells you there are fish out there just waiting for you to catch. Then hop in a small boat. It wobbles from side to side, but you quickly steady yourself. Untie the boat and shove off from the pier and begin to row away from shore. Although the boat has a motor you decide to row. One oar splashes you as it hits the water. The exercise energizes you. *(Pause)* Soon you find a spot that looks good for fishing. Drop anchor. The water is clear, but soon the anchor disappears from sight, right before it hits bottom. See yourself baiting your hook, setting your bobber, and throwing your line to a perfect spot. The sun has melted the haze and now glints off the waves like tiny white diamonds. Notice for the first time the music of song birds echoing across the lake.

The setting is beautiful and, although you have no fish, you have plenty of patience to keep trying. *(Pause)* Look way across the lake and see a large, weedy, marshy area. You are sure the fish are hiding there. Without a moment's thought, you pull up anchor. The marsh is so far away that you will have to use the motor. You pull the cord on the motor and it starts up right away. You enjoy the rhythmic motion of the boat as it skims across the water. The wind whistles in your ear. *(Pause)* You are finally at the edge of the marsh. It seems as big as the lake itself.

You use the oars to navigate deep within the marsh. The cattails and other vegetation are so high you cannot see the storm on the horizon. Each place you stop looks good for fish, but after a few unsuccessful casts, you decide to move deeper in.

Feel a nibble on your hook. *(Pause)* Now set the hook, and begin to reel furiously. Your rod dips and dances. Your body is filled with adrenaline and excitement. Your fish is almost to the boat. See yourself grabbing the net from the bottom of the boat. Your rod looks like a horseshoe as you make one last reel and pull. Feel yourself jerk back. *(Pause)* Your line has broken and the fish has gotten away. *(Pause)* You have no time to be sad, because suddenly thunder rumbles in the distance. You look up and notice the sky is dark. A cool breeze rustles through the tall vegetation all around you. You must get back home quickly. Even though you are rushing you are able to stay relaxed. The storm is closer as it begins to rain and the wind picks up.

You continue to stay relaxed and focus your efforts to get home safely. Despite your surroundings you are able to stay calm.

Your heartbeat slows, and you are able to ignore the noise and chaos around you. You are focused. *(Pause)* Look up and see a large tree in the distance. Calmly and confidently row toward the tree. Look across the water and see home. Pull the cord and start your motor. The boat travels swiftly. You arrive home safely as the storm continues.

Take a deep breath and say to yourself three times: **I make good decisions under stress...** Remember that you can stay cool under pressure.

Take a deep breath and return to the room. Open your eyes and stretch your arms, your legs and your mind.

≫ Discussion/Reflection

- Think of a time that you made a good decision under stress.
- What are some things you can do to avoid panic in a stressful situation?

≫ Activities

Program local emergency phone numbers into your phone / cell phone.

Make a list of emergency/safety items needed for home, car, vacation, etc. If possible, get some of these items.

≫ Alternate Affirmations

- **I manage stress by thinking positively.**
- **I think clearly in a crisis**

Subject: Empowerment

Into Focus: It is important to like yourself. Others enjoy being around and are attracted to people who like themselves. Be sure to compliment yourself every day!

Affirmation: I like who I am.

INTO FOCUS

≫ Introduction

Sit comfortably with your eyes closed. Take three long, deep breaths. *(Pause)* Feel yourself relaxing more and more with each breath. Let the rhythm of the music calm you. Feel your muscles relax and your heart rate and breathing slow. Say to yourself, "I am calm and relaxed."

≫ Script

Imagine lying in your bed sleeping when you suddenly hear buzzing. It's seems way too early in the morning for your alarm to be going off. You hope the sound you are hearing is only a dream, but it is not. See yourself reaching over, hitting the snooze button, pulling the covers over your head and falling back asleep. Ten sleepy minutes seem like one second as the alarm awakens you again.

Squint and see that the numbers on the clock are telling you that it's time to get up. Your body is tired, but your mind seems wide awake as you think about ways that will allow you to stay in bed longer. You look over at the clock again and see the display dimly flashing the words of advice, "you snooze, you lose." As you rub your eyes and recheck the clock, you realize you must get up. In your mind's eye see yourself sitting up and slowly sliding off the bed until your feet hit the floor. In an almost sleeping state you walk to the bathroom. As you click on the lights you begin to wake up.

Now, see yourself step into the shower and turning on the water. Listen to the water as it gurgles down the drain. Feel the warmth of the water as it runs down your face and the rest of your body. Imagine any worry or stress flowing down through your body from your head to your toes. It flows out the bottom of your feet and swirls around in the water and then down the drain. You now feel so awake and alive you begin to hum and then sing to yourself or out loud one of your favorite songs.

Now turn off the shower and reach out and grab a large towel. Use it to first dry your eyes then face. Step out of the shower and begin to dry off your entire body. You want to look in the mirror, but it is all steamed up. See yourself draw a happy face or a funny face on the mirror. *(Pause)* Turn on the hair dryer and point it at the mirror. Soon a small circle becomes clear. Slowly the circle grows and your entire face comes into focus. The circle on the mirror has framed your face and created a portrait of you. Your hair is wet and uncombed but you are pleased with the reflection.

Like any great artist, sign your name in the corner of the mirror next to your portrait. *(Pause)* Continue to get ready for your day feeling good about yourself and the day ahead. Each time you take a shower you are reminded of the importance of complementing yourself. Next time you look in the mirror, smile and it's guaranteed that your reflection will smile back.

Now say you yourself three times: **I like who I am...**

Come back to the room, open your eyes and stretch your arms, your legs and your mind.

» Discussion/Reflection

- Arlo Guthrie said in the song "Garden Party," that "you can't please everyone so you've got to please yourself." What is the wisdom in these words?

» Fast Fact

It takes 17 muscles to smile and 43 to frown.

»Alternate Affirmations

- **I like what I see in me.**
- **I believe in myself.**

Subject: Empowerment

Into Focus: Getting your drivers license is one of the great joys of adolescence. Driving a car brings mobility but also adds responsibility.

Affirmation: I have inner strength and confidence.

JOY RIDE

≫ Introduction

Sit comfortably with your eyes closed. Take three long, deep breaths. (*Pause*) Feel yourself relaxing more and more with each breath. Let the rhythm of the music calm you. Feel your muscles relax and your heart rate and breathing slow. Say to yourself, "I am calm and relaxed."

≫ Script

Imagine that you recently passed your driver's test after much studying and practicing. You were waiting to get your driver's license and now you finally have it. You worked hard to earn money for car insurance. You kept up your grades and stayed out of trouble to demonstrate that you are responsible enough to have your own car. With each relaxing breath enjoy a feeling of pride in all of your accomplishments. (*Pause*) You have saved enough money and you decide to buy your own car. Imagine walking around a used car lot. There are cars of every color and shape lined up before you. The vehicles shine like emeralds as they reflect the sun's rays. One of these gems will soon be yours. You start to look around.

You are discouraged as you look at the high prices painted on the windshields. You are feeling sticker shock! Walk down the rows. You continue hoping that you will see one car that is in your price range. Just as you are about to leave, you see it. Parked in a corner is a modest little car with your name on it, and at a price you can afford. You are excited as you begin to look closely at the car. Although it's not your favorite color and has a lot of miles of wear and tear, you sit in the front seat and feel comfortable. You quickly learn the location of all the knobs and controls. The steering wheel fits perfectly in your hands. This car fits you and you buy it. (*Pause*)

As you are driving home, you think about all the things you like about this car. The cup holder is in just the right place, the air conditioner seems to work and the speakers sound great.

As you near home, you drive by a group of kids from your school. They seem to be laughing and pointing at your car. You think you hear one of them say that it is a piece of junk. Normally you would worry about the reaction of others but you feel strong in your car. You decide not to worry about the reaction of people you hardly know.

You feel proud knowing you have the courage to walk or drive away from others who may try and hurt your feelings or take away from your feeling of accomplishment.

You remain calm and relaxed and repeat three times to yourself: **I have inner strength and confidence...**

Take a deep breath and open your eyes. Stretch your arms and legs and your mind.

» Discussion/Reflection

· What are some reasons that people make fun of other people?

» Fast Fact

Each day Americans spend an average of 55 minutes driving.

» Alternate Affirmations

· **I believe in myself.**
· **Others can not define me..**

Subject:	Empowerment
Into Focus:	What do you do when life throws you a curve? As the expression goes, can you take lemons and make lemonade?.
Affirmation:	I have good luck.

RAIN DELAY

≫ Introduction

Sit comfortably with your eyes closed. Take three long, deep breaths. *(Pause)* Feel yourself relaxing more and more with each breath. Let the rhythm of the music calm you. Feel your muscles relax and your heart rate and breathing slow. Say to yourself, "I am calm and relaxed."

≫ Script

Pretend that there is a mall close to where you live. Now imagine that it's Saturday and the mall is calling you to you to make a visit. You have been saving your money for a new computer and want to buy one today. You have some time to spare so you decide to walk. Take a relaxing breath and notice the dampness in the air as it fills your lungs. Your mind is clear and it begins to drift from one carefree thought to another. Time passes with a simple easiness until you notice a cool trickle on the bridge of your nose.

You look up and discover it is beginning to rain. You start walking faster hoping to get to your destination without getting soaked. As your breathing deepens and heart rate increases, the raindrops actually cool your body. The faster you walk the harder it seems to rain. You see a newspaper lying on a bench and quickly pick it up and use it to cover your head. Listen to the raindrops as they pelt your makeshift paper umbrella. You are in the middle of a full blown downpour!

Imagine looking for cover. Just up ahead is a bus shelter with a bench. You feel relieved when you reach the shelter. The newspaper has kept you amazingly dry and comfortable. This tiny space leaves you with nothing to do but to sit and watch the rain until it stops.

Hear the rain beating on the thin fiberglass roof of the shelter. The rhythm of the rain gets faster and louder *(Pause)* then slows a bit *(Pause)* then gets faster and louder again. Listen to the beat. *(Pause)* Now add the sound of thunder crashing. *(Pause)* Take a breath and smell the dampness of the soil and grass around you. *(Pause)*

Look out of the shelter into the gray mist. Focus on the raindrops as they bounce off the pavement. Each one bounces off the ground and makes a different shape. *(Pause)* You wonder if, like snowflakes, each raindrop is different.

Follow the stream of water as it rushes down the curb in front of you. Watch as the current quickly carries a leaf down the street to places unknown. The rain has a cleansing effect that relaxes you.

Reach over the bench and pick up the wet newspaper. The top sections of the paper, including your favorite sections, are soaked through and are unreadable. The dark, wet newspaper tears in your hands as you try to turn the pages. Layer after layer is wet until you get to the middle of the paper, the want ads. You glance over the ads until you come to one that says "computer for sale." You read it and find out that it is exactly the computer you have been looking for at almost half the advertised store price.

Rip out the small ad and put it in your pocket. The sound of the rain is beginning to quiet. The thunder is only a faint sound in the distance. The rain now has stopped and the sun is starting to peek through the clouds. There is no need to head to the mall because you have found your computer.

Say to yourself three times: **I have good luck...**

Take a deep breath and return to your room. Open your eyes and stretch your arms, your legs and your mind.

» Discussion/Reflection

- Think of a day that went in a completely different direction than planned. Were you able to take something positive from this experience?
- Explain the quote by the famous golfer Gary Player, "the more I practice, the luckier I get."

» Activity

Come up with the titles of as many songs as possible with the theme of rain.

» Fast Fact

The first domain name ever registered was Symbolics.com on March 15, 1985.

» Alternate Affirmations

- **I am open to new opportunities.**
- **I am a positive person and enjoy life.**

Subject: **Empowerment**

Into Focus: Sometimes the hardest person to please is yourself. How do you look at yourself?

Affirmation: **I believe in myself and appreciate who I am.**

SELF PORTRAIT

≫ Introduction

Sit comfortably with your eyes closed. Take three long, deep breaths. *(Pause)* Feel yourself relaxing more and more with each breath. Let the rhythm of the music calm you. Feel your muscles relax and your heart rate and breathing slow. Say to yourself, "I am calm and relaxed."

≫ Script

Imagine that you are getting ready to go on a hike. You pack a day pack and put in everything that you will need: some water, sunscreen, and a snack. Strap on your pack. See yourself putting on comfortable shoes with plenty of support. You are ready to start your hike.

Now imagine yourself on a trail. The path is clearly marked. The sky is crystal blue. Many beautiful sights and experiences lay ahead. As you walk, you notice the trees form a canopy above you. It is getting darker, yet you feel safe and protected. It is perfectly still. Look down and notice little blue and white wildflowers beneath a long ray of sunlight. As you bend over to smell the flowers, you notice various layers of thick moss which seem to form a soft green carpet all around you. As you breathe in take in all of the oxygen and beautiful fragrance of the flowers. As you continue walking you feel calm and relaxed. There is a clearing ahead. As you walk toward the sunlight, the relaxing sound of water becomes louder and louder. You are on the bank of a beautiful stream. The water sparkles like diamonds as it makes its way over and around the smooth rocks. A gentle breeze floats over the water. Nature's air conditioning cools your entire body.

You have discovered a special place. Sit on a cool rock and dangle your feet over a smooth and perfectly still pool of water just beyond the stream's current. Look down and see a reflection of you as clear as a mirror. The blue sky makes a perfect background for your self-portrait. The clear water lets you see deep within you. This in depth look allows you to go beyond the surface reflection and see your inner strength and your other inner qualities. Regardless how you see your outside reflection, you know that your inner beauty is the most important. Stick your toe in the water and distort your reflection. Watch as your image becomes clear again. A calm, contented feeling comes over you, like the breeze off the stream. You feel at peace, knowing you can not change how you look, but you can change how you look at yourself.

The trip back seems all downhill. Your feet seem to glide down the trail. The next time you look into a mirror you will see all of you, not just the image of your face. Continue to relax and repeat to yourself three times: **I believe in myself and appreciate who I am....**

Now return to your room. Open your eyes and stretch. *(Pause)* Take a few moments to enjoy the good feeling that comes with relaxation.

CALVIN AND HOBBES   by Bill Watterson

≫ Discussion/Reflection

- What is meant by the expression, "Beauty is only skin deep."
- Do you sometimes fall victim to the pressures and commercialization of today's society?

≫ Activity

Next time you look in a magazine, think about how many of the advertised products you really, truly need.

≫ Alternate Affirmations

- **I look at myself and feel proud.**
- **I look beneath the surface in myself and in others.**

Subject: Empowerment

Into Focus: Sometimes when people move to a place that is warm year round they say they miss the change of seasons. What is it they miss?

Affirmation: Things change for the better.

SPRING FEVER

» Introduction

Sit comfortably with your eyes closed. Take three long, deep breaths. *(Pause)* Feel yourself relaxing more and more with each breath. Let the rhythm of the music calm you. Feel your muscles relax and your heart rate and breathing slow. Say to yourself, "I am calm and relaxed."

» Script

Imagine that it is early spring and the landscape around you is still dull and lifeless. Last year's leaves and dead plants and grass have created a gloomy brown quilt over the entire yard. Take a relaxing breath and picture yourself outside raking leaves.

The temperature is cool and you are wearing a sweatshirt. Listen as the spring breeze rattles through the empty trees. Watch as a few leaves swirl around your feet.

Raking is hard work and you feel yourself begin to warm up. You decide to take off your sweat shirt. Now see yourself pull the brown leaves toward you. Each pull of the rake seems to become easier. Pull and relax, *(Pause)* pull and relax, *(Pause)* pull and relax. *(Pause)* Hold the rake upright and take a short break. Breathe in the fresh air. Feel the breeze cool your arms, which ache from raking. *(Pause)*

Look up at the bright blue sky. Feel the sun warm your face and arms. Listen as the birds chirp with excitement and anticipation. You feel calm, relaxed and ready to finish the job.

Reach out once again and pull the brown leaves toward you. For the first time notice the ground beneath the leaves. Little green shoots and buds seem to appear in the wake of your rake. Reach out and pull your rake. You have freed another tiny green colony from its blanket of darkness. Your raking becomes effortless and with each pull of the rake you become more and more relaxed.

The work seems easy as you clear your entire back yard. Imagine each bud and blade of grass cheering as it reaches up to face the sun. You are on a mission to give each plant space to grow. You know they will return the favor by producing oxygen. Breathe in slowly and smell the new life all around you. Your rake now seems to glide on the surface. Soon your mission is accomplished.

There seems to be a giant weight off your shoulders as you fall back into a soft pile of leaves. You feel calm and relaxed. Look up at the clear blue sky and say to yourself three times: **Things change for the better...** Growing is an exciting adventure. Enjoy life and value it.

Take a deep breath and return to your room. Open your eyes. Stretch your arms, your legs and your mind.

» Discussion/Reflection

- Name some tasks you do that are mundane and repetitious, but are necessary.
- What are some of the similarities between humans and plants?
- What is cabin fever? What is spring fever? How are they alike? Have you had them before?

» Fast Fact

Laughing lowers levels of stress and strengthens the immune system. Six year olds laugh an average of 300 times a day. Adults laugh as little as 15 times a day.

» Alternate Affirmations

- **I give myself opportunities for new growth.**
- **I am optimistic.**

Subject: Empowerment

Into Focus: When you get in a funk or a rut it is important to stay positive.

Affirmation: I breathe out problems and breathe in hope.

UP IN SMOKE

» Introduction

Sit comfortably with your eyes closed. Take three long, deep breaths. *(Pause)* Feel yourself relaxing more and more with each breath. Let the rhythm of the music calm you. Feel your muscles relax and your heart rate and breathing slow. Say to yourself, "I am calm and relaxed."

» Script

Imagine that you are out walking on a sidewalk on a cold and cloudy autumn afternoon. Feel the brisk wind against your face. You are cold and feel "goose bumps" on your arms. You are not in a very good mood. Something is bothering you. See yourself rubbing your hands together and stomping your feet to warm up. The brisk walk begins to warm you up and forces you to breathe deeply. You notice that the rhythm of breathing helps you relax. Take a deep breath and let it out slowly. *(Pause)* With each breath you become more and more relaxed. Feel your body become even warmer and more relaxed. *(Pause)* As you breathe slowly, watch as your warm breath turns to steam as it mixes with the cold outside air. Feel you hands warming. Look around, the trees are almost bare. They rise up around you, tall, thin giants. Listen to them as they make hollow creaking noises in the wind. The few brown leaves remaining seem to be holding on for dear life. As the cold wind whistles through the branches, you can hear the leaves shiver. Watch as a leaf lets go of the limb and races down the road and out of sight.

A large noisy truck passes slowly by you. You feel the ground vibrate beneath your feet. It, too, heads down the road. You notice the black, sooty exhaust as it streams out and rises into the air. The exhaust twists and turns with the wind, then disappears.

The cold wind seems to be pushing you down the winding road. You are glad the wind is behind you. As you breathe, you notice a smell of something burning. Look up to see that someone is burning a pile of leaves.

Listen as the leaves crackle. You are soon close enough to feel the warmth of the fire on your face and hands. Rub your hands together. Watch as the billows of smoke rise up in the air like small clouds. Imagine you are sending smoke signals to an out-of-town friend. You are explaining with the smoke signals the problem that has been bothering you.

Think of a problem or worry that you sometimes have. *(Pause)* Imagine that with each breath you exhale you send that problem "up in smoke." It feels good to get that problem out in the open and watch it drift away and disappear. Take another breath and repeat to yourself three times: **I breathe out problems and breathe in hope...**

It's time to head home. The walk has made you feel better. The physical exercise, using your imagination and being out in nature helped you resolve what was bothering you.

Come back to the room now, open your eyes and stretch your arms, your legs and your mind.

>> Discussion/Reflection

· What are some things you can do if you are feeling down or depressed?

>> Activity

Develop a list of people and organizations in your community who are helpful to teens who are feeling depressed.

>> Fast Fact

Statistics show that 77% of students have said they have been bullied mentally, verbally or physically.

>> Alternate Affirmations

· **Staying busy helps me cope.**
· **I cope when things go bad.**

**esponsibility**

Making good choices for yourself and
your relationships.

**mpowerment**

Feeling positive about yourself and competent
with peers. Feeling supported by others.

earning

**Developing skills to acquire and retain knowledge.
Finding enjoyment in creative pursuits.**

**ttitudes**

Developing and practicing the attitudes and
values needed to become a complete person.

**-pand**

Exploring your ability to feel calm and centered.

Subject: Learning

Into Focus: The key to doing well on tests is being prepared, and picturing yourself as confident and relaxed.

Affirmation: **I stay calm and relaxed while taking tests.**

TEST PREPARATION ACHIEVEMENT TESTS - DAY I

» Introduction

Sit comfortably with your eyes closed. Take three long, deep breaths. *(Pause)* Feel yourself relaxing more and more with each breath. Let the rhythm of the music calm you. Feel your muscles relax and your heart rate and breathing slow. Say to yourself, "I am calm and relaxed."

» Script

As you breathe slowly, imagine that today is the day to take your group achievement tests. You feel confident and relaxed and look forward to the challenge. Slowly relax all of the muscles in your body. Notice any tension or anxiety that you may have and release it. Taking tests is a reminder for you to think about remaining calm, confident and relaxed. When and if you feel any tension or worry think of the words "calm and relax" and release the tension. *(Pause)* Imagine a special place where you always feel safe, calm and worry free. This can be somewhere you've been or an imaginary place. *(Pause)*

In your mind's eye, see your teacher passing out the test booklets. Watch them come to your desk. As each booklet is passed out you become more and more relaxed. Feel the tension drain from your body. If you notice any tension or anxiety, simply keep your breathing slow and relaxed and say to yourself, "I am calm and relaxed." As you relax you gain more confidence.

The test booklet is on your desk. The teacher asks you to open it to the first page of instructions. Each turn of the page is a signal for you to relax. Now see yourself reading the test instructions and complete the sample questions. Your teacher tells you it is time to begin the first test. Do the easiest questions first and then come back to the harder ones. Notice how you stay relaxed by breathing slowly. When you notice yourself getting worried or anxious you simply slow down your breathing and say the words "calm and relax." If you are not sure which one is the correct answer, you make the best guess by reading the question with each possible choice and choosing the one that makes the most sense. Once you have completed each item, see yourself going back over them to check your answers. To you, testing is becoming easier because of your ability to stay relaxed. Say to yourself three times: **I stay relaxed and calm while taking tests.**

The next test is called _____. Again, see yourself carefully reading the sample question. Stay relaxed, breathing slowly. Feel your arms and shoulders relaxing even more. Go to your special place and say to yourself, "I am confident and relaxed. I enjoy the challenge of taking achievement tests. I try my hardest. I stay relaxed. When I don't know the correct answer, I make the best guess possible. I check my work." Say to yourself three times: **I stay relaxed and calm while taking tests.**

Today's test is over. You have done the best you can do and feel proud of your hard work. You compliment yourself for taking your time, staying relaxed and following directions. Open your eyes now and get ready to listen to your teacher.

» **Discussion/Reflection**

· Why is it important to stay relaxed during tests? What steps should you take if you feel yourself getting worried or tense? What questions do you have about upcoming achievement tests?

» **Alternate Affirmations**

· **I check my work.**
· **I am confident when I take tests.**

Note: **For more information on testing and test anxiety refer to pages 19, 24, and 47.**

Subject:	Learning
Into Focus:	This script can be used to help students remain relaxed while completing group achievement tests.
Affirmation:	**I find answers by staying relaxed.**

TEST PREPARATION ACHIEVEMENT TESTS – DAY 2

›› Introduction

Sit comfortably with your eyes closed. Take three long, deep breaths. *(Pause)* Feel yourself relaxing more and more with each breath. Let the rhythm of the music calm you. Feel your muscles relax and your heart rate and breathing slow. Say to yourself, "I am calm and relaxed."

›› Script

Take another deep breath and, as you exhale, feel your whole body let go of any tension. Arms and shoulders relaxed. Hands and fingers warming. Relax your neck and all the muscles in your face. Feel the relaxation spread to your chest, stomach and hips.

Relax your legs. Let go of any tension in your ankles and feet. As you continue to relax, let yourself drift with the music. Take a deep breath and as you let it out slowly, imagine your teacher telling you that it is time to take more achievement tests. You stay calm and relaxed. You feel confident and know what to expect. Breathing slowly, relaxing. Be aware of any tension that creeps into your body and release it by relaxing that area.

Now in your mind picture your teacher passing out the test booklets and see yourself staying relaxed. Your teacher tells you to open your test booklets. When you open your test you feel even more relaxed. You feel confident and relaxed.

Today's tests are _____. On each section you read the directions carefully. Next, see yourself completing the sample questions. Finally, see yourself reading the questions while staying relaxed. Imagine a great book of facts in your special place. When you feel stuck simply say to yourself, "relax and calm," and go to your special place. Imagine the book of facts that contains all of the things you have learned. You feel confident about the answer you choose. Say to yourself three times: **I find answers by staying relaxed.**

Breathe slowly and stay relaxed. During each time you take tests you will do your best. Stay relaxed by being aware of your breathing. Slow breathing, calm and relaxed. Tonight at home practice relaxing by releasing all the tension in your muscles. Open your eyes and listen carefully to your teacher.

» Discussion/Reflection

- Why do schools give achievement tests? Do you ever get nervous before tests? What are some things you plan on doing if you feel nervous?

» Activity

Tonight at home practice relaxing by releasing all the tension in your muscles.

» Alternate Affirmations

- **I am confident about my answers.**

Subject: Learning

Into Focus: This script can be used to help students remain relaxed and feel confident about completing group achievement tests.

Affirmation: **I am relaxed and confident about taking tests.**

TEST PREPARATION ACHIEVEMENT TESTS - DAY 3

>> Script

Sit comfortably with your eyes closed. Take three long, deep breaths. *(Pause)* Feel yourself relaxing more and more with each breath. Let the rhythm of the music calm you. Feel your muscles relax and your heart rate and breathing slow. Say to yourself, "I am calm and relaxed."

Take another deep breath and slowly release it. Imagine your teacher telling you that the last day of testing is today. The word "testing" signals you to relax. Let go of all the tension in your body. Relax your upper body. Release any tension in your face, neck, shoulders, arms, hands, fingers. Relax your lower body. Legs relaxed. Feet relaxed. As you become more relaxed imagine your teacher passing out the test booklets.

Today's tests are _____. You feel confident and relaxed. See yourself open your test booklet and stay relaxed. See yourself read the instructions carefully and then complete the sample questions. See yourself staying relaxed and completing the entire test. Complete each item by looking carefully at all the possible answers. You feel confident that the answer you choose is the correct one. Say to yourself three times, **"I am relaxed and confident about taking tests."** Open your eyes and be ready to listen to your teacher.

>> Discussion/Reflection

· Discuss any questions students may have about the upcoming achievement tests.

>> Alternate Affirmations

· **I consider all possible answers and choose the best selection.**

Subject:	Learning
Into Focus:	This script provides a brief relaxation exercise in preparation for taking a test.
Affirmation:	**I stay calm and relaxed when taking tests.**

TEST PREPARATION ACHIEVEMENT TESTS OR GENERAL TESTING

» Introduction

Sit comfortably with your eyes closed. Take three long, deep breaths. *(Pause)* Feel yourself relaxing more and more with each breath. Let the rhythm of the music calm you. Feel your muscles relax and your heart rate and breathing slow. Say to yourself, "I am calm and relaxed."

» Script

Sit comfortably with your feet on the floor and your eyes closed. Take three long, deep breaths. Feel yourself relaxing more and more with each breath.

Let the rhythm of the music calm you. Feel your muscles relax and your heart and breathing slow. Say to yourself, "I am calm and relaxed."

In your mind's eye see a special place where you always feel safe, calm and worry free. This can be somewhere you've been or an imaginary place. *(Pause)*

Take a deep breath and as you release it, relax even more. In your mind, look over your test. You are feeling calm and relaxed. Imagine that you have a great book of facts in your special place.

When you look in your book of facts, you can find all the answers you need. Continue to breathe slowly, and relax. You are confident that you can do well on today's test. The book of facts is open. You may go back to it whenever you need it. Say to yourself three times: **"I stay relaxed and calm when taking tests."**

Take a deep breath and open your eyes. Stretch your arms, your legs and your mind.

» Discussion/Reflection

• Why is it important to tell yourself that you will do well on tests?

Subject: Learning

Into Focus: Do you take time to notice the small things around you? Do you miss the chance to learn things and make new relationships because you are moving too fast?

Affirmation: I enjoy learning new things.

BEACHED

≫ Introduction

Sit comfortably with your eyes closed. Take three long, deep breaths. *(Pause)* Feel yourself relaxing more and more with each breath. Let the rhythm of the music calm you. Feel your muscles relax and your heart rate and breathing slow. Say to yourself, "I am calm and relaxed."

≫ Script

Imagine yourself alone on a beach by the ocean. Listen to the sound of the waves as they hit the shore. *(Pause)* Feel the warm sun on your back. *(Pause)* You have no music, books or friends to disturb your thoughts. Your cell phone is turned off. As you walk along the shore the soft, wet sand oozes under your bare feet. The sound and sight of the wave's rhythmic pattern relaxes you. Pick up a small shiny rock, blow the sand off and put it in your pocket. Pick up another larger stone and throw it into the seemingly endless water. *(Pause)*

Now imagine sitting on the dry sand and taking handfuls of the sand and letting it sprinkle through your fingers. Soon you move to the water's edge and start doodling with your finger in a pile of seaweed and small shells that have washed up next to you. Notice the bright colors and intricate patterns on the tiny shells. You decide to sort them by color. *(Pause)* Now sort them by their kind and shape. *(Pause)* Make a mosaic pattern in the sand with the shells. *(Pause)* Notice that there are two different types of seaweed that the waves have intertwined together. You wonder to yourself and ask these questions: Where did it grow? *(Pause)* What does the ocean floor look like? *(Pause)* Now see very small crabs eating the seaweed. When your shadow moves over them they scurry to hide in the vegetation. They must quickly adapt to any condition. Your mind is full of questions and you can't wait to find a book or get on the internet to learn more about ocean life.

As you get ready to leave you see another person walking slowly toward you. Her skin has been darkened by the sun. As she gets closer you can see that her face is lined with white, almost salty, wrinkles. As she nods while passing you decide to ask her some of your questions. She seems to know everything about the ocean and in particular this stretch of beach. You enjoy listening to her and as you say goodbye, you realize that she gave you more in-depth, practical information than you could ever find in a book or on the internet. *(Pause)* Watch now in your mind's eye as the old woman walks away and seems to disappear into the sunset.

You feel proud that you are curious about your surroundings and learn new things. It feels good to step out of your comfort zone and try something new. While staying relaxed say to yourself three times: **I enjoy learning new things**...

Take a deep breath open your eyes and stretch your arms, legs and your mind.

» Discussion/Reflection

· How do you learn best? Is there a person you look to for wisdom?

» Activity

Make a list of two or three things that you would like to learn about in depth. Explore these things when you have free time.

» Fast Fact

The vocabulary of the average person consists of 5,000 to 6,000 words.

»Alternate Affirmations

· **I ask questions to learn more.**
· **I slow down and see things in depth.**

Subject: Learning

Into Focus: Do you ever wish that you had a photographic memory?

Affirmation: **I store and retrieve information easily.**

FREEZE FRAME

≫ Introduction

Sit comfortably with your eyes closed. Take three long, deep breaths. *(Pause)* Feel yourself relaxing more and more with each breath. Let the rhythm of the music calm you. Feel your muscles relax and your heart rate and breathing slow. Say to yourself, "I am calm and relaxed."

≫ Script

Imagine yourself walking into a large library. You're carrying a book from school along with some notes you took to study for a test. As you walk through this library you notice the tall bookshelves. They seem to form a long and complicated maze. You are astounded by the thousands of books that surround you. Slowly zig- zag through the towers of books until you find a quiet, secluded place in a far corner. There is only one chair and it looks very comfortable. See yourself sit down and take a moment to enjoy the silence. *(Pause)* Listen… you can almost hear the books and the other library media whisper to you. *(Pause)* Past, present and future ideas are together in one place. You feel important and energized at being surrounded by all this knowledge.

Open the book and the notes you brought and begin to read. The silence helps you concentrate. Continue to breathe in a calm and relaxed way… breathing in and out, in and out. Now imagine that your mind is like a sponge — light, open and ready to soak up information. Now as you study, focus on the important vocabulary and concepts. They seem to pop right out at you. Focus, blink, and freeze in your mind the important information and concepts. Imagine that your memory has an enter button. See yourself push this button as all of the information is stored in your memory.

Now continue reading. Focus on another piece of information. Again, it seems to pop right out at you. As you continue to relax, focus, blink and freeze the important information in your mind. Push enter and everything is stored in your memory.

Continue this routine until you are finished studying. Look at all of the books on the shelves around you. They are not so intimidating anymore. In fact, they look quite friendly. They are filled with information ready for you to learn. Say to yourself three times: **I store and retrieve information easily.**

Take a deep breath and return to your room. Open your eyes. Stretch your arms, your legs and your mind. You feel confident that you can use this technique to store and retrieve important information.

» Fast Fact

73 percent of all books in libraries are never checked out.

» Alternate Affirmations

- I focus on what is important.
- I remember what I study.

Subject:	Learning

Into Focus: Some people need constant activity or entertainment or they quickly become bored. Here is an example of using imagination as a form of entertainment.

Affirmation: My imagination helps me to see the world in creative ways.

SNOWFLAKE SYMPHONY

>> Introduction

Sit comfortably with your eyes closed. Take three long, deep breaths. *(Pause)* Feel yourself relaxing more and more with each breath. Let the rhythm of the music calm you. Feel your muscles relax and your heart rate and breathing slow. Say to yourself, "I am calm and relaxed."

>> Script

Imagine that you are on a winter vacation. You are at a resort staying in a cabin that overlooks a lake. It's freezing outside and a storm is blowing in. Everyone has gone snow skiing, but you decided to stay back and enjoy the solitude. Look out at the cold clear sheet of ice that covers the lake. The sun bouncing off the ice makes it so bright you have to squint. Listen as the cold wind rattles the windows in front of you. *(Pause)* Listen to the wind howl like wolves in the night. *(Pause)* It is much too cold to go outside. You are glad that you are warm and snug indoors.

As you get up to close the drapes, you notice a change outside. Puffy grey clouds cover the sun, so you no longer have to squint. Breathing slowly and easily you feel relaxed and calm. As you look out the window, you notice beautiful, large lacy snowflakes that begin to dance in the wind. With your mind's eye, focus on just the snowflakes.

Imagine that you move your hand to the left and the snowflakes follow. Now move your hand to the right and they follow. Now make them go up, now down. *(Pause)* When you move your hand in a circle the faithful flakes follow your command. Thousands of snowflakes move in perfect harmony - first left, then right, then back, then forth. Their rhythm relaxes you. Use your arms and direct a snowflake symphony. You are using your imagination and your creativity and are filled with the rhythm of music and the awe of nature. Millions of snowflakes have gathered on the ice. They stream and dance in many directions as the wind directs them. Sit back and enjoy a snowflake dance. *(Pause)* You marvel as the snowflakes dance to form any pattern, word or object you want. *(Pause)* Your imagination and creativity are wonderful gifts that need exercise. Use them to help you enjoy life.

Now take a deep breath and as you slowly release it, repeat to yourself three times: **My imagination helps me to see the world in creative ways...** Take a breath and blow the snowflakes away.

Open your eyes and stretch. *(Pause)* Take a few moments to appreciate the good feeling that comes with relaxation.

» Discussion/Reflection

- In most cases, a human being does not direct external forces such as the weather, poverty, war, etc. Is it possible to have more control over internal forces, such as your feelings, emotions, happiness, health, etc.? What are some ways you can practice control over these internal forces?
- What are some of the benefits of having a good imagination?

» Activity

For fun, do this script using rap music, country music or your favorite kind of music.

» Resources

Classical music (select music that features tempo changes such as selections from *Fantasia* or the *Nutcracker Suite.*

» Alternate Affirmations

- **I have an active and healthy imagination.**
- **I enjoy different types of music.**

Subject: Learning

Into Focus: Thinking "outside the box" is needed in today's world more than ever.

Affirmation: I am able to see things from more than one perspective.

STAR CRUISE

≫ Introduction

Sit comfortably with your eyes closed. Take three long, deep breaths. *(Pause)* Feel yourself relaxing more and more with each breath. Let the rhythm of the music calm you. Feel your muscles relax and your heart rate and breathing slow. Say to yourself, "I am calm and relaxed."

≫ Script

Imagine that you are sitting in a chair on the deck of a large cruise ship. The temperature is perfect and the sun is beginning to set. As you gaze across the bow of the ship you see clear blue water all around you. The forward motion of the boat creates waves that glisten like diamonds in the setting sun. Feel the fresh ocean breeze on your face. The air holds a faint smell of marine life.

Look out toward the sky and enjoy a magnificent sunset. The huge orange sun sinks slowly on the horizon. *(Pause)* The sun melts behind the curve of the earth until all that is left is a fading orange glow. In a few minutes, darkness surrounds you. You feel the gentle swaying of the ship as it glides over the water. The slight breeze blankets you with relaxation. Take a moment to enjoy this comfortable breeze. *(Pause)*

Now notice how relaxed and calm you feel as you reach down and recline your chair all the way back. Look up at the sky. One dim star catches your attention. Now scan the sky with your eyes wide open to see as much as possible. Notice another star, then another, then a few more. Soon the entire sky is dotted with tiny white lights. *(Pause)* Watch as one of the lights shoots across the sky.

Pretend you have a laser that can connect the stars. Point it to the sky and use it to form a large circle of stars. Now imagine it is a three dimensional ball. Make it bounce all across the sky like a beach ball. *(Pause)* Look at all the stars again. With your laser, connect some stars to form any picture you want. *(Pause)* Take a moment to appreciate your creation. *(Pause)*

The whole sky is filled with pictures and each person can see something different in the stars. Everyone is different and born with their own vision. You can always close your eyes and go on a "star cruise" to see things from a different perspective. The world is full of opportunities to "connect the dots" and create interesting opportunities for yourself. Follow your own unique path. Breathe slowly and say to yourself three times: **I am able to see things from more than one perspective...**

Take a deep breath and return to your room. Open your eyes and stretch your arms, your legs and your mind

» Discussion/Reflection

- What does the statement "Follow your own unique path" mean?
- How do you express your creativity? Have you ever hidden your creativity?
- What does the phrase "connect the dots" mean to you?

» Activity

On a clear night, lay on your back and look at the stars. Look for constellations or make up your own.

» Resources

Music: Vincent by Don McLean
When You Wish Upon a Star - Disney

» Fast Facts

Astronomers estimate there are about 100 thousand million stars in the Milky Way galaxy alone. Outside that, there are millions upon millions of other galaxies.

» Alternate Affirmations

- **Diversity makes life interesting.**
- **I celebrate differences.**

Subject: Learning

Into Focus: Having a study place set aside where you can focus and concentrate is important.

Affirmation: I am able to focus when needed.

WELCOME WEB

≫ Introduction

Sit comfortably with your eyes closed. Take three long, deep breaths. *(Pause)* Feel yourself relaxing more and more with each breath. Let the rhythm of the music calm you. Feel your muscles relax and your heart rate and breathing slow. Say to yourself, "I am calm and relaxed."

≫ Script

Picture yourself studying in your favorite room. This may be in your school, in your home or somewhere else. Although you have a big reading assignment due tomorrow and are having some trouble concentrating, you are confident that you will regain your focus. It is quiet, which helps you begin to concentrate.

Breathing slowly, feeling calm and relaxed, see yourself opening your book. *(Pause)* There is much to do, but you feel confident that you will receive some inspiration to begin. While waiting you become aware of the extreme quiet and notice the words on the page start to run together. Remaining confident, you allow your mind to wander. *(Pause)* You find yourself looking around the room. *(Pause)* You notice a little harmless spider just outside the window. The spider is just beginning to spin a web. You look at the spider and it scurries to the corner to hide. You want to see the spider work on its web, but it stays in a little ball, hiding.

Remaining calm and relaxed, see yourself refocusing on your book. You start to read and finish part one of your required reading. When you are done, you remember the spider. You look over as the spider runs to hide. You are amazed at the work she has already done. The web is much bigger than it was before. You can't wait to see what happens next. You purposely ignore the spider and continue your work. You find your reading even more interesting now and time passes quickly.

Continue to enjoy what you are reading. *(Pause)* You are done with part two and glance over at the spider. She slowly moves back to her hiding place. She has been busy weaving a web about the size of your fist. You see a series of growing circles, held together with thin, almost invisible thread.

You look away feeling that both of you need to get back to work. Before long you have finished your reading and have enjoyed and remembered everything in the book.

Look over and see that your spider friend has also finished. Her masterpiece is as big as your outstretched hand. It has hundreds of splendid spokes that seem to float on air. This time the spider doesn't hide, feeling safe in her web as a result of her hard work. You have also finished your work and you enjoy the feeling of accomplishment. While enjoying this feeling say to yourself three times: **I am able to focus when needed**...

Take a deep breath and open your eyes. Stretch your arms and legs and your mind.

» Discussion/Reflection

- Do you ever play games to help you study?
- How do you study best – quiet, music, etc.?
- What other members of the animal kingdom are known for their work habits?

» Activity

Sit on a swing, bench or chair for two minutes. What do you hear, smell, see? Do some homework and come back to this spot. What were the changes around you?

» Fast Fact

If you read just 15 minutes a day for one year, you can complete 20 average size books.

» Alternate Affirmations

- I remember what I read.
- I focus when I need to complete a task.

Responsibility

Making good choices for yourself and
your relationships.

Empowerment

Feeling positive about yourself and competent
with peers. Feeling supported by others.

Learning

Developing skills to acquire and retain knowledge.
Finding enjoyment in creative pursuits.

Attitudes

**Developing and practicing the attitudes and
values needed to become a complete person.**

X-pand

Exploring your ability to feel calm and centered.

Subject: Attitudes

Into Focus: Left to its own resources, nature can be as exciting as any type of entertainment.

Affirmation: Nature is amazing.

BIO BAY

≫ Introduction

Sit comfortably with your eyes closed. Take three long, deep breaths. *(Pause)* Feel yourself relaxing more and more with each breath. Let the rhythm of the music calm you. Feel your muscles relax and your heart rate and breathing slow. Say to yourself, "I am calm and relaxed."

≫ Script

You are on vacation in a warm topical country. You have spent the past few days lying in the warm sand and listening to the soothing sea sounds. You feel relaxed, refreshed and ready for an adventure. You signed up for an evening tour to the far end of the island and the time has arrived. Your destination is to see an amazing feat of nature that take place in water. Feel excited as you climb on a small bus and head out to the highway.

Look out the window and notice the lush vegetation in all shades of green on the mountains that surround you. Notice that a warm, gentle rain has begun to fall. Take a deep breath and smell the thick, damp air. Look past the raindrops on the bus windows and notice that the sky is brightening. Then right before your eyes, the clouds break up and the sun appears. The large plants and tall trees sparkle as the sunlight reflects off their wet leaves.

The hum of the highway and the gentle rocking of the bus relax you. The sun is now getting lower and an orange and yellow light tints the landscape. A voice breaks the silence and announces you will soon reach your destination.

The bus stops in a small parking lot. You smell fresh salt water as you step off. You are handed a life vest, a two ended paddle and are told you will be kayaking to Bio Bay. After a short lesson, you are led to the edge of the water and asked to get in one of the many identical kayaks bobbing up and down. Your small vessel balances easily as you get in.

It is now almost dark. Your guide clips a green glow stick to your vest and says, "Follow me." Any nervousness you may have had quickly dissipates as you begin to paddle. Left, right – left, right – left, right. *(Pause)* Your deep breathing invigorates you and you soon glide over the water.

It is now completely dark except for the moon and flickering stars above. Look back and see a winding line of small green glowing lights. You are not alone on your journey. *(Pause)* As you focus on the green light of your guide ahead you feel the shadows begin to close in around you. *(Pause)* The light ahead stops and you stop. *(Pause)* Using the light of the moon you can see that you have entered a secluded bay. *(Pause)* The bay is now dotted with glow sticks like fireflies on a warm summer's night. It is quiet and peaceful. *(Long pause)*

Your guide breaks the silence and says, "It is time." Before you can say, time for what, the water below begins to light up in a beautiful blue-green color. You now see the other boats scattered throughout the bay and hear the excited voices of their passengers. Look on with amazement. *(Pause)*

Dip your oar and watch the water around it light up even more. Now put your hand in the warm glowing water. Move it back and forth and watch as little particles of light trail closely behind. Make an X in the water and watch as it slowly fades away. The guide says this amazing phenomenon is caused by tiny algae in the water that receive energy from sunlight during the day. At night, at a certain time, the algae emit light in response to movement in the water. There are only a few places in the world where conditions are just right to allow this remarkable thing to happen.

Breathe slowly and say to yourself three times: **Nature is amazing.**

The glow of the water begins to fade and your guide says it is time to leave. The moon the stars and a winding stream of glow stick lights will show you the way. You feel energized as you paddle and glide back.

Take a deep breath and return to your room. Left to it's own resources, nature is truly amazing.

» Discussion/Reflection

- Why might this wonderful discovery become endangered in the future? What are some hints of this in the story?
- Why is it that some of the best things in life require a little effort?

» Books, Music, Websites etc.

Look up "Bioluminescent Bays" to find out more information on this phenomenon.

» Alternate Affirmations

- **Being with nature relaxes me.**
- **I like to learn and explore.**

Subject: Attitudes

Into Focus: There are many sides to each of us.

Affirmation: I appreciate the many sides of who I am.

EXTRA EXTRA

>> Introduction

Sit comfortably with your eyes closed. Take three long, deep breaths. *(Pause)* Feel yourself relaxing more and more with each breath. Let the rhythm of the music calm you. Feel your muscles relax and your heart rate and breathing slow. Say to yourself, "I am calm and relaxed."

>> Script

Imagine that it's the time of day when you can take some time to relax. Picture yourself in a living room. Choose a newspaper from a stack of reading material next to a comfortable reclining chair. Sit down, see yourself sink into the cushions, and feel them wrap around your thighs and back. Reach down and pull the reclining lever. Feel your feet elevate and relax. Pull the lever again and the entire chair tilts back. The comfort of the cushions surrounds you. As you relax, tilt your head slightly back. Take time to enjoy this total comfort. *(Pause)*

After a while, you reach down and grab the newspaper. Begin to read your favorite section. It is full of interesting news and features. When you turn the page a different section of the newspaper falls on your lap. You pick it up and read the headline. To your surprise it says in large bold letters, "THIS IS YOUR LIFE." Next to it is a hologram picture of you. As you tilt the picture, it winks at you.

You are intrigued and begin to read. The first article is about an accomplishment you worked hard to achieve. It is something you feel good about. Put yourself in the picture and see yourself enjoying your accomplishment. Imagine now what are you doing? *(Pause)* This accomplishment could be anything that you feel proud about. It may have been the 1st time you rode a bike by yourself, or doing well in a class, or making a new friend.

You read the story under the title, "Good News." You see yourself doing something to help others. Put yourself in the story and imagine what are you doing? *(Pause)* Enjoy the good feeling that comes when you help others.

You read on. Toward the bottom of the page is the leisure section. A picture begins to appear. As it comes into focus you see a crystal clear 3D picture of you practicing a hobby or activity that you enjoy. *(Pause)*

At the bottom of your special edition is your quote of the day. As you continue to be relaxed say to yourself three times: **I appreciate the many sides of who I am.**

Bring your chair into the upright position. There are many articles in a newspaper just like there are many sides of you. You strive to be a well-rounded person. Come back to your room and open your eyes. Stretch your legs, your arms and your mind.

» Discussion/Reflection

- Pretend that your namc is in print or your picture is printed in the paper for a special achievement or community service? How would you feel about it?
- A noteworthy achievement does not always have to be in sports, academics or entertainment. In what other aspects of life can we achieve? What devices are changing the way people read newspapers, magazines and books?

» Alternate Affirmations

- **I find interests that are relaxing and fulfilling.**
- **Reaching out to help others makes me feel good.**

⊘ ◄ ►

Subject:	Attitudes
Into Focus:	Have you heard the saying, if you have good health you have everything you need?
Affirmation:	**I am thankful for each day of good health.**

HEADS UP

≫ Introduction

Sit comfortably with your eyes closed. Take three long, deep breaths. *(Pause)* Feel yourself relaxing more and more with each breath. Let the rhythm of the music calm you. Feel your muscles relax and your heart rate and breathing slow. Say to yourself, "I am calm and relaxed."

≫ Script

Imagine that you are at school and that you are early for class and are waiting for everyone else to arrive. You lean back in your chair and watch as the other students trickle in. One by one the chairs fill.

The teacher walks in. Listen as the classroom noise slowly goes from loud *(Pause)* to medium *(Pause)* to soft *(Pause)* to quiet.

The teacher clears her throat and says there is a special assignment today. Everyone is to leave the classroom and go on a long walk by him or herself. You each must return to the classroom in one hour and report one thing you have learned on your brief journey. The class cheers and quickly files outside. Some of your classmates treat this opportunity as free time, but you are willing to give it a chance.

As you leave the building you notice a slight cool breeze on your face. There are odd shaped shadows on the pavement. Look up and see large white clouds directly above you. The cloud shadows escort you down the sidewalk and into a park. These shadows disappear as you reach the lush green grass. The cool breeze is now at your back. The walk has made your breathing deepen. You feel relaxed yet full of energy. Your mind is open and free. Your head is clear and focused. Look up to notice the clouds again. They continue to slowly float and change in size and shape. The clouds are much more interesting and complex than the shadows they create. You see different shades of white and gray on an endless blue background.

Suddenly you trip on a rock and go head over heels down a small embankment. You are shocked, shaken up, embarrassed, but unhurt. As you lay on your back the clouds continue to drift by overhead. You can almost feel their shadows. Sit up and brush yourself off. You were feeling so good and then in a moment so scared. Life can change so quickly. You wonder, "what if you had been seriously hurt?" You then picture a person you could count on to support you no matter what

condition you were in. *(Pause)*

The hour is almost over so you walk back to school happy that you were not hurt and carefully watching your step along the way.

Now repeat to yourself three times: **I am thankful for each day of good health…**

Take a deep breath and let it out as you return to the room. Open your eyes and stretch your arms, your legs and your mind.

>> Discussion/Reflection

- Where were you when you learned a lesson you will always remember? Where was it? What did you learn?
- What do the phrases "life is too short," or "don't sweat the small stuff" mean to you? How do they relate to this story?
- Is there symbolism in the clouds in this story?
- If you had an accident and became disabled, would you become a different person?
- Have you ever had a friend who held you back or restricted you?
- Do you currently have a friend who shows true patience and understanding? Is this friend your age or an adult? Have you not found a true friend yet?

>> Resources

Music: Don't Laugh at Me — Peter, Paul and Mary

>> Alternate Affirmations

- **I make friends easily.**
- **I am thankful for my good health.**

Subject:	Attitudes

Into Focus: We meet people every day who are different from us. We can use this opportunity to learn from each other as well as to reach past difference and make connections.

Affirmation: The world is a diverse and interesting place.

DIVERSITY = STRENGTH

≫ Introduction

Sit comfortably with your eyes closed. Take three long, deep breaths. *(Pause)* Feel yourself relaxing more and more with each breath. Let the rhythm of the music calm you. Feel your muscles relax and your heart rate and breathing slow. Say to yourself, "I am calm and relaxed."

≫ Script

Picture yourself walking into a mall. You turn right and enter the first store you see a clothing store called Universal. As you look through the racks, you notice that everything is offered in just one color and one style. You decide to find a store with more variety.

As you walk down the broad corridor of the mall, you are surprised to see that every store is called Universal. You peer into the shops, one after the other, and see that each one is selling the exact same color and style of clothes as the first. You notice how frustrated you feel by the lack of choices and how dull this mall seems to you.

You keep walking. You can detect the smell of pizza coming from the food court up ahead. You begin thinking of the many different kinds of food you like and hope they have a variety of different options. You turn the corner into the food court and see eight food counters. They are all identical pizza shops. You look around at the people seated at the tables and notice that everyone is eating a slice of cheese pizza. You look more closely and realize that every person looks just like you. You slump down into a chair feeling bored by all of the sameness.

You remember that you saw another mall across the parking lot and hurry over there hoping that it's different. You open the front door and walk in. You breathe a sigh of relief as you are surrounded by a diversity of sights, sounds, and smells. Each store is unique, selling many different styles of clothing in many different colors. The food court is a cacophony of smells coming from food of various regions around the world. All of the people sitting at the food court and walking past you look different and interesting—you notice distinct styles of clothing, people of different ages and cultures, and you hear people speaking many languages.

You notice a group of students from your school sitting at a table near you. Usually you don't hang out with them because you think they're too different from you, but now you feel grateful for the chance to talk to them. They are happy to have you join them. You tell them about the other mall and explain how boring and monotonous it felt. You end up having an engaging conversation with them on this topic and agree that diversity is a strength.

Take a moment to feel grateful and say to yourself three times: **the world is a diverse and interesting place.**

Take a deep breath, open your eyes and stretch your arms, legs and mind.

≫ Discussion/Reflection

· Are you a perceptive person who can read different situations? Why is this an important skill to have?

≫ Fast Fact

There are 41,000 spoken languages in the world today.

≫ Alternate Affirmations

· **I see diversity as strength**
· **I enjoy learning about other people.**

Subject:	Attitudes
Into Focus:	There are many smart people making a fortune trying to get you to buy all kinds of goods and services. What type of consumer are you?
Affirmation:	I know what is best for me.

MEDIA MADNESS

≫ Introduction

Sit or lay comfortably with your eyes closed. Take three long, deep breaths. *(Pause)* Feel yourself relaxing more and more with each breath. Let the rhythm of the music calm you. Feel your muscles relax and your heart rate and breathing slow. Say to yourself, "I am calm and relaxed."

≫ Script

Imagine now that you have just awakened after sleeping in on a Saturday morning. It's been a long week and you are looking forward to doing nothing but relaxing. Picture yourself sitting on the edge of your bed. You are trying to decide if you should get up or continue relaxing in bed. *(Pause)* You decide to lay back down. Feel the mattress relax your legs, hips and back. Fluff your pillows and put them behind your head. You are comfortable, relaxed and without a care in the world. *(Pause)*

While you are relaxing you reach over and grab the TV remote off the nightstand. Turn on the TV and begin to channel surf. Everywhere you stop there is a commercial. You see "get rich quick" schemes and ways to get out of debt. You view fantastically fatty fast foods followed by ads for exercise machines and crash diets. If you drink this certain beverage you will do superhuman things and be super cool. Athletes, models and movies stars all tell you how you should look, eat and act.

There is nothing good on TV so you turn it off. As you reach to put back the remote control, the phone on the nightstand rings. You answer it and it is someone trying to sell you something you don't need. They are persistent, but you quickly say "no thanks" and hang up.

Now imagine reaching down and picking up your favorite magazine. Fluff your pillows and lean back. As you flip through the magazine you notice almost every page has an advertisement. You are encouraged to buy clothes, cars, hygiene items, cigarettes and other goods. You know that the models are all air-brushed and the situations in the ads are all staged. You also notice the ads send you the message that you're not good enough as a ploy to get you to buy their product. You choose to tune them out and put the magazine down.

As you relax say to yourself three times: **I know what is best for me...**
Look down at the back of the magazine and see a short poem called "Media and Me."

> I switch the channel and turn the page, Hang up, delete or walk away.
> They tell me what to do and be. But only I know what's best for me.

You know that it is more difficult to ignore the influence of advertisements than this poem suggests, but you feel empowered to resist. You know that you can resist outside pressure and make choices that are good for you.

Take a deep breath and return to your room. Open your eyes. Stretch your arms, your legs and your mind

» Discussion/Reflection

- What does it mean to compare yourself to your potential and not to others?
- What was the strangest thing someone ever tried to sell you?
- Have you ever purchased something you later regretted?
- What does the following expression mean? "If it sounds too good to be true, it probably is."

» Activities

Design an ad that does not exaggerate the benefits of a product. (i.e. 50/50 Aspirin – works about half the time.)

Take some clothes to your local mission, Goodwill or St. Vincent DePaul store.

» Fast Fact

In the course of a year the average young person is exposed to over 40,000 advertisements on television.

» Alternate Affirmations

- **I can resist pressure from others.**
- **I make good choices because I think things through.**

CALVIN and HOBBES   **by Bill Watterson**

Subject:	Attitudes
Into Focus:	Did you know that the earth is 70 percent water? Our body is also 70 percent water.
Affirmation:	**I believe one person can make a difference.**

MELTING AWAY

≫ Introduction

Sit comfortably with your eyes closed. Take three long, deep breaths. *(Pause)* Feel yourself relaxing more and more with each breath. Let the rhythm of the music calm you. Feel your muscles relax and your heart rate and breathing slow. Say to yourself, "I am calm and relaxed."

≫ Script

Imagine standing at the railing of a large ship on a sunny day. You arms are crossed because the air is chilly. Look down into the cold blue water. You can see the reflection of huge puffy white clouds above. You are traveling way up north to Greenland. Take a deep breath and enjoy the cool oxygen rich air free of any pollutants. Look out to see majestic white mountains in the distance. You wonder why they call it Greenland when so much of it is ice.

Look down over the railing of the ship and see that little chunks of ice are now floating by. These "ice cubes" soon become "ice boxes" as you get nearer to your destination. A short distance away is an iceberg. It glistens in the sun as it slowly and quietly floats. *(Pause)*

The ship slows down so you can have a good look. As you drift closer, the iceberg is as large as three or four domed stadiums. Your ship looks like a toy boat next to this massive structure of snow and ice. The air is cold but still. You can now see the cracks and the edges where snow has broken off. The shadows make it look even more beautiful. Where the water meets the iceberg solid ice is formed. This ice reflects the water and beautiful blue streaks dance around the entire iceberg. You have that most of an iceberg lies below the surface of the water. Look down and imagine the beautiful sea caves below the surface of the water carved by the ocean tides. *(Pause)*

The picturesque scene is broken by a huge avalanche of snow cascading down one of the peaks of the iceberg. A rumbling sound echoes all around and you feel the vibration beneath your feet. *(Pause)* As the ship moves away, you notice something white moving on the iceberg. You focus your eyes, look again and see a large polar bear pacing at the edge of the ice. *(Pause)*

You are amazed at all that is unfolding in front of you and you make a promise to help preserve the balance and the beauty of nature.

Breathe slowly and say to yourself three times: **I believe one person can make a difference.**... Take a deep breath and return to your room. Open your eyes.

≫ Discussion/Reflection: Read the following short story

A man was jogging down the beach after a major storm had just come through the area. He was dismayed by the huge number of starfish that the storm had washed up on the beach. He thought that there was nothing he could do because of the immense numbers. As he continued down the beach he saw an old man throw something into the water. As he got closer, he saw the old man walk a little farther down the beach, bend over, pick up a starfish and throw it back into the water. As the jogger approached, the old man stopped again, bent over, picked up another starfish and was about to throw it into the water. The jogger stopped and asked "Why are you doing that? There are thousands of starfish on the beach. You can't possibly make a difference." The old man looked at the starfish, threw it back into the water, and then replied, " I made a difference to that one, didn't I?"

Adapted from *"The Star Thrower"* By Loren Eiseley.

- Think of someone you know who has made a difference
- Why is it easy to get overwhelmed by such a large problem as pollution or other problems that affect the entire world?
- What is a cause or concern that you feel passionate about?

≫ Activities

Brainstorm ten ways a person can help the environment. Post these ideas or email them to friends.

For fun, draw a picture of an iceberg. What does it look like below the water?

Subject:	Attitudes
Into Focus:	There are some things in life that are very hard to prepare for, even though you know they will happen someday.
Affirmation:	**Those who are gone live on in my memory.**

MEMORIES

≫ Introduction

Sit comfortably with your eyes closed. Take three long, deep breaths. *(Pause)* Feel yourself relaxing more and more with each breath. Let the rhythm of the music calm you. Feel your muscles relax and your heart rate and breathing slow. Say to yourself, "I am calm and relaxed."

≫ Script

Imagine you are alone in your bedroom. Sit on the edge of your bed. Put on your headphones and play your favorite soft music. The music is just the right beat and you begin to relax. Now concentrate on the soothing music. Hear it softly glide up and then trickle gently back down. *(Pause)* As the melody waves back and forth, in and out, your mind begins to open up.

You notice things around the room. See a worn out ball sitting in the corner of your bookcase. This ball brings to mind images of all the fun you had playing with your childhood friends. *(Pause)* Notice on a shelf above the ball an old dusty book. It is a book that was read to you when you were young. You remember the good feeling of reading it with someone who loved you.

As the light music continues to relax you, notice an item on the top of your dresser. It is one of your most prized possessions and brings back good memories. Stand up and walk over and pick it up. Holding it makes your memories even more vivid. *(Pause)*

Now set the object down on the dresser right next to a photograph in a frame. It is a picture of someone you really cared about, but who is no longer in your life. It hurts to think about them. You feel sad for a moment, and then your mind goes right to a happy time you shared with this person. Take a moment and think of this special time. *(Pause)* The music from your headphones serves as a perfect sound track for your happy memory. *(Pause)* With this in mind, take a deep breath and say to yourself three times: **Those who are gone live on in my memory...**

Look up from the photo and into the mirror attached to your dresser. As you look at yourself, you also see a reflection of the face in the photograph behind you. You know that your life is better because of this person and feel honored for having known them. Take a few moments to enjoy this good feeling. *(Pause)*

Now it is time to come back to the room, open your eyes. Stretch your arms and legs and your mind.

>> Discussion/Reflection

- How has losing a loved one affected you?
- Have you known anyone your age that has died? Why is this so hard?
- What was the symbolism of seeing your loved one next to you in the mirror at the end of the story?
- Explain the famous line: "It is better to have loved and lost than to have never loved at all."

>> Resources

Piano music by David Lanz, David Benoit, George Winston.

>> Alternate Affirmations

- **Life is ever changing.**
- **I find the good even in bad times.**

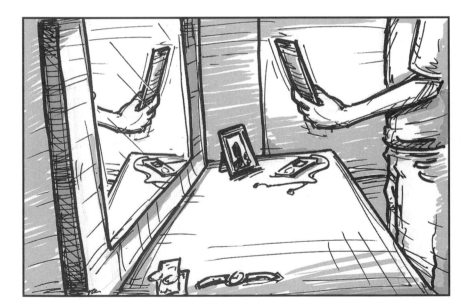

Subject: Attitudes

Into Focus: It's important for all of us to do what we can to clean up our environment.

Affirmation: I take pride in myself and my surroundings.

PERSONAL JUNKET

» Introduction

Sit comfortably with your eyes closed. Take three long, deep breaths. *(Pause)* Feel yourself relaxing more and more with each breath. Let the rhythm of the music calm you. Feel your muscles relax and your heart rate and breathing slow. Say to yourself, "I am calm and relaxed."

» Script

Imagine that it's the first day of class. You are excited because your teacher has the reputation of being cool and interesting. Look around and see most of your friends sitting around the room. Hear the bell ring and watch as the teacher enters. The room becomes quiet with anticipation. Your teacher says your first assignment is to collect junk and trash from around your neighborhood and bring it to school. You are ready for something different. As you leave the room you are handed a pair of gloves and a large plastic bag. You wonder how long it will take you to fill it.

After getting home you head out to begin your trash collection. See yourself walking briskly down your street. It doesn't take long to spot your first piece of trash. Put on your gloves. Now reach down and grab the fast food wrapper at your feet. It is saturated in grease. Put it in the plastic garbage bag. Your breathing continues to be relaxed and calm as you continue your walk. It is not long before you have to swerve to avoid stepping on a broken beer bottle. Reach down and carefully pick up the larger pieces of glass and then add them to your bag. Hear a clank and feel the bag become heavier.

You decide to walk towards the highway where there is sure to be a wide variety of trash. Along the way, notice an almost nonstop trail of discarded cigarette butts. You pick up as many of them as you can. Listen to the whirling sound of traffic as you come upon a large amount of garbage by the busy road. You have never noticed that there was this much junk around. Reach down and pick up candy wrappers, potato chip bags, styrofoam coffee cups and soda cans. *(Pause)*

Before no time your bag is full. Start walking back home holding the bag as far away from you as possible. As you think about all this junk that has littered your neighborhood, you feel proud of your efforts to clean it up. As you walk you think that most of what you collected is packaging for things that are not healthy for your body. You make a commitment to keeping your neighborhood clean. You also pledge to cut down on "fast food" to avoid putting "junk" into your body.

Take a deep breath and say to yourself three times: **I take pride in myself and my surroundings...**

Before you know it you are back home. Take a deep breath, open your eyes and stretch. Stretch your arms, your legs and your mind.

Chad was oblivious to the fact that he
had a very large carbon footprint.

≫ Discussion/Reflection

- What is meant by the expression "garbage in, garbage out?"
- What are things you can do to help keep your environment litter free?

≫ Activities

Organize a walk or pick up litter in your neighborhood. Separate it into like groups. Chart the types of trash found in your area.

Make signs to remind people not to litter. (Try to use a positive message.) Get permission to post them in your neighborhood.

≫ Fast Fact

The colors yellow, red and orange are used in fast food restaurants because those are the colors that stimulate hunger.

≫ Alternate Affirmations

- **I stay away from things that are harmful to my mind or body.**
- **A balanced diet leads to good physical and emotional health.**

Subject: Attitudes

Into Focus: You've heard the expression "you can't judge a book by its cover." Do you make quick judgments about others based on what you see on the surface?

Affirmation: I look and think before I form opinions.

SCRATCH THE SURFACE

≫ Introduction

Sit comfortably with your eyes closed. Take three long, deep breaths. *(Pause)* Feel yourself relaxing more and more with each breath. Let the rhythm of the music calm you. Feel your muscles relax and your heart rate and breathing slow. Say to yourself, "I am calm and relaxed."

≫ Script

Imagine that you are walking along the seashore on a perfect day. The shoreline consists of sand, smooth rock and bits of thin seaweed. The sun is shining and the temperature is just right. You have walked away from the crowded beach and are by yourself. In the near distance you see the remnants of what looks like a small lighthouse.

As you walk toward it, you take time to enjoy the feel of the wet sand as it cools the bottoms of your feet. Feel this sensation extend up your legs, thighs, waist, back and entire upper body. You walk at a relaxed pace and barely notice your destination is just ahead.

The old lighthouse sits on a small, rocky peninsula. Carefully step over and around the large smooth rocks until you reach the old crumbled structure. It's easy to get inside because the wall facing the ocean has collapsed and is already part of the seawall. The remaining wall hides you from view.

Imagine how this old structure looked when it was once a watchtower for incoming ships. Close your eyes and see tall sailing vessels gliding on the horizon. *(Pause)* You might even imagine seeing a pirate ship or perhaps a beautiful schooner.

There is one rock nearby that is surrounded by water and sand that looks like an inviting place to sit. It offers a panoramic view. You decide to sit down on this rock. Feel the cool ocean breeze on your face and body. *(Pause)* Listen to the sound of the water as it washes against the rocks then swirls and retreats. The rhythm of the waves further relaxes you. White bubbles dance then disappear. Look closer at the rocks. They are different shades of gray, brown, yellow and red. When the dry rocks are washed by a wayward wave they become a shiny, bright color.

Look down below the surface of the water to discover a new world. Bright green algae clings to the rocks and dances in unison to the rhythm of the underwater currents. Now look even more closely. *(Pause)* See camouflaged fan-shaped shells attached to the rocks. One, two, three, the more you look the more you find. You are surprised to see a small crab eating on a rock just above the water line. Now look between the rocks to see many more small crabs hiding in the shadows.

You are discovering new things on a single rock at the edge of the ocean. Two-thirds of the earth is covered by water. Imagine what lies below. You are glad you made this journey. You appreciate what you can discover when you take the time to look deeper. You now realize there is so much to find below the surface in all things in nature. You decide to be more patient and curious about things and other people. Often there is more to learn under the surface. You decide to withhold judgment until you have all the information possible.

As you relax by the sea shore say to yourself three times: **I look and think before I form opinions...**

Take a deep breath and return to your room. Open your eyes and stretch your arms, legs and your mind.

» Discussion/Reflection

- Give an example in your life when a first impression of someone or something proved to be wrong.
- What is your favorite book or movie that partially or totally takes place underwater.

» Alternate Affirmations

- **I do not judge others.**
- **I have an open mind to new experiences.**

Subject: Attitudes

Into Focus: You can find a positive in almost any circumstance.

Affirmation: **I appreciate and respect the efforts of others.**

THREE CHEERS

» Introduction

Sit comfortably with your eyes closed. Take three long, deep breaths. *(Pause)* Feel yourself relaxing more and more with each breath. Let the rhythm of the music calm you. Feel your muscles relax and your heart rate and breathing slow. Say to yourself, "I am calm and relaxed."

» Script

Imagine that you are seated high up in the bleachers in a football stadium. It's a chilly night, but everyone is too excited and nervous to be cold. Your team has a chance at the championship if they win this game. There is a buzz in the air. Everyone is focused on the lighted field below.

A roar erupts as your team races on the field. You stand and clap as the band plays the school song. See your school colors on the uniforms. *(Pause)* See the cheerleaders and mascot do their best to get the crowd revved up.

Everyone screams as your team kicks off. Watch as your opponent bounces back and forth like a pinball. Get him! Get him! He's all the way in for a score. Listen as an eruption of noise from the other side of the field fills the air. *(Pause)* By halftime your side of the stadium is quiet. Some people have already left. Your team is so far behind that they will never catch up. Despite your optimism, inside you know there will be no miracle finish to this story. *(Pause)* Despite the score you look forward to hearing the marching band perform.

Watch as the band members gather their enthusiasm and march, heads held high to the center of the field. The music makes you feel better. Hear the sound of crunching peanut shells as your foot begins to tap to the beat.

The band begins to make designs on the field. With perfect precision they spin and twirl to the music. Watch closely as they begin to form letters. First the letter R, then E, L appears, then A, then two lines cross to make an X. Take a relaxing breath and say the word RELAX. *(Pause)* The trumpets, drums, and flags all work in harmony. They begin to play your favorite song. *(Pause)* As you continue to relax, enjoy the entertainment. You appreciate all the practice and teamwork that went into the halftime show. As the final note sounds you jump to your feet and join with the others for a standing ovation.

You are in a much better mood. Soon the game is over. You join in with the other fans and give your team a standing ovation for their effort. They lost this game but never quit trying. Look up to see an airplane pulling a message. As you continue to relax say this message to yourself three times: **I appreciate and respect the efforts of others...**

Take a deep breath and return to your room. Open your eyes, stretch your arms and legs and your mind. You have the ability to look for positives in almost any situation.

» Discussion/Reflection

· Have you ever become worried about something you thought at the time was important, but really wasn't?
· Do you agree with the Vince Lombardi statement "Winning isn't everything, it's the only thing."

» Activities

As a group, make a banner or sign to hold up at a school event.

Play your favorite board or card game with a friend or family member. What is the most important part about playing games?

» Resources

Music: Don't Worry, Be Happy by Bobby McFarren

» Alternate Affirmations

· **I keep things in perspective.**
· **I recognize the efforts of others.**

Subject:	Attitudes
Into Focus:	If you want to go fast, go alone. If you want to go far, go with others.
Affirmation:	**I work with others to accomplish goals.**

V FOR VICTORY

>> Introduction

Sit comfortably with your eyes closed. Take three long, deep breaths. *(Pause)* Feel yourself relaxing more and more with each breath. Let the rhythm of the music calm you. Feel your muscles relax and your heart rate and breathing slow. Say to yourself, "I am calm and relaxed."

>> Script

Imagine that it is very late at night and you are lying on your back in your bed with your eyes open. It is dark. The dim red light of your alarm clock faces you from across the room. The alarm will be buzzing before you know it. Your mind is racing with thoughts of what needs to be done tomorrow. It seems that nothing ever gets done without you leading the way. You stare at the clock as one minute melts into
the next.

Then all the numbers change. See yourself squinting as you try to make out the new time. The new time is not in numbers but in digital letters. It says: R, E, L, A, X. Rub your eyes and look again. It says: RELAX.

Become aware of your breathing… inhaling through your nose and exhaling through your nose. Slow and gentle, the controlled breathing makes you more and more relaxed. The muscles in your face begin to let go and relax. Feel your shoulders, arms and legs begin to melt into the mattress. As you relax you feel yourself let go of the pressure of time. *(Pause)* Feel yourself begin to doze off.

You fall asleep and begin to dream. In your dream you are sitting on a hillside on a blanket of soft green grass. It is a perfect day. The sun warms your face and puts your whole body at ease. Look toward the horizon and see a ribbon of color coming at you from a distance.

As the color winds closer, you see that it is actually hundreds of bicycle riders in a race.

Watch as the leader slows down and waves to another to take her place. After a short time another moves up the lead. Soon many have faced the wind and shared the lead. The lead biker helps the others by breaking the wind. They move as a group with little effort. You feel a cool breeze as the bikers spin by you in a blur of color and speed. Soon it is quiet.

As you continue to sleep you begin to hear a faint honking sound. In your dream you look down but see no cars on the road. You calmly look up and are surprised to see a large flock of geese cutting through the sky in a perfect V formation. Watch as the lead goose falls back and another takes his place. Then without any argument, another goose leads. The loud honking seems to encourage and motivate the group as they glide past. See that V formation in your mind's eye. *(Pause)* Remember it as a cue for cooperation.

Some of the pressure is off. You don't have to do everything. You realize you can let others take the lead. Together you can cut the wind of resistance and accomplish great things. Your alarm buzzes and wakes you from your dream. You feel relieved and energetic and look forward to the new day.

You enjoyed your dream. As you continue to relax and say to yourself three times: **I work with others to accomplish goals...**

Take a deep breath and return to your room. Open your eyes, stretch your arms, your legs and your mind.

›› **Discussion/Reflection**

· What are signs of being too active or involved?
· What are the pros and cons of working as a team?
· What are some of the characteristics of a good leader?
· How many hours of sleep per night do you average? Do you feel it is enough?

›› **Activity**

Go on a bike ride. Imagine that your team just won the Tour de France.

›› **Fast Fact**

During migration, geese may cover up to 600 miles per day.

›› **Alternate Affirmations**

· **I can both lead and follow for the good of the group.**
· **I pace myself for the long run.**

Subject:	Attitudes

Into Focus:	There is no word in the English language that rhymes with the word orange. In this story, you are about to eat an orange like no other.

Affirmation:	**When I am relaxed, I see things below the surface.**

VITAMIN SEE

» Introduction

Sit comfortably with your eyes closed. Take three long, deep breaths. *(Pause)* Feel yourself relaxing more and more with each breath. Let the rhythm of the music calm you. Feel your muscles relax and your heart rate and breathing slow. Say to yourself, "I am calm and relaxed."

» Script

Picture yourself sitting in one of your classrooms at school. It's been a busy morning and you are ready for a break. Imagine leaving your classroom and walking to the library. See a comfortable couch in the library. Sit down and feel yourself sink down to a very comfortable position. The soft cushions surround you and you feel your whole body begin to relax. Your breathing is slow and time seems to stand still. *(Pause)* This library allows you to have food. Reach into your pocket and take out an orange you brought for a snack. Holding the orange in both hands, use your thumbs and begin to peel it. Feel the orange peel come off easily in your hands. Breathe in and enjoy the sweet citrus smell. *(Pause)* Set the orange peelings in your lap. As you separate the slices some juice squirts on to your upper lip. As you lick your lips you begin to taste the juicy orange. *(Pause)* Break off a segment of the orange and imagine how wonderful it will taste. Pop it into your mouth and experience a wonderful, sweet and tangy taste. You have never tasted anything like this before. Your entire body feels energized and invigorated.

See yourself now looking down at the peelings on your lap to see what type of special orange this is. You see a small sticker that simply says, "Filled with Vitamin See" spelled s-e-e. You wonder if this is a misprint. Break off another piece of this delicious fruit. This time it squirts you in the eyes, but does not burn. Imagine rubbing your eyes and feeling a cool soothing sensation. *(Pause)*

Things around you seem to look different. Notice some interesting and colorful artwork on the walls that you had never noticed before. *(Pause)* Now picture one of your classmates sitting alone in the corner. You have often ignored this person but you now see and feel that you would like to get to know them better. As you smile at your potential friend, you feel open and accepting and happy that you are able to see below the surface. You notice all the differences in the other students in the library and realize how lucky you are to go to school with such a diverse student body.

You feel thankful for your dose of vitamin s-e-e. You finish your orange feeling excited about the new relationships that lie ahead. Use your ability to see the good in others regardless of their differences.

Take a deep breath and say to yourself three times: **When I am relaxed, I see things below the surface...**

Take a deep breath and open your new and improved eyes. Stretch your arms, your legs and your mind.

≫ Discussion/Reflection

- How can "vitamin s-e-e" lead to a healthy happy lifestyle?
- Reflect on a time when you ignored someone. How do you feel when someone ignores you?

≫ Alternate Affirmations

- **I accept others.**
- **I see below the surface.**

Responsibility

Making good choices for yourself and your relationships.

Empowerment

Feeling positive about yourself and competent with peers. Feeling supported by others.

Learning

Developing skills to acquire and retain knowledge. Finding enjoyment in creative pursuits.

Attitudes

Developing and practicing the attitudes and values needed to become a complete person.

X-pand

Exploring your ability to feel calm and centered.

Subject: X-Pand

Into Focus: Stress can overheat you. Take a trip to cool off by riding in your personal elevator.

Affirmation: I take time to calm myself when needed.

ELEVATOR MUSIC

≫ Introduction

Sit comfortably with your eyes closed. Take three long, deep breaths. *(Pause)* Feel yourself relaxing more and more with each breath. Let the rhythm of the music calm you. Feel your muscles relax and your heart rate and breathing slow. Say to yourself, "I am calm and relaxed."

≫ Script

In your imagination see yourself in a place that is very noisy and chaotic. People around you are rushing everywhere and they appear stressed. You hear many different noises at the same time. You want to avoid getting stressed out yourself. You remember that when a person gets stressed their muscles tense up, their hands feel cold and clammy, their face gets flushed, and their body may begin to sweat. You have a plan to deal with situations when you feel stressed and know that you can calm yourself. When you begin to feel stressed you imagine yourself taking an elevator ride.

In your mind's eye, imagine an elevator appearing. You have a choice to either ride up or ride down the elevator. Walk over and push either the button to ride up or the button to ride down. The door quickly opens and you step inside. The doors close and soft relaxing music begins to play. Now push the lighted button. Feel the elevator slowly begin to go in the direction you chose. Look up at the lights above the door. As you begin to move, the first light is the letter R. Enjoy the soft sound of the music. Notice how the music slows your heart rate and breathing. Now the letter E lights up. Feel your hands warming and your arms getting heavy and relaxed. Now comes floor L. Feel your muscles loosen and your shoulders and neck relax. The button for floor A now is glowing. Enjoy a warm, calm feeling throughout you entire body. X now lights up. Look up and see the word RELAX in lights above you. The elevator gently stops. You have let go of the tension of the noisy crowd. Your elevator ride is always there for you when you need to relax.

Take a deep breath and as you slowly exhale say to yourself three times: **I take time to calm myself when needed.**

You now feel relaxed and ready to face the challenges of the day. Picture yourself being in a noisy, stressed out crowd, but being able to keep yourself relaxed and calm. Take the relaxation elevator any time you need to calm yourself.

If you need more time, stop on any floor.

Open your eyes and return to your room. Stretch your arms, your legs and your mind.

≫ Discussion/Reflection

- Why do some people call quiet music, like you listened to, "elevator music?" What type of music relaxes you?
- Think of a situation when you can benefit by taking time to relax and calm yourself.

≫ Fast Fact

As of 2010, the fastest pedestrian elevator is in the world's tallest building, the Burj Khalifa in Dubai. It ascends over 58 feet per second.

≫ Alternate Affirmations

- **When I am anxious, I calm myself.**
- **I avoid unnecessary confrontations.**

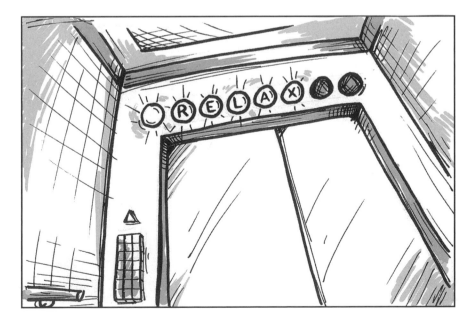

Subject: X-Pand

Into Focus: Here is a quick exercise you can do when you feel like you are getting filled up with stress.

Affirmation: **I release stress and pressure by expressing my feelings.**

PRESSURE VALVE

›› Introduction

Sit comfortably with your eyes closed. Take three long, deep breaths. *(Pause)* Feel yourself relaxing more and more with each breath. Let the rhythm of the music calm you. Feel your muscles relax and your heart rate and breathing slow. Say to yourself, "I am calm and relaxed."

›› Script

Place one hand gently on your stomach. Breathe deeply and feel your hand move up and down… up and down. Breathe in through your nose. Breathe out through your mouth. Feel your stomach rise as you breathe in. Feel your stomach "fall" as you exhale.

Imagine that your stomach is like a balloon. Blow up the balloon by breathing in slowly and deeply. Hold it in. *(Pause)* Now slowly breathe out and empty all the air from your balloon. *(Pause)*

Blow up the balloon again with a long, deep breath. Hold it in. *(Pause)* Let the air escape quietly as you slowly exhale. *(Pause)* Blow up the balloon again. *(Pause)* Notice that with each breath, you become more and more relaxed. As you become relaxed, you will notice your hands warming. You may feel your fingertips tingling as your blood flows into your hands. Continue to inhale and exhale through your nose.

Relaxed breathing helps keep you calm. Focus on your breathing, keeping it slow and steady as you now think of something that upsets you or makes you feel stressed. Now imagine yourself as a giant soda bottle. The more you think about this problem situation without expressing your feelings, the more the bottle begins to shake. This shaking of the bottle causes more and more pressure to build up. You realize you must release the pressure slowly. Take a deep breath, and as you slowly let the air out, imagine the cap on your bottle slowly loosening. Listen as the pressure begins to escape. Take another deep breath. As you exhale, feel the cap open a bit more allowing more pressure to quietly release and disappear. You continue to release pressure slowly until you are able to unscrew the cap and take it off. Breathing slowly and easily you are relaxed and calm. Now say to yourself three times: **I release stress and pressure by expressing my feelings…**

It feels good to be able to control your tension and not "blow your top."

Come back to the room. Open your eyes and stretch your arms, your legs and your mind.

≫ Discussion/Reflection

- This exercise can help you to get through a time when you are feeling frustrated or angry about something. For example, if you are being teased. By ignoring teasing and using ways to calm yourself you are demonstrating that the other person or group does not have power over your reactions or emotions. However, if you are being threatened, sexually harassed or bullied, you will need to get help from others as soon as you recognize the problem. Name some people you could turn to for help.
- What are some things you do when people tease or make fun of you?
- Do you know anyone who holds things in like a soda can that has been shaken until they finally explode?

≫ Alternate Affirmations

- **I breathe out tension.**
- **I express anger in a healthy way.**

Subject: X-Pand

Into Focus: Here is a quick progressive muscle relaxation exercise you can do almost anytime in almost any place.

Affirmation: **Relaxing my body keeps my mind fresh.**

RELAXATION ANGLE

>> Introduction

Sit comfortably with your eyes closed. Take three long, deep breaths. *(Pause)* Feel yourself relaxing more and more with each breath. Let the rhythm of the music calm you. Feel your muscles relax and your heart rate and breathing slow. Say to yourself, "I am calm and relaxed."

>> Script

Sit in a chair of your choice. With your knees extended and heels on the ground continue to think of the words "calm" and "relaxed." *(Pause)* While staying relaxed, point your toes straight up and then pull them toward your knees. Feel your lower leg muscles stretch. *(Pause)* Continue to breathe in a slow, relaxed way. Now, with your knees extended and heels on the ground, point your toes away from your knees. *(Pause)* Feel the muscles on the top of your shins stretch. Now bring your toes back to a relaxed comfortable position.

Sit back in an upright position again. Now this time take a deep breath and, as you slowly exhale, extend your arms straight above your head and reach toward the ceiling. Feel the muscles in your hands, your arms and your shoulders stretch upward. *(Pause)* Now, put your arms back on your desk or on your lap in a relaxed position. Become aware of any tension in your body and release it and relax. *(Pause)* Now again, take a deep breath. *(Pause)* While exhaling, slowly stretch your neck muscles by rotating your head slowly to the right *(Pause)* and then to the left. *(Pause)* Find the most comfortable position for your neck and relax those muscles. Again, scan your body for any tense muscles and release them and relax. *(Pause)*

Now while relaxing your entire body, take a deep breath and as you breathe out say to yourself three times: **Relaxing my body keeps my mind fresh...** *(Pause)* Sit up straight in your chair and enjoy the feeling of relaxation. You have new energy to face the challenges of the day.

While staying relaxed open your eyes and come back to the room.

>> Discussion/Reflection

· Think of a time you could have used a relaxation exercise. Try to remember to do it next time you are in that situation.

>> Activities

Use the beginning progressive muscle relaxation exercise at any time during the day to relax and focus, (i.e. before a test, during a work break, to relieve tension).

>> Alternate Affirmations

· **I have tools to help me relax, focus and stay on task.**
· **I recognize when I'm tense and relax myself.**

Subject: X-Pand

Into Focus: Sometimes the hardest part is just to start.

Affirmation: I am a self-starter.

TAPS

» Introduction

Sit comfortably with your eyes closed. Take three long, deep breaths. *(Pause)* Feel yourself relaxing more and more with each breath. Let the rhythm of the music calm you. Feel your muscles relax and your heart rate and breathing slow. Say to yourself, "I am calm and relaxed."

» Script

Imagine that you are home and not much is going on. You can't go out because you have too much homework to do. Everything seems to be in slow motion. You are worried about getting your work done, but lack motivation to get started. You are sitting at the kitchen table with your books spread open in front of you. There is no one else around. Although you are a little worried, you are able to stay relaxed and calm. You are practicing breathing slowly, inhaling through your nose and exhaling through your mouth. This slow, rhythmic breathing helps you begin to focus.

While staying relaxed, imagine putting your hands on the flat surface of the table. Imagine tapping one finger repeatedly. *(Pause)* Now feel your other fingers joining in. One, two, three, four; one, two, three, four; one two, three, four. Your fingers move in perfect cadence. Faster and faster your fingers rap until they sound like wild galloping horses or the motor of a racing car.

As your fingers continue to move, your body begins to generate energy. The energy starts at your fingertips and spreads through your fingers, hands, arms, shoulders, and soon your entire body. Even now, as you imagine this energy, you feel it spreading through your body. *(Pause)*

Now imagine that you are so energized that you begin to tap out a song. As you think of a favorite song you can see yourself playing it by tapping out the rhythm using your fingers. You add sound with your fingernails or rings. Imagine tapping, snapping your fingers or clapping as you play your song.

Now see yourself tapping your feet to the beat. *(Pause)* Your whole body feels in tune and alive with energy. Finish your song, but continue to feel the beat of the music within you. You are now ready to begin your work.

Take a deep breath and as you breath out say to yourself three times: **I am a self starter**...Remember, when you feel unfocused or unmotivated, use finger taps to get your engine started. Take a deep breath and open your eyes. Stretch your arms, your legs and your mind.

» Discussion/Reflection

· What are some things you do to motivate yourself when you don't want to do something?
· What is your favorite type of music? Do you put on music when you work? Study? Relax?

» Activity

Create a tap, snap, clap or rap to motivate you.

» Alternate Affirmations

· **I motivate myself to get started.**
· **I control my energy level.**

PART III

Appendices and References

APPENDIX A

Separation Anxiety Disorder

Many children experience separation anxiety between 18 months and three years of age, when it is normal for a child to feel some anxiety when a parent leaves the room or goes out of sight. Usually he/she can be distracted from these feelings. Crying when first being left at daycare or pre-school is also common, and the crying subsides when the child becomes engaged in his/her surroundings.

Usually four year olds are able to leave their parents. If not, the problem could be separation anxiety disorder, which affects approximately four percent of children. With separation anxiety disorder, a child experiences extreme anxiety when away from home or separated from parents or caregivers. In this case, the desire to be in contact with missed persons is excessive, extreme homesickness and feelings of misery at not being with loved ones are common. While separated, it is not uncommon for these children to have fears regarding the health and safety of their parents.

Children suffering from separation anxiety disorder may:
- Try to avoid going places by themselves;
- Refuse to go to school or camp;
- Be reluctant or refuse to participate in sleepovers;
- Follow a parent around;
- Demand that someone stay with them at bedtime, or "appear" in their parent's bedroom during the night;
- Awake from nightmares about being separated from loved ones.

Onset of separation anxiety disorder can occur any time before age 18, but it is most common in children between the ages of seven and nine.

Specific Phobias

A specific phobia is defined as the intense, irrational fear of a specific object, such as a dog, or a situation, such as flying. Fears of animals, situations and natural occurrences are common in childhood and often go away. A phobia is diagnosed if the fear persists for at least six months and interferes with a child's daily routine. An example of this is a child who refuses to play outdoors for fear of encountering a dog. Common childhood phobias include:

- Animals
- Storms
- Heights
- Water
- Blood
- The dark
- Medical procedures

Unlike adults with specific phobias, children do not usually recognize that their fear is irrational or out of proportion to the situation and they may not articulate their fears. Children will avoid situations or things that they fear, or endure them with anxious feelings, which can manifest as:

- Crying
- Tantrums
- Freezing
- Clinging
- Avoidance
- Headache
- Stomachache

Generalized Anxiety Disorder (GAD)

Generalized anxiety disorder usually affects children between the ages of six and 11. It is characterized by excessive worry and anxiety over a variety of things, including, but not limited to:

- Grades
- Performance in sports
- Punctuality
- Family issues
- Earthquakes
- Health

The affected child cannot control his/her worry and it interferes with normal activities. Physical symptoms of GAD include:

- Restlessness
- Fatigue/Inability to sleep
- Difficulty concentrating
- Irritability
- Muscle tension

Children with GAD tend to be very hard on themselves, striving for perfection, sometimes redoing tasks repeatedly. They may also seek constant approval or reassurance from others.

Social Anxiety Disorder

Social anxiety disorder, or social phobia, is characterized by an intense fear of social and performance situations. The most commonly feared situations include initiating conversations, unstructured peer activities, performing in front of others, speaking up in class, and inviting others to get together. Avoiding these activities significantly interferes with the quality of a child's or teen's life, often impairing his/her school performance and attendance, as well as his/her ability to socialize with peers and develop and maintain relationships.

The onset of social anxiety disorder peaks in adolescence, when establishing and managing friendships independently is a crucial part of healthy development. Untreated, the disorder can persist into adulthood and may increase the risk for depression or alcohol abuse.

Parents and teachers may not be aware of the warning signs of social anxiety disorder, or they may not consider extreme shyness a problem warranting professional attention.

Signs to watch for:
- Hesitance, passivity and discomfort in the spotlight
- Avoidance or refusal to initiate conversations, perform in front of others, invite friends to get together, telephone others for homework or other information or order food in restaurants
- Avoiding eye contact
- Speaking very softly or mumbling
- Minimal interaction and conversation with peers
- Appearing isolated or on the fringes of the group
- Sitting alone in the library or cafeteria or hanging back from a group in team meetings
- Overly concerned with negative evaluation, humiliation or embarrassment
- Difficulty with public speaking, reading aloud or being called on in class

When faced with anxiety-producing situations, a child or teen can suffer from these symptoms:

- Sweating
- Racing heart
- Somachache
- Dizziness
- Crying
- Tantrums
- Freezing

Tips for Parents

- Expose your child to play groups, birthday parties, after-school activities or other social situations where the child will have opportunities to interact with peers.
- Encourage your child to speak up, such as ordering food in a restaurant. Don't speak for your child.
- Praise or offer rewards for speaking up. For example, offer a trip to the movies if he or she asks for the tickets at the box office.
- Lead by example. Teach your child by showing how you handle social situations.

Tips for Teachers

Implement procedures to get socially anxious students more involved, such as calling on them in class.

- Explain to these students beforehand that you want to help them feel more comfortable in class, not more embarrassed.
- Coach them, if necessary, to make sure they know the answers.
- Remind them that speaking up in class will get easier with practice.
- Do not single out a student; call on all of them for answers.
- Incorporate oral presentations into your curriculum to help all your students develop confidence in public speaking.

Tips adapted from Triumph Over Shyness, by Murray B. Stein, MD, and John R. Walker, PhD

Panic Disorder

Panic disorder is diagnosed when a child suffers at least two unexpected panic attacks, followed by at least one month of concern over having another attack, losing control or "going crazy." The most common age of onset for panic disorder is the early-to-mid 20s. It is not common in young children, but can begin in adolescence.

A panic attack is defined as the abrupt onset of an episode of intense fear or discomfort, which peaks in approximately 10 minutes, and includes at least four of the following symptoms:

- A feeling of imminent danger or doom
- The need to escape
- Palpitations
- Sweating
- Trembling
- Shortness of breath or a smothering feeling
- A feeling of choking
- Chest pain or discomfort
- Nausea or abdominal discomfort
- Dizziness or lightheadedness
- A sense of things being unreal, depersonalization
- A fear of losing control or "going crazy"
- A fear of dying
- Tingling sensations
- Chills or hot flushes

Children, like adults, often become apprehensive when in situations or places where they have previously had attacks and may begin to avoid these situations and places. Agoraphobia can develop when the child begins to avoid situations in which he/she has had a panic attack previously or situations and places from which the child feels that he/she would not be able to escape if experiencing a panic attack.

Obsessive-compulsive Disorder (OCD)

OCD is characterized by repeated, intrusive and unwanted thoughts (obsessions) and/or rituals that seem impossible to control (compulsions). Adolescents may be aware that their symptoms don't make sense and are excessive, but younger children may be distressed only when they are prevented from carrying out their compulsive habits. Compulsive behaviors often include counting, arranging and rearranging objects, and excessive hand washing.

Post-traumatic Stress Disorder

Persistent symptoms of this disorder occur after experiencing a trauma such as abuse, natural disasters or extreme violence. Symptoms include nightmares; flashbacks; the numbing of emotions; depression; feeling angry, irritable, and distracted; and being easily startled.

APPENDIX B

YOGA: A piece of the puzzle

Yoga is an ancient practice that shows great promise for helping teens self-regulate stress. Yoga helps to shut the door on the outer "noise" and encourages the teen to focus on self-awareness. The gentle quiet focus on the breath allows the teen to shift her mental and physical state from one of anxiety to one of calm focus and balance. The Pranayama (Prana = breath or life force, yama = discipline or regulation) helps lead the way to self-discovery through controlling the breath.

The Yoga poses (asana) give rise to a quieter mind and self-connection. The poses (asana) give the mind something to do to draw it away from anxious or obsessive thinking. Asana keep the body strong, flexible and relaxed. When holding a pose, especially balance poses, the mind must shift to the here and now and the physical reality of what is going on with the body. It cannot worry about the fight you had with your friend or your upcoming test. The physical act of aligning the body into the correct form along with continuing focus on the breath draws the mind away from the unproductive and often damaging effects of what is termed "stress" or "obsessive thinking".

Stress is exacerbated when we feel no outlet for frustration and no sense of control. Yoga helps teens associate an action that relieves stress with a feeling of control or self-regulation. They learn a "tool box" of poses and breathing techniques that give them a feeling of releasing tension. Teens come to realize with practice that they can release tension rather than allowing it to increase.

As in the other techniques reviewed, Yoga helps teens to access the healing power of the relaxation response.

Yoga can be the practice for all of us to come to a level of stillness where we can become aware of each passing moment. We can notice the quality of our interactions, increase focus and find a state of alert calmness.

An excellent resource to teach children and teens these techniques is the book, Yoga Calm for Children: Education Heart, Mind, and Body by Lynea Gillen, MS and Jim Gillen, RYT. This book is available on our website at www.innercoaching.com.

APPENDIX C

ROGER J. KLEIN, Psy. D.

The Effects of Sedative Music, Muscle Relaxation, and Success Imagery on Self-Report of Anxiety, Self-Concept, and Depression Among Elementary School Children

A stress-management program entitled Ready...Set...R.E.L.A.X. (Release, Expand, Learn, Appreciate, X-pand) used a combination of sedative music, muscle relaxation, and success imagery for the purpose of reducing the harmful effects of anxiety among elementary age children and subsequently increasing their performance on the Metropolitan Achievement Test (MAT).

The experimental (E) group subjects were 123 1st through 6th grade students enrolled in a Catholic school. The control (C) group subjects were 120 1st through 6th grade students enrolled in a second Catholic school in the same city. The two groups represented the entire enrollment of their schools and were matched in socioeconomic levels, ability levels, and age.

Pre- and post-testing was completed at grades one through three using the Revised Children's Manifest Anxiety Scale (RCMAS), Depression Inventory for Children and Adults, and the MAT. Children in grades four through six completed the RCMAS, the Piers-Harris Self-Concept Inventory, and the MAT.

The Ready...Set...R.E.L.A.X. program consisted of the following components: a. an educational inservice program held separately for the parents of the subjects, teaching staff and students; b. the principal reading the original relaxation and success imagery scripts over the intercom with follow-up discussion led by the classroom teacher; c. relaxing music and a quiet reading time on days scripts were not read. The first year program did not include follow-up discussion nor any scripts dealing with preparation for taking the MAT. Both the first year and the second year were included in the analysis of data.

Within- and between-group comparisons of anxiety, depression, and self-concept suggested that children in grades 1-5 benefited most from the program. In particular, grade one and two subjects showed a significant treatment effect in all measured categories. Results of the MAT indicated significant gains for both the E group and the C group from year one to two. However, the E group scores were significantly higher than the C group in every instance except at the sixth-grade level. Finally results of between-year comparison showed that self-report of anxiety, depression, and self-concept remained generally stable between post-testing the first year to pre-testing the second year.

The Ready, Set, R.E.L.A.X. program was intended to help elementary-age children reduce harmful levels of anxiety. The current project provides an economical and easily implemented procedure that can be used with small or large groups of students.

Subjects

The experimental subjects in the pilot year of the current study were 123 first through sixth grade students enrolled in a Catholic school in a small Midwestern rural community of 20,000, primarily of middle to lower-middle income status. All subjects were white, had female teachers, and represented the portion of the enrollment of the school that remained stable over two years.

The control group subjects were 120 students enrolled in another Catholic grade school in the same community. All subjects were white, had female teachers, and represented the entire enrollment of the school that remained stable over two years. Children in both schools were similar in chronological age, intelligence, as measured by the cognitive index of the Metropolitan Achievement Test (Prescott, G., Irving, B., Hogan, T., & Farr, R., 1986) and socioeconomic level, as assessed by the Hollingshead Two Factor Index of Social Position (1958). The subjects during the second year of the study remained the same with the exception of an additional set of first grade students and graduation of sixth grade students.

Materials

There were six main types of materials used:

1. Pre- and post-testing was completed using various self-report inventories. Children in Grades 1-3 were administered the Revised Children's Manifest Anxiety Scale and the Depression Inventory for Children and Adults, while children in Grades 4-6 were administered the Revised Children's Manifest Anxiety Scale and the Piers-Harris Children's Self Concept Scale.

The Piers-Harris Children's Self Concept Scale entitled, "The Way I Feel About Myself," is a self-report instrument designed to measure self-concept in elementary through high school age students. It requires approximately a third-grade reading ability. The scale has been judged to have good internal consistency (.87-.90) and adequate temporal stability (.72-.77). Validity was established through comparison with other self-report, self-concept instruments. Content validity was established by defining the universe to be measured as the areas which children reported qualities they liked or disliked about themselves (Jersild, 1952).

The Revised Children's Manifest Anxiety Scale, subtitled "What I Think and Feel," is a 37-item, self-report instrument designed to assess the level and nature of anxiety in children and adolescents from 6 to 19 years old. Reliability estimates using the KR20 formula ranged from .83 to .85 in the norm group indicating acceptable internal consistency between individual items and the Total Anxiety Score.

The Depression Inventory for Children (Battle, 1987) is a self-report instrument comprised of 25 items selected from a pool of 80 items previously identified on the basis of their ability to measure characteristics or symptoms of depression. In research, the scales have proven to be valid, reliable measures that correlate strongly with effective states such as self esteem and have demonstrated that they are sensitive to change (Battle, 1987). Reliability estimates ranging from .77 to .80 were obtained using seven hundred sixty-four boys and girls in the norm group.

2. A series of original success imagery and progressive muscle-relaxation scripts written by this author and Mr. Jeff Allen, principal of the test school.

3. An introductory letter to introduce the program to parents.

4. In-service programs for staff, parents, and students.

5. Music selections, including Baroque classics as well as sedative music. The music selected was based on the research already cited in Chapter Two.

6. A questionnaire to obtain feedback from participants (teachers and students) in the R.S.R. program.

Procedure

To obtain permission to implement the program an overview of the program was presented to the school board of each of the targeted schools for their formal endorsement. After school-board approval, a letter explaining the program was sent to each parent. An in-service program was then held with the faculty of the experimental school to explain data-gathering procedures and to provide an introduction to the Ready, Set, RELAX (R.S.R) program and materials. This was followed by pre-testing during the second week of school using the Revised Children's Manifest Anxiety Scale (RCMAS), the Depression Inventory for Children, and the Piers Harris Children's Self-Concept Scale. Students in grades one through three were given the RCMAS and the Depression Inventory. Teachers at these levels were asked to read the items to their students and define unfamiliar words. Students in grades four through six were asked to complete the RCMAS and the Self-Concept Scale. Teachers in these grades monitored the testing and answered questions or defined words as needed. The same instruments were administered and the same instructions were used with all students grades one through six in the control-group school.

Next a workshop was presented to the experimental school students in order to give factual information about stress and lead them in discussion about its psychological and physiological effects. The R.S.R. program was explained to the students by the principal and the group was led through a relaxation/imagery experience by the author.

The R.S.R. program was implemented during the fourth week of school and ran through April of the following spring. During the first month, first through third graders listened to R.S.R. scripts on Monday, Wednesday and Friday from 12:45 p.m. to 1:00 p.m., while fourth through sixth graders listened on Tuesday, Wednesday and Thursday at the same time. The scripts were read over the intercom by the school principal. The R.S.R. session was introduced by the principal stating over the intercom, "Boys and girls it is time for Ready, Set, RELAX", which was followed by two minutes of the music selection. The classroom teachers turned off the classroom lights and instructed their students to clear their desks, place their feet flat on the floor, place their hands on their thighs, bow their heads slightly forward and close their eyes. At the end of the two minutes, the principal began reading the script while the music continued in the background. The principal was trained by this author in appropriate pacing when reading scripts. At the end of the script each teacher led the class in a brief discussion using the questions at the end of the script. (The teachers had written copies of all scripts and follow-up questions.) All grades listened to sedative music and had a quiet reading time on the days R.S.R. was not presented. In the second year of the study, the test preparation scripts were read each day for one week preceding administration of the Metropolitan Achievement Tests. Initially scripts were read three times a week (M, W, F) in an effort to help students achieve proficiency in obtaining a relaxation response. After October 19th,

R.S.R. scripts were read only twice a week so as to present only original scripts over the course of the entire academic year.

A workshop on stress and the R.S.R. program was presented to all interested parents at the test school during the first week in October in both years.

Other than the pre- and post-testing, nothing out of the normal routine occurred at the control school.

The procedure during the pilot year differed in several ways. First, all grade levels listened to the same scripts on the same days. This was changed because of the feedback from fifth and sixth grade students indicating that some scripts were more appropriate for the younger grades. Second, there was no follow-up discussion, which became one of the more valuable opportunities to integrate the R.S.R. messages during the second year. Third, no test preparation scripts were available. The hope during the second year was to increase students' overall performance on the Metropolitan Achievement Tests by using relaxation and success imagery prior to the students completing the testing.

The following null hypotheses were postulated:

1. No significant differences will occur for experimental subjects' self-reports of anxiety and depression (grades 1-3) or anxiety and self-concept (grades 4-6) when compared to students in the control school.

2. No within-group significant differences will occur in experimental subjects' self-reports of anxiety and depression (grades 1-3) and anxiety and self-concept (grades 4-6).

3. No significant differences will occur in self-report of anxiety, depression or self-concept on post-test results from the pilot year to pre-test results in the second year in the experimental and control groups.

4. The addition of scripts directly related to testing during the second year will not significantly increase achievement test results in the experimental group.

For a complete statistical analysis of results please email Dr. Klein at rogerjklein@charter.net

APPENDIX D

Positive self talk examples

- I listen to good advice
- I control myself and make good decisions
- I set goals and work toward achieving them
- I improve with practice
- I work hard to do the right things
- I appreciate who I am
- I like how I look
- I am fair
- I accept other's differences
- I am learning
- I recall important information
- I am helpful to others
- I deserve to be happy and successful
- I have the power to change myself
- I forgive and understand others and their motives
- I am confident in my own choices and decisions
- I make healthy choices and decisions
- I choose happiness whenever I wish no matter what my circumstances
- I am flexible and open to change in every aspect of my life
- I act with confidence having a general plan and accept plans are open to alteration
- It is enough to have done my best
- I deserve to be loved
- I am as capable as anyone else out there
- I know with time and effort I can accomplish my goals
- I am comfortable in front of people and say the right things
- I know who I am and I am unique
- Anyone who meets me will remember how interesting I am

- I can accomplish any task set out before me
- I find things out when no clear answer is defined
- I am worthwhile, succesful, and happy
- I have all the time in the world to do all the things I need to do
- I eat healthy food
- Vegetables and fruits strengthen me and I love to eat them
- I enjoy going for a walk and being in nature
- Exercise makes me feel good
- I am generous with my time and talents
- I stay calm and understanding in difficult times
- I always observe and think things through before reacting
- I am organized and know what I need to do
- I know where I am going in life
- I accept the choices of other people
- I am learning and growing
- I enjoy being quiet and listening to my own as well as others advice
- I am optimistic.

Responsibility — Making good choices for yourself and your relationships.

- I make healthy choices and decisions
- I choose happiness whenever I wish no matter what my circumstances
- I make good decisions in making friends
- I am responsible in my actions
- I accept responsibility for my choices

Empowerment — Feeling positive about you and competent with peers and feeling supported by others.

- I appreciate who I am
- I like how I look
- I deserve to be happy and successful

- I act with confidence having a general plan and accept plans are open to alteration
- I deserve to be loved
- I am as capable as anyone else out there
- I know with time and effort I can accomplish my goals
- I know who I am and I am unique
- Anyone who meets me will remember how interesting I am
- I can accomplish any task set out before me
- I am worthwhile, successful, and happy
- I have all the time in the world to do all the things I need to do
- I know where I am going in life
- I enjoy being quiet and listening to my own as well as others advice
- I release the need to prove myself to anyone
- I am my own person and accept who I am
- I deserve all that is good

Learning — Developing skills to acquire and retain knowledge. Finding enjoyment in creative pursuits.

- I set goals and work toward achieving them
- I improve with practice
- I am learning
- I find things out when no clear answer is defined
- I am organized and know what I need to do
- I am learning and growing
- I recall important information
- Studying comes easy to me
- I love studying
- I understand that this is the age to learn and prepare for the future
- I make a positive contribution to my class

Attitudes — Developing and practicing the attitudes and values needed to become a complete person.

- I listen to good advice
- I work hard to do the right things
- I am fair
- I accept other's differences
- I am helpful to others
- I forgive and understand others and their motives
- I am confident in my own choices and decisions
- I am flexible and open to change in every aspect of my life
- I eat healthy food
- Vegetables and fruits strengthen me and I love to eat them
- I enjoy going for a walk and being in nature
- Exercise makes me feel good
- I am generous with my time and talents
- I accept the choices of other people
- I am optimistic
- I am a wise yet humble person

X-Pand — Exploring your ability to feel calm and centered.

- I control myself and make good decisions
- I have the power to change myself
- It is enough to have done my best
- I am comfortable in front of people and say the right things
- I always observe and think things through before reacting
- I stay calm and understanding in difficult times
- I stay focused despite interruptions and distractions
- I let go when something is out of my control
- I calm myself when needed
- I express anger in a healthy way

APPENDIX E

Stress Inventory

Following is a list of stressful events as adapted from the Holmes-Rahe Life Stress Inventory (modified for children/teens). These events are ranked in descending order starting with the most stressful events.

To take the test check any of the events that have occurred in the teen's life in the past twelve months. The total score measures the amount of stress the teen has been subjected to in the one year period and can be used to predict his/her chance of suffering serious illness within the next two years. For example, a total score less than 150 means that the teen has approximately a 37 percent chance of becoming ill. A score from 150-300 increases the chance of getting sick to 51 percent. A score over 300 increases the odds of getting sick to eighty percent.

The Holmes-Rahe Life Stress Inventory.
The Social Readjustment Rating Scale.
(modified for children/teens)

Life Event	Mean Value
1. A parent has died.	100
2. Parents have divorced.	73
3. Parents have separated.	65
4. Separation from parents (at boarding school or living with another family).	63
5. Death of a close family member.	63
6. Major personal injury or illness.	53
7. Remarriage of a parent (getting a new parent).	50
8. A parent was fired from a job or you were expelled from school.	47
9. Parents got back together after separating.	45
10. One parent stops working to stay at home or parent goes back to work.	45
11. Major change in health or behavior of family member.	44
12. Pregnancy of family member.	40
13. Problems in school.	39
14. Gaining a new family member (e.g., birth, adoption, grandparent moves in).	39
15. Major school change (e.g., class or teacher change, failing subjects).	39
16. Family financial state changes a great deal (much better or much worse off).	38
17. Death or serious illness of a close friend.	37

Life Event	Mean Value
18. A new activity begins (one that takes up a lot of time and energy, e.g., dance or music lessons, sports team, computer classes after school).	36
19. Major change in the number of arguments with parents or brothers and sisters.	35
20. Feeling threatened (trouble with a bully or a gang).	31
21. Losing or being robbed of a valuable or important possession.	30
22. Major changes in responsibilities at home (e.g., must help with many chores or with raising a younger child).	29
23. Brother or sister leaves home (e.g., runs away, joins army, goes away to school).	29
24. Trouble with relatives other than parents or siblings (e.g., grandparents, aunt, uncle).	29
25. Outstanding personal achievement and recognition	28
26. Major changes in living conditions (e.g., neighborhood gets much improved, fire damages part of home).	25

The Holmes-Rahe Life Stress Inventory.
The Social Readjustment Rating Scale.
(modified for children)

Life Event	Mean Value
27. Personal habits change (e.g., style of dress, manners, people you hang out with)	24
28. Trouble with a teacher	23
29. Major change in your school schedule or conditions (e.g., new school schedule, more work demanded, using a temporary building).	20
30. Change in where you live (even in the same building).	20
31. Changing to a new school.	20
32. Major change in usual type or amount of recreation (e.g., more or less time to play).	19
33. Major change in religious activities.	19
34. Major change in school activities (e.g., clubs, movies, visiting friends).	18
35. Major change in sleep habits.	16
36. Major change in family get-togethers (many more or less).	15
37. Major change in eating habits.	15
38. Vacation.	13
39. Christmas or birthday.	12
40. Punished for doing wrong.	11

Signs of Stress

Following are symptoms of stress often exhibited by children

1. Headaches
2. Stomach problems - diarrhea, constipation, nausea, heartburn,
3. Heart pounding
4. Aches and pains
5. Muscle jerks or tics
6. Eating problems - no appetite, constant eating, full feeling without eating
7. Sleeping problems - unable to fall asleep, wake up in middle of the night, nightmares
8. General feeling of tiredness
9. Shortness of breath
10. Dry mouth or throat
11. Teeth grinding
12. Stuttering
13. Uncontrollable crying or not being able to cry
14. General anxiety, nervous feelings, or tenseness
15. Dizziness and weakness
16. Irritable and easily set off
17. Depressed
18. Accident prone
19. Feeling angry in general
20. Feeling overwhelmed and unable to cope - want to run away,
21. Nervous laughter, easily startled, jumpy
22. Bored
23. Feeling rejected all the time
24. Unable to concentrate or finish things
25. Never laugh
26. Does not have friends
27. Does not finish homework

Any symptom observed as happening often may indicate need for followup by a teacher, counselor, or parent.

References

[1]Substance Abuse and Mental Health Services Administration, Office of Applied Studies. (2007). Detailed Tables of 2006 National Survey on Drug Use and Health. Available at: http://oas.samhsa.gov/NSDUH/2k6NSDUH/tabs/TOC.htm.

[2]Gagnon, D., Hudnell, L., & Andrasck, F. (1992). Biofeedback and related procedures in coping with stress. In A. La Greca, L. Siegell, J. Wallander, & E. Walker (Eds.), *Stress and Coping in Child Health* (303-326). New York: Guilford Press.

[3]Murphy, J. (1992). Psychophysiological responses to stress in children and adolescents. In A. La Greca, L. Siegel, J. Wallander, & E. Walker (Eds.), *Stress and Coping in Child Health* (45-71). New York: Guilford Press.

[4]Matthews, D. (1989). Relaxation theory for rural youth. *Research Bulletin*. No. 46, South Carolina State College, Orangeburg.

[5]Barrett, P. M. & Turner, C. (2001). Anxiety disorders of childhood and adolescence: A critical review. *Journal of the American Academy of Child and Adolescent Psychiatry*, 30, 519-552.

[6]Allen, J. & Klein, R. (1996). *Ready, Set, R.E.L.A.X. A research based program of relaxation, learning, and self esteem.* Inner Coaching, Watertown, WI.

[7]Speidel, G. E. & Troy, M. E. (1985). The ebb and flow of mental imagery in education. In A.A. Sheikh and S. Sheikh (Eds.), *Imagery in Education*, (pp. 11-38). Farmingdale, N.Y.: Baywood Publishing.

[8]DeMarco – Sinatra, Jan. (2000). *Relaxation training as a holistic nursing intervention.* Holistic Nursing Practice, Vol. 14, #3, p. 30-39.

[9]P.C., Benson, P.L., Leffert, N., & Blyth, D.A. (2000). The contribution of developmental assets to the prediction of thriving outcomes among adolescents. *Applied Developmental Science*, 4, 27-46.

[10]Nelson, Jill R. & Kjos, Sarah. (2008). *Helping Teens Handle Tough Experiences: Strategies to Foster Resilence*. Search Institute Press, Minneapolis, MN.

[11]Mc Cafffrey, Ruth, Lacsin, Rozzano C. (2002). Music listening as a nursing intervention: a symphony of practice. *Holistic Nursing Practice:* Vol 16, #3, p 70-77.

[12]Levine, B.H. (1991). *Your Body Believes Every Word You Say: The Language of the Body/Mind Connection*. Boulder Creek, CA: Aslan.

[13]Murphy, J. (1992). Psychophysiological responses to stress in children and adolescents. In A. La Greca, L. Siegel, J. Wallander, & E. Walker (Eds.), *Stress and Coping in Child Health* (45-71). New York: Guilford Press.

[14]Citation listed by Kenneth Bell at the Governors Conference on Gangs in Los Angeles, CA.

[15]Kaiser Family Foundation National Survey (2010). Generation M2: *Media in the Lives of 8-18-Year-Olds*. www.kff.org/entmedia/8010.cfm.

[16]Cauchon, Dennis (2005). Childhood pastimes are increasingly moving indoors: Fishing, biking and sports giving way to video games. *USA Today*, McLean, VA: July 12th. Pg. A.1.

[17]Crespo, Carlos, Smit, Ellen, et. Al. (2001). Television Watching Energy Intake and Obesity in US Children. *Archives in Pediatric Adolescent Medicine*. 155: pp. 360 -365.

[18]Paik H., Comstock G. (1994). The effects of television violence on antisocial behavior: a meta-analysis. Commun Res; 21: 516-546.

[19]Wood W., Wong FY., Chachere JG. (1999). Effects of media violence on viewers' aggression in unconstrained social interaction. *Psychological Bulletin*; 109: 371-383.

[20]Berliner, D. & Amrein, A. (2003). The effects of high stakes testing on student motivation and learning. *Educational Leadership*, 60 (5) 32-38.

[21]Raley, R.K. & Bumpass, L. (2003). The topography of the divorce plateau: Levels and trends in union stability in the United States after 1980. *Demographic Research*, 8, 245-260.

[22]U.S. Department of Health and Human Services. National Institute on Alcohol Abuse and Alcoholism. *Journal: Alcohol Research & Health: Highlights From the Tenth Special Report to Congress, Health Risks and Benefits of Alcohol Consumption* (Volume 24, Number 1, 2000 ed.) Washington, DC: U.S. Government Printing Office. Retrieved October 07, 2002 from the World Wide Web: http://pubs.niaaa.nih.gov/publications/arh24-1/05-11.pdf.

[23]McDonald, Renee & Jouriles, ernest N., E. (2006). Estimating the number of American children living in partner-violent families. *Journal of Family Psychology*, Vol. 20. No. 1, 137-142.

[24]http://www.cdc.gov/nccdphp/ace/prevalence.htm ACE Study – Prevalence – Adverse Childhood Experiences.

[25]CDC. Youth Risk Behavior Surveillance – United States, 2007 [pdf 1m]. *Morbidity & Mortality Weekly Report* 2008; 57(SS-4):1–131.

[26]Tomb, Meghan & Hunter, Lisa (2004). Prevention of anxiety in children and adolescents in a school setting: The role of school-based practitioners. *Children & Schools*. Volume 26, p 87.

[27]Greenberg, M. T., Domitrovich, C., & Bumbarger, B. (2001, March). The prevention of mental disorders in school-age children: Current state of the field. *Prevention and Treatment*, 4, Article 1. (Online serial). http://www.journals.apa.org/prevention directory: vol. 4/pre0040001a.html.

[28]Rushton, J. L., Forcier, M. & Schecktman, R. M. (2002). Epidemiology of DepressiveSymptoms in the National Longitudinal Study of Adolescent Health. *Journal of the American Academy of Child and Adolescent Psychiatry*, 41(2). 199-205.

[29]Youth Risk Behavior Surveillance System, Division of Adolescent and School health, Centers for Disease Control and Prevention. (2007). Youth Online: http://aps.nccd.cdc.gov/yrbss/.

[30]Aviva Laye-Gindhu and Kimberly A. Schonert-Reichl (2004). Nonsuicidal Self-Harm Among Community Adolescents: Understanding the "Whats" and "Whys" of Self-Harm. *Journal of Youth and Adolescence*, Vol.34, Number 5, 447 – 457.

[31]Youth Risk Behavior Surveillance System, Division of Adolescent and School Health, Centers for Disease Control and Prevention. (2007). Youth Online: http://aps.nccd.cdc.gov/yrbss/.

[32]Johnston,L.D. O'Malley, P.M., Bachman, J. G., et al. (2007). Monitoring the Future National Survey Results on Adolescent Drug Use: Overview of Key Findings, 2006. Bethesda, MD: National Institute on Drug Abuse.

[33]Kilpatrick, D.G., Ruggerio, K. J., Acierno, R., et al. (2003). Violence and risk of PTSD, major depression, and substance abuse: Results from the National Survey of Adolescents. *Journal of Consulting and Clinical Psychology*, 71(4), 692-700.

[34]National Adolescent Health Information Center. (2007b). National Survey on Drug Use and Health, 2006. http://www.icpsr. umich.edu/cocoon/ICPRSR/SERIES/00064.xml.

[35]Selye, H. (1956). *The Stress of Life*. New York: McGraw-Hill Book Co., Inc.

[36]Cannon, W. B. (1914). The emergency function of the adrenal medulla in pain and major emotions. *American Journal of Physiology*, 33, 356-372.

[37]Sandler, Irwin, Tein, Jenn-Yun, West S. (1994). Coping, stress and the psychological symptoms of children of divorce: A cross-sectional and longitudinal study. Child Development, 65, 1744-1763.

[38]Wagner, Barry and Compas, Bruce. (1990). Gender, instrumentality, and expressivity : Moderators of the relation between stress and psychological symptoms during adolescence. American Journal of Community Psychology. 18. no. 3, pp. 383-486.

[39]Benson, H. (1977). Systemic hypertension and the relaxation response. *New England Journal of Medicine*, 296, 1152-1156.

[40]Shepard, R. N. & Cooper, L. A. (1982). *Mental Images and Their Transformations*. Cambridge, Mass.: MIT Press.

[41]Hume, D. (1748). *An inquiry concerning human understanding*. Chicago: Open Court, Reprinted 1907, 252-254.

[42]Huth MM, Broome ME, Good M. (2004). Imagery reduces children's post-operative pain. *Pain*. Jul;110(1-2):439-48.

[43]Olness, K (1991). "Imagery (self-hypnosis) as adjunct therapy in childhood cancer." *Am. Journal of Pediatric Hematology/Oncology* 3 (3) 313-320.

[44]Gregg, M., Hall, C., & Nederfof, E. (2005). Imagery ability, imagery use, and performance relationship. *The Sport Psychologist*, 19, 93-99.

[45]http://altmed.od.nih.gov/cam/methods/Imagery.html.

[46]Garfield, Charles (1987). *Peak Performers*. Avon Books, New York, New York.

[47]Sullivan, George. (1985) *Mary Lou Retton*. New York: Julian Messner.

[48]Covey, Steven. (1996). *The 7 Habits of Highly Effective People*. Simon & Schuster, UK Ltd.

[49]Helmstetter, Chad. (1982). *What to say when you talk to yourself*. Pocket Books, Simon & Schuster, Inc., New York, New York.

[50]Levine, B.H. (1991). *Your Body Believes Every Word You Say: The Language of the Body/Mind Connection*. Boulder Creek, CA: Aslan.

[51]Meichenbaum, D. (1977). *Cognitive-behavior modification: An integrative approach*. New York: Plenum.

[52]Jacobson, E. (1944). *Progressive Relaxation*. Chicago: University of Chicago Press.

[53]Lazarus, R. S. (1971). The concepts of stress and disease. In L. Levi (Ed.), *The psychosocial environment and psychosomatic disease* (pp. 53-58). London: Oxford University Press.

[54]Chang, J., & Hiebert, B. (1989). Relaxation procedures with children: A review. *Medical Psychotherapy*, 2, 163-176.

[55]Porter, S. S., & Omizo, M. M. (1984). The effects of group relaxation training/large muscle exercise, and parental involvement on attention to task, impulsivity, and locus of control among hyperactive boys. *Exceptional Child*, 31, 54-64.

[56]Brown, R. H. (1977). An evaluation of the effectiveness of relaxation as a treatment modality for the hyperactive child. *Dissertation Abstracts International*, 38 (6B), 2847.

[57]Reynolds, S. B. (1984). Biofeedback, relaxation training, and music: Homeostasis for coping with stress. *Biofeedback and Self-Regulation*, 9, No. 2.

[58]Goldbeck, Lutz, Schmid, Katharina. (2003). Effectiveness of autogenic relaxation training on children and adolescents with behavioral and emotional problems. *Journal of the American Academy of Child and Adolescent Psychiatry*, 42: 1046.

[59]Reynolds, William M. (1986). A comparison of cognitive-behavioral therapy and relaxation training for the treatment of depression in adolescents. *Journal of Consulting Psychology*, v54 n5 pp653-660.

[60]Schilling, D. J. & Poppen, R. (1983). Behavioral relaxation training and assessment. *Journal of Behavior Therapy and Experimental Psychiatry*, 14, 99-107.

[61]Rasid, Z., Parish, T. (1998). The effects of two types of relaxation training on students' levels of anxiety. Vol. 33, *Adolescence*, 99(3).

[62]Field, T., Grizzle, N., Scafidi, F., and Schanberg, S. (1996). Massage and relaxation therapies effects on depressed adolescent mothers. Vol. 31, *Adolescence*, 903 (9).

[63]Klein, Roger & Allen, Jeffrey. (1996). *Ready, set, R.E.L.A.X.: A research based program of relaxation, learning and self esteem for children.* Inner Coaching, Watertown, WI.

[64]Kabat-Zinn, J., Massion, A. O., Kristeller, J., Peterson, L. G., Fletcher, K. E., Lenderking, W. R., & Santorelli, S. F. (1983). Effectiveness of a mediation-based stress reduction program in the treatment of anxiety disorders. *American Journal of Psychiatry.* 149, 936-943.

[65]Benson, H. (1977). Systemic hypertension and the relaxation response. *New England Journal of Medicine*, 296, 1152-1156.

[66]Liserman, J., Stuart, E. M., Marnish, M. E., & Benson, H. (1989). The efficacy of the relaxation response in preparing for cardiac surgery. *Behavioral Medicine*, Fall, 111-117.

[67]Engel, J. M. (1992). Relaxation training: A self-help approach for children with headaches. *American Journal of Occupational Therapy*, July, Vol. 46, 591-596.

[68]Singer, H. S. (1994). Migraine headaches in children. *Pediatric Review*, March, Vol. 15, Issure 3, 94-101.

[69]Kohen, d. (1987). A biobehavioral approach to managing childhood asthma. *Children Today*, Vol. 16, N. 2, 6-10.

[70]Carroll, D. & Seers, K. (1998). Relaxation for the relief of chronic pain: a systematic review. *Journal of Advanced Nursing.* 27: 476-487.

[71]Morrow, G. R., & Hickok, J. T. (1993). Behavioral treatment of chemotherapy – induced nausea and vomiting. *Oncology*, 1993, December, Vol. 7. Issure 12, 83-9.

[72]Carroll, D. & Seers, K. (1998). Relaxation for the relief of chronic pain: a systematic review. *Journal of Advanced Nursing.* 27: 476-487.

[73]Kearney, C. & Silveman, W. (1990). A prelininary analysis of a functional model of assessment and treatment of school refusal behavior. *Behavior Modification*, July, Vol. 14. Issure 3, 340-66.

[74]Reynolds, W. & Stark, K. (1987). School-based intervention strategies for the treatment of depression in children and adolescents. *Special Services in the Schools*, V. 3, n. 3-4. 69-88.

[75]Powers, S. W. (1999). Empirically supported treatments in pediatric psychology; procedure-related pain. *Journal of Pediatric Psychology*, April, Vol. 24. Issure 2, 131-45.

[76]Klein, N. (2001). *Healing Images for Children: Teaching Relaxation and Guided Imagery to Children Facing Cancer and Other Serious Illnesses*. Inner Coaching, Watertown, WI.

[77]Achterberg, J. (1985). *Shamanism and modern medicine*. Boston: Shambhala.

[78]Andrews, T. (1996). *Sacred sounds: Transformation through music & word*. St. Paul, MN: Llewellyn Publishers.

[79]Morninweg, U. C. (1992). Effects of music preference and selection on stress reduction. *Journal of Holistic Nursing*, 10(2): 101-109.

[80]Campbell, D. (1992). *Music for being born into death*. Weaton, IL: Quest Books.

[81]Rolla, G. (1993). *Inner music: creative analysis and music memory*. Wilmette, LL: Chiron Publications.

[82]Ostrander, S. & Schroeder, L. (1979). *Super learning*. New York: Dell Publishing Co., 84.

[83]Peretti, P. O., & Swenson, K. (1974). Effects of music on anxiety as determined by physiological skin responses. *Journal of Research in Music Education*. 22, 278-283.

[84]Landreth, J. E., & Landreth, H. F. (1974). Effects of music on physiological response. *Journal of Research in Music Education*, 22, 4-12.

[85]Webster, C. (1973). Relaxation music and cardiology: the physiological and psychological consequences of their interrelation. *Australian Occupational Therapy Journal*. 20, 9-20.

[86]Foster, E., & Gamble, E. A. M. (1906). The effect of music on thoracic breathing. *American Journal of Psychology*. 17, 406-416.

[87]Prager-Decker, I. J. (1979). The relative efficacy of progressive muscle relaxation, EMG biofeedback, and music for reducing stress arousal of internally vs. externally controlled individuals. *Dissertation Abstracts International*, 7, 3177.

[88]Furman, C. E. (1978). The effect of musical stimuli on the brainwave production of children. *Journal of Music Therapy*, 15, 108-117.

[89]Middleton, W. W., Ray, P. W., Kerry, W. A., & Amft, R. (1944). The effect of music on feelings of restfulness-tiredness and pleasantness-unpleasantness. *Journal of Psychology*, 17, 299-318.

[90]Robb, S. L. (2000). The effect of therapeutic music interventions on the behavior of hospitalized children in isolation: developing a contextual support model of music therapy. *Journal of Music Therapy*, 37(2), 118-46.

[91]Gold, C., Voracek, M. & Wigram, T. (2004). Effects of music therapy for children and adolescents with psychopathology: A meta-analysis. *Journal of Child Psychology and Psychiatry and Allied Disciplines*. 45(6), 1054-1063.

[92]Kibler, V. E. (1983). Effects of progressive muscle relaxation and music on stress as measured by finger temperature response. *Journal of Clinical Psychology*, 39, No. 2, 213-215.

[93]Reynolds, S. B. (1984). Biofeedback, relaxation training, and music: Homeostasis for coping with stress. *Biofeedback and Self-Regulation*, 9, No. 2.

[94]Wesecky, A. (1986). Music therapy for children with Rett syndrome. *American Journal of Medical Genetics*, 24, 253-257.

[95]Cratty, B. J. (1972). *Physical expressions of intelligence.* Englewood Cliffs: Prentice-Hall Inc., 144-145.

[96]Logan, T. G., & Roberts, A. R. (1984). The effects of different types of relaxation music on tension level. *Journal of Music Therapy,* 21, 177-183.

[97]Smith, Jonathan & Carol, Joyce. (2004) Mozart versus new age music: relaxation states, stress, and ABC relaxation theory. *Journal of Music Therapy:* Vol. 41, No. 3, Page 215.

[98]Gentile, Douglas, editor (2003). *Media violence and children: A complete guide for parents and professionals.* Praeger, Westport, Connecticut.

[99]Wells, Alan & Hakanen, Ernest (1990). The emotional use of popular music by adolescents. *Mass Media & Society,* Ablex Publishing, New York, New York.

[100]Gentile, Douglas, editor (2003). *Media violence and children: A complete guide for parents and professionals.* Praeger, Westport, Connecticut.

[101]Matthews, D. (1989). Relaxation theory for rural youth. *Research Bulletin.* No. 46, South Carolina State College, Orangeburg.

[102]Barrett, P. M. & Turner, C. (2001). Anxiety disorders of childhood and adolescence: A critical review. *Journal of the American Academy of Child and Adolescent Psychiatry,* 30, 519-552.

[103]Allen, J. & Klein, R. (1996). *Ready, Set, R.E.L.A.X. A research based program of relaxation, learning, and self esteem.* Inner Coaching, Watertown, WI.

[104]Speidel, G. E. & Troy, M. E. (1985). The ebb and flow of mental imagery in education. In A.A. Sheikh and S. Sheikh (Eds.), *Imagery in Education,* (pp. 11-38). Farmingdale, N.Y.: Baywood Publishing.

[105]Forman, S., O'Malley, P. (1985). A school-based approach to stress management education of students. *Special Services in the Schools,* 1, 61-71.

[106]Weigel, C., & Wertlieb, D. (1986). Social support as a moderator of children's stressful life experiences. *Psychosomatic Medicine*, 48, 3-4.

[107]Cauce, A. M., Comer, J. P., & Schwartz, D. (1987). Long term effects of a systems-orientated school prevention program. *American Journal of Orthopsychiatry*, 57 (1), 127-131.

[108]Allen, J. & Klein, R. (1996). *Ready, Set, R.E.L.A.X. A research based program of relaxation, learning, and self esteem.* Inner Coaching, Watertown, WI.

[109]Larsson, B. (1987). Therapist-assisted versus self-help relaxation treatment of chronic headaches in adolescents: A school-based intervention. *Journal of Child Psychology and Psychiatry*, 28 (1), 127-136.

INDEX

ORDER FORM

Inner Coaching Products for Teens

ITEM	QTY X	PRICE	= TOTAL
RELAX.calm Book	___ x	$24.95 =	_____
Motivation & Academic Achievement			
RELAX.calm Teen CD......	___ x	$15.95 =	_____
Self Confidence & Bully Resistance			
RELAX.calm Teen CD......	___ x	$15.95 =	_____
Attitudes & Asset Development			
RELAX.calm Teen CD......	___ x	$15.95 =	_____
Special Packages:			
Book and 3 CDs	___ x	$59.95 =	_____
Set of all 3 CDs	___ x	$39.95 =	_____

Inner Coaching Products for Children

Ready...Set...R.E.L.A.X.			
Book	___ x	$23.95 =	_____
Ready...Set...Release			
CD	___ x	$15.95 =	_____
Special Package:			
Book and CD	___ x	$35.95 =	_____

Relaxation for All Ages

Relaxation & Success			
Imagery CD	___ x	$12.95 =	_____

Music for Relaxation

Pianoscapes: Music CD			
(2 Discs)	___ x	$15.95 =	_____
Pachelbel w/Ocean:			
Music CD	___ x	$15.95 =	_____
Ocean Odyssey: (20 page booklet included)			
Music CD	___ x	$15.95 =	_____
The Fairy Ring:			
Music CD	___ x	$15.95 =	_____
Set of all 4 CDs	___ x	$49.95 =	_____

Music for Accelerated Learning, by Steve Halpren

Music CD	___ x	$15.95 =	_____

Relaxation Suite, by Steve Halpren

Music CD	___ x	$15.95 =	_____

Healing Images Products for Children Facing Serious Illnesses

ITEM	QTY X	PRICE	= TOTAL
Healing Images for			
Children Book	___ x	$24.95=	_____
Healing Images for			
Children CD	___ x	$15.95=	_____
Healing Images			
Activity Book	___ x	$12.95=	_____
Special Package:			
above 3 items	___ x	$47.95=	_____
Comforting			
Your Child...................	___ x	$4.95 =	_____
Healing From			
Burn Injuries	___ x	$4.95 =	_____
All Tucked In:			
Hints for			
Falling Asleep................	___ x	$4.95 =	_____
Relaxation Stories			
& Strategies:			
for Surgery	___ x	$4.95 =	_____
Libro de Actividades.......	___ x	$7.95 =	_____

Products Recommended by Inner Coaching

Yoga Calm for			
Children Book	___ x	$29.95=	_____
Let's Roll Yoga	___ x	$23.95=	_____

*Add 10% of total cost. SHIPPING		_____
WI Residents add 5.5% SALES TAX		_____
TOTAL=		_____

Ship to (this information will not be released to others).

Name _____

Address _____

City State Zip _____

Phone _____

Email _____

Visa/MasterCard # Exp Date _____

Shop online at www.innercoaching.com

Mail or fax orders must be accompanied by purchase order,
credit card information, check or money order payable to Inner Coaching.
Guaranteed – return within 30 days for refund if dissatisfied.
Inner Coaching | 1108 Western Avenue | Watertown, WI 53094
phone (920) 262-0439 | fax (920) 261-8801 | email kids@readysetrelax.com

ORDER FORM

Inner Coaching Products for Teens

ITEM	QTY X PRICE = TOTAL
RELAX.calm Book .... ___ x $24.95 = _____	
Motivation & Academic Achievement	
RELAX.calm Teen CD...... ___ x $15.95 = _____	
Self Confidence & Bully Resistance	
RELAX.calm Teen CD...... ___ x $15.95 = _____	
Attitudes & Asset Development	
RELAX.calm Teen CD...... ___ x $15.95 = _____	

Special Packages:
Book and 3 CDs .... ___ x $59.95 = _____
Set of all 3 CDs .... ___ x $39.95 = _____

Inner Coaching Products for Children

Ready...Set...R.E.L.A.X.
Book .... ___ x $23.95 = _____
Ready...Set...Release
CD.......................... ___ x $15.95 = _____
Special Package:
Book and CD .... ___ x $35.95 = _____

Relaxation for All Ages

Relaxation & Success
Imagery CD .... ___ x $12.95 = _____

Music for Relaxation

Pianoscapes: Music CD
(2 Discs) .... ___ x $15.95 = _____
Pachelbel w/Ocean:
Music CD .... ___ x $15.95 = _____
Ocean Odyssey: (20 page booklet included)
Music CD .... ___ x $15.95 = _____
The Fairy Ring:
Music CD .... ___ x $15.95 = _____
Set of all 4 CDs .... ___ x $49.95 = _____

Music for Accelerated Learning, by Steve Halpren
Music CD .... ___ x $15.95 = _____
Relaxation Suite, by Steve Halpren
Music CD .... ___ x $15.95 = _____

Healing Images Products for Children Facing Serious Illnesses

ITEM	QTY X PRICE = TOTAL
Healing Images for	
Children Book .... ___ x $24.95= _____	
Healing Images for	
Children CD .... ___ x $15.95= _____	
Healing Images	
Activity Book .... ___ x $12.95= _____	

Special Package:
above 3 items .... ___ x $47.95= _____
Comforting
Your Child................... ___ x $4.95 = _____
Healing From
Burn Injuries .... ___ x $4.95 = _____
All Tucked In:
Hints for
Falling Asleep .... ___ x $4.95 = _____
Relaxation Stories
& Strategies:
for Surgery .... ___ x $4.95 = _____
Libro de Actividades....... ___ x $7.95 = _____

Products Recommended by Inner Coaching

Yoga Calm for
Children Book .... ___ x $29.95= _____
Let's Roll Yoga .... ___ x $23.95= _____

*Add 10% of total cost. SHIPPING   _____
WI Residents add 5.5% SALES TAX   _____
                              TOTAL= _____

Ship to (this information will not be released to others).
Name _____
Address _____
City State Zip _____
Phone _____
Email _____
Visa/MasterCard # Exp Date _____

Shop online at www.innercoaching.com

Mail or fax orders must be accompanied by purchase order,
credit card information, check or money order payable to Inner Coaching.
Guaranteed—return within 30 days for refund if dissatisfied.
Inner Coaching | 1108 Western Avenue | Watertown, WI 53094
phone (920) 262-0439 | fax (920) 261-8801 | email kids@readysetrelax.com

This chapter, which is similar in scope to the other chapters in this book, provides an overview of some of the self-defending components of the ASA product line, with an emphasis on how to manage the device using management products such as the device manager. This chapter is intended to be an overview and a pointer to more detailed or advanced publications, as provided in the References section. In this chapter, you will learn about the antispoofing, IPS, application or protocol inspection, antivirus, antispam, antiphishing, and antispyware protection on the ASA product line.

Antispoofing

Cisco ASA contains several features to enhance the ability of the network to be self-defending. One example of these features is the ability for the ASA to implement an antispoofing function. Antispoofing helps to protect an interface of the ASA by verifying that the source of network traffic is valid.

The antispoofing feature protects an individual interface from IP address spoofing by creating filters to confirm both source address and route integrity. The antispoofing feature creates an **ip verify reverse-path** command-line interface (CLI) command. The antispoofing feature verifies route integrity by performing a route lookup on the source address of an incoming packet. This packet is dropped if a route does not exist back to the source address or if the route does not match the interface of the incoming packet. The inability to have a route back to the source address for an interface is considered to be suspect for a denial-of-service (DoS) attack because many attacks use IP spoofing to disguise the true source IP address of the attacker.

Figure 3-2 displays an example of where to enable antispoofing on an interface by selecting the interface and selecting the Enable button under Antispoofing in ASDM. This antispoofing feature is also called Unicast Reverse Path Forwarding (uRPF).

CHAPTER 3

Cisco Adaptive Security Appliance Overview

The Cisco Adaptive Security Appliance (ASA) line combines the functions of a firewall, Virtual Private Network (VPN), and intrusion prevention system (IPS) in a single appliance. This product line is adaptive, which means that it provides several mechanisms that enable the network to be self-defending. The ASA product line is also built to be extensible to add new self-defending capabilities like antivirus, antispam, antiphishing, and antispyware protection, which are supported in the Content Security and Control Security Services Module (CSC-SSM) on the ASA product line.

The ASA product line contains several models, including the Cisco ASA 5505, Cisco ASA 5510, Cisco ASA 5520, Cisco ASA 5540, and the Cisco ASA 5550. Each of these ASA models has a different capacity and price point. The ASA is managed by an easy-to-use Adaptive Security Device Manager (ASDM). ASDM is a follow-on release to the popular PIX Device Manager (PDM). ASDM features several enhancements over PDM, including a near real-time syslog viewer. Figure 3-1 shows the ASDM main screen.

Figure 3-1   *ASDM Main Screen*

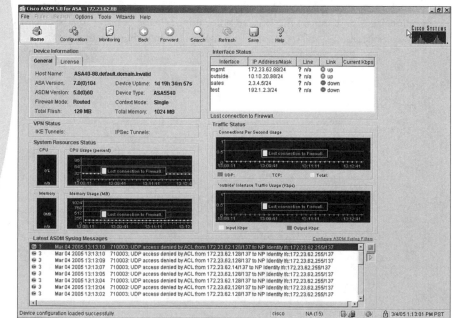

The Traffic Anomaly Detector and Guard combine to form a comprehensive solution that protects a zone. A zone can be an IP address, subnet, network, or ISP. The Traffic Anomaly Detector and Guard participate in a learning phase that creates a baseline of valid network traffic for each zone. This learning phase is composed of a policy creation phase to create policies to protect the zone and a threshold-tuning phase. The threshold-tuning phase creates minimum threshold values for each configured protocol that are based on the sample network traffic observed during the learning phase. Once network traffic for a specific application exceeds the tuned threshold, the Guard can create a dynamic filter or leverage a user filter to attempt to protect the zone against the DDoS attack. The specific DDoS attack traffic for that zone is diverted to the Guard, often with a BGP routing update mechanism. This DDoS traffic is then scrubbed by the Guard and reinjected back to the zone, often with a tunneling or VLAN mechanism. Both the Traffic Anomaly Detector and the Guard WBM features a rich-set of status and attack reports to visualize the DDoS attack and mitigation process for the protected zone.

References

Cisco Systems, Inc. DDoS Attack Prevention. http://www.cisco.com/en/US/netsol/ns480/networking_solutions_sub_solution_home.html

Cisco Systems, Inc. Cisco Traffic Anomaly Detector User Guide. http://cisco.com/application/pdf/en/us/guest/products/ps5887/c2001/ccmigration_09186a00803bd0d8.pdf

Cisco Systems, Inc. Cisco Traffic Anomaly Detector Web-Based Management User Guide. http://cisco.com/application/pdf/en/us/guest/products/ps5887/c2001/ccmigration_09186a00802d7255.pdf

Cisco Systems, Inc. Cisco Traffic Anomaly Detector Web-Based Management User Guide (Software Version 5.0). http://www.cisco.com/en/US/products/hw/modules/ps2706/products_module_configuration_guide_chapter09186a00804bef24.html

Cisco Systems, Inc. Cisco Guard Configuration Guide (Software Version 3.1(0)). http://www.cisco.com/en/US/products/ps5888/products_configuration_guide_book09186a00803bed03.html

Cisco Systems, Inc. Cisco Guard Web-Based Management User Guide (Software Version 3.1(0)). http://www.cisco.com/en/US/products/ps5888/products_configuration_guide_book09186a00802d1baf.html

Cisco Systems, Inc. Cisco Anomaly Guard Module Web-Based Management Configuration Guide, Glossary. http://www.cisco.com/en/US/products/hw/modules/ps2706/products_module_configuration_guide_chapter09186a00803f3ee7.html

BOOKS ONLINE
ENABLED

THIS BOOK IS SAFARI ENABLED

INCLUDES FREE 45-DAY ACCESS TO THE ONLINE EDITION

The Safari® Enabled icon on the cover of your favorite technology book means the book is available through Safari Bookshelf. When you buy this book, you get free access to the online edition for 45 days.

Safari Bookshelf is an electronic reference library that lets you easily search thousands of technical books, find code samples, download chapters, and access technical information whenever and wherever you need it.

TO GAIN 45-DAY SAFARI ENABLED ACCESS TO THIS BOOK:

- Go to **http://www.ciscopress.com/safarienabled**

- Complete the brief registration form

- Enter the coupon code found in the front of this book before the "Contents at a Glance" page

If you have difficulty registering on Safari Bookshelf or accessing the online edition, please e-mail customer-service@safaribooksonline.com.

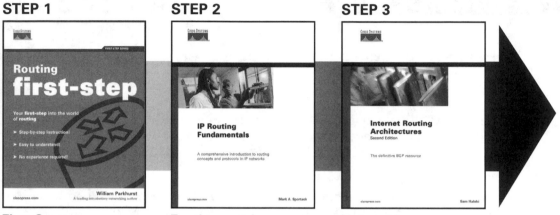

Figure 3-6 *Create Traffic Class*

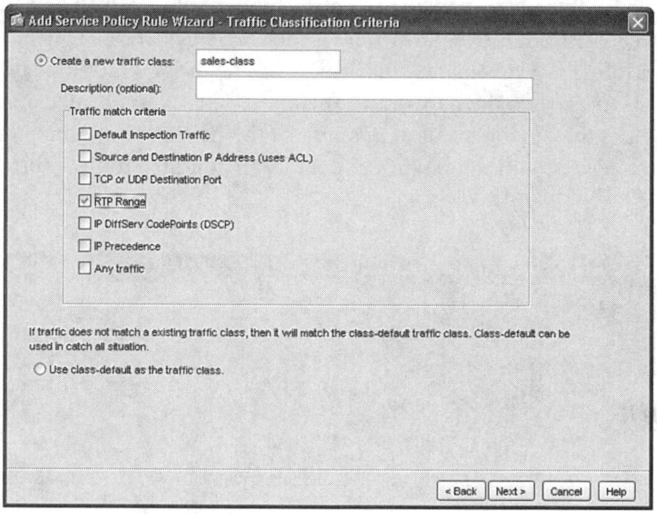

Figure 3-7 *Define Network Traffic for Traffic Class*

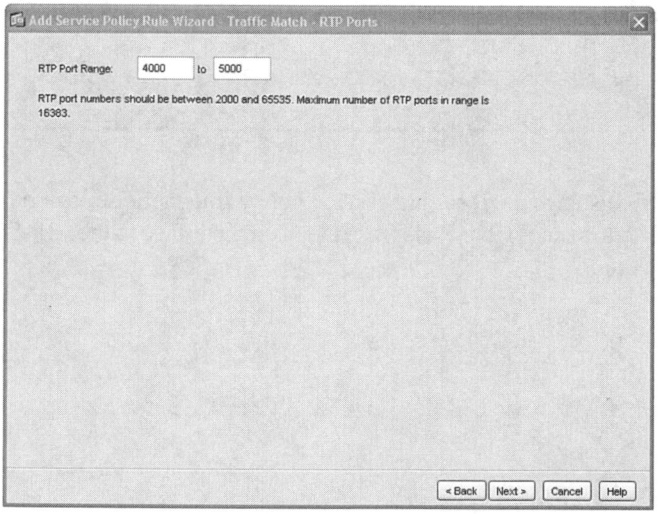

Figure 3-8 defines how to configure IPS inspection for this traffic flow. Configuring IPS prevention for this traffic flow in the service policy rule sends the matched traffic class from the ASA chassis to the AIP-SSM module for IPS inspection. This example defines IPS to be inline. Inline IPS means that this traffic can be dropped for a match of an IPS signature for packets that match the network traffic class. This example also defines IPS to fail-open, which means that, in the event of a failure of the AIP-SSM module, this traffic class for the specified interface will not be dropped and will continue to flow through the ASA.

Figure 3-8 *Enable IPS for Traffic Flow*

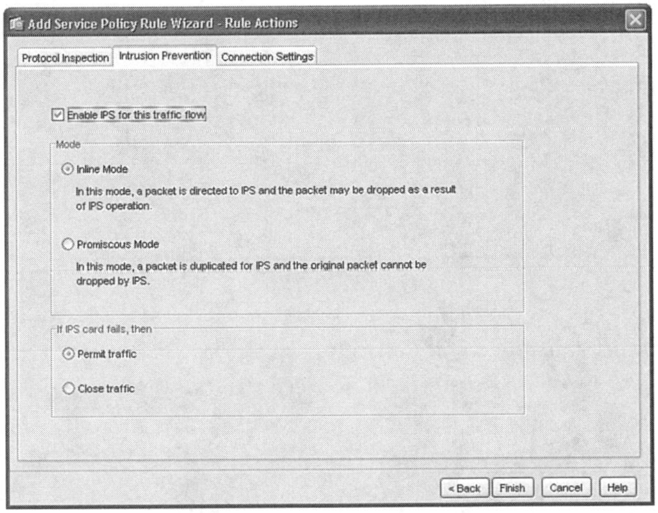

Figure 3-9 displays the resulting service policy rule in the service policy table for the new traffic class to send RTP packets from the inside interface to the AIP-SSM module for inline IPS inspection.

Figure 3-9 *Service Policy Rule Table Entry*

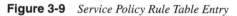

Example 3-2 displays the resulting **class-map**, **policy-map,** and **service-policy** CLI commands on the base ASA platform.

Example 3-2 *CLI for Service Policy Rule*

```
class-map sales-class
 match rtp 4000 1000
 !
 !
policy-map sales-policy
 class sales-class
   ips inline fail-open
 !
service-policy sales-policy interface inside
```

Define IPS Signatures

After configuring any specific service policy rules, you next configure the specific IPS signatures that will be used to inspect the network traffic for a potential network attack. IPS can be inline, which means that the ASA product deals with the real network packet of a possible attack in real time, as opposed to a copy of the network traffic from a span port on a Catalyst LAN switch as typically implemented with an intrusion detection system (IDS) solution. IPS signature configuration is initiated by selecting the Signature Configuration option in ASDM as shown in Figure 3-10.

Figure 3-10 *IPS Signature Configuration*

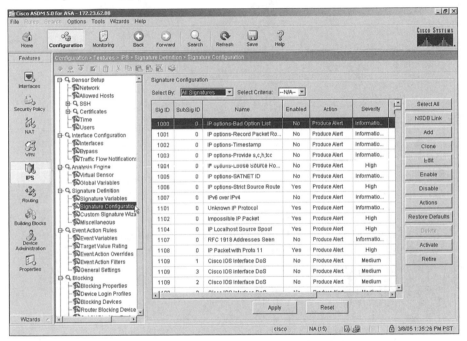

IPS signatures are divided into several subcategories, including Layer 2/Layer 3/Layer 4 (L2/L3/L4) protocol, attack, and operating system (OS) platforms. Target OS platform signatures include Linux, Windows, MacOS, Netware, and Cisco IOS. Figure 3-11 displays the signatures subcategories.

Figure 3-11   *IPS Signature Subcategories*

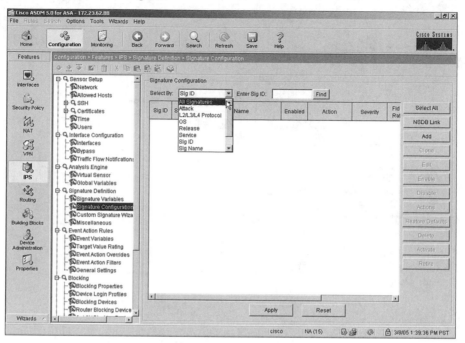

The attack signatures are composed of several attack subcategories including adware/ spyware, distributed denial of service (DDoS), DoS, and file access. Figure 3-12 shows an example of these attack subcategories.

Figure 3-12 *Attack Signature Subcategories*

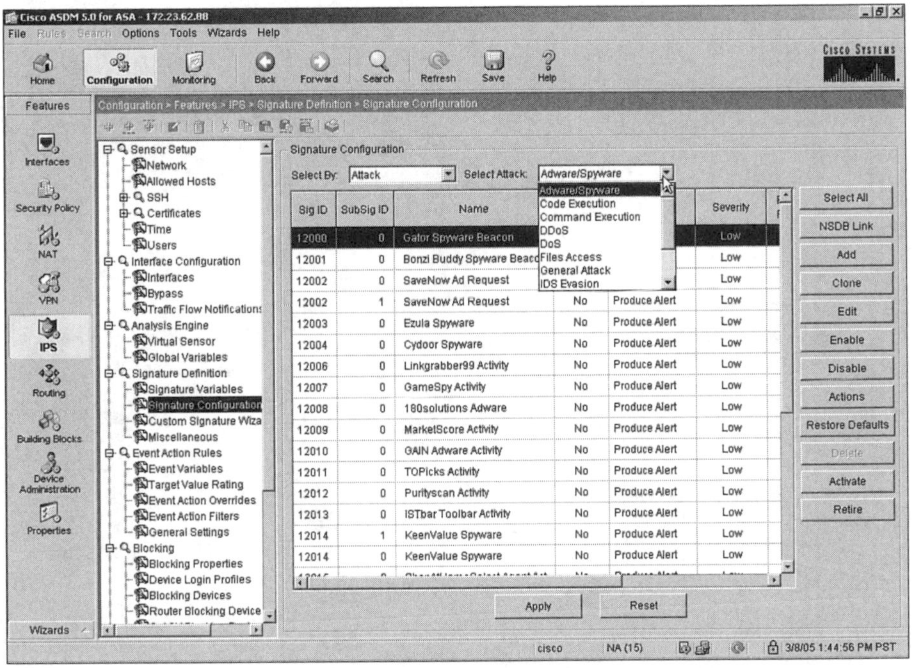

Let's say that a user wants to deploy the attack signatures to detect spyware. The process to deploy the attack signature is as simple as selecting the spyware category, highlighting the spyware signature, and then selecting the Enable and Apply buttons. The location in ASDM to select a spyware signature and to select the Enable and Apply buttons in ASDM is shown in Figure 3-13.

Figure 3-13 *Applying Spyware Detection Signatures*

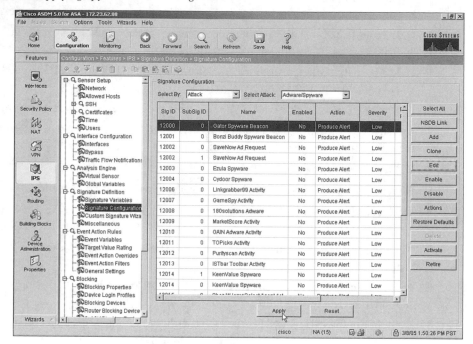

Protocol Inspection Services

Cisco ASA features the ability to perform application or protocol inspection on specific Layer 4–Layer 7 protocols. Many network attacks attempt to exploit a vulnerability in the handling of a network protocol. The ability for the ASA to inspect the contents of network packets for certain protocols can enable the ASA to identify a potential attack and be self-defending. Protocol inspection can also verify dynamic port assignments and rewrite embedded network addresses within the protocol data packets. The protocols that are supported for protocol inspection in ASA include the following:

- **Computer Telephone Interface Quick Buffer Encoding (CTIQBE)**—CTIQBE is used by Cisco IP SoftPhone and Cisco CallManager.

- **Domain Name System (DNS)**—DNS translates a name to an IP address.

- **Enhanced Simple Mail Transport protocol (ESMTP)**—ESMTP adds Extended Hello to SMTP.

- **File Transfer Protocol (FTP)**—Use FTP to transfer files across a network using PUT and GET.

- **GPRS Tunneling Protocol (GTP)**—GPRS is a 3G data service for GSM mobile phones. A separate license is required to enable GTP protocol inspection on ASA.

- **H.323 and H.225**—H.323 are endpoints that participate in a Voice over IP (VoIP) call, and H.225 is the ITU call control signaling protocol.

- **H.323 Registration, Admission, and Status (RAS)**—This is the H.323 gatekeeper discovery and registration protocol.

- **Hypertext Transfer Protocol (HTTP)**—This protocol enables web browsing.

- **Internet Control Message Protocol (ICMP)**—ICMP ping is used to determine if there is connectivity to an IP address across the network.

- **ICMP Error**—Ping error codes.

- **Internet Locator Service (ILS)**—ILS is used in Microsoft NetMeeting.

- **Media Gateway Control Protocol (MGCP)**—MGCP controls media gateways from controllers and call agent.

- **Network Basic Input/Output System (NetBIOS)**—NetBIOS is used for Windows print sharing.

- **Point-to-Point Tunneling Protocol (PPTP)**—PPTP was the first VPN protocol supported by Microsoft dial-up networking.

- **Remote Shell (RSH)**—RSH is the UNIX utility to remotely execute commands.

- **Real Time Streaming Protocol (RTSP)**—RTSP is the IETF protocol for streaming media such as video on a network.

- **Session Initialization Protocol (SIP)**—SIP is the IETF protocol for voice over IP (VoIP).

- **Skinny Call Control Protocol (SCCP)**—SCCP is the voice communication protocol between Cisco CallManager and VoIP phones.

- **Simple Network Management Protocol (SNMP)**—SNMP is used for network monitoring and management by reading and writing to Message Information Blocks (MIBs).

- **SQLNET**—This is the SQL*NET protocol for Oracle database.

- **Sun Remote Procedure Call (SunRPC)**—This is the Sun client/server protocol for distributed computing. Network File System (NFS) also uses this protocol.

- **Trivial File Transfer Protocol (TFTP)**—TFTP is the protocol to transfer a file accross a network or boot a network device.

- **X Display Manager Control Protocol (XDMCP)**—This is the protocol for communication between a display manager and X server.

HTTP Inspection Engine

HTTP or web traffic is one of the most popular types of traffic on networks today. ASA includes the ability to inspect HTTP traffic flows to detect possible network attacks. You can initiate the process to configure the inspection of an HTTP traffic flow under the Service Policy Rules section. This process to initiate the creation of a traffic flow for HTTP inspection is similar to the process to define a traffic flow with Service Policy Rules for IPS inspection as described in the "Intrusion Prevention Service" section earlier in this chapter. The configuration to inspect a certain HTTP traffic flow results in a class-map and policy-map statement, similar to the CLI output for the IPS Service Policy Rule configuration.

The HTTP inspection engine allows the ASA to mitigate potential network attacks that are tunneled over TCP port 80, the HTTP port. The HTTP inspection engine also verifies that the network traffic is RFC-compliant and not a series of malformed or handcrafted packets designed to potentially launch a network attack. URL length is also inspected to help detect any handcrafted large URLs that can be designed to create a network attack.

ASDM features an easy-to-use wizard to walk you through the Service Policy Rule definition process. You can configure HTTP inspection globally for all traffic through the ASA, or you can configure protocol inspection for a single interface. In the Add Service Policy Rule Wizard, as shown in Figure 3-14, you can configure a rule to be global, which applies to all interfaces on the ASA.

Figure 3-14   *Global Rule to Inspect HTTP*

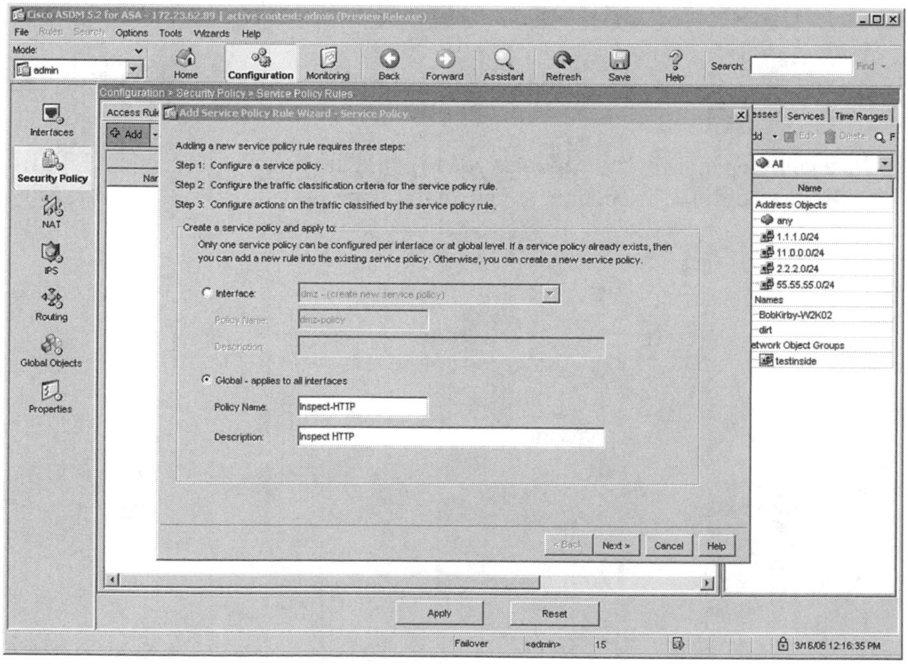

The next step is specification of what traffic or ports will be inspected. Figure 3-15 displays an example of how to select the inspection of TCP packets, and Figure 3-16 configures the HTTP/web service to inspect HTTP/WWW, or TCP port 80.

Figure 3-15 *Inspect TCP*

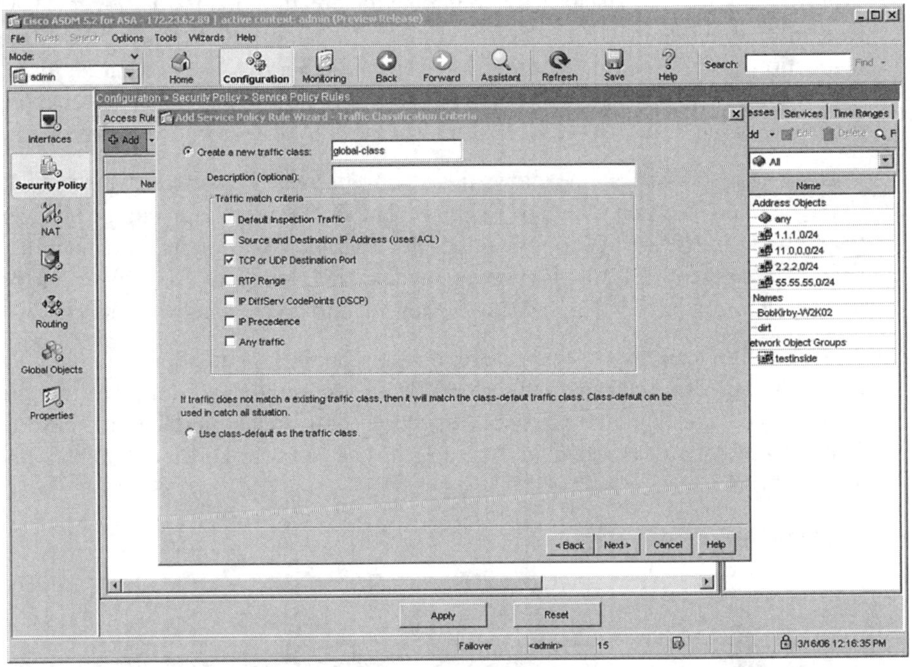

The next step in the wizard enables you to configure protocol inspection. HTTP inspection can be selected for inspection, as shown in Figure 3-17.

Figure 3-16 *Inspect HTTP/Web Service*

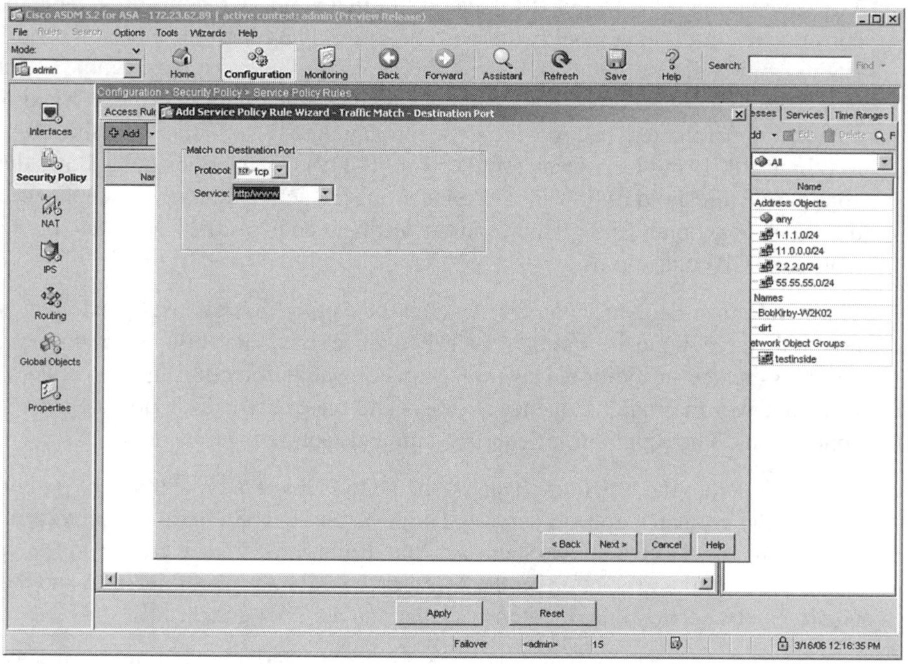

Figure 3-17 *Select HTTP for Protocol Inspection*

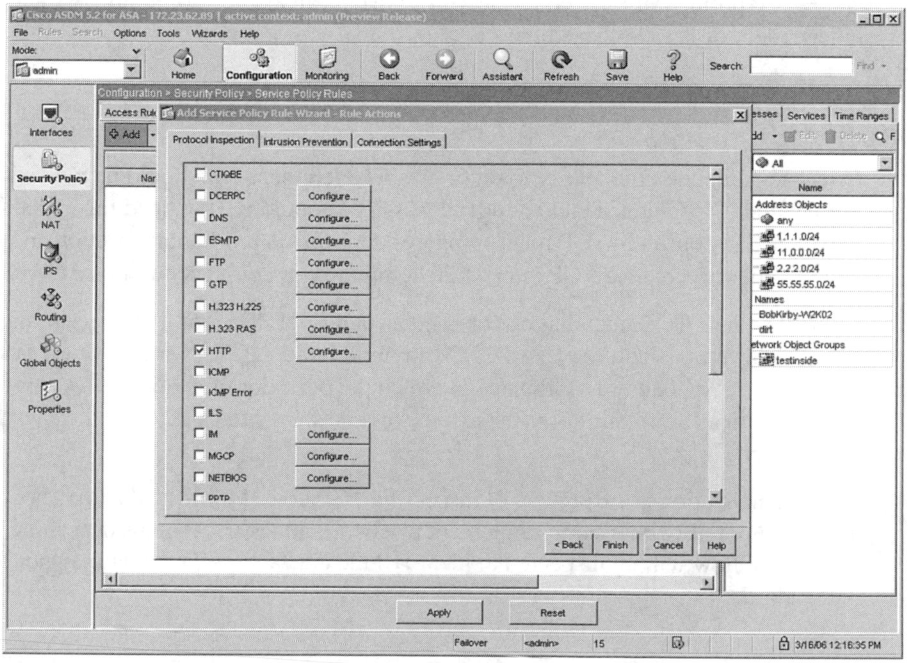

Several DDoS attacks send only part of the TCP handshake to initiate but never complete a TCP connection. This DDoS attack can result in a large TCP connection table that can consume resources that would otherwise go to servicing legitimate network traffic. The ASA supports the ability to configure a threshold for the maximum number of embryonic, or developing, connections that are allowed at one time by the appliance. Maximum connection parameters can provide protection against DDoS attacks on the ASA. The Maximum TCP and User Datagram Protocol (UDP) Connections field allows the ASA to configure a threshold of how many connections are active through the appliance at one time. The Maximum Embryonic Connections field controls the size of the internal state table for TCP connections.

The Randomize Sequence Number feature allows the ASA to create random, nonpredictable sequence numbers for TCP connections. The ability to randomize sequence numbers creates an additional layer of abstraction and protection against network attackers who endeavor to predict sequence numbers and masquerade as legitimate network connections. The Randomize Sequence Number feature is on by default.

As mentioned in the previous chapters, the DDoS Guard is typically deployed upstream close to the protected zone or servers. The ASA and DDoS Guard can provide a layered defense against DoS and DDoS attacks. Max Embryonic Connections and Randomize Sequence Number protection on the ASA can be the first line of defense, and the DDoS Guard can be second line of defense against the network attack.

A TCP Map is used to configure the customized inspection and protection for TCP connections. A TCP Map can be configured as part of the HTTP inspection to provide TCP and HTTP protection for web traffic. A TCP Map can also be configured separately and independent of HTTP inspection.

TCP Map

Cisco ASA features the ability to tailor how TCP connections should be policed and normalized. TCP maps dictate how TCP sessions should be managed for a specific traffic flow. You can configure TCP maps as part of application protocol inspection, as evidenced by the ability to create a TCP map while defining protocol inspection for HTTP.

To create a new TCP map that can be used as part of HTTP protocol inspection, select the connection settings and the **Use TCP Map** option under TCP Normalization as shown in Figure 3-18. You can use TCP maps to police the behavior of a connection to reduce vulnerabilities and to minimize the chance of a network attack through the specified TCP connection.

TCP normalization is the process of inspecting TCP flows for traffic that may not be normal and could possibly be used to implement a network attack. TCP maps determine what part of the TCP flow will be inspected to identify fields in TCP packets that may not be normal or standard.

Figure 3-19 displays an example of TCP Map configuration options.

Figure 3-18 *Use TCP Map*

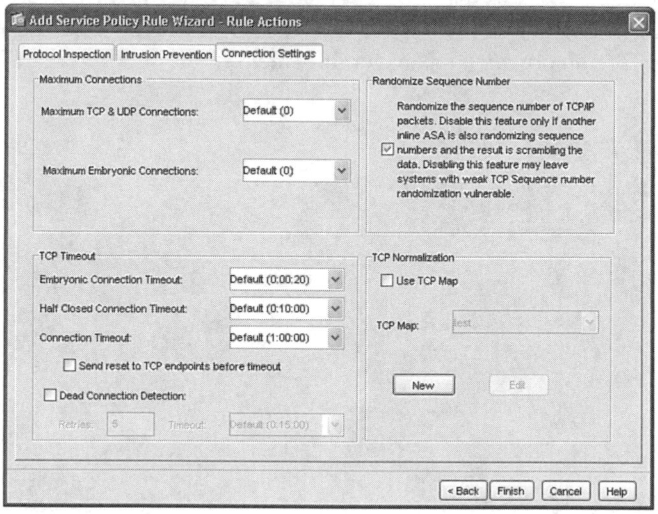

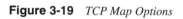

Figure 3-19 *TCP Map Options*

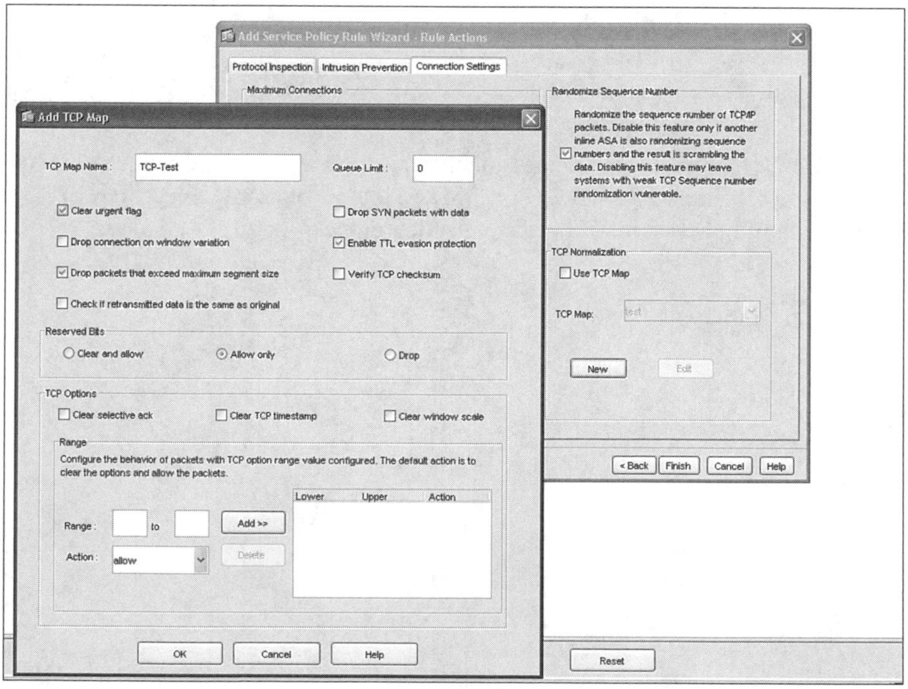

HTTP Map

Figure 3-20 displays an example of selecting protocol inspection for HTTP and the location to configure or select a customized HTTP map. An HTTP map is used to define the parameters of the inspection for HTTP. Multiple HTTP maps are allowed in order to have different HTTP normalization and enforcement rules for different traffic flows on different interfaces.

Figure 3-20 *Configure HTTP Map*

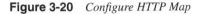

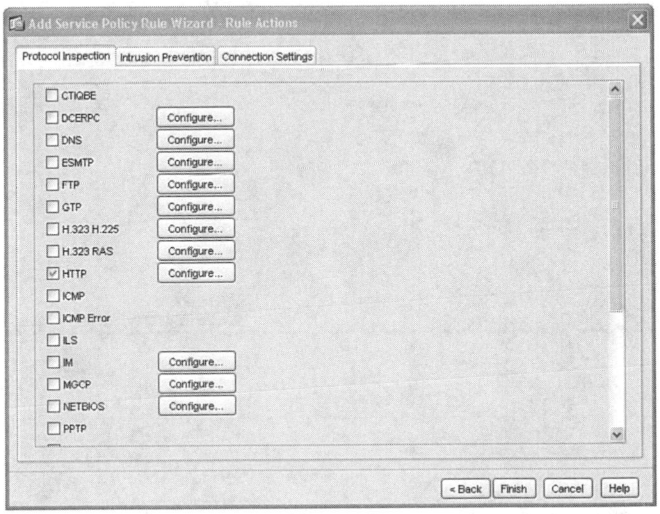

An HTTP map can be configured to allow customized or specific processing for an HTTP protocol violation. Figure 3-21 displays an example of how to select an HTTP Map and the location of how to initiate the customization process for an HTTP map.

Figure 3-21 *Select HTTP Map*

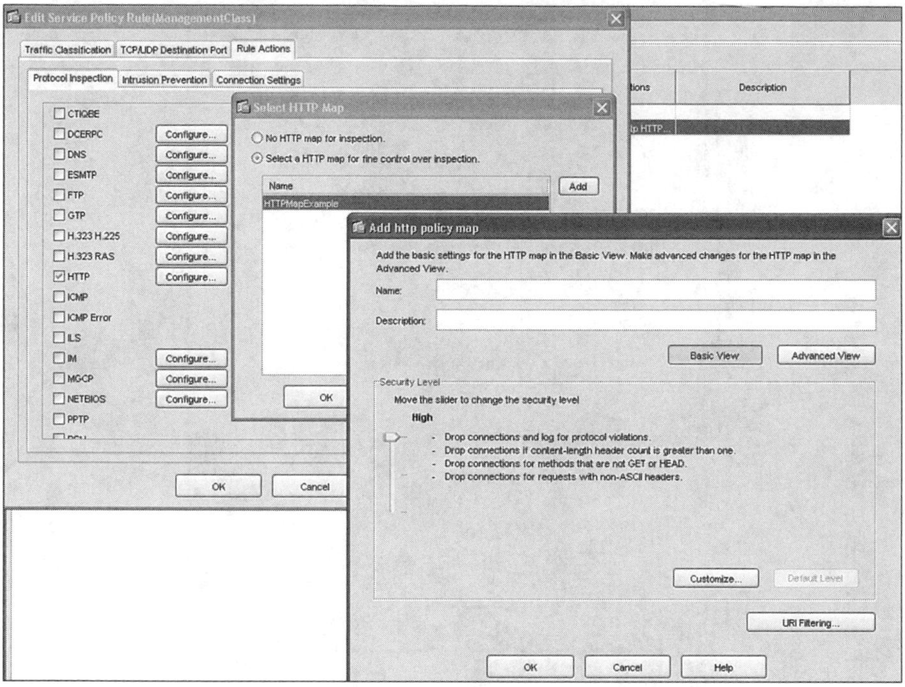

An HTTP connection can be allowed, reset, or dropped, depending on conformance to the RFC standard. A syslog can also be generated for an HTTP connection that triggers the defined condition. ASDM can reset any HTTP connection that does not conform to the HTTP protocol. This stance to reset an HTTP connection in an HTTP Map enables the ASA to be self-defending by automatically resetting the nonconforming or suspect HTTP connection that could be used for a potential network attack. Figure 3-22 displays an example of the customizable options under the basic view of an HTTP Map and the basic protocol violation parameters in an HTTP map.

Figure 3-22 *HTTP Map Protocol Violation Customization*

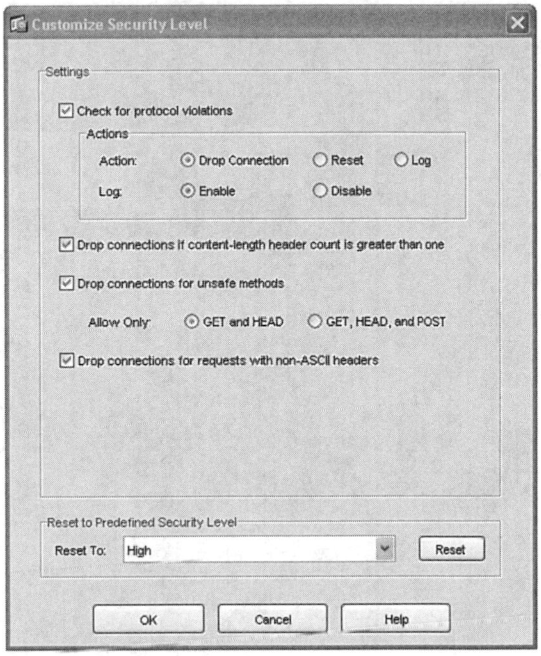

The advanced view of an HTTP Map allows additional customization features, including the ability to restrict certain content or application types in an HTTP connection. For example, Figure 3-23 displays an example of how an HTTP Map can be customized to prevent or block MP3 download through an HTTP connection.

Figure 3-23 *HTTP Content Type Inspection*

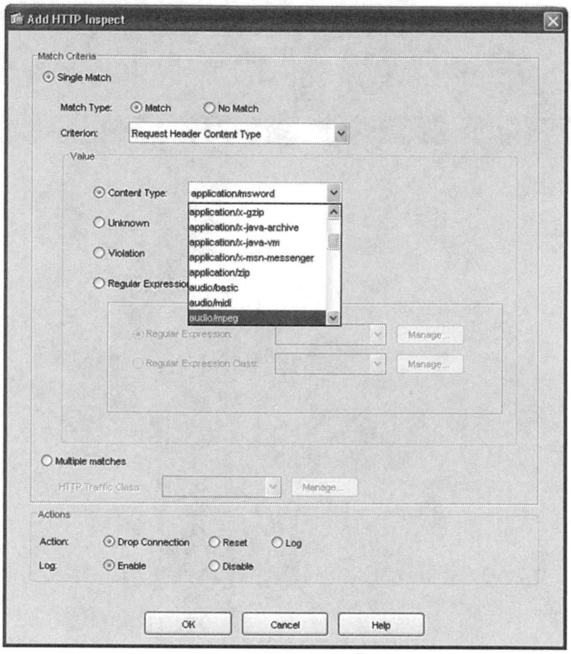

Figure 3-24 provides an example of a configured service policy rule to inspect TCP and HTTP traffic and references the corresponding TCP and HTTP maps.

Figure 3-24 *Service Policy Rule for TCP and HTTP Protocol Inspection*

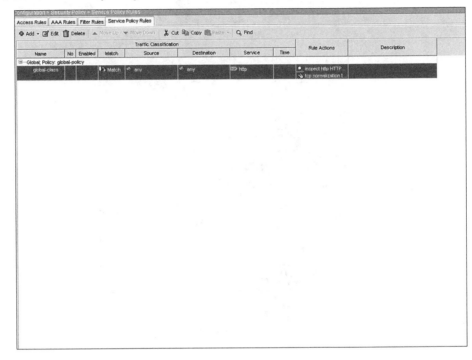

Configuring Content Security and Control Security

The partnership between Cisco Systems and Trend Micro has enabled the creation of the Content Security and Control Security Module for the ASA product line. This Content Security and Control Security Service Module (CSC-SSM) implements many of the advanced virus, phishing, spam, and spyware control functions on the ASA platform. The functions that are implemented on the CSC-SSM Module include the following:

- Antivirus
- Antiphishing
- Antispam
- Antispyware
- URL filtering/blocking
- Content filtering
- File blocking

The base CSC-SSM license contains support for the antivirus, antispyware, and file-blocking features. An additional plus license is required to enable the antiphishing, antispam, URL filtering/blocking, and content filtering features. You can implement these base and plus functions on the following network protocol types that are supported by the CSC-SSM module:

- POP3
- SMTP
- HTTP
- FTP

The CSC-SSM module can be managed with ASDM. The CSC-SSM module management through ASDM uses the IP address, username, and password for the CSC-SSM module. Figure 3-25 displays the Trend Micro Content Security icon in ASDM and the initial logon to the Content Security SSM. In addition to ASDM management, the CSC-SSM modules can also be centrally managed by Trend Micro's Trend Micro Control Manager (TMCM) centralized management product.

Figure 3-25 *Content Security Icon and CSC-SSM Logon in ASDM*

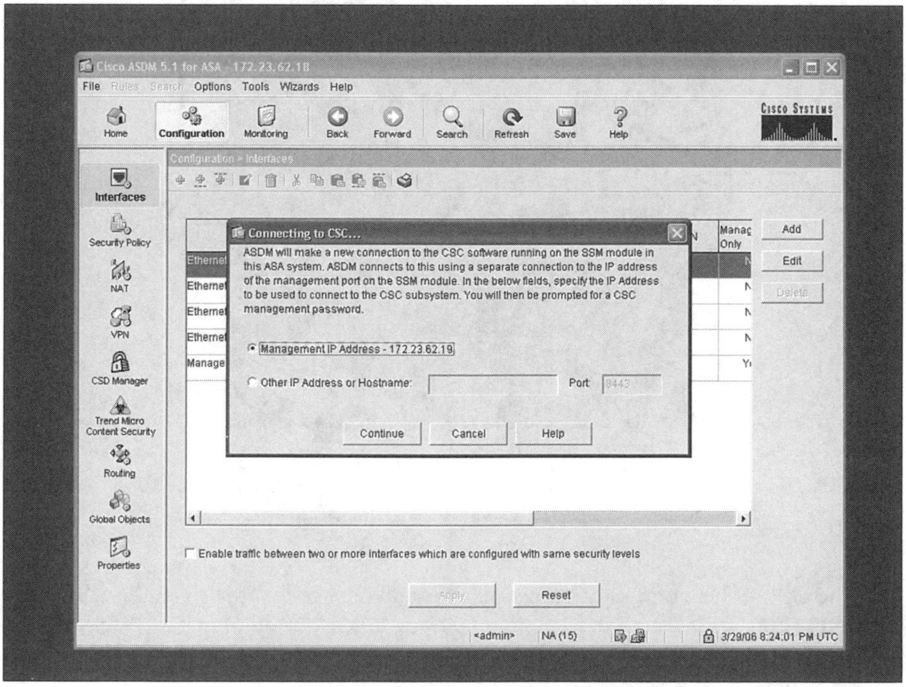

The main Content Security tab on the ASDM homepage features a near real-time update of the security threats that have been detected by the Content Security module. These security threats are divided into the following categories:

- Virus
- Spyware
- URL filtered/blocked
- Spam

Figure 3-26 displays the graphs in ASDM for virus detection. Similar threat graphs are also available for spyware detection, spam detection, and URL filtering/blocking protection. The threat graphs can be accessed from the Monitoring area in ASDM by selecting the Threat option under the Trend Micro Content Security icon.

Figure 3-26 *Threat Graphs*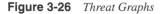

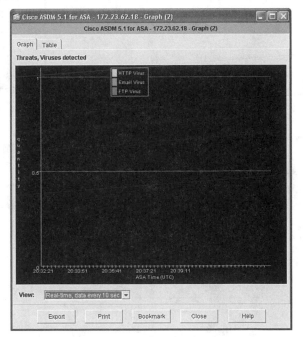

The CSC-SSM configuration process to send network traffic from the ASA chassis to the CSC-SSM is similar to that of other features in ASA, including the IPS-SSM module. CSC-SSM, like IPS-SSM, uses the service policy rules described earlier in the "Intrusion Prevention Service" and "Protocol Inspection" sections of this chapter to specify what network traffic should be sent from the ASA chassis to the CSC-SSM module. The user can initiate configuration of the CSC-SSM module by selecting Configuration from the top of

the ASDM GUI and then selecting the Trend Micro Content Security option from the left side of the ASDM GUI. Selecting the Configuration option for Trend Micro Content Security will result in the display of the items that can be configured on the CSC-SSM module including Content Security and Control Services Module (CSC-SSM) setup, web (URL filtering/blocking), mail (scanning, content filtering, antispam), file transfers (scanning, blocking), and updates.

Content Security and Control Services Module (CSC-SSM) Setup

CSC Setup options include the following:

- Activation/license
- IP configuration
- Host/notification settings
- Management access host/networks
- Password
- Setup Wizard

The CSC-SSM Setup Wizard walks the user through each of the CSC-SSM setup steps. Figure 3-27 displays CSC Setup options in the GUI and the launch point for the Setup Wizard screen of the CSC-SSM Setup Wizard.

Figure 3-27   *CSC-SSM Setup Wizard*

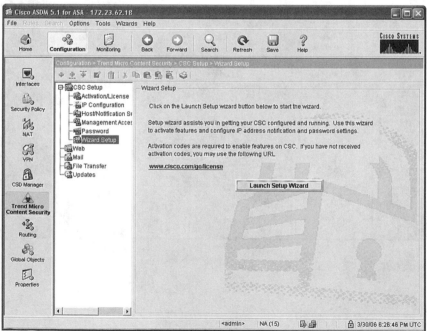

Web

The CSC-SSM module features the following web or HTTP functions:

- URL blocking (antiphishing and antispyware)
- URL filtering
- HTTP/web scanning
- File blocking

The configuration of these web features requires ASDM to launch the integrated Trend Micro InterScan for Cisco CSC-SSM management.

Trend Micro InterScan requires an additional password to be entered to log on. Figure 3-28 displays the web options in ASDM for CSC-SSM, and Figure 3-29 provides the resulting logon screen to Trend Micro InterScan. Figure 3-30 displays the Summary page in Trend Micro InterScan, which can be displayed after logon to Trend Micro InterScan from ASDM.

Figure 3-28 *Trend Micro Content Security Options*

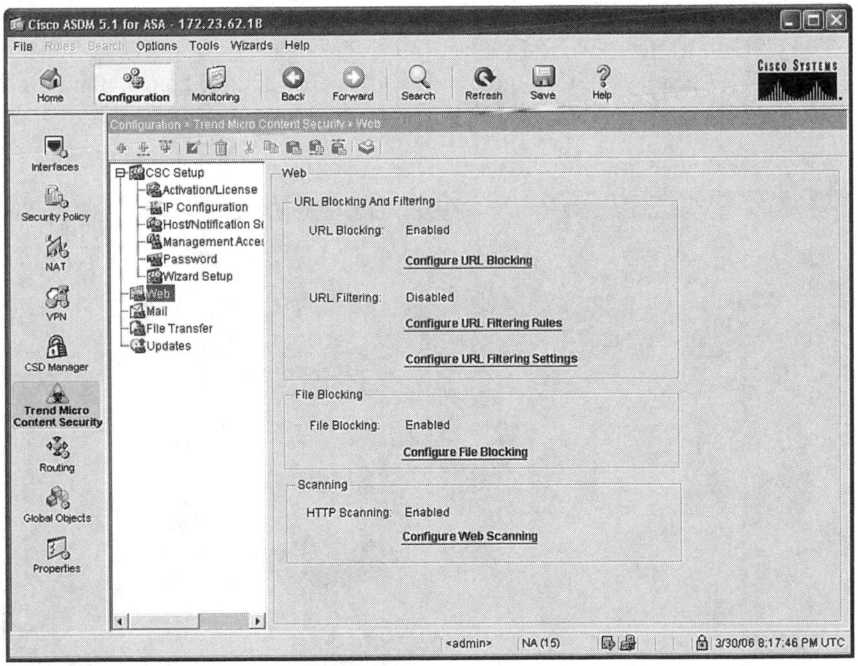

Figure 3-29   *Log on to Trend Micro InterScan for Cisco CSC-SSM*

TREND MICRO™ InterScan™ for Cisco CSC SSM

TREND MICRO
InterScan for Cisco CSC SSM

Please type your password to access the product console.

Password: [_____] [Log on]

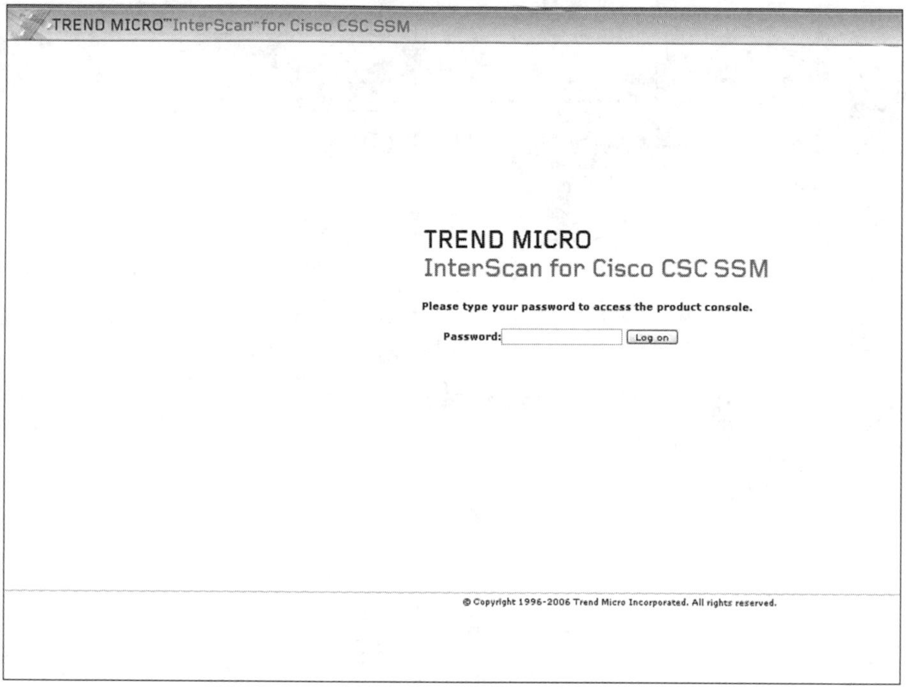

Figure 3-30   *Trend Micro InterScan Summary*

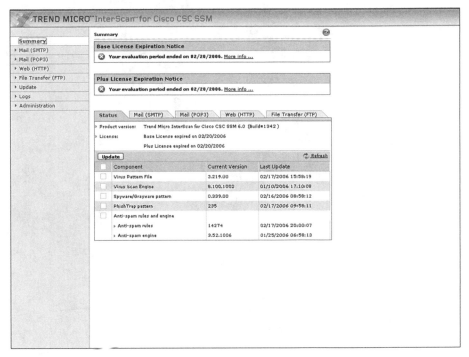

URL Blocking

URL Blocking allows a specific URL to be blocked, thus preventing a user from accessing a specific website or webpage. ASDM, through the launch of the integrated Trend Micro InterScan Device Manager, allows the URL blocking feature to be configured including blocking on wildcards and the ability to always allow a specific list of URLs.

Figure 3-31 displays the location to select web URL blocking configuration and the resulting configuration options that are displayed in Trend Micro InterScan.

Figure 3-31 *URL Blocking in Trend Micro InterScan*

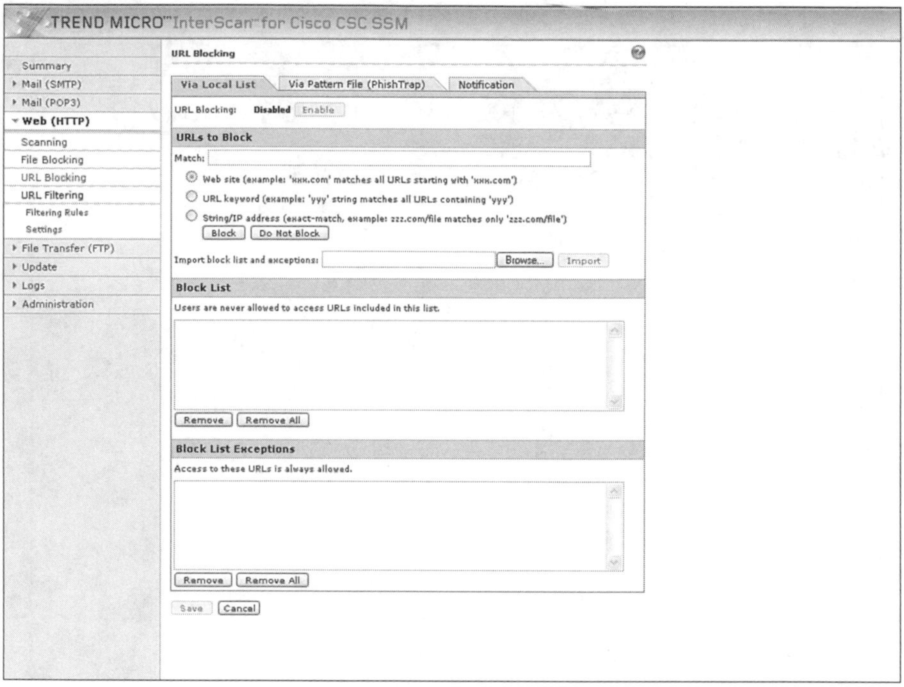

Phishing is a type of malware with which an e-mail is sent to an unsuspecting user with a link to a fake website. These phishing e-mails can attempt to trick the user to log on to what appears to be a valid banking or e-commerce site. However, what the user is really logging on to is a fake website, and the attacker's purpose is the gathering of the user's account information.

Trend Micro collects and maintains a list of these phishing or fake websites. The CSC-SSM module can block the HTTP connection and protect the user from accessing one of these known phishing websites. Trend Micro also collects a list of known websites that harbor spyware. Network attackers often plant spyware on more vulnerable websites and attempt to download spyware to unsuspecting users that frequent these websites. The CSC-SSM module also features the ability to block URL access to prevent users from accessing one of these known websites that are rife with spyware.

Figure 3-32 provides an example of how antiphishing and antispyware can be enabled for URL inspection through the ASA CSC-SSM. Figure 3-32 also displays how you can identify a specific phishing site and update Trend Micro's phishing sites list.

Figure 3-32 *Antiphishing and Antispyware*

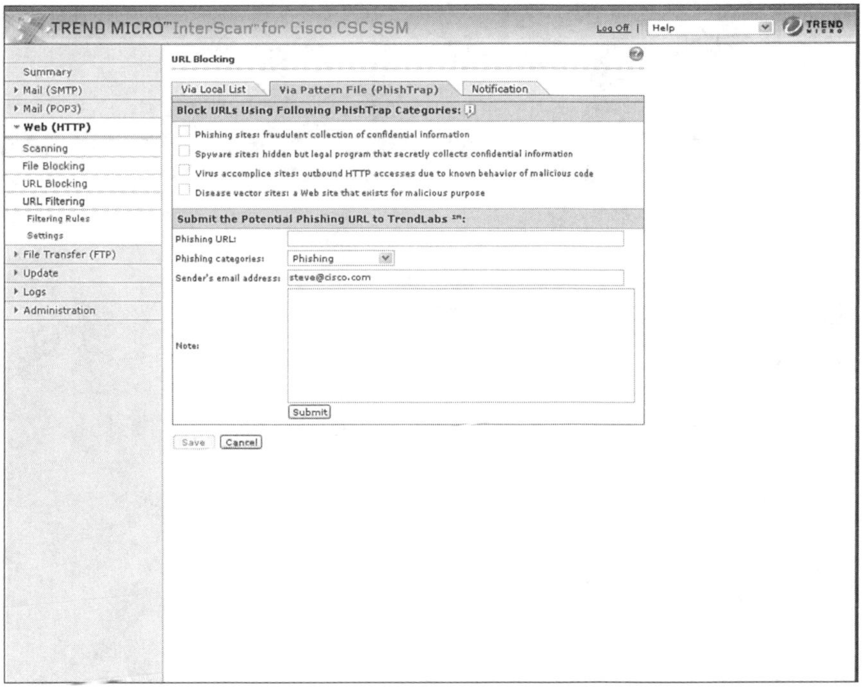

URL Filtering

CSC-SSM supports the use of predefined types of websites that can be filtered, including entertainment, gambling, job search, and so on. The websites within these categories are updated and maintained through Trend Micro. These categories of websites can also be filtered based upon the time of day to permit certain sites during leisure time but not during standard work hours.

Scanning

Scanning enables the CSC-SSM module to scan HTTP traffic, including that for web mail, and to detect and remove certain viruses or spyware that could be used to implement a network attack. CSC-SSM also features the ability to clean an infected file or to delete the infected file before it is transported to the user over the scanned HTTP or web connection.

File Blocking

File blocking enables certain file types or file extensions to be blocked so they are not transported over an HTTP or web download connection. File types that can be blocked include MP3, JPG, EXE, java, and Microsoft Office applications.

Mail

CSC-SSM can provide protection for the POP3 and SMTP mail protocols. The CSC-SSM module supports the following mail security functions for incoming and outgoing POP3 and SMTP network traffic:

- Scanning
- Spam protection
- Content filtering

Scanning

Scanning allows incoming and outgoing e-mail to be scanned for viruses, spyware, and other malware. Infected attachments can be either cleaned or deleted before they are delivered to the user.

Figure 3-33 displays an example of configuring virus and other malware scanning for incoming SMTP mail.

Figure 3-33 *Scanning Configuration for Incoming SMTP Mail*

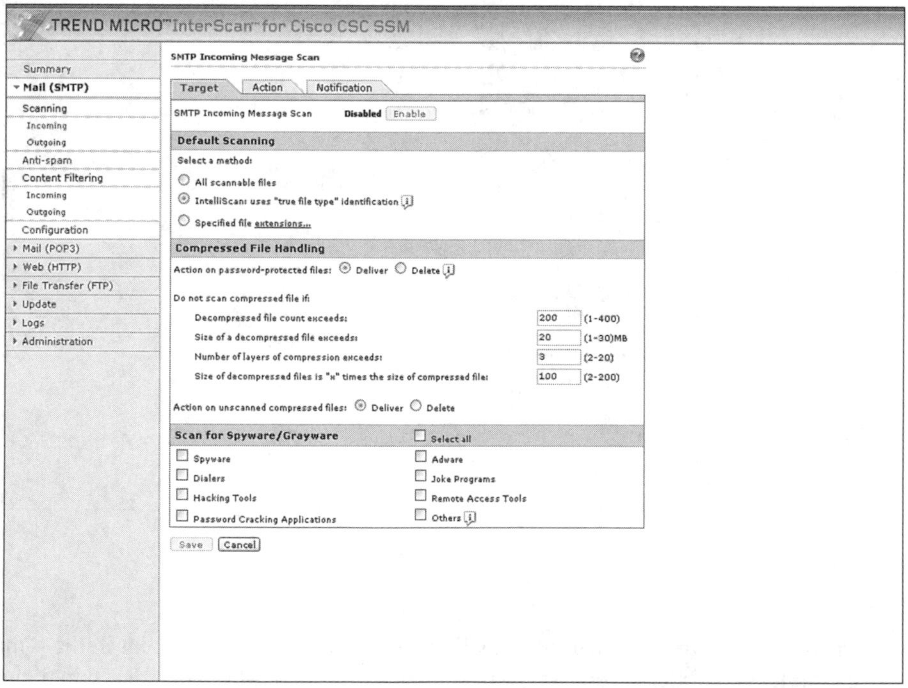

Antispam

The Mail configuration option in Trend Micro InterScan for CSC-SSM also contains the ability to protect e-mail users from spam. Spam messages can contain a potential network threat, in addition to being a nuisance. The antispam capability in ASA CSC-SSM can both reduce the exposure to spam-based network attacks and increase productivity by reducing spam to users of a network.

The antispam capability enables the administrator to define spam threshold buckets of high, medium, or low. The easy-to-use configuration of Antispam through the integration of ASDM and Trend Micro InterScan also enables the administrator to permit specific e-mail sources or block specific e-mail sources/spammers. Figure 3-34 displays the Antispam configuration options of ASA CSC-SSM.

Figure 3-34 *Antispam Configuration*

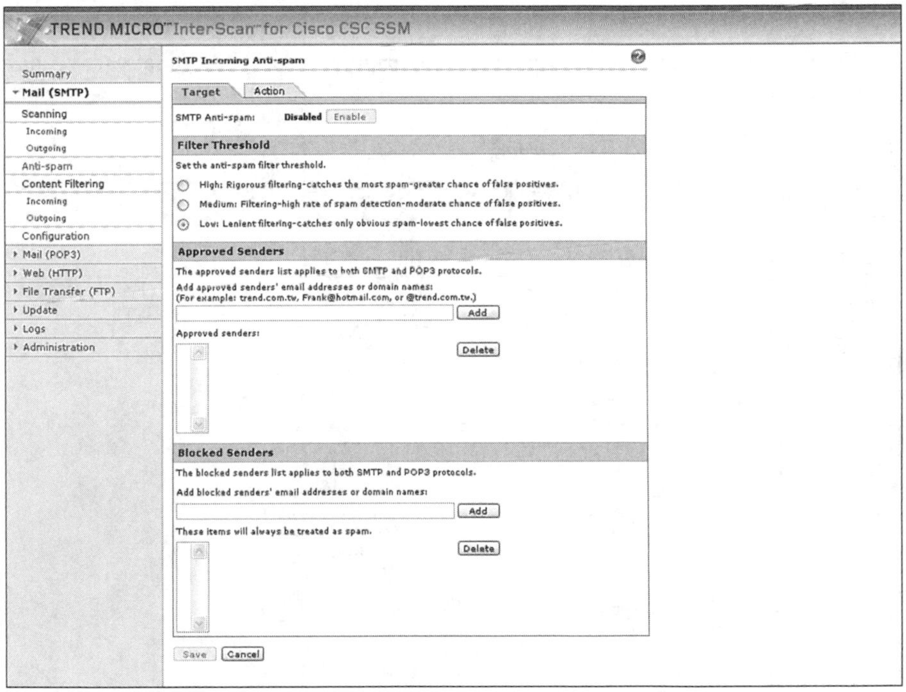

Content Filtering

The CSC-SSM module can filter mail based upon the type of content in the e-mail. For example, mail that exceeds a certain size can be filtered. Mail with a certain filename on an attachment or an attachment of a certain file type, like MP3, JPG, or EXE, can also be

filtered or removed from an e-mail before delivery to the user. Figure 3-35 displays an example of the content filtering options.

Figure 3-35   *Content Filtering Configuration*

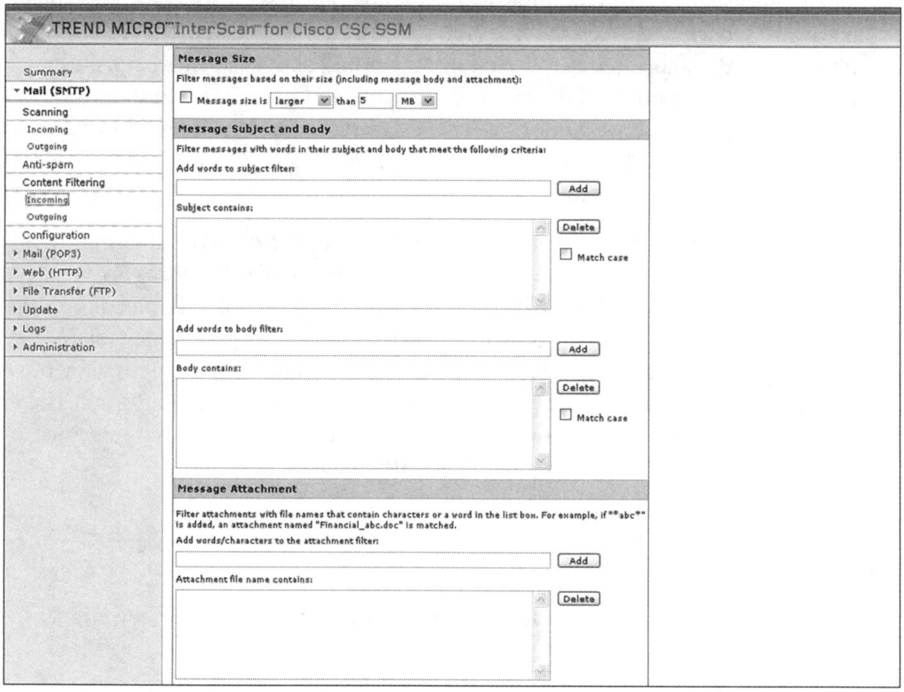

File Transfer

CSC-SSM provides protection for file transfers using FTP. CSC-SSM allows both the scanning of FTP network traffic for viruses and other malware and the blocking of file transfers based upon file types. File types that can be blocked include MP3, JPG, EXE, Java, and Microsoft Office file extensions. The file transfer, or FTP, scanning, and blocking configuration options are very similar to the web scanning and file blocking features described in the "web" section for CSC-SSM in this chapter.

Summary

The Cisco ASA product line offers an extensive list of security features in a single appliance, including firewall, antispoofing, protocol inspection, VPN, IPS, content security, and control security. IPS, content security, and control security are implemented as a hardware security services module (AIP-SSM and CSC-SSM). The CSC-SSM module implements advanced security functions, including antivirus, antispam, antiphishing, URL filtering and blocking, and file transfer scanning and blocking. The extensible architecture of the ASA product line, combined with the partnership with Trend Micro on the Content Security and Control Security Service Module (CSC-SSM), enable the ASA product to be the platform for future security innovations.

The different footprint, capacity, and price points of the ASA product line enable the ASA to be used in both remote branches and the data center. ASA features an easy-to-use device manager, ASDM, that allows new users to get up-to-speed quickly on configuring the ASA. ASA is also centrally managed by the Cisco Security Manager, which enables hundreds of ASA appliances to be managed with thousands of routers for a single view of security configuration, integration, and enforcement between these two platforms. The Cisco Security Manager can also centrally manage the IPS signature configuration on the ASA AIP-SSM module along with other Cisco IPS devices.

References

Abelar, Greg. Securing Your Business with Cisco ASA and PIX Firewalls. Cisco Press, 2005.

Cisco Systems, Inc. Cisco Adaptive Security Appliance Command Line Configuration Guide, Version 7.0. http://www.cisco.com/en/US/products/ps6120/products_configuration_guide_chapter09186a00804522f6.html

Cisco Systems, Inc. Cisco Security Appliance Command Reference, Version 7.0 http://cisco.com/application/pdf/en/us/guest/products/ps6120/c2001/ccmigration_09186a0080666332.pdf

Cisco Systems, Inc. Content Security and Control SSM Administrator Guide. http://www.cisco.com/en/US/partner/products/ps6120/products_administration_guide_book09186a00805ac11d.html (Requires Cisco.com registration.)

Cisco Incident Control Service

Cisco and Trend Micro have partnered to create several security components. One component of the partnership is the antivirus signatures in Cisco Intrusion Prevention System (IPS) products. Another component of the partnership is the Content Security and Control Security Services Module for the Adaptive Security Appliance (ASA) as discussed in Chapter 3, "Cisco Adaptive Security Appliance Overview." A third component of the partnership is the automatic download of access lists and new incident signatures for attacks such as worms and viruses from Trend Micro to Cisco router, ASA, and IPS devices. The download of access lists and signatures for new security incidents from Trend Micro helps to enable Cisco networks to be self-defending against new network attacks. Cisco Incident Control Service (Cisco ICS) manages the worm and virus access list and signature download service from Trend Micro.

Cisco ICS enables the automatic or manual download of access lists and IPS signatures to security devices. The download of access lists from Trend Micro can enable a new attack to be identified and stopped or slowed in less than one hour. Trend Micro maintains a database of new attacks, such as worms. Trend Micro, through the Cisco ICS and the service with Trend Micro, attempts to define an access list that will stop the new network worm within one hour of the discovery of the worm. This access list provides the broad protection against the worm, while Trend Micro creates a specific, custom signature to stop the worm. Trend Micro attempts to define a custom signature to stop the incident within several hours of identifying the incident or worm. This signature can also be either automatically or manually downloaded to the IPS device to stop the newly identified network incident.

Chapter 3 discusses the ASA appliance with support for IPS signatures, access lists, and antivirus protection. Cisco ICS, with the update service from Trend Micro, provides an extra layer of protection in the self-defending network by deploying or recommending access lists and IPS signatures when a new network outbreak such as a worm is identified. In addition to using TrendLabs to identify a new network attack, Cisco ICS also is a product in the self-defending network that focuses on worm mitigation.

This chapter describes the role of Cisco ICS in controlling network incidents and explains the different options, including outbreak prevention access control lists (OPACLs), outbreak prevention signatures (OPSigs), outbreak prevention reports, and logs.

Implementing Outbreak Management with Cisco ICS

Cisco ICS is a centralized management product from Cisco that manages the automated IPS signature update service with Trend Micro for new security incidents. Cisco ICS can deploy a broad access control lists (ACLs) to stop the spread of a newly identified infection through the network. These ACLs are known as OPACLs.

After analysis of the new network incident by Trend Micro, Cisco ICS can also deploy a specific signature to mitigate a new network infection outbreak such as a worm. These signatures are known as OPSigs. OPSigs can be deployed to IOS routers with IPS signatures and other Cisco IPS systems.

The first step in the ICS system is the identification of a new network threat. After a network threat is identified, Trend Micro will post on its website the information required to mitigate or reduce the impact of the network attack. The typical list of events that transpires to control the network incident includes the following items:

1 Trend Micro's TrendLabs identifies a new network threat or attack.

2 Trend Micro's TrendLabs creates an outbreak management task file. This outbreak management task file contains a broad OPACL that will prevent the outbreak from spreading throughout the network.

3 Cisco ICS can automatically download this outbreak management task file for the new network threat.

4 The OPACL in the task file can be either automatically deployed or manually deployed after human intervention. There is also an exception list that will prevent Cisco ICS from applying an ACL for a specific port for common network traffic, such as HTTP (TCP Port 80).

5   TrendLabs releases an OPSig to enable IPS devices to detect the new network threat. Typically the OPSig is released within a few hours of the release of the outbreak management task file with the OPACL.

6   Cisco ICS downloads the OPSig, either automatically or manually.

7   The original OPACL expires after the download of the OPSig.

8   Cisco ICS uses IPS events to determine if a host is sending network traffic that is considered to be a network threat and could possibly be infected. If a host is determined to be infected, the infected host is added to the watch list in Cisco ICS.

Cisco ICS is a Windows server application, and the client GUI is a web browser. Internet Explorer is required as the web browser since ActiveX is used as part of the client GUI. The logon screen for the Cisco ICS is displayed in Figure 4-1.

Figure 4-1   *Cisco ICS Logon*

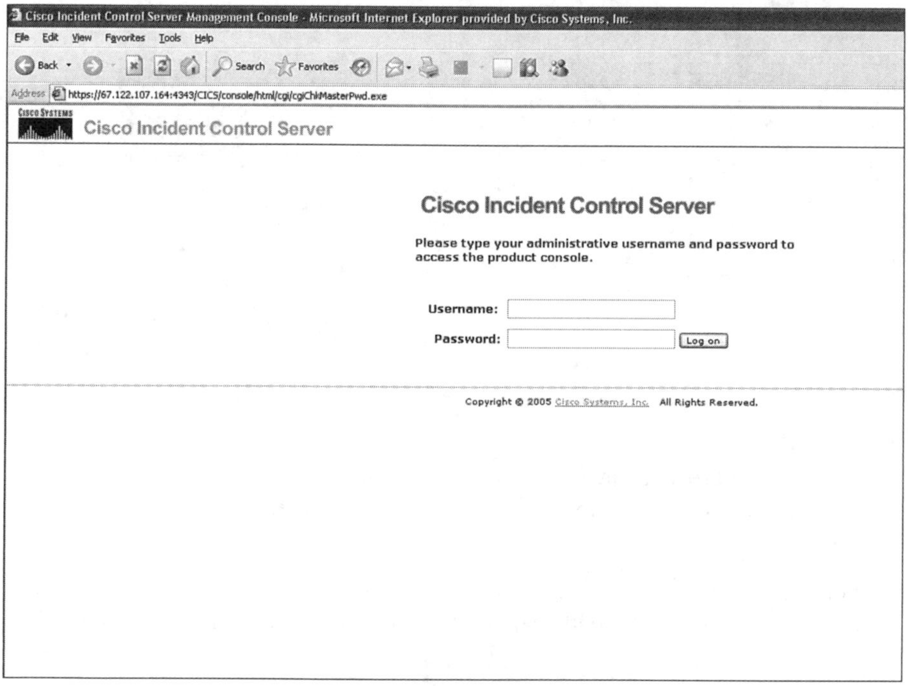

Outbreak Management Summary

The Cisco ICS summary page shown in Figure 4-2 provides a summary of the tasks to manage a network outbreak. The Outbreak Management Summary page is divided into the following areas:

- Active Outbreak Management Tasks
- Automatic Outbreak Management Tasks
- OPACL
- OPSigs

Figure 4-2 *Cisco ICS Summary Page*

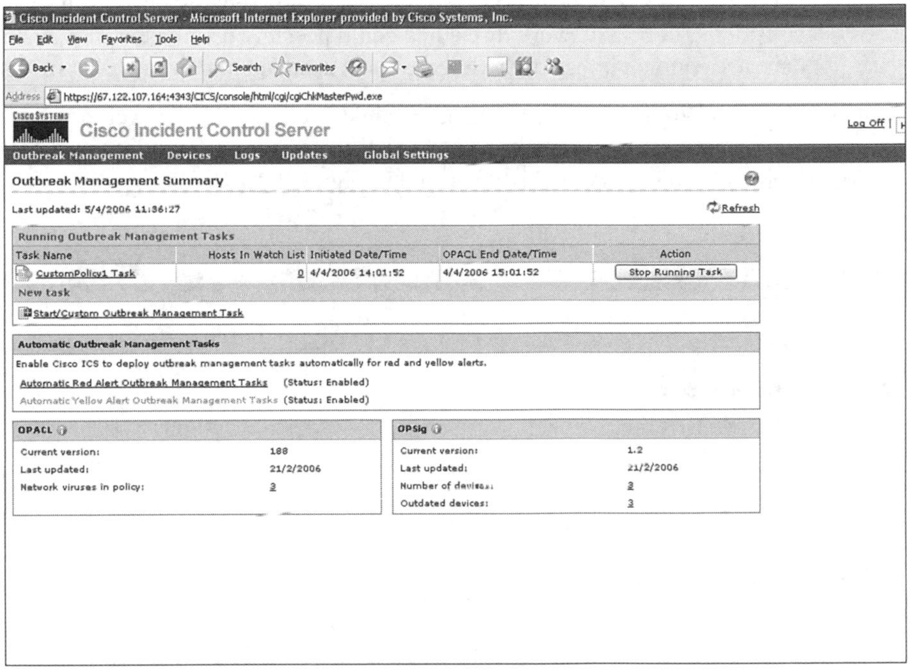

Any new outbreak management tasks are highlighted at the top of the Active Outbreak Management Tasks. The location to select a new outbreak management task is displayed in Figure 4-3.

Selecting a new outbreak management task results in the display of network threats with the new threat or corresponding outbreak management task selected, as shown in Figure 4-4.

Figure 4-3   *Selecting a New Outbreak Management Task*

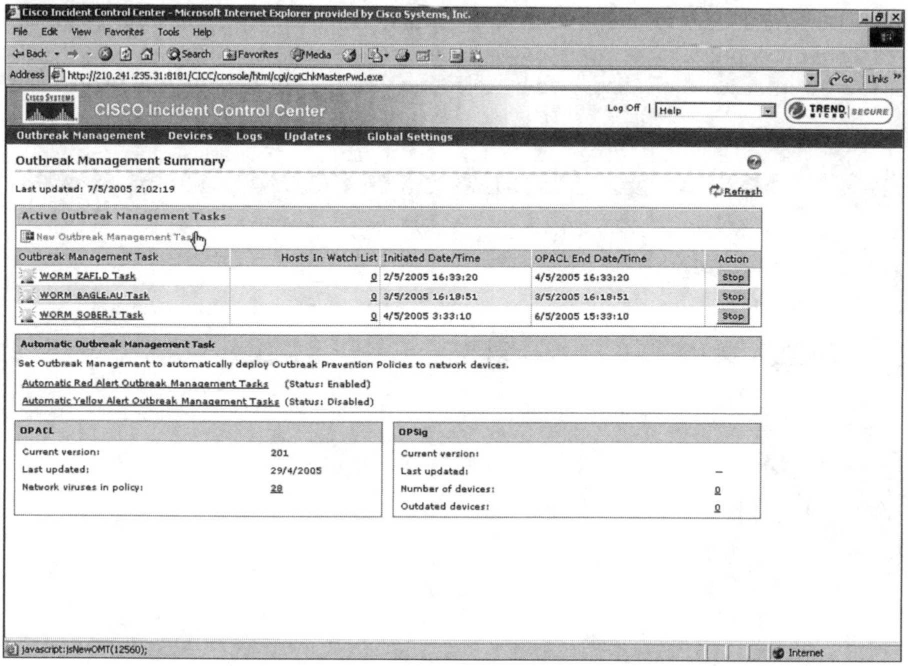

Figure 4-4   *Selecting Name of Threat*

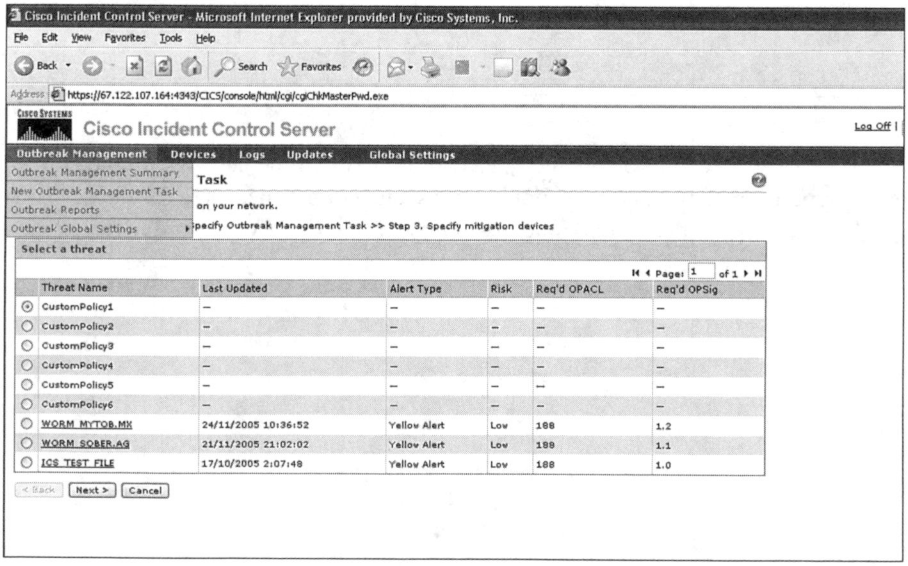

Information and Statistics on Network Threats from Trend Micro

Each threat name contains a link to information about that threat from Trend Micro. Figure 4-5 provides an overview of the network threat from Trend Micro. The network threat information is displayed by selecting the name of the threat or incident.

Figure 4-5 *Overview of Threat*

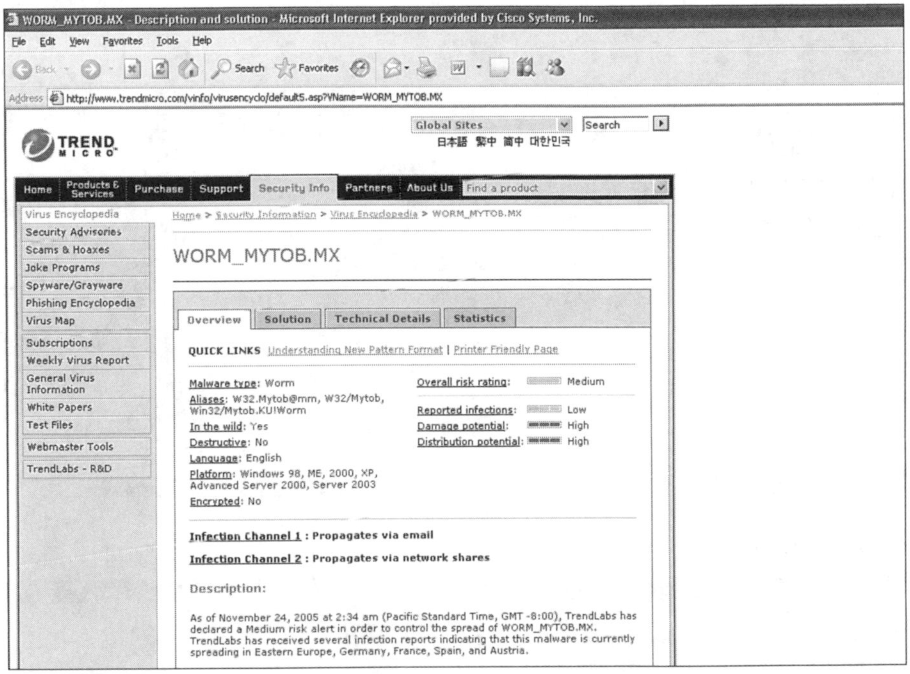

The overview can also contain a behavior diagram of the network threat. A behavior diagram can contain actions, implications, and countermeasures for the network threat. Figure 4-6 provides an example of a behavior diagram from Trend Micro.

Figure 4-6   *Behavior Diagram of Threat*

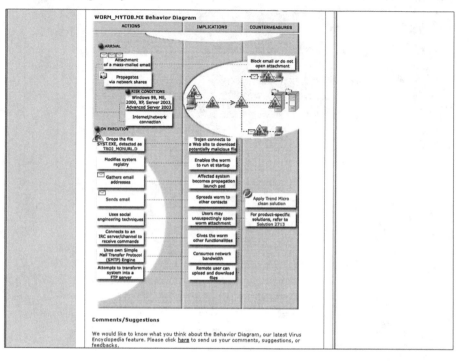

The security information about the threat from Trend Micro can also contain technical details of the network threat. Figure 4-7 shows a technical details sample.

Figure 4-7 *Technical Details of Threat*

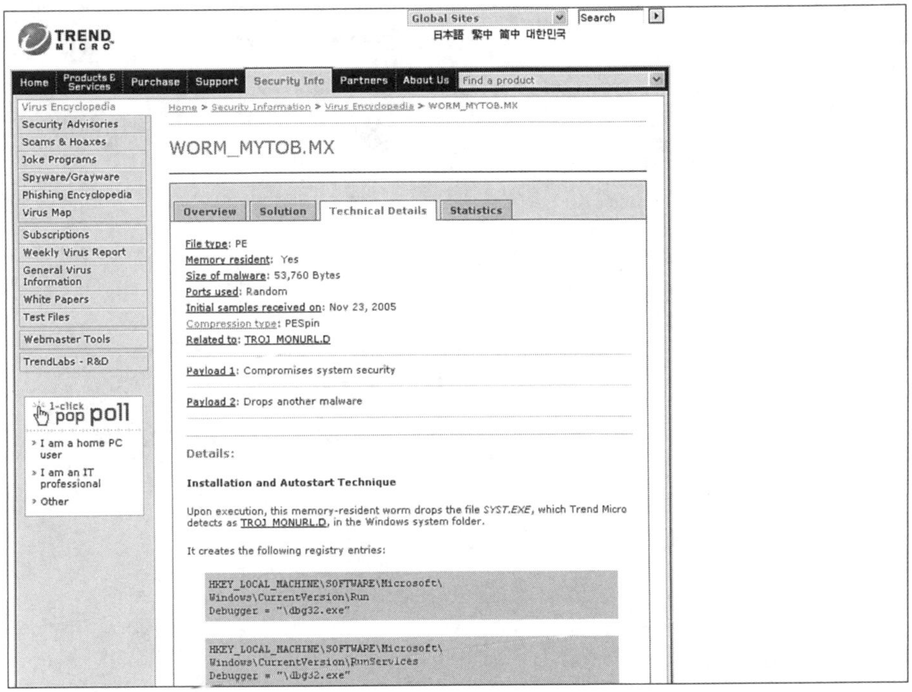

Statistics of the threat are also provided in the security information from Trend Micro. Information like the number of computers infected by the network threat and a one-day trend of how many computers are infected by the threat can be provided in the Statistics option. These statistics tend to be global and based upon aggregate information from Trend Micro. Figure 4-8 displays an example of statistics on a network threat.

Figure 4-8   *Statistics of Threat*

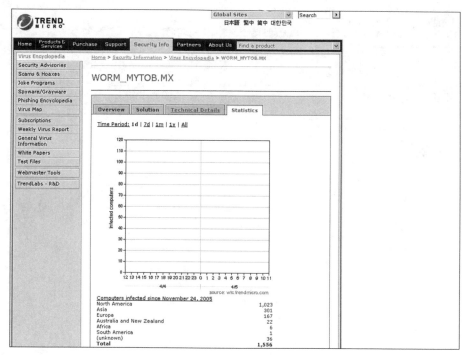

New Outbreak Management Task

Selecting Next from the New Outbreak Management Task list in Figure 4-4 displays information about the recommended OPACL deployment to stop the network attack. OPACL information includes the time or end date at which the OPACL should expire, the ability to configure a custom OPACL, and the ability to view the OPACL configuration. An example of a display of this OPACL information for a new outbreak management task is provided in Figure 4-9.

Figure 4-9 *OPACL Information for Threat*

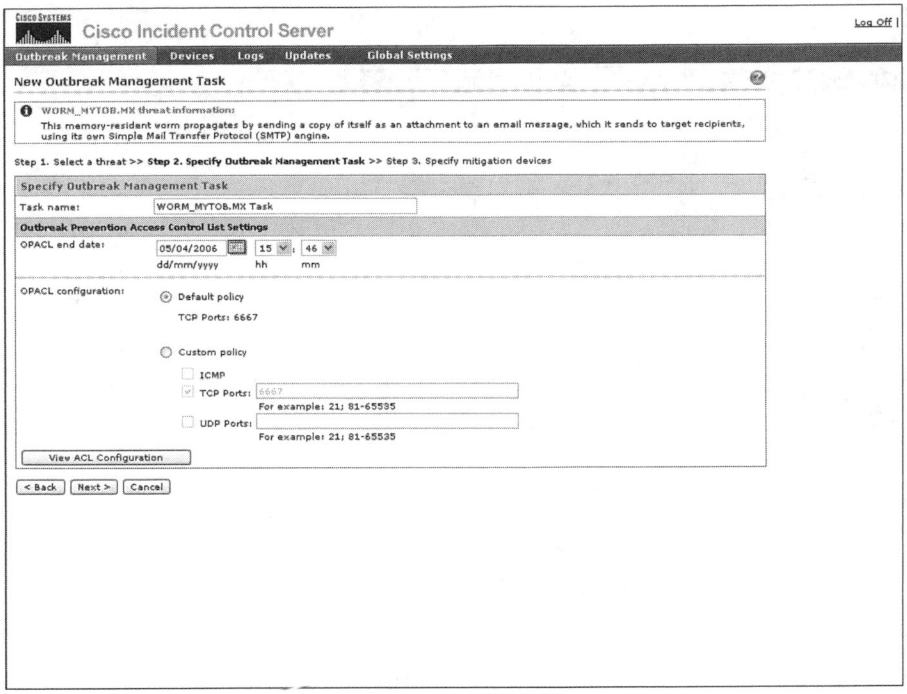

The next step in setting up a new outbreak management task is defining the target devices that will receive the OPACL. The wizard, by default, will select a default set of devices with an option to change the set of target devices. An example of the target device configuration for the OPACL is provided in Figure 4-10.

Figure 4-10 *Select Target Device for OPACL*

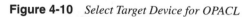

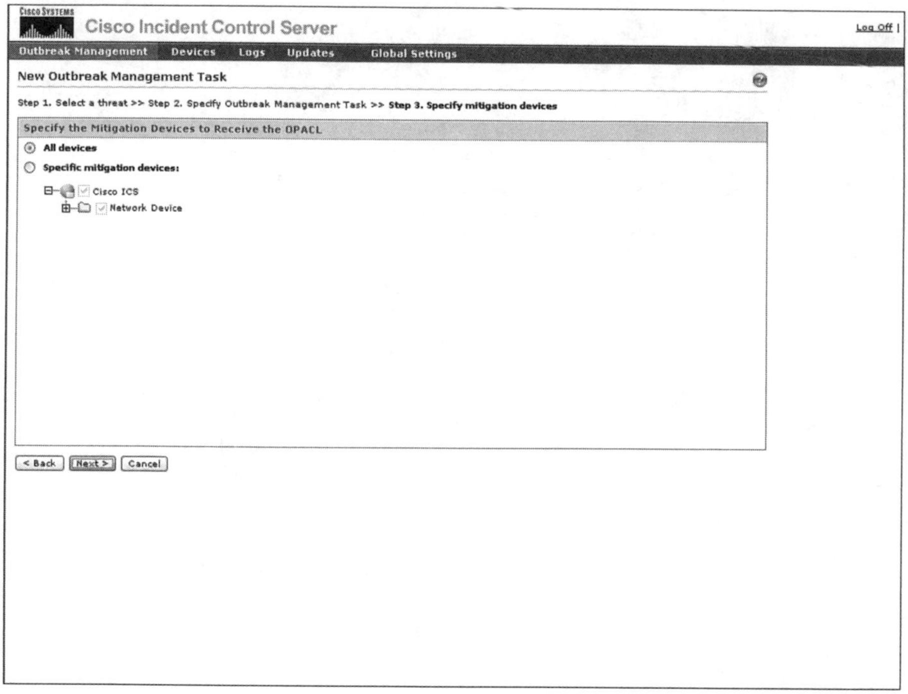

Selecting the target devices and then clicking Finish will result in the running of a new outbreak management task. Figure 4-11 displays an example of a summary that indicates that a New Outbreak Management Task is now running.

Figure 4-11 *New Outbreak Management Task Running*

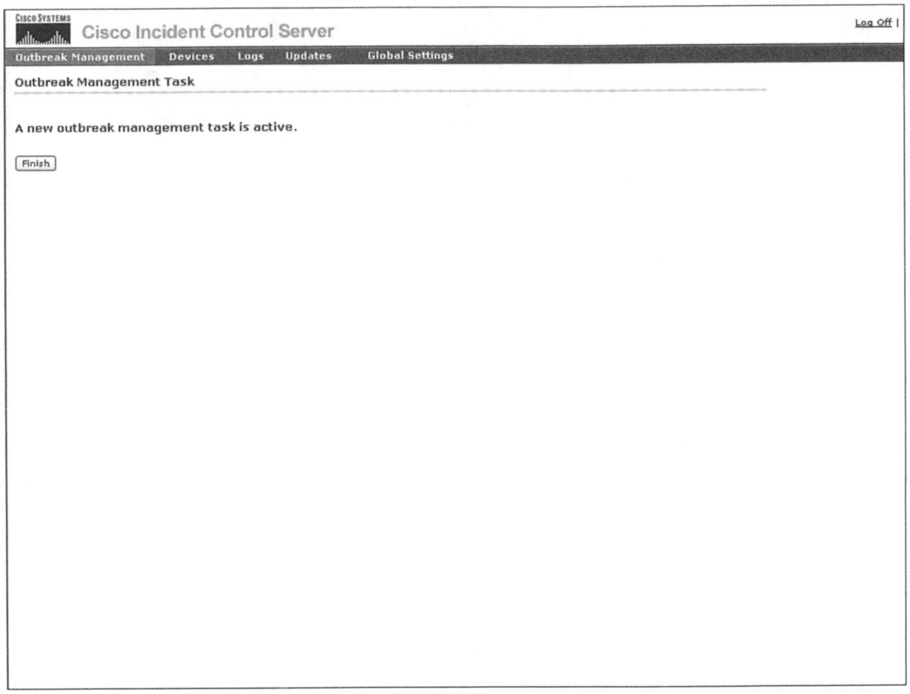

The network threat that was identified in the New Outbreak Management Task list should now be listed in the Outbreak Management Task List. Information for each network threat in the Outbreak Management Task List includes the following:

- Task name
- Hosts in watch list
- Initiated date/time
- OPACL end date/time
- Action to stop task

You can stop an outbreak management task by clicking the Stop button in the Action column, as shown in Figure 4-12.

Cisco ICS features the ability to recommend an OPACL or to automatically deploy an OPACL in the event of a detected network threat. Cisco ICS enables the automatic deployment option to be configured by type of alert. These alerts can be divided into two classes: red and yellow. Red alerts are more mission-critical, whereas yellow alerts are less impactful.

Figure 4-12 *Stop Management Task*

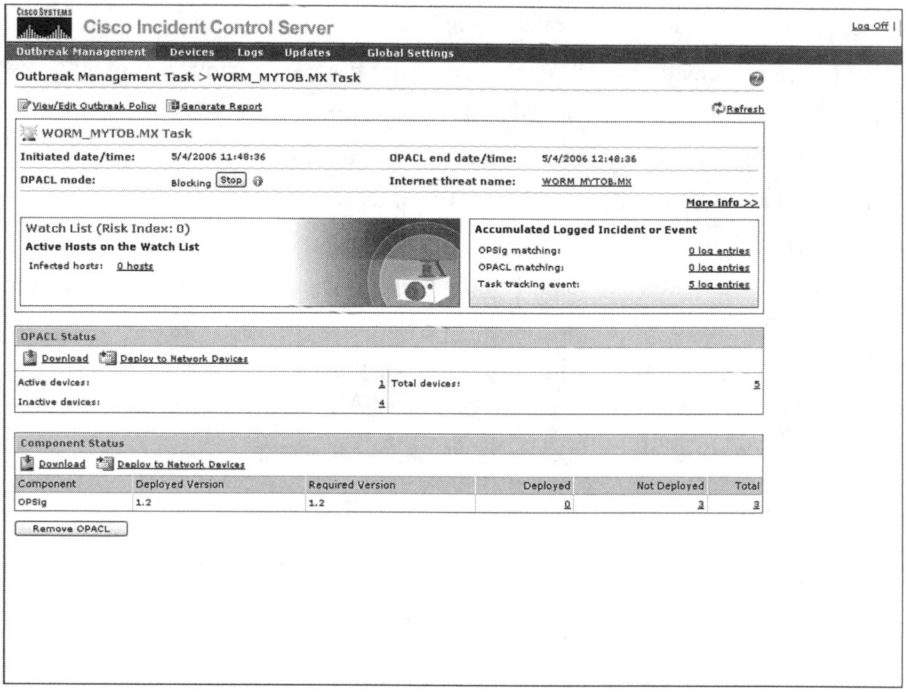

Figure 4-13 displays how the task automation default status per red and yellow alert class is shown to the user.

Figure 4-13 *Automated Outbreak Management Alert Level*

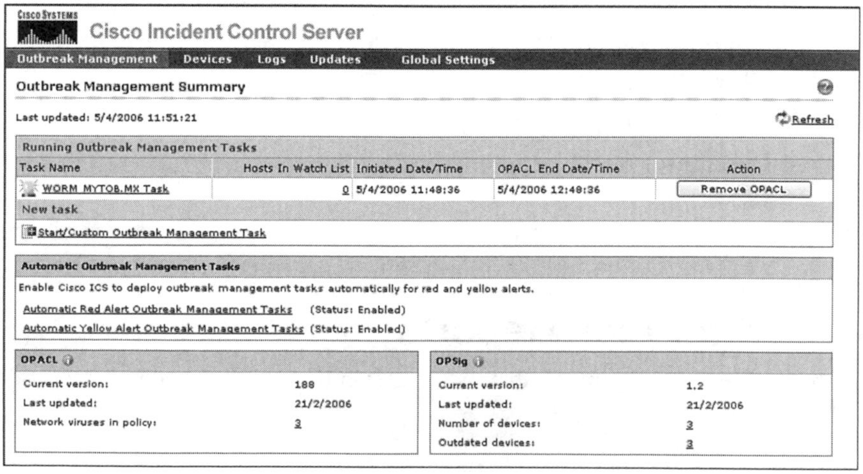

Outbreak Settings

Specific parameters for outbreak settings include the following:

- Automatically stop OPACL when OPSig has been deployed
- Automatically overwrite OPACL settings for new OPACL
- Enable automated outbreak management task for red and yellow alerts
- End OPACL after a specific number of days
- Default target devices for OPACL deployment

Figure 4-14 provides an example of the configurable outbreak settings for automated task deployment.

Figure 4-14 *Automatic Outbreak Management Tasks Outbreak Settings*

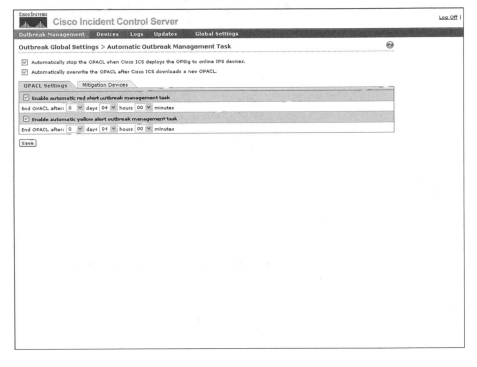

Displaying Outbreak Reports

The Outbreak Management tab provides a drop-down link to outbreak reports, as shown in Figure 4-15.

Figure 4-15   *Select Outbreak Reports*

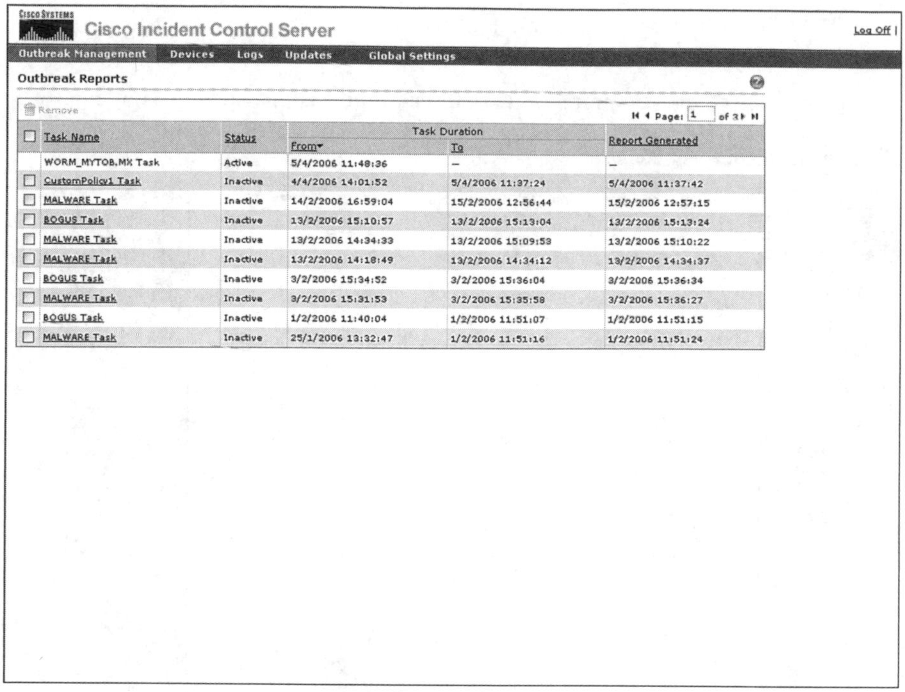

The selection of the incident or worm from the Outbreak Management Task from this list will display the outbreak report for that outbreak management task. Information in outbreak reports includes the following:

- Executive summary
- Initiated date and time
- OPACL end date and time
- OPACL mode
- Threat name
- Alert type
- Threat information
- Risk index graph
- Hosts on watch list
- Infected hosts
- IPS virus incident status
- OPACL matching status

- Accumulated log incident
- OPACL status
- Service component status

An example of the beginning of an outbreak report is provided in Figure 4-16.

Figure 4-16 *Sample of Outbreak Report*

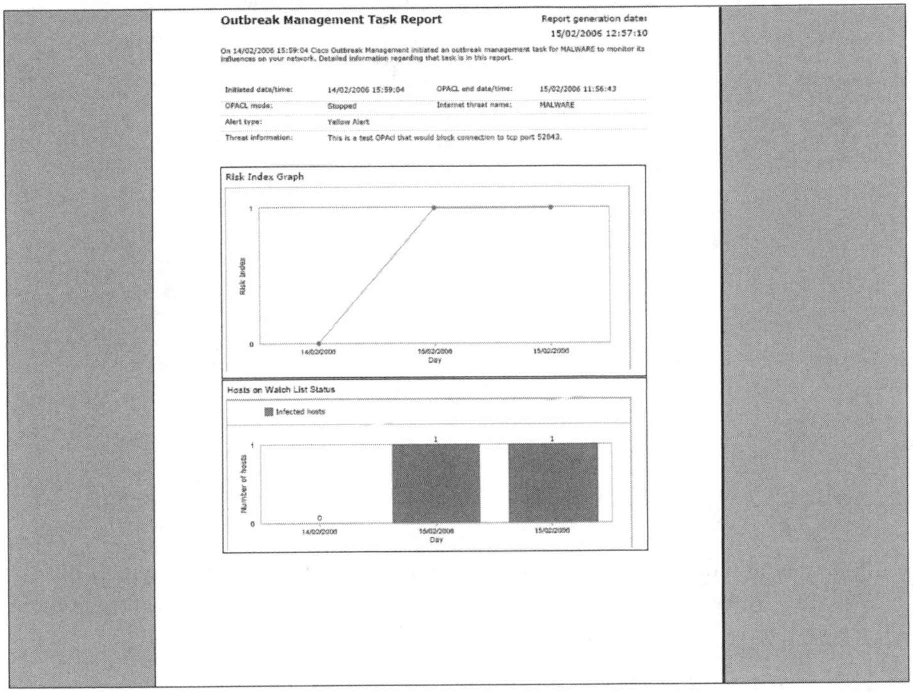

Cisco ICS includes configurable settings to manage the self-defending characteristics of the network to contain a network incident. To access the outbreak settings that are a part of Cisco ICS, select Outbreak Settings from the Outbreak Management list, as shown in Figure 4-17. Components of outbreak settings include the following:

- **OPACL Settings**—Use for blocking or logging
- **Exception List**—Define ports that will not receive OPACLs
- **Report Settings**—Define how automatic reports are generated
- **Watch List Settings**—Indicate which hosts or networks will be watched for attack
- **Automatic Outbreak Management Task**—Define whether OPACLs and OPSigs will be automatically deployed for alert classes

Figure 4-19 *Exception List*

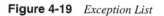

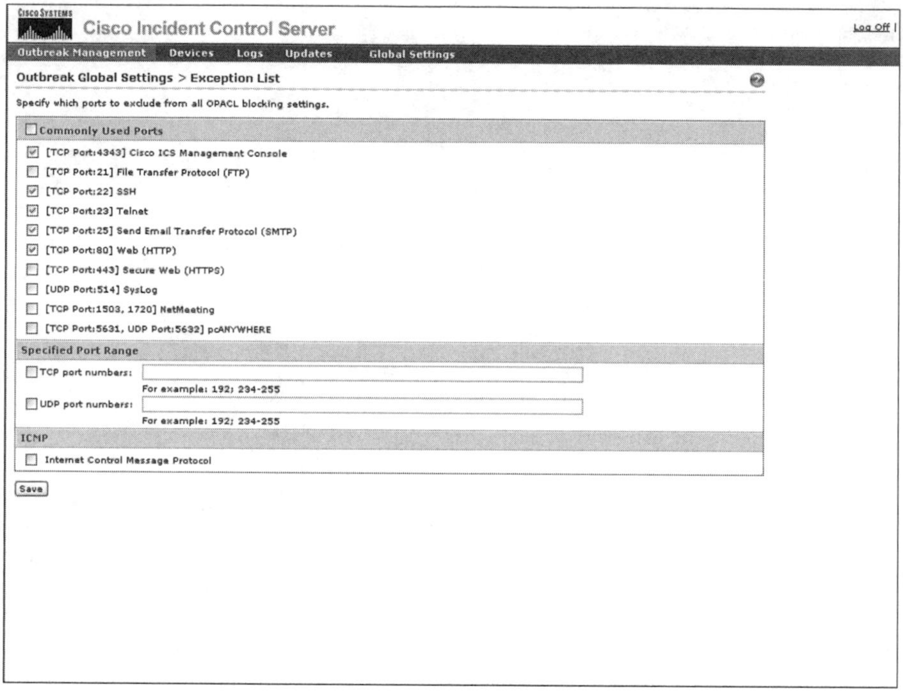

Report Settings

As indicated in Figure 4-20, Report Settings provides a mechanism to configure the automatic generation or reports and the frequency of report generation.

Figure 4-20 *Report Settings*

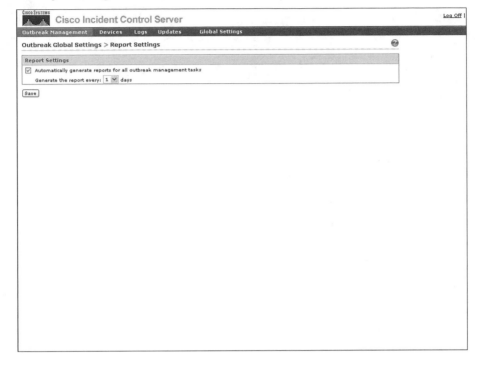

Watch List Settings

The watch list is intended to indicate which hosts in the network may have been infected by a network attack. Figure 4-21 shows that you can configure the watch list for an IP address or a range of IP addresses. Cisco ICS will use the IPS signatures to determine if a host is sending network traffic that could be due to an infection and will add this host to the watch list.

Figure 4-21   *Watch List*

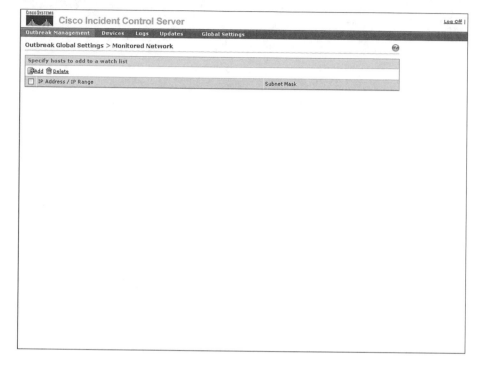

Automatic Outbreak Management Task

The Outbreak Settings link under Outbreak Management provides a way to access the Automatic Outbreak Management Task configuration. This Automatic Outbreak Management Task configuration specifies whether yellow and red alerts can receive automatic OPACL and OPSig deployment by Cisco ICS or if an operations person must manually review and deploy the OPACLs and OPSigs. The Automatic Outbreak Management Task configuration is identical to Automatic Outbreak Management Task configuration that was displayed earlier in Figure 4-13.

Displaying Devices

The Devices drop-down list provides a way to display the list of devices that are managed by the Cisco ICS. The Devices drop-down list also provides a mechanism to add a device to the list of devices under management. Figure 4-22 displays the Devices drop-down list to view the device list and to add a device.

Figure 4-22   *Devices*

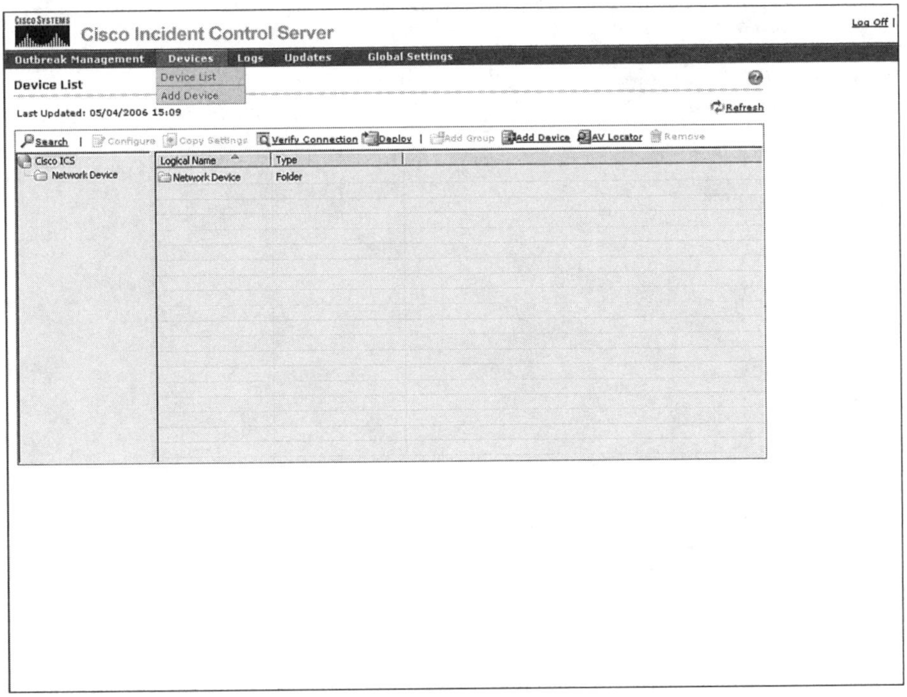

The following sections describe the Device List and Add Device options.

Device List

The Device List contains a list of devices that will be managed by Cisco ICS. These devices in the list can receive OPACLs and OPSigs and can be self-defending against a network incident. An example of a Device List is shown in Figure 4-23.

Figure 4-23 *Device List*

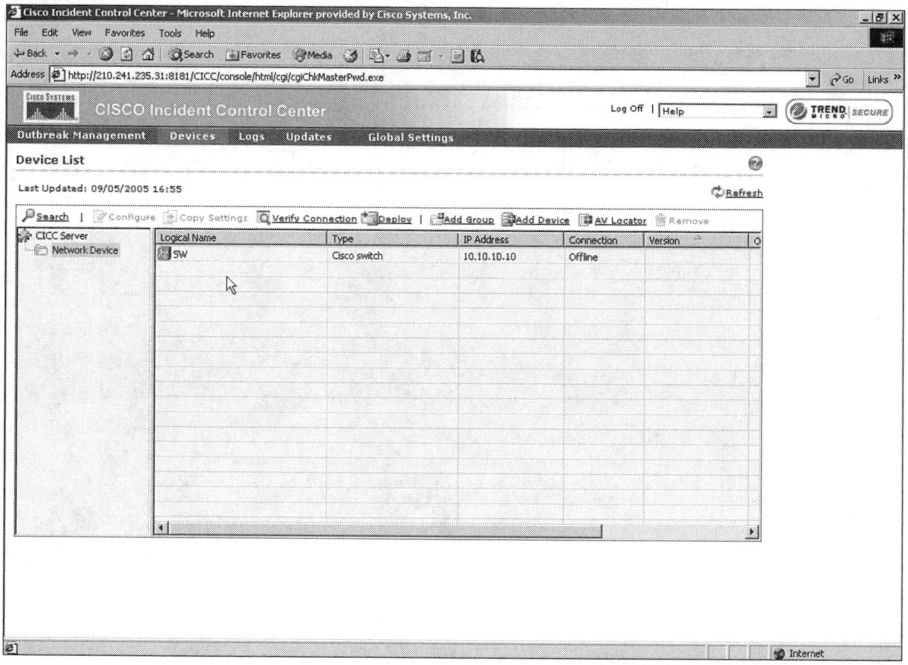

Add Device

The Add Device function enables a Cisco IPS, router, or switch to be added to the Cisco ICS server. There is also an Add Device link from the Device List in addition to the link from the main Device tab. Figure 4-24 displays the parameters related to how to add a device to the Cisco ICS server.

Figure 4-24 *Add Device*

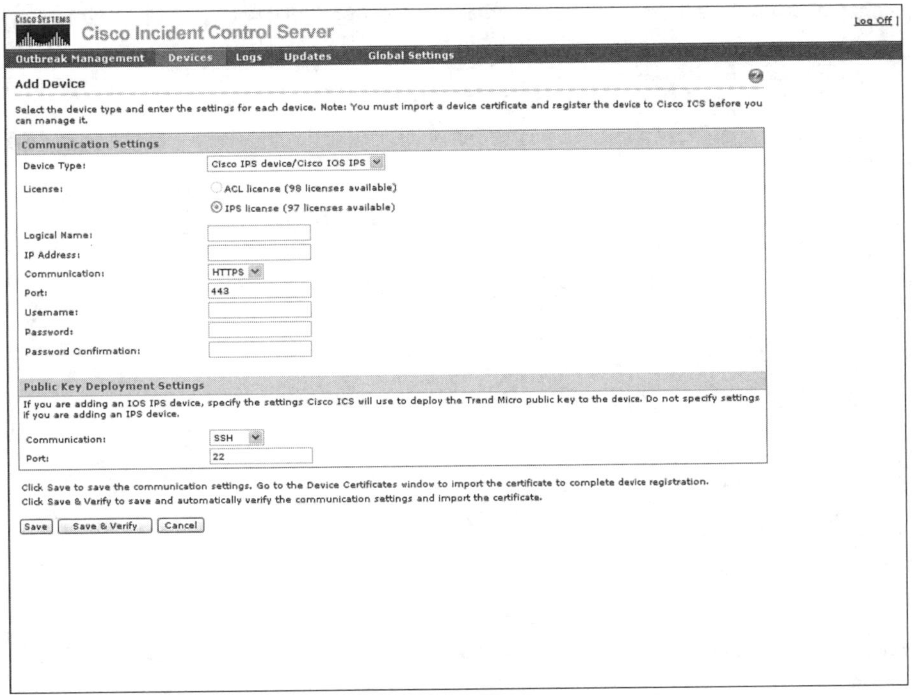

Viewing Logs

Cisco ICS provides a variety of log functions including the following:

- Incident Log Query
- Event Log Query
- Outbreak Log Query
- Log Maintenance

An example of the log functions from the Logs drop-down list is provided in Figure 4-25.

Figure 4-25 *Logs*

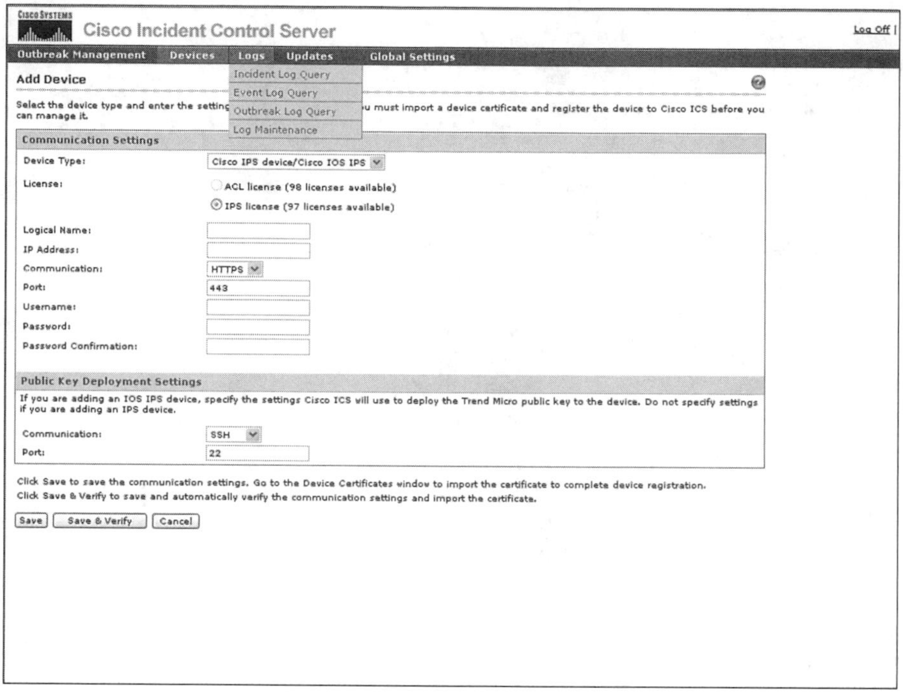

The following sections describe each log function in more detail.

Incident Log Query

The Incident Log Query function provides a way to display the logs from IPS Virus Detection or an OPACL Matching during a specific range of dates. Figure 4-26 displays an example of the configuration parameters for an Incident Log Query.

Figure 4-26 *Incident Log Query*

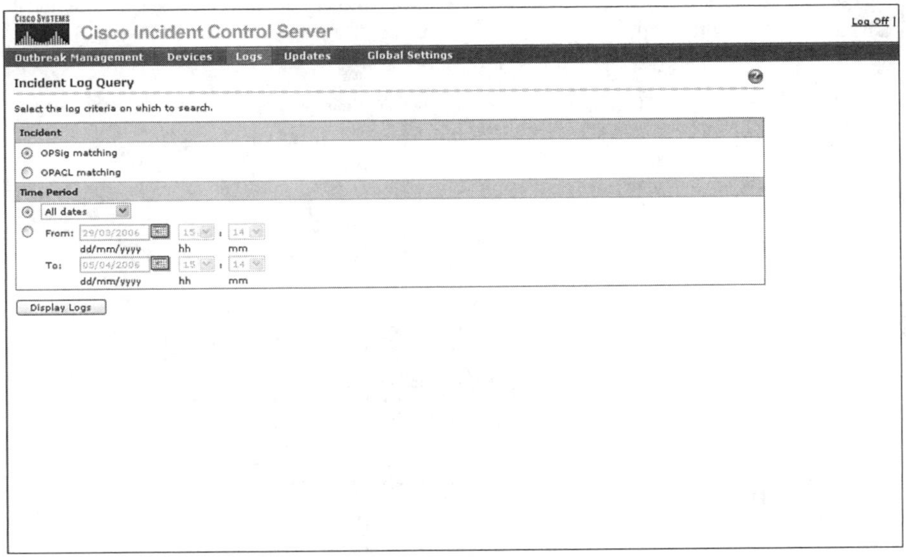

Event Log Query

The logs in Cisco ICS can be queried based upon event type and date range. An example of the types of event logs includes the following:

- System Events
- Outbreak Events
- Server Update Events
- Deployment Events
- Connection Status Event
- Host Event

Figure 4-27 provides a sample of the result from an Event Log Query.

Outbreak Log Query

The Outbreak Log Query provides a way to display all logs that relate to a certain outbreak management task, as shown in Figure 4-28. Outbreak log query can be considered a subset of the event log query.

Figure 4-27 *Event Logs*

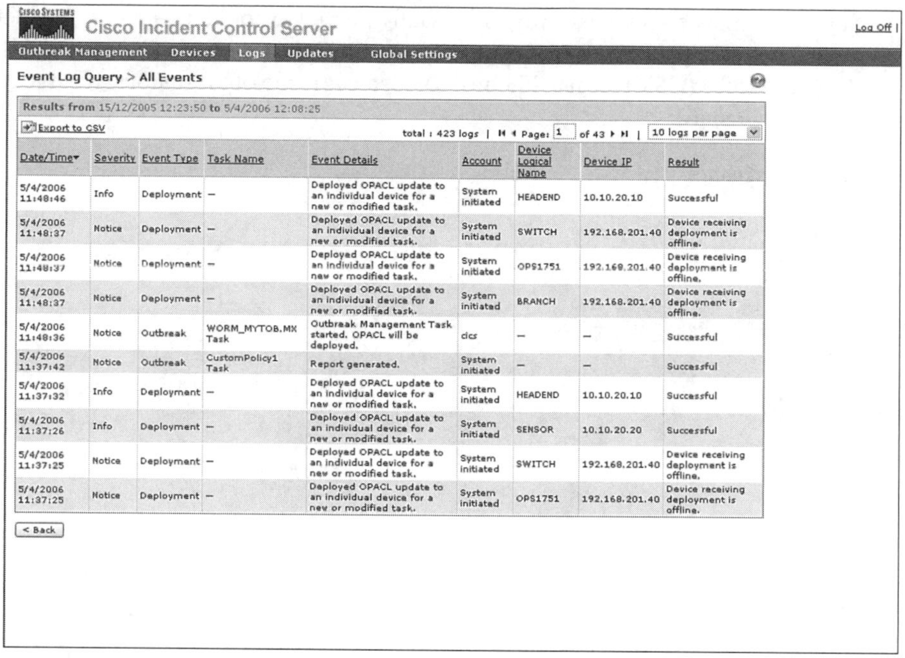

Figure 4-28 *Outbreak Log Query*

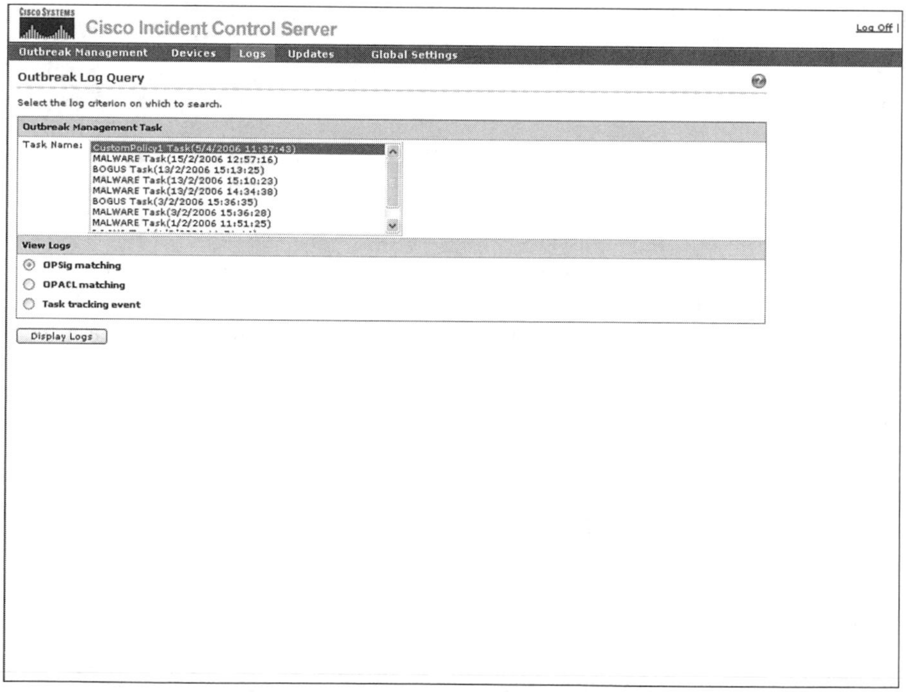

Log Maintenance

Log Maintenance provides a way to manually purge logs of certain types or to define time periods to automatically purge logs from Cisco ICS. Logs can also be exported in comma-separated value (CSV) format. Figure 4-29 displays some of the options to purge logs under Log Maintenance.

Figure 4-29   *Log Maintenance*

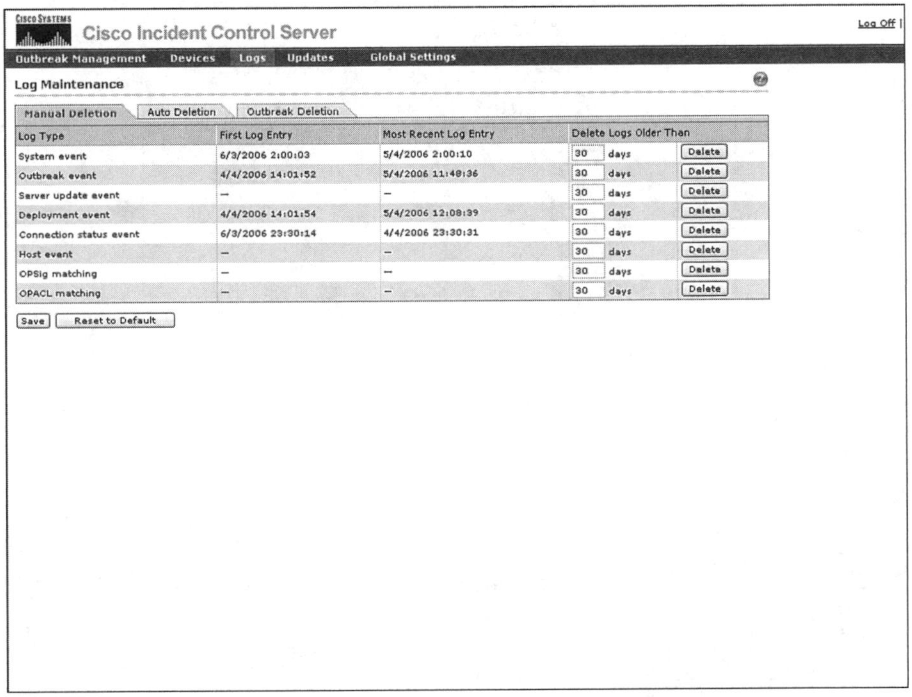

NOTE   Cisco ICS also features Update and Global Setting tabs in the main GUI. This chapter does not focus on the update global setting feature because this tends to be more generic and related to product maintenance and less specific to the self-defending characteristics of the Cisco ICS product.

Summary

The Cisco ICS is created by the partnership between Cisco and Trend Micro. Cisco ICS provides an additional layer of self-defense that can contain network incidents with a focus on preventing networkwide virus and worm outbreaks. Cisco ICS works in concert with a subscription service from Trend Micro where Trend Micro monitors and identifies new network threats. Trend Micro first creates a broad access list, or OPACL, to stop the network outbreak. Trend Micro further investigates the new network threat and then creates an IPS signature, or OPSig, as a very specific mechanism to stop the outbreak or worm.

Cisco ICS can deploy OPACLs and OPSigs either automatically, without user intervention, or manually, with user approval. OPACLs and OPSigs can also be applied automatically or manually, based upon classes of events, as designated by the red and yellow alert levels. Cisco ICS complements the base level of access lists and IPS protection as described in Chapter 3. In addition to the ASA platform, Cisco ICS can also apply OPACLs to routers and switches and OPSigs to IPS devices, including routers, appliances, and Catalyst 6500/7600 IPS service modules.

References

Cisco Systems, Inc. Administrator Guide for Cisco Incident Control Service. http://www.cisco.com/univercd/cc/td/doc/product/iaabu/ics/ics10/admin/index.htm

Demystifying 802.1x

802.1x is a public standard that defines port-based user authentication. 802.1x is also a mechanism for user identity and authentication over both wired and wireless network infrastructures. 802.1x is considered by many to be fairly complex, with several Extensible Authorization Protocol (EAP) types that define how authentication is implemented on the network. This chapter attempts to demystify 802.1x, provide an overview of Cisco Identity-Based Networking Services (IBNS) and machine authentication, and discuss how 802.1x can complement Network Admission Control (NAC). In this chapter, you also learn the basics of some of the most popular EAP types and how 802.1x can participate in an EzVPN network for telecommuting and remote branch offices.

Fundamentals of 802.1x

The IEEE 802.1x standard is designed to provide port-based user authentication onto a network. Prior to the 802.1x standard, many mechanisms existed to determine if a user was authorized to join the network. However, these mechanisms were often proprietary and typically were often independent of the port or entrance point in to the network. The ability to define port or link-layer authentication to the network allows the ability to assign a user or group of users network access policy attributes including virtual LAN (VLAN) and access control lists (ACLs) when the user authenticates and logs on to the network. IEEE 802.1x provides a standard mechanism for port or link-level user authentication and works in concert with traditional port-level security.

An example of traditional port-level security is the ability to specify what MAC addresses, or layer 2 addresses, are allowed through a particular Catalyst LAN switch port. In addition to user-based authentication, IEEE 802.1x can also support device-based authentication to authenticate a device name to a certificate authority or to a Windows Active Directory system prior to user authentication. The IEEE 802.1x standard was designed to provide an open, secure, and scalable mechanism for port-based or link-layer user authentication.

802.1x comprises the following three major components:

- **Authentication server**—The authentication server is an 802.1x server and often contains other user authentication services like Remote Authentication Dial-In User Service (RADIUS). The authentication server often provides user authentication services for both 802.1x and other access methods like remote access IPSec VPNs. Cisco Secure Access Control Server (ACS) is an example of an authentication server.

- **Authenticator**—The authentication client, or authenticator, is the network component that receives the initial request for port-based user authentication. The authenticator is typically a switch or wireless access-point.

- **Supplicant**—The supplicant resides on the end-device, like a laptop, desktop computer, or PDA. Some end-device platforms, including the pervasive Microsoft XP, contain a native 802.1x supplicant. Full-featured 802.1x supplicants can also be purchased from third parties for Windows and other platforms, including Linux and MacOS.

IEEE 802.1x defines a PPP connection between the end-device supplicant (for example, PC) and authenticator (for example, Catalyst LAN switch). IEEE 802.1x allows EAP messages to be transported between the supplicant and the authentication server. Communication between the authenticator and authentication server (for example, Cisco Access Control Server [ACS]) is performed with the RADIUS protocol. Figure 5-1 displays an example of the 802.1x components in a network.

Figure 5-1   *802.1x Network*

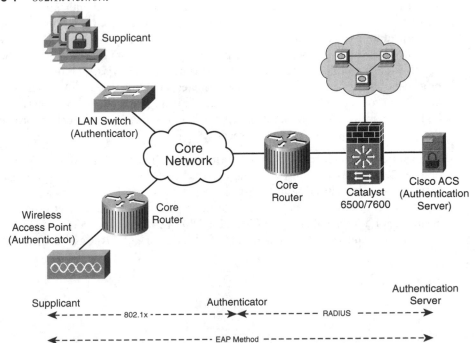

Introducing Cisco Identity-Based Networking Services

Cisco Identity-Based Networking Services (IBNS) is the product suite that implements 802.1x identity-based networking on Cisco networks. Cisco IBNS implements the capabilities defined in the IEEE 802.1x standard, which acts as a foundation for identity-based networking. For example, a Cisco switch can be an authenticator, and a Cisco ACS can be an authentication server in an IBNS/802.1x Cisco network.

IBNS also adds a layer of additional functionality that is not contained in the IEEE 802.1x standard. Cisco IBNS networks allow a user to be placed in a specific VLAN and apply specific ACLs after 802.1x port-based user authentication. Cisco IBNS also implements the advanced functionality including the Wake-on-LAN (WoL), Guest VLAN, and MAC authentication bypass features. WoL enables a remote server within the trusted network to reboot or initiate a connection to a remote 802.1x client that is not currently connected to the LAN in order to remotely install software updates. Guest VLAN allows unknown users to be placed into a Guest VLAN with restricted network permissions. MAC authentication bypass features allow devices that do not have an 802.1x supplicant (for example printers) to be granted or denied network access based upon MAC address.

Prior to IBNS with 802.1x, Cisco offered a proprietary identity management solution. This proprietary solution leveraged VLAN Management Policy Server (VMPS) as a VLAN distribution and assignment mechanism with the User Registration Tool (URT) for management. The introduction of the open 802.1x standard has enabled Cisco to implement an identity network solution, or IBNS, on the open 802.1x and RADIUS standards.

Machine Authentication

802.1x features the ability to authenticate a machine during the system boot of that machine. This machine authentication happens prior to dynamic IP address assignment and prior to port-based user authentication. Machine-based authentication supports only Windows machines because the machine name is authenticated against an Active Directory server. Microsoft's support for specific EAP types enables 802.1x to support machine authentication for multiple EAP types. An overview and details about the variety of EAP types that are supported in Cisco 802.1x are provided later in this chapter in the "EAP" section.

802.1x and NAC

802.1x can use information including the machine name, client-side digital certificate, and username and password to identify and authenticate a user onto a port in the network. The authentication process can include any of the identity credentials or even a combination of these credentials. For instance, digital certificates can be used for device authentication, and username and password can be used for user authentication.

Network Admission Control (NAC) is also a form of authentication and can be considered a superset of the authentication of 802.1x. NAC can use 802.1x as a base for identity authentication. NAC then extends the authentication process to check the security posture or other posture credentials to ensure that the device has the latest operating system (OS) service pack (SP), hot-fix, and antivirus updates. The additional security checks that are performed by NAC are often referred to as a security posture or posture credential check of the endpoint or device.

NAC also offers the ability to quarantine a machine for remediation. Remediation involves the process of allowing the machine to join a quarantined part of the network, such as a specific VLAN or quarantine VLAN. NAC can also enable the display of instructions of how to download the required OS SP and antivirus updates to join the network safely and be removed from the guest or quarantine VLAN. Chapter 6, "Implementing Network Admission Control," provides a detailed overview of the NAC framework that is implemented with routers, switches, and Cisco ACS. The integration between 802.1x and NAC enables the identity and posture credential check to occur in a single 802.1x transaction. NAC can use 802.1x as a base for identify authentication, but then extend the authentication process to include other posture credentials such as OS patches and antivirus updates.

Using EAP Types

EAP is a component of an 802.1x network. EAP is designed to create a mechanism to provide authentication types that leverage existing authentication, authorization, and accounting (AAA) solutions. EAP messages can be transferred from the 802.1x supplicant to the authenticator or authentication server. The communication between the authenticator to the authentication server, such as Cisco ACS, is performed with RADIUS messages. These RADIUS messages are often transported over User Datagram Protocol (UDP). EAP is defined in RFC 2284, "PPP Extensible Authentication Protocol (EAP)." Examples of EAP types include the following:

- **EAP MD5**—EAP MD5 supports one-way authentication, similar to Challenge Handshake Authentication Protocol (CHAP). CHAP is defined in RFC 1994 and uses a shared secret for authentication. The authenticator can receive an MD5 hash derived from the shared secret in order to verify the validity of the authentication request.

- **EAP Transport Layer Security (TLS)**—EAP TLS uses digital certificates

- **LEAP**—Wireless EAP supports mutual authentication

- **Protected EAP (PEAP)**—PEAP was coauthored by Microsoft and Cisco. Microsoft Windows also includes a native PEAP supplicant. PEAP can also be used for Layer 3 NAC, or NAC with the authentication client on an IOS router. PEAP also supports both MSCHAPv2 and Generic Token Card (GTC). MSCHAPv2 is Microsoft CHAP version 2 and implements addition support for changing passwords. Microsoft's

Active Directory is an example of a directory that supports the MSCHAPv2 protocol for authentication. GTC allows authentication to be based upon one-time passwords and logon passwords and does not require a directory to support MSCHAPv2.

- **EAP FAST**—EAP FAST is the EAP type for Layer 2 NAC (authentication client on a Catalyst LAN switch) with 802.1x (NAC-L2-802.1x). EAP FAST is also good on wireless networks since EAP FAST is tunneled LEAP.

The following sections describe each type of EAP in more detail.

EAP MD5

EAP MD5 is one of the simplest authentication mechanisms. EAP MD5 uses one-way authentication, which means that only the supplicant has to provide authentication to the authenticator. In other words, the supplicant is not protected from a rogue authenticator. EAP MD5 is not the best choice for wireless LANs because it is a one-way authentication protocol. EAP MD5 uses the MD5 hash that was originally defined in 1992. Microsoft Windows XP contains a native EAP MD5 802.1x supplicant and uses a password on the end-user workstation.

EAP TLS

EAP Transport Layer Security (TLS) uses digital certificates for user authentication and key generation. TLS uses both the certificate of the client and authentication server to implement mutual authentication. EAP TLS verifies that the user possesses an RSA key pair that is signed in the certificate. EAP TLS generates a unique key per session for each user. EAP TLS is defined in RFC 2716, "PPP EAP TLS Authentication Protocol."

LEAP

LEAP is an EAP type designed to authenticate users attempting gain access to a wireless network. LEAP can use Cisco ACS as the authentication server. LEAP provides a secure wireless connection and promotes a unique session key for encryption for each user. The Cisco Aironet Client contains a LEAP supplicant for 802.1x wireless networks.

PEAP

PEAP was designed to provide a more secure or protected form of EAP as an alternative to EAP MD5. PEAP is supported by Microsoft and provides a protected EAP for authentication on both wireless networks and LANs. PEAP uses digital certificates on the server-side to provide secure and encrypted authentication. PEAP can use EAP GTC to provide two-factor user authentication with one-time passwords. PEAP can also use MSCHAPv2 to provide a unique session key without the overhead of a client-side digital certificate solution.

PEAP is a popular EAP type on 802.1x networks today because it enables a Microsoft machine with an 802.1x supplicant to authenticate on both wireless and wired (Ethernet LAN) networks. The popularity of PEAP can also be attributed to the fact that Microsoft XP contains a native PEAP 802.1x supplicant. PEAP MSCHAPv2 in addition to EAP TLS described earlier are two EAP types that support Windows machine authentication.

EAP FAST

EAP FAST is a technology that can use Cisco ACS as the authentication server. EAP FAST allows the EAP protocol to be transmitted over a secure, encrypted TLS tunnel. EAP FAST is also highly secure through the use of strong secrets, or Protected Access Credentials (PAC). Cisco ACS uses a master key to generate these credentials. PACs can be provisioned both in-band and out-of-band for the authentication process.

In addition to being a strong security solution, EAP FAST can be a higher-performing solution than some of the other EAP protocols because EAP FAST can use shared secrets rather than more resource-intensive mechanisms, like digital certificates or public key infrastructure (PKI). EAP FAST can be an attractive candidate for embedded devices with low processor power since it does not have to process digital certificates. EAP FAST can be used in Layer 2 or LAN switch NAC deployment. EAP FAST can also be used for 802.1x authentication to both wired and wireless networks.

VPN and 802.1x

Port-based user authentication is very useful in a remote-access or teleworker environment. The ability for people to work at home after hours or on weekends can provide a major boost in productivity. However, the ability for people to work from home also has risks because the home network is typically not controlled by the IT staff of the employer. Due to security risks, the IT staff of the employer would like only the employee to access the corporate network, and not the PCs or PDA of that employee's spouse or kids. For example, the employee's daughter takes her laptop to college and downloads MP3s. Unfortunately, in this process she also downloads the latest virus in addition to the latest tune from her favorite band. She goes home for the weekend to get her laundry done and uses the wireless network at home to IM with her college friends. In this process, she inadvertently places the virus on the employer's network through the tunneled connection from the employee's house that first goes through the employer's corporate network prior to the Internet.

802.1x authentication can be used to allow only the employee's laptop to join the VPN connection to the corporate network, while allowing the college student at home to use the Internet through the home network. An 802.1x authenticator is embedded or included in the home router as an IOS feature. In this example, the home router receives information from the 802.1x supplicant on the laptop. The home router, or 802.1x authenticator, sends the authentication request to the authentication server at the corporate network. The authentication server in many Cisco self-defending networks is the Cisco Secure ACS.

Figure 5-2 shows an example of a teleworker network with a VPN to the corporate network using 802.1x authentication. In Figure 5-2, the at-home college student can access the Internet through the same home network router that the employee uses to access the corporate network. She does not risk infection to the corporate network because her network traffic goes directly to the Internet rather than going first to the corporate network and then to the Internet.

Figure 5-2   *Teleworker VPN with 802.1x*

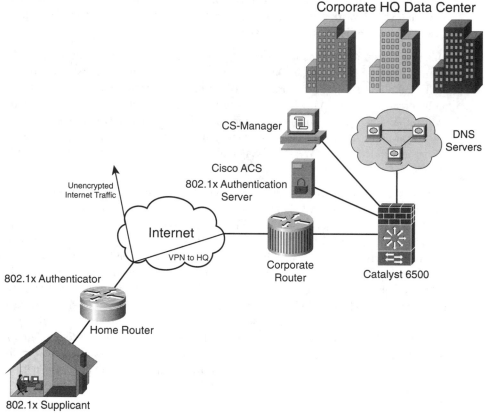

This teleworker network supports the ability for the VPN tunnel to remain active between the home network router and the access router at the corporate network. The IT staff at the employer's network can define an IP pool for valid employee devices that need to connect to the corporate network and a separate IP pool for nonemployee machines. The dual IP pool solution has the advantage that the employee machines can use the corporate DNS server and the nonemployee machines can use the ISP DNS server.

Summary

802.1x is an IEEE standard that defines how to identify a user and grant a user access to a network. 802.1x is a link layer, or Layer 2, authorization protocol that defines how a user is granted port-based access to a network. 802.1x is composed of three major components: supplicant, authenticator, and authentication server. The supplicant resides on the end-device to identify the user. The authenticator can exist in a Catalyst LAN switch, wireless access point, or router and forwards authentication requests from the supplicant device to the authentication server. The authentication server contains knowledge of the authorized users and the network privileges that should be granted to a user for network access. The Cisco ACS server is an example of an authentication server.

802.1x communication occurs between the supplicant and the authenticator. Communication between the authenticator and authenticator server is in the form of RADIUS records. EAP types are used to communicate between the supplicant and the authentication server. Many EAP types exist for different network scenarios, including one-way authentication (supplicant authenticates to authenticator), two-way authentication (protects supplicant devices against rouge authenticators), support for both wired (Ethernet) and wireless (WiFi) networks, and support for either passwords or digital certificates.

802.1x is a good base for user authentication. Other functionality can complement 802.1x user authentication. 802.1x also supports device or machine authentication. Machine authentication uses Microsoft's Active Directory, so machine authentication is only supported for Microsoft Windows PCs. Cisco IBNS layers additional functionality on to an 802.1x network, including the ability to bypass authentication based upon MAC address and the WoL feature to activate and reboot an idle computer in order to remotely install software applications, patches, and updates. NAC can also leverage an 802.1x network to provide additional checks of the security posture on the authenticating device to ensure that the device has the proper antivirus, service packs, and hotfix updates to safely join the network. 802.1x is also supported in Cisco's IOS routers and can implement additional security for remote employees and teleworkers by using 802.1x to allow the employee to safely access the corporate network while allowing other users on the home network to access the Internet without connecting through the corporate network.

References

Cisco Systems, Inc. User Guide for Cisco Secure ACS for Windows Server 3.3. http://cisco.com/en/US/products/sw/secursw/ps2086/products_user_guide_book09186a00802335e2.html

Aboba, B., and D. Simon. RFC 2716, PPP EAP TLS Authentication Protocol. 1999.

Cisco Systems, Inc. Cisco IOS Easy VPN Remote with 802.1x Authentication. http://cisco.com/en/US/tech/tk583/tk372/technologies_white_paper 09186a00801fdef9.shtml

Cisco Systems, Inc. Layered Security in a VPN Deployment. http://www.cisco.com/en/US/products/ps6660/products_white_paper0900aecd8046cbc4.shtml

Cisco Systems, Inc. FAQ: How Does 802.1x Work with Cisco IBNS? http://www.cisco.com/application/pdf/en/us/guest/netsol/ns75/c685/ccmigration_09186a0080259020.pdf

Cisco Systems, Inc. FAQ: Using Cisco Secure ACS with Cisco IBNS. http://www.cisco.com/application/pdf/en/us/guest/netsol/ns75/c685/ccmigration_09186a0080259063.pdf

Cisco Systems, Inc. FAQ: Overview of 802.1x and Cisco IBNS Technology. http://www.cisco.com/application/pdf/en/us/guest/netsol/ns75/c685/ccmigration_09186a0080258e2f.pdf

Cisco Systems, Inc. FAQ: VLAN Assignment with Cisco IBNS. http://www.cisco.com/application/pdf/en/us/guest/netsol/ns75/c685/ccmigration_09186a0080259047.pdf

Cisco Systems, Inc. Cisco LEAP. http://www.cisco.com/en/US/products/hw/wireless/ps430/products_qanda_item0900aecd801764f1.shtml

This chapter covers the following topics:

- Network admission control overview
- NAC Framework benefits
- NAC Framework components
- Operational overview
- Deployment models

Implementing Network Admission Control

Network Admission Control (NAC) is a technology initiative led by Cisco Systems working in collaboration with many leading security vendors, including antivirus and desktop management. Their focus is the creation of solutions that limit security threats, such as worms and viruses.

This technology provides a framework using existing Cisco infrastructure to enforce network admission policies on NAC-enabled endpoint devices, guaranteeing software compliance before network access is granted. If an endpoint device is determined noncompliant, a variety of admission actions are available to administrators, and how the actions are implemented is at the discretion of the network administrator. For example, a noncompliant endpoint may be placed in a quarantine area of the network and redirected to a remediation server to load the necessary software or patches. A notification is displayed to the user warning that their device is not compliant or, in the worse case, that they are denied network access entirely.

This chapter describes the Cisco NAC Framework, identifies benefits, describes the solution components and how they interoperate, and describes common deployment models.

Network Admission Control Overview

Worms and viruses continue to be disruptive, even though many businesses have significantly invested in antivirus and traditional security solutions. Not all users stay up to date with the many needed software security patches of antivirus files. Noncompliant endpoints are frequent and the reasons vary; for example:

- A user might choose to wait and install a new update later because they don't have the time

- A contractor, partner, or guest needs network access; however, the business may not control the endpoint

- The endpoints are not managed

- The business lacks the capability to monitor the endpoints and determine whether they are updated to conform to the business's security policy

When infected endpoints connect to the network, they unsuspectingly spread their infections to other improperly protected devices. This has caused businesses to examine how they should implement endpoint compliance enforcement besides user authentication before granting access to their networks.

Cisco Systems provides two network admission control solution choices:

- NAC Appliance
- NAC Framework

Chapter 7, "Cisco Clean Access," describes NAC Appliance, which was originally marketed as Cisco Clean Access (CCA). NAC Appliance is a turnkey self-sufficient package that does not rely on third-party products for determining and enforcing software compliance. This chapter focuses on NAC Framework.

NAC Framework is an integrated solution that enables businesses to leverage many of their existing Cisco network products, along with many third-party vendor products such as antivirus, security, and identity-based software. Vendor products must be NAC-enabled in order to communicate with the NAC-enabled network access devices. NAC Framework is extremely flexible because it can enforce more features available from other vendors' products. A comparison of customer preferences for choosing the NAC Appliance and NAC Framework is shown in Table 6-1.

Table 6-1 *NAC Customer Profile*

NAC Framework	NAC Appliance
Uses an integrated framework approach, leveraging existing security solutions from other vendors	Prefers bundled, out-of-the-box functionality with preinstalled support for antivirus and Microsoft updates
Complex network environment, leveraging many types of Cisco network access products	Heterogeneous network infrastructure
Longer, phased-in deployment model	Rapid deployment model
Can integrate with 802.1x	Independent of 802.1x

Source: Cisco Systems, Inc.[1]

NAC Framework Benefits

Following are some benefits that can be recognized by businesses that have implemented NAC Framework:

- **Protects corporate assets**—Enforces the corporate security software compliance policy for endpoints.

- **Provides comprehensive span of control**—All the access methods that endpoints use to connect to the network are covered, including campus switching, wireless, router WAN links, IP Security (IPSec), and remote access.

- **Controls endpoint admission**—Validates all endpoints regardless of their operating system, and it doesn't matter which agents are running. Also provides the ability to exempt certain endpoints from having to be authenticated or checked.

- **Offers a multivendor solution**—NAC is the result of a multivendor collaboration between leading security vendors, including antivirus, desktop management, and other market leaders. NAC supports multiple security and patch software vendors through APIs.

- **Leverages existing technologies and standards**—NAC extends the use of existing communications protocols and security technologies, such as Extensible Authentication Protocol (EAP), 802.1x, and RADIUS services.

- **Leverages existing network and antivirus investments**—NAC combines existing investments in network infrastructure and security technology to provide a secure admission control solution.

NAC Framework Components

The initial release of the Cisco NAC Framework became available in June 2004 and continues to evolve in phases. The functions of the solution architecture remain consistent; however, as each phase is introduced, more capabilities and deeper integration are added to the NAC Framework architecture. To stay up to date with NAC and partner products, refer to the URL www.cisco.com/go/nac.

NAC Framework includes the following main components, as shown in Figure 6-1:

- Endpoint security application
- Posture agent
- Network access devices
- Cisco Policy server
- Optional servers that operate as policy server decision points and audit servers
- Optional management and reporting tools are highly recommended (not shown)

Figure 6-1 *NAC Framework Components*

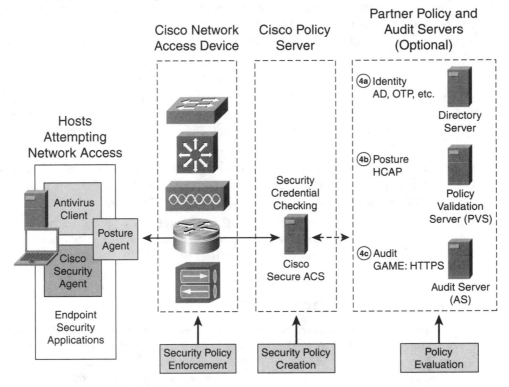

The next sections describe the main components in more detail.

Endpoint Security Application

An endpoint security application is security software that resides on a host computer. Depending on the application, it can provide host-based intrusion prevention system (HIPS), antivirus scanning, personal firewall, and other host security functions. Cisco Security Agent is a HIPS example.

NAC partners provide NAC-enabled security applications that use a posture plug-in that communicates their credentials and state with a posture agent, both residing on the same endpoint. Many endpoint security applications provide antivirus capabilities, and some provide additional identity-based services. For a list of NAC partners, refer to www.cisco.com and search for "Network Admission Control Current Participants."

Posture Agent

A posture agent is middleware or broker software that collects security state information from multiple NAC-enabled endpoint security applications, such as antivirus clients. It communicates the endpoint device's compliance condition. This condition is referred to as the *posture* of an endpoint. The posture information is sent to Cisco Secure Access Control Server (ACS) by way of the Cisco network access device.

The *Cisco Trust Agent* is Cisco's implementation of the posture agent. Cisco has licensed the trust-agent technology to its NAC partners so that it can be integrated with their security software client products. The trust agent is free and is also integrated with the Cisco Security Agent. Cisco Trust Agent can work with Layer 3 Extensible Authentication Protocol over User Datagram Protocol (EAPoUDP), and Cisco Trust Agent (CTA) version 2 can also work with Layer 2 with Extensible Authentication Protocol over 802.1x (EAPo802.1x) or Extensible Authentication Protocol over LAN (EAPoLAN).

Network Access Devices

Network access devices that enforce admission control policy include Cisco routers, switches, wireless access points, and security appliances. These devices demand endpoint security credentials and relay this information to policy servers, where network admission control decisions are made. Based on customer-defined policy, the network will enforce the appropriate admission control decision—permit, deny, quarantine, or restrict. Another term for this device is security policy enforcement point (PEP).

Policy Server

A policy server evaluates the endpoint security information relayed from network access devices (NADs) and determines the appropriate admission policy for enforcement. The Cisco Secure ACS, an authentication, authorization, and accounting (AAA) RADIUS server, is the foundation of the policy server system and is a requirement for NAC. Cisco Secure ACS is where the admission security policy is created and evaluated to determine the endpoint device's compliance condition or posture.

Optionally, Cisco Secure ACS may work in concert with other policy and audit servers to provide the following additional admission validations:

- **Identity**—User authentication can be validated with an external directory server and the result is communicated to Cisco Secure ACS. Examples include Microsoft Active Directory and one-time password (OTP) servers.

- **Posture**—Third-party, vendor-specific credentials such as antivirus and spyware can be forwarded using the Host Credential Authorization Protocol (HCAP) to NAC-enabled Policy Validation Servers (PVS) for further evaluation. This enables

businesses to leverage existing policies maintained in their PVS to validate and forward the software compliance result to Cisco Secure ACS, ensuring that a consistent policy is applied across the entire organization.

- **Audit**—Determines the posture for a NAC Agentless Host (NAH), which is a host without the presence of a posture agent such as Cisco Trust Agent. The Audit server works out of band and performs several functions:
  - Collects posture information from an endpoint.
  - Acts as a posture validation server to determine compliance of an endpoint and determine the appropriate compliance result in the form of a posture.
  - Communicates the result to Cisco Secure ACS using Generic Authorization Message Exchange (GAME) over an HTTPS session. GAME uses an extension of Security Assertion Markup Language (SAML), a vendor-neutral language enabling Web services to exchange authentication and authorization information.

The optional validation policy servers communicate the user authentication status or compliance status or both to Cisco Secure ACS, which makes the final determination as to the admission policy for the endpoint. *Policy decision point* is a term used to describe the function Cisco Secure ACS performs.

Management and Reporting Tools

In addition to the required NAC components, a management system is recommended to manage and monitor the various devices. Reporting tools are available to operation personnel to identify which endpoints are compliant and, most importantly, which endpoints are not compliant. Examples include Cisco Security MARS and CiscoWorks Security Information Manager Solution (SIMS).

Operational Overview

This section describes how NAC determines admission compliance and how it then uses the network to enforce the policy to endpoints.

Network Admission for NAC-enabled Endpoints

This section describes the process in which a noncompliant endpoint device is discovered and is denied full access until it is compliant with the admission policy. This scenario is shown in Figure 6-2.

Figure 6-2   *Admission Process for Noncompliant Endpoint*

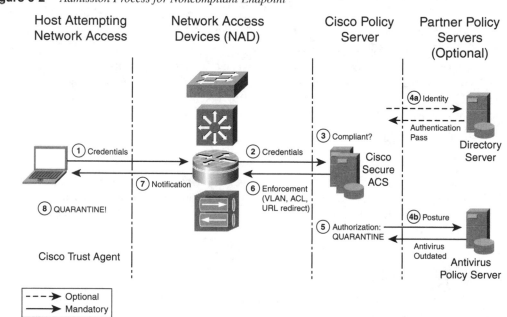

The following list is a summary of the admission process for a noncompliant endpoint shown in Figure 6-2:

1   An endpoint attempts to access the network.

2   The NAD notifies the policy server (Cisco Secure ACS) that an endpoint is requesting network access.

3   Cisco Secure ACS checks the NAC policy to determine whether the endpoint is compliant.

4   Cisco Secure ACS forwards specific information to other partner policy servers.

   a   Identity information is sent to a directory server for authentication validation.

   b   Host credentials are sent to an antivirus policy server for posture determination.

5   Cisco Secure Access uses information from the all-policy servers and decides the endpoints authorization. In this example, the endpoint is not compliant and is assigned a quarantine posture.

6   Quarantine enforcement actions are sent from Cisco Secure ACS to the NAD servicing the endpoint.

7   NAD enforces admission actions and communicates posture to Posture Agent.

8   Posture Agent notifies the user that the endpoint is quarantined.

The following sections explain each step in more detail.

Endpoint Attempts to Access the Network

In step 1, the admissions process begins when an endpoint attempts to access the network. What triggers the process is dependent upon the NAD's capabilities and configuration. The NAD initiates posture validation with Cisco Trust Agent using one of the following protocols:

- EAPoUDP
- EAPo802.1x

The protocol used is dependent upon the NAD to which the endpoint connects. Both of these protocols serve as a communication method between the endpoints using Cisco Trust Agent and the NAD. Cisco Trust Agent gathers credentials from NAC-enabled security applications such as antivirus.

NAD Notifies Policy Server

In step 2, the NAD notifies the policy server (Cisco Secure ACS) that an endpoint is requesting network access. A protected tunnel is set up between the policy server and the endpoints posture agent. Once communication is established, the credentials from each of the posture plug-ins are sent to Cisco Secure ACS.

Cisco Secure ACS Compares Endpoint to NAC Policy

In step 3, Cisco Secure ACS looks at the admission control policy and compares the endpoint credentials to the policy to determine whether it is compliant. It determines which of the following posture states to assign to the endpoint:

- **Healthy**—Endpoint is compliant; no network access restrictions.
- **Checkup**—Endpoint is within policy, but an update is available. This state is typically used to proactively remediate a host to the Healthy state or to notify a user that a more recent update is available and recommend remediation.
- **Transition**—This state became available in NAC phase 2. The endpoint posturing is in process; provide an interim access, pending full posture validation. This state is applicable during an endpoint boot in which all services may not be running or audit results are not yet available.
- **Quarantine**—Endpoint is out of compliance; restrict network access to a quarantine network for remediation. The endpoint is not an active threat but is vulnerable to a known attack or infection.

- **Infected**—Endpoint is an active threat to other endpoint devices; network access should be severely restricted or totally denied all network access.

- **Unknown**—Endpoint posture cannot be determined. Quarantine the host and audit or remediate until a definitive posture can be determined.

Cisco Secure ACS Forwards Information to Partner Policy Servers

In step 4, Cisco Secure ACS can optionally send user login (4a) and credentials (4b) to other policy decision servers. When this is done, Cisco Secure ACS expects to receive authentication status and a posture state from each of the policy decision servers.

In step 4a when NAC L2-802.1x is used, Cisco Secure ACS can send identity information to an authentication server. It confirms that the username and password are valid and returns a passed authentication message to Cisco Secure ACS. If identity authentication fails, no posture is checked and the endpoint fails authentication, resulting in no network access.

In step 4b in this example, an antivirus policy server determines that the device is out of compliance and returns a quarantine posture token to Cisco Secure ACS.

Keep in mind that NAC partner policy servers vary and offer a variety of compliance checks besides antivirus. For example, some vendors offer checking for spyware and patch management.

Cisco Secure ACS Makes a Decision

In step 5, Cisco Secure ACS compares all the posture states and determines which posture is the worst; infected is the worst and healthy is the best. It always assigns the worst state and takes the action for that posture. In this example, the user has passed authentication but the endpoint has been assigned a quarantine posture.

Cisco Secure ACS Sends Enforcement Actions

Cisco Secure ACS takes the actions assigned to a quarantine state. In this quarantine example, they can include the following:

- Enforce quarantine access; this varies based on the NAD.

  — For NADs using NAC-L3-IP, the enforcement actions include a quarantine Access Control List (ACL) being applied to the endpoint.

  — For NADs using NAC-L2-IP, the enforcement actions include a quarantine ACL being applied to the endpoint.

  — For NADs using NAC-L2-802.1x, the enforcement action includes a quarantine virtual LAN (VLAN) being applied to the endpoint device.

- Optionally, the endpoint device may be assigned a URL redirect to the remediation server.

- Optionally, a notification message can be sent to the user, indicating that their device is not compliant and is being redirected for remediation.

NAD Enforces Actions

In step 7, the NAD receives the quarantine policy enforcement from Cisco Secure ACS and responds accordingly. In this example, such a response would be to quarantine the endpoint, enforce an endpoint URL redirect to the remediation server, and send a quarantine message to the posture agent.

Posture Agent Actions

In step 8, the posture agent displays the quarantine message, and the user is redirected to the remediation server.

Actions available vary by NAC partner products. Cisco Secure ACS is capable of sending different application actions from HCAP-compliant policy servers to their specific application plug-ins. This can trigger actions such as the following:

- Force an auto-remediation to a designated remediation server

- Force an auto-patch by instructing the host to download and apply a patch automatically

- Restart a stopped application service

In this example, the endpoint is now quarantined, and the user has been notified by a message. The user can elect to do nothing and remain quarantined, or comply and allow their computer to be updated.

The admission control process can take very little time, as little as milliseconds. The time varies and is based on many factors, including:

- Where the endpoint is located in relation to the policy server and optional partner policy servers

- Where the remediation server is located

- NADs performance capability

- Network bandwidth

- How busy the policy servers are

As shown in Figure 6-3, an endpoint is changing from quarantine to healthy posture state.

Figure 6-3   *Admission Process for Endpoint Changing from Quarantine to Healthy State*

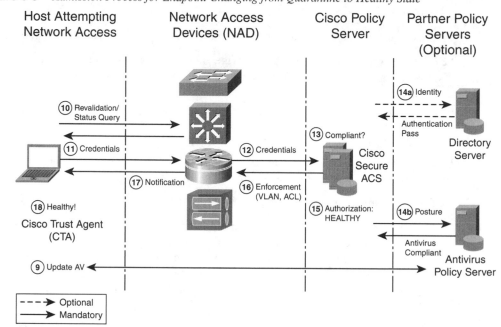

The following list explains the process shown in Figure 6-3:

9 Endpoint remediated.

10 Endpoint polled for change of compliance.

11 Host credentials gathered from endpoint.

12 Host credentials passed to Cisco Secure ACS.

13 Cisco Secure ACS rechecks the NAC policy to determine whether the endpoint is compliant.

14 Cisco Secure ACS forwards specific information to other partner policy servers.

 a Identity information is sent to a directory server for authentication validation.

 b Host credentials are sent to an antivirus policy server for posture determination.

15 Cisco Secure Access uses information from all policy servers and decides the endpoints authorization. In this example, the endpoint is compliant and is assigned a healthy posture.

16 Healthy enforcement actions are sent from Cisco Secure ACS to the NAD servicing the endpoint.

17 NAD enforces admission actions and communicates healthy posture to Posture Agent.

18 Posture Agent can notify the user that the endpoint is healthy. Many businesses prefer that a healthy posture be transparent to the user with no message notification displayed.

Endpoint Polled for Change of Compliance

Once an endpoint has been assigned a posture, it stays in effect and is not checked again until a NAC timer has expired or a posture agent trigger occurs.

The following are configurable timers for NAC:

- **Status Query**—Ensures that an endpoint remains compliant with the admission policy. The timer begins at policy enforcement for the endpoint; compliance is rechecked after the timer expires. Different Status Query timers can exist for different posture states. A shorter amount of time is beneficial for noncompliant states such as quarantine; the device can be rechecked sooner than a healthy device, in order to regain full network access.

- **Revalidation**—A time in which the posture remains valid. It can be set lower when an outbreak occurs, to force all endpoints to go through the admission policy process again. This enables endpoints to timeout at different intervals depending on where their timers are, versus forcing all endpoints to go through the validation process at the same time.

  In phase 2 with NAC-L2-802.1x, there is no capability to send a status query from the NAD by way of 802.1x. To overcome this, beginning with version 2 of Cisco Trust Agent, an asynchronous status query capability exists. Cisco Trust Agent can send an Extensible Authentication Protocol Over Lan (EAPOL)-Start to the NAD, or CTA can frequently poll all registered NAC application posture plug-ins looking for a change in credentials. If a change exists, it will trigger an EAPOL-Start signaling for a new posture validation.

  In step 10 of Figure 6-3, the quarantine status query timer has expired.

The NAD is aware that the timer has expired for the endpoint, so it begins rechecking for compliance. The posture agent gathers credentials from the posture plug-ins of NAC-enabled security applications such as antivirus.

Revalidation Process

From step 11 through step 18, the process is the same as the example described in Figure 6-2. The NAD notifies the policy server (Cisco Secure ACS) that an endpoint requests network access. This time, the Cisco Secure ACS determines that the posture is healthy for

all admission checks and that the user login is valid. Authentication is successful, and Cisco Secure ACS assigns the healthy policy.

The NAD receives the healthy policy enforcement from Cisco Secure ACS and responds accordingly by allowing full network access. The timers begin for the healthy state.

The NAD informs the posture agent of the healthy status, but no message is sent to the user this time. The user can now resume normal network activity.

Network Admission for NAC Agentless Hosts

The previous example described the admission process for a NAC-enabled endpoint running a posture agent, such as Cisco Trust Agent. This section describes the process for endpoints that do not have a posture agent.

NAC agentless hosts (NAH) can be accommodated by several methods, as shown in Table 6-2. A NAH exception list and whitelist can be created to identify known endpoints that do not have a posture agent installed and running. The option chosen is dependent upon the NAC Framework component and the NAD enforcement method used.

Table 6-2   *NAC Agentless Host Exceptions and Whitelisting*

Component	Administration Model	NAC-L2 IP	NAC-L3 IP	NAC-L2 802.1x
NAD	• Distributed, managed at the device level • Does not scale	Device Type, IP, or MAC Enforcement by intercept ACL (IP/MAC)	Device Type, IP, or MAC Enforcement by intercept ACL (IP)	MAC-Auth-Bypass (identity + posture)
Cisco Secure ACS whitelist	• Centralized • Scales	MAC (posture only)	MAC (posture only)	MAC-Auth-Bypass (identity + posture)
Audit	• Centralized • Scales	Active network scan, remote login, browser object, hardware/software inventory	Active network scan, remote login, browser object, hardware/software inventory	Not supported at the time of this writing

Source: Cisco Systems, Inc.[2]

The audit server can be used for NAH in all enforcement methods and is a single centrally managed server. As shown in Figure 6-4, an audit server can be included as a decision policy server for NAH. The audit server can determine the posture credentials of an endpoint without relying on the presence of a posture agent.

Figure 6-4 *Admission Control for NAC Agentless Host*

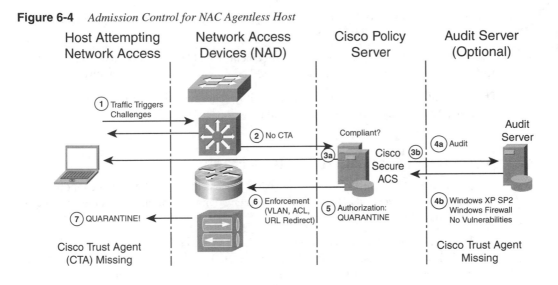

The following list explains the process shown in Figure 6-4:

1 An endpoint attempts to access the network. The trigger mechanism is dependent upon the NAD's capabilities and configuration. The NAD attempts to initiate posture validation with the posture agent, but no posture agent (Cisco Trust Agent) exists.

2 The NAD notifies the policy server (Cisco Secure ACS) that an endpoint is requesting network access with no Cisco Trust Agent (CTA) present.

3 Cisco Secure ACS cannot determine whether the NAH is compliant because no posture agent exists. Cisco Secure ACS performs the following:

   a Assign a transition posture to grant a temporary, limited network access to the agentless host while the audit server is determining the full posture validation. The NAD enforces the transition admission policy.

   b Notify the external audit server that the NAH is requesting admission.

4 Cisco Secure ACS cannot determine whether the NAH is compliant, so it notifies the audit server using GAME to conduct a scan on the endpoint.

   a The audit server scans the endpoint. It evaluates the endpoint's software information against the audit server's compliance policy. It determines that the operating system patch level is compliant or healthy, but the posture agent is missing, so it is considered noncompliant.

   b Quarantine is the application posture token (APT) assigned by the audit server for this NAH and is communicated to Cisco Secure ACS.

5 Cisco Secure ACS uses quarantine as the final posture, which is referred to as the system posture token (SPT), and takes the actions assigned to a quarantine state. The actions can include the following:

— **Enforce quarantine access**—This varies based on the NAD.

For NAC-L3-IP, the enforcement actions include a quarantine ACL being applied to the endpoint.

For NADs using NAC-L2-IP, the enforcement actions include a quarantine ACL being applied to the endpoint.

For NADs using NAC-L2-802.1x, the enforcement action includes a quarantine VLAN.

— **Enforce Redirection (optional)**—In this example, the endpoint device is assigned a URL redirect to the remediation server.

6 The NAD receives the quarantine policy enforcement from Cisco Secure ACS. It quarantines the endpoint and sends the endpoint a redirect URL to go to the remediation server.

7 The endpoint is now quarantined and redirected to a remediation server. With NAH, the URL redirect is the only way to provide feedback to the user because there is no posture agent present. At this point, the user can elect to do nothing and remain quarantined, or comply and allow their host to remediate by installing Cisco Trust Agent.

From this point, the NAC Framework process is the same as the example in which the endpoint state changed from quarantine to healthy as shown in Figure 6-3.

Deployment Models

Cisco NAC Framework is a flexible solution providing protection to connected endpoints regardless of network connectivity. As shown in Figure 6-5, it operates across all access methods including campus switching, wired and wireless, WAN and LAN links, IP Security (IPSec) connections, and remote access links.

Figure 6-5 *NAC Deployment Scenarios*

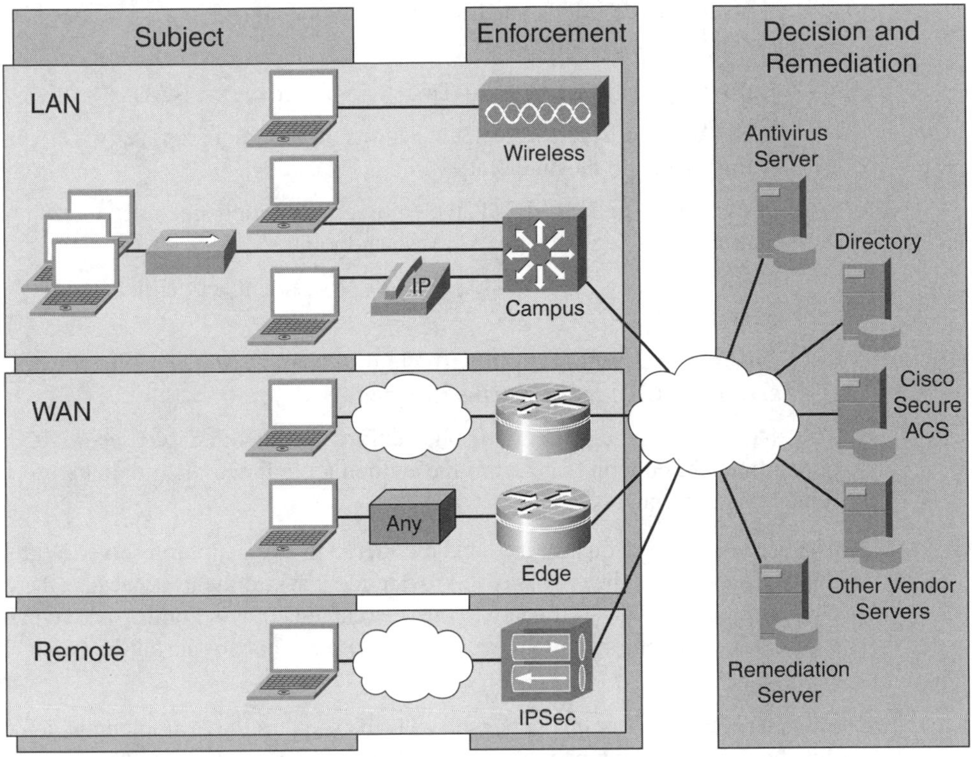

Source: Cisco Systems, Inc.[3]

The first NAC Framework deployment rule of thumb is to use the NAC-enabled NAD closest to the endpoints for checking compliance, helping enforce a least-privilege principle. The second rule is that compliance checking for an endpoint should occur at one NAD (closest to the endpoint), not throughout the network. The NAD might not be capable of performing compliance checks or enforcing the admission policy. Examples include non-Cisco devices or an older NAD that does not support NAC. As a result, NAC deployments will vary.

The following sections describe common NAC deployment scenarios.

LAN Access Compliance

NAC monitors desktops and servers within the office, helping to ensure that these endpoints comply with corporate antivirus and operating system patch policies before granting them LAN access. This reduces the risk of worm and virus infections spreading within an organization by expanding admission control to Layer 2 switches.

NAC Framework can also check wireless hosts connecting to the network to ensure that they are properly patched. The 802.1x protocol can be used in combination with device and user authentication to perform this validation using the NAC-L2-802.1x method. Some businesses might not want to use the 802.1x supplicant, so instead they may choose to use the NAC-L2-IP method using either IP or MAC.

NAC can be used to check the compliance of every endpoint trying to obtain network access, not just those managed by IT. Managed and unmanaged endpoints, including contractor and partner systems, may be checked for compliance with antivirus and operating system policy. If the posture agent is not present on the interrogated endpoint, a default access policy can be enforced limiting the endpoint to a specific subnet, thus limiting its ability to infect other devices on the entire network.

WAN Access Compliance

NAC Framework can be deployed at branch or home offices to ensure that endpoints comply with the latest antivirus and operating system patches before allowing them access to WAN or Internet connections to the corporate network. Alternatively, compliance checks can be performed at the main office before access is granted to the main corporate network.

Remote Access Compliance

NAC Framework helps to ensure that remote and mobile worker endpoints have the latest antivirus and operating system patches before allowing them to access company resources through IP Security (IPsec) and other virtual private network (VPN) connections.

Summary

The Cisco Network Admission Control is a framework comprising Cisco networking infrastructure along with a variety of partner products to enforce network admission policies on NAC-enabled endpoint devices, guaranteeing software compliance before granting network access.

The Cisco NAC Framework consists of the following components:

- NAC-enabled security applications such as antivirus and host intrusion protection systems such as Cisco Security Agent
- Posture agents such as Cisco Trust Agent
- Network access devices such as routers, switches, and wireless access points
- Cisco Secure ACS, which is the Cisco Policy Server
- Optional third-party validation policy servers
- Optional management and reporting tools

NAC allows the appropriate level of network access only to compliant and trusted endpoint devices such as PCs, servers, and PDAs. NAC can also identify noncompliant endpoints, deny them access, and place them in a quarantined area or give them restricted access to computing resources.

NAC agentless hosts can be identified by exception lists, whitelisting, or audit servers and can be evaluated before granting network access.

NAC Framework operates across all network access methods including campus switching, wired and wireless, router WAN and LAN links, IPSec connections, remote access, and dial-up links.

References

[1] Cisco Systems, Inc. NAC Customer Profile Reference by Russell Rice. Network Admission Control (NAC) Cisco Security SEVT Update. April 6, 2005.

[2] Cisco Systems, Inc. NAC Agentless Host Exceptions and Whitelisting. 2005.

[3] Cisco Systems, Inc. Network Admission Control (NAC). 2005.

Network Admission Control Appliance

In Chapter 6 you learned about the Network Admission Control (NAC) framework that is implemented with Cisco IOS routers and Catalyst LAN switches. Because NAC Framework is implemented with routers and switches, it leverages the existing network infrastructure.

This chapter describes the NAC appliance, which is also marketed as Cisco Clean Access (CCA). The NAC appliance offers a dedicated NAC deployment option that provides admission control functions including authentication, posture validation, and remediation. The NAC appliance is composed of a server and manager component. The NAC appliance server implements the admission control features, whereas the NAC appliance manager configures the policies on the NAC appliance servers. The NAC appliance also features an optional client agent for the Windows end stations within the network. The client agent provides additional security posture validation options, including Windows registry value, file, service, and application checks. The client agent can also assist the remediation process to help the end station download the necessary software updates to authenticate and safely join the network.

There are several deployment options for the NAC appliance. The NAC appliance server can be deployed in-band or out-of-band. An in-band deployment ensures that all data from the authenticated client flows through the NAC appliance server. An out-of-band deployment allows the NAC appliance server to be removed from data flow from the client after a successful authentication and subsequent network scans for posture validation.

NAC Appliance Features

NAC appliance is a dedicated, or turnkey, NAC deployment option that is implemented with dedicated server and management appliances. The option of a dedicated NAC appliance provides the ability to have a turnkey NAC deployment that does not use resources from existing network components like routers or switches. NAC appliance may also be considered to be a simpler NAC deployment option as a dedicated, self-contained appliance suite. For example, NAC appliance does not use a router or switch as the authentication client. NAC appliance also does not require 802.1x as a port-based user authentication mechanism and does not require an 802.1x authentication server. NAC appliance also does not require the customer to purchase third party vendor servers for policy validation, audit, and remediation.

NAC appliance offers several features, including the following:

- Authenticates device attributes and users for network admission.
- Provides an all-in-one NAC deployment option with a dedicated server appliance, manager appliance, and optional appliance agent for Windows PCs and laptops.
- Scans PCs, servers, and laptops on the network to identify infected or vulnerable hosts.
- Identifies vulnerabilities and views registry key values with an optional client agent. At the time of this writing, the client agent is offered at no additional cost.
- Quarantines vulnerable machines and facilitates remediation.
- Provides DHCP, DHCP Relay, and Network Address Translation (NAT) services to users on untrusted networks.
- Supports floating devices like public kiosks that require each new user to authenticate after the logoff of the previous user.
- Terminates VLANs between trusted and untrusted networks.
- Supports "bump-in-the-wire" and acts like an Ethernet bridge in addition to IP gateway scenarios. *Bump-in-the-wire* means that the NAC appliance server acts in a pass-through mode and does not require IP readdressing. IP gateway provides a routed option for the NAC appliance deployment.
- Allows IP Security (IPSec), Layer 2 Transport Protocol (L2TP), and Point-to-Point Tunneling Protocol (PPTP) encryption from PCs and laptops to be terminated on NAC appliance server between untrusted and trusted networks. The IPSec/L2TP/ PPTP functionality requires specific software on the client system.
- Provides exemption or filters so that certain devices (based upon Layer 2 MAC address) and users do not have to be authenticated.
- Denies a specific device (MAC address), user, IP address or subnet from authenticating to the network.
- Allows the enforcement of bandwidth restriction for certain user classes.
- Incorporates a native high availability (HA) solution between two servers.
- Provides NAC Message Information Block (MIB) to integrate with Hewlett-Packard OpenView (HP OV) SNMP systems.
- Offers a subscription service for automatic Microsoft OS, antivirus, and antispyware updates.
- Allows single sign-on with remote-access VPN.

NAC Appliance Manager

The NAC appliance servers are managed by the NAC appliance manager. NAC appliance also offers optional subscription services for automatic OS, antivirus, and antispyware updates.

A web browser is used as the client GUI to the NAC appliance manager. Configuration from the web GUI client is secured by using HTTPS between the client web browser and the NAC appliance manager. Users must provide a username and password to log on to the NAC appliance manager. Usernames and passwords can be stored in an external LDAP database or can be stored locally on the NAC appliance manager server. In addition to LDAP, Kerberos is also supported as an external administrator authentication method.

The NAC appliance manager can be ordered as an appliance or as standalone Linux software. The NAC Appliance (CCA) Manager contains a monitoring summary page that contains information about product version and online users. This monitoring summary is displayed in Figure 7-1.

Figure 7-1   *NAC Appliance Manager Monitoring Summary*

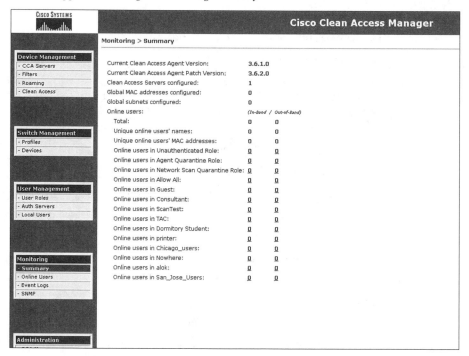

The main functional areas of the manager homepage are organized under the five categories, as follows:

- Device Management
  - — Configure network and local settings for each server
  - — Configure filters for device names, MAC addresses, IP addresses, and subnets
  - — Configure agent scanning parameter
- Switch Management
  - — Is enabled for out-of-band (OOB) deployments only
  - — Profile to add OOB LAN switches including Simple Network Management Protocol (SNMP) configuration
  - — Receive SNMP traps from the OOB switches when configured to do so
  - — Include list of OOB switches
  - — Include discovered clients behind the OOB switches
- User Management
  - — Define types of user roles, including quarantined and temporary users
  - — Define authentication parameters for user groups
  - — Specify external authentication servers including Lightweight Directory Access Protocol (LDAP), Remote Authentication Dial-In User Service (RADIUS), Windows NT LAN Manager (NTLM), Kerberos, and transparent 802.1x
  - — Associate assigned VLANs with user groups
  - — Configure RADIUS accounting
  - — Define local users for authenticating directly on NAC appliance server
- Monitoring
  - — View summary of recent policy deployment and quarantines
  - — View status of user categories and specific users
  - — Display event notification and warning logs
- Administration
  - — Configure manager settings, failover, digital certificates, and license key
  - — Define the logon page that is presented to user groups during authentication
  - — Specify admin privilege roles for managing the manager
  - — Back up the manager database

Device Management

Device Management is the first item displayed in the manager. Device Management features are configured in the following categories:

- CCA Servers
- Filters
- Clean Access

CCA Servers

The CCA Servers option displays a list of managed servers and also allows the ability to define a new server to be managed. The process to add a new server and select the server mode is displayed in Figure 7-2.

Figure 7-2   *Add New CCA Server with Server Type*

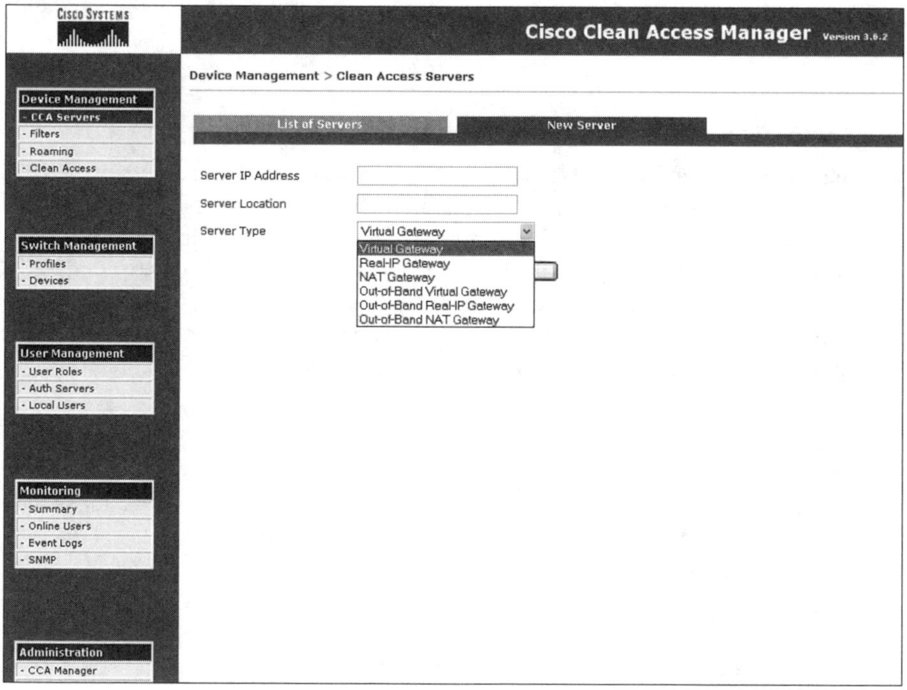

The Cisco Clean Access Server can be configured in the following modes:

- Real IP Gateway (in-band_)
- Virtual IP Gateway (in-band)

- NAT Gateway (in-band)—demo only
- Out-of-band (OOB) Real IP Gateway
- OOB Virtual IP Gateway
- OOB IP NAT Gateway—demo only

The next sections describe each mode in detail.

Real IP Gateway

In the Real IP Gateway mode, the server sits between an untrusted subnet and a trusted subnet. The IP addresses for the server interfaces must be configured. Static routes must be configured since the server is not a router and does not broadcast routes. Both DHCP server and DHCP relay functions are supported in this mode. The server can either assign authenticated users an IP address from a DHCP pool or allow the DHCP-assigned process to relay through the server from the internal DHCP server on the trusted network to the end point on the untrusted network. Architecturally, this is similar to the functionality of a router.

Virtual IP Gateway

The Virtual IP Gateway mode is essentially a bump-in-the-wire deployment. In this mode, the server is inserted inline into an existing network segment. No readdressing of subnets or IP addresses is required for the Virtual IP Gateway, or bump-in-the-wire, deployment. In this mode, both interfaces on the server can share the same IP address. Only DHCP relay is supported because the Virtual IP Gateway does not allow a native DHCP server. VLAN termination also is not supported in Virtual mode. The manager must reside on a different subnet from the server, even in Virtual IP Gateway mode.

NAT Gateway

The NAT Gateway includes a NAT function that enables the user IP address on the untrusted network to be translated to a new IP address on the trusted network. If you select NAT Gateway, you will be presented with a pop-up window that indicates that NAT Gateway is recommended only for testing/demo purposes. The CCA (NAC Appliance) 3.6 documentation takes this idea a step further and indicates that NAT Gateway mode is not supported for production network deployment.

OOB Real IP Gateway, OOB Virtual IP Gateway, and OOB NAT Gateway

Cisco introduced support for out-of-band (OOB) deployments with the CCA 3.5 release. Prior to OOB support, the server was always inline with all user traffic from the client. This user traffic includes the initial authentication traffic and all of the actual data traffic from

the client. OOB support allows the server to participate only in the authentication, scanning, and remediation flows for the user client and not the data traffic from the client for web browsing, e-mail, and so on. OOB support enables the implementation of a NAC deployment with fewer servers and can result in a more scalable solution, as all data traffic does not have to travel through a server after authentication. The OOB solution requires a separate license key. A server can be deployed in OOB Real IP Gateway, or OOB Virtual IP Gateway modes.

An OOB deployment can remove the bottleneck of the processing power of the server for data traffic. OOB deployment enables greater than 1 Gbps, because all data traffic does not have to flow through the server after successful authentication. In an OOB deployment, only network traffic for authentication, security posture validation, and any required remediation flow through the NAC appliance server. OOB is an option only for wired (LAN) networks because OOB is not supported on wireless networks. It is also not recommended to enable 802.1x on a LAN switch interface that will participate in an OOB NAC appliance deployment due to potential conflicts with VLAN assignments.

The OOB deployment modes work in concert with the supported line of Layer 2 LAN switches. The manager defines which VLAN on the LAN switch will be assigned to the authenticating device. The manager uses SNMP v2c and v3 to obtain MAC address table information and to assign VLANs to authentication devices. The out-of-band modes also support VLAN quarantine because the server performs device remediation and can reside on the quarantine VLAN. Supported Catalyst LAN switches for OOB deployments include the following device models:

- Cisco Catalyst Express Series 500 (3.6.1+ only)
- Cisco Catalyst 2900 XL (3.5.4+ only)
- Cisco Catalyst 2940 (3.5.4+ only)
- Cisco Catalyst 2950
- Cisco Catalyst 2950 LRE
- Cisco Catalyst 2960 (3.5.7+ only)
- Cisco Catalyst 3500 XL (3.5.4+ only)
- Cisco Catalyst 3550
- Cisco Catalyst 3560 (3.5.1+ only)
- Cisco Catalyst 3750
- Cisco Catalyst 4000 (3.5.8+ only)
- Cisco Catalyst 4500
- Cisco Catalyst 6500

Filters

Filters provide the ability to exclude devices or subnets from the authentication process. Many security operators will want to provide filters to nonPC devices like printers and IP phones in order to ensure easy access to the network without going through the authentication process. Filters can be configured based upon device MAC address. A filter enables the ability to automatically allow or deny a device on to the network. Device filters also enable the ability to put a machine into a specific user role, such as employee or consultant, based upon MAC address. Figure 7-3 provides an example of device filters.

Figure 7-3   *Device Filters*

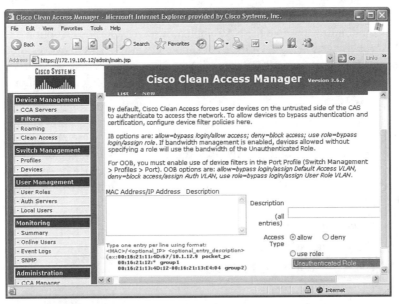

In addition to MAC address device filters, the manager also supports the configuration of filters based upon subnet or IP address. The Device Management area of the manager allows the configuration of a user to bypass authentication based upon the user's IP address. This subnet filter capability also supports the mechanism to permit or deny a user access to the network based upon IP address. Similar to device filters, a user can also be assigned a user role such as employee or consultant based upon the source IP address. An example of how to configure a subnet filter is provided in Figure 7-4.

NOTE   Previous versions of the NAC appliance managed wireless access points and allowed mobile users to roam between different access points and maintain an authenticated connection. Roaming and wireless access point management is now performed by the wireless LAN controller (WLC) management product and is no longer configured by the NAC appliance manager.

Figure 7-4 *Subnet Filters*

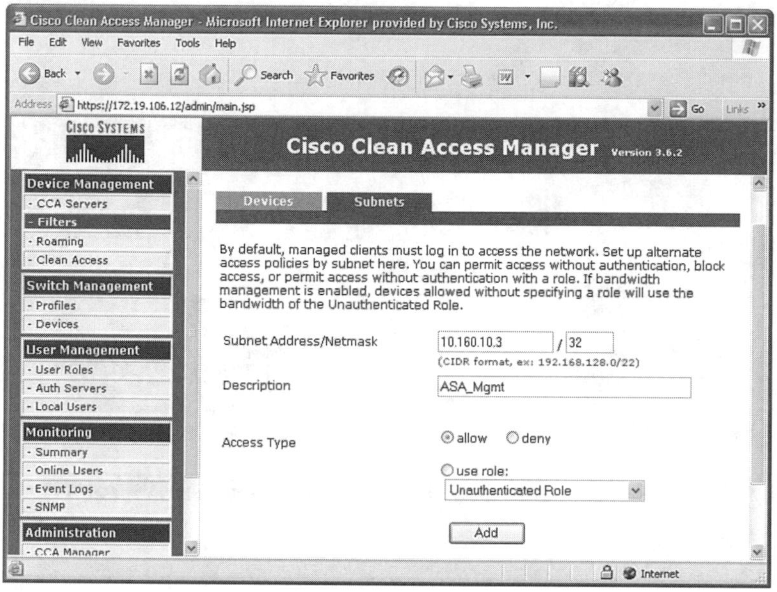

Clean Access

The Clean Access area under Device Management in the manager allows the display and configuration of exempt devices, floating device, general setup, network scanning, and agent configuration. Exempt devices are devices that are exempt based upon MAC address as discussed earlier in this chapter. Floating devices are designed for public places like online kiosks. Floating devices are authenticated during the user session. Once the user logs off, the next user on that device—even if it is the same user—must be reauthenticated. Floating devices are defined by their L2 MAC address. An example of the location to configure a floating device by adding its MAC address is displayed in Figure 7-5.

General setup involves configuring the logon or restriction information that is displayed for the users in the various user roles. General setup also specifies whether the agent is required for a specific user role. Figure 7-6 displays an example of the General setup configuration parameters for a particular user role.

Figure 7-5 *Floating Device*

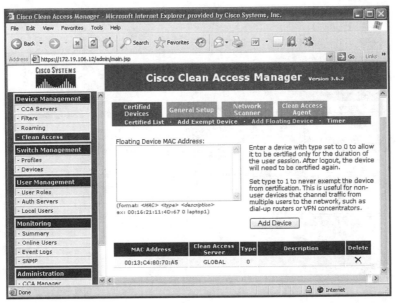

Figure 7-6 *General Setup*

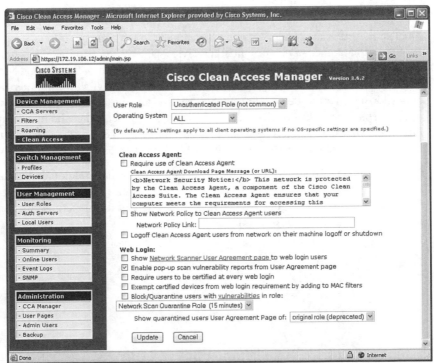

The NAC appliance contains an embedded Nessus network scanner. The NAC appliance server supports Nessus plug-ins and provides a mechanism for users to download new Nessus plug-ins. Figure 7-7 provides the configuration options for the user-agreement that is displayed to the user to access a network, based upon a network scan.

Figure 7-7 *User Agreement*

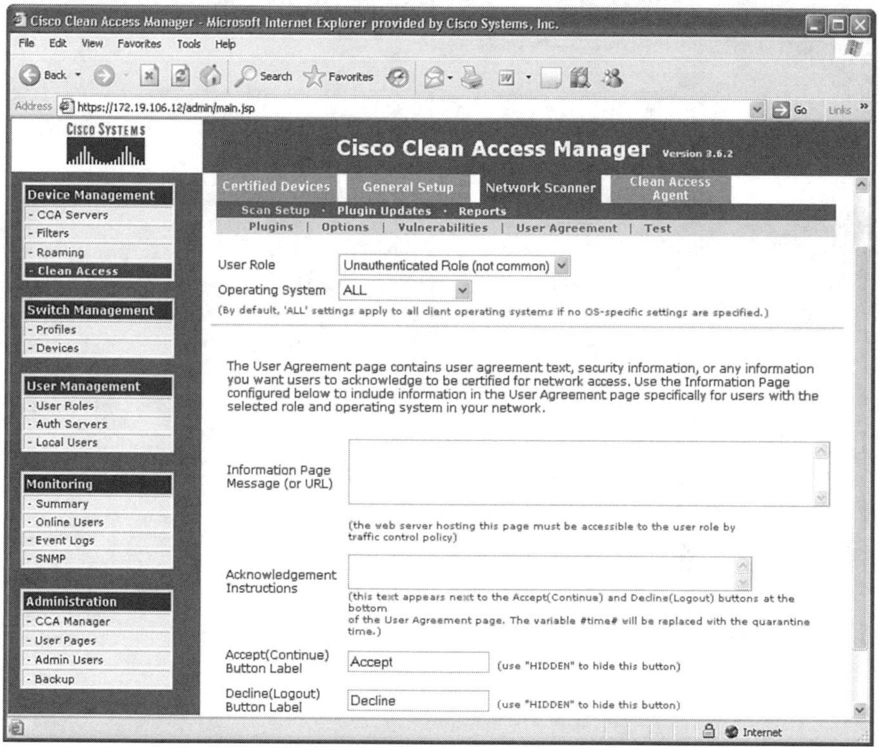

The optional agent provides an extra dimension of scanning and authentication to Windows clients. The agents can be distributed to Windows clients directly from the server. Agents allow registry checks to determine if OS hotfixes are applied. These registry checks can also be used to determine the existence of a specific software application and the inspection for a potential worm or virus infection.

In addition to registry checks, rules can also be defined in the manager to check if an end station with the agent has a specific file on the machine, or if a specific service or application is active on the Windows end station. Figure 7-8 displays some of the rules check list to determine if specific Windows hotfixes have been applied to a client with the agent. Figure 7-9 shows the parameters used to create a rule to inspect a client for a specific registry key. Figure 7-10 displays rules for checking the presence of specific antispyware products on clients with the agent installed.

Figure 7-8 *Rules Check List*

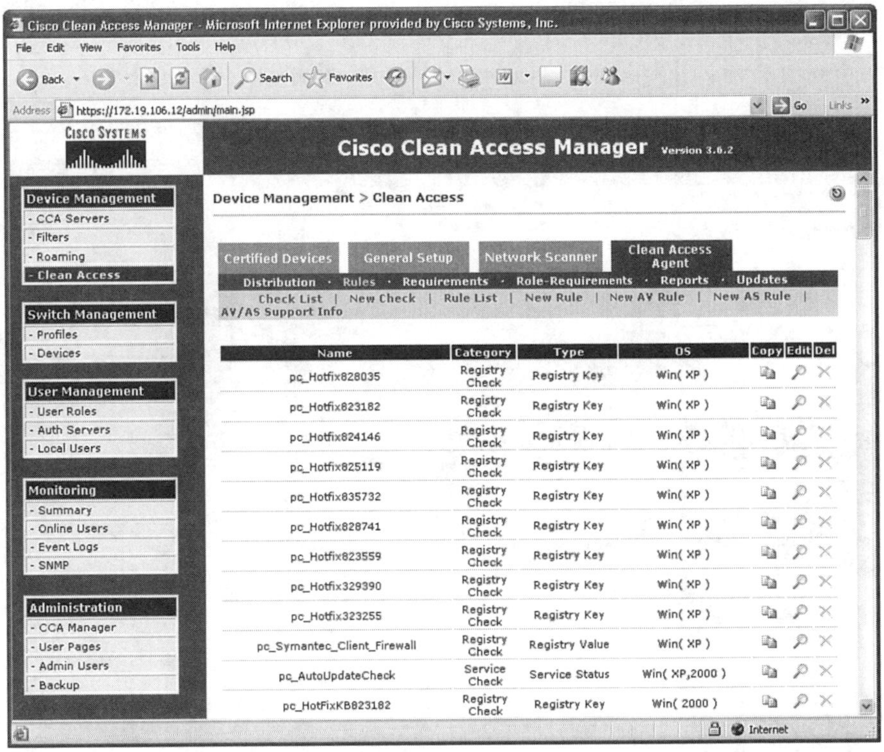

Figure 7-9   *Registry Check*

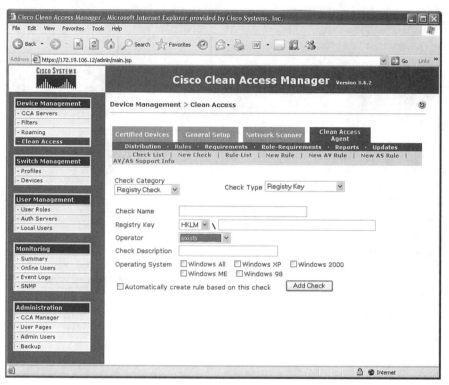

Figure 7-10 *Antispyware Check*

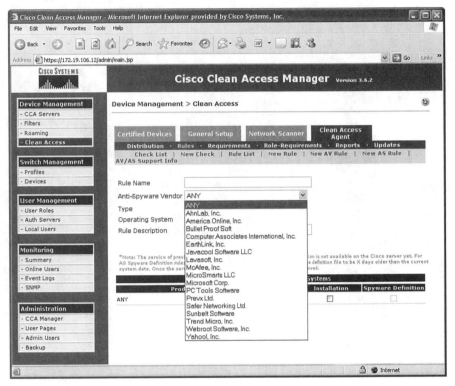

Switch Management

The switch management function is designed to configure LAN switches that will be used in an OOB NAC appliance deployment. The NAC appliance manager uses SNMP to manage the OOB LAN switches. Switch management is composed of the profiles and devices categories. A profile defines the type of LAN switch and the SNMP parameters that are used to manage the LAN switch. Figure 7-11 displays an example of the location and settings to configure a LAN switch profile.

Figure 7-11 *Profile*

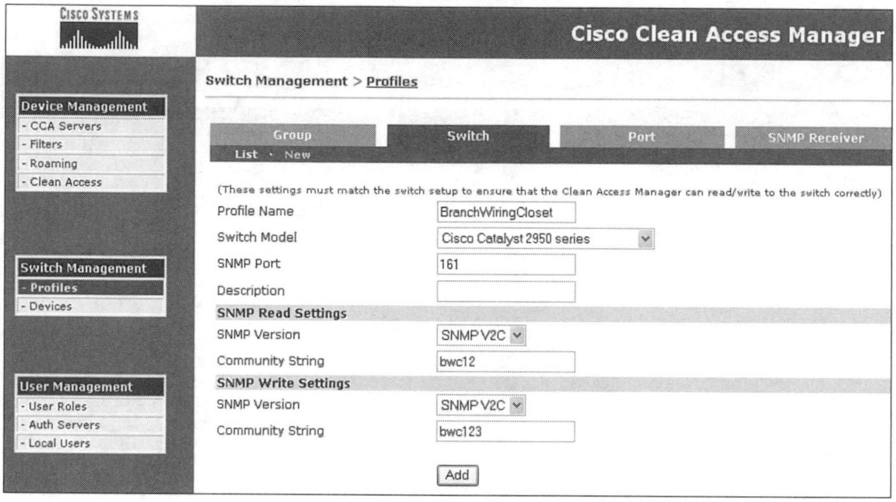

The device option under switch management enables the user to define or discover LAN switches that can be used for an OOB deployment. The IP address of a LAN switch can be defined, or the user can enter a range of IP addresses to search and discover LAN switches that can be used for OOB. The device option also displays the discovered clients or end stations of the OOB LAN switch. The clients are discovered based upon SNMP MAC notification updates or Link-up/Link-down SNMP traps from the LAN switch to the NAC appliance manager.

User Management

Each user is classified to participate in a specific user role. User roles are both predefined and customized. User roles are used to determine what an authenticated user can do on a network. Some of the parameters associated with user roles include the following:

- VLAN ID
- allowed networks and ports
- bandwidth permission
- session timeout
- host registry key restrictions

By default all user traffic is denied unless explicitly permitted by a global or local policy for authenticated users. Figure 7-12 displays a sample list of user roles.

Figure 7-12 *List of Roles*

NAC appliance has a quarantine role for Windows users with the agent and a quarantine role for users with a vulnerability that was discovered during a network scan by the NAC appliance. The vulnerable user is placed in the quarantine role until they update their device to remove the identified vulnerability. Users will be moved from the quarantine role after remediation and a successful logon. One of the main drivers behind the different user roles is the definition of what a specific type of user is allowed to do on the network. The quarantine role allows users to access only a part of the network in order to download the required software updates to address the identified vulnerability in order to be remediated and be removed from the quarantine role.

Figure 7-13 displays an example of how the quarantine role is allowed permission to access only the remediation server. Users who are placed in the quarantine role must be remediated before they can join one of the other user roles that are designed for successful authentication and certification.

Figure 7-13 *Traffic Control of Agent Quarantine Role*

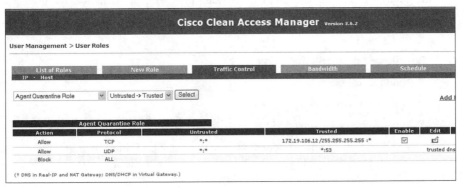

Several mechanisms can associate, or map, a user to a user role during the authentication process. One example is the ability to map a user to a role based upon their VLAN ID.

The NAC appliance can authenticate users who are locally defined on the NAC appliance or leverage an external LDAP, RADIUS, or NTLM (Windows NT LAN Manager) database for user authentication. The NAC appliance manager allows the ability to define a local user, a user's logon password, and mapping to a specific user role that will define what the user can do once authenticated into the network. Figure 7-14 displays an example of defining a new user on the local user database and mapping that user to the consultant user role.

Figure 7-14 *Create a Local User and Map to User Role*

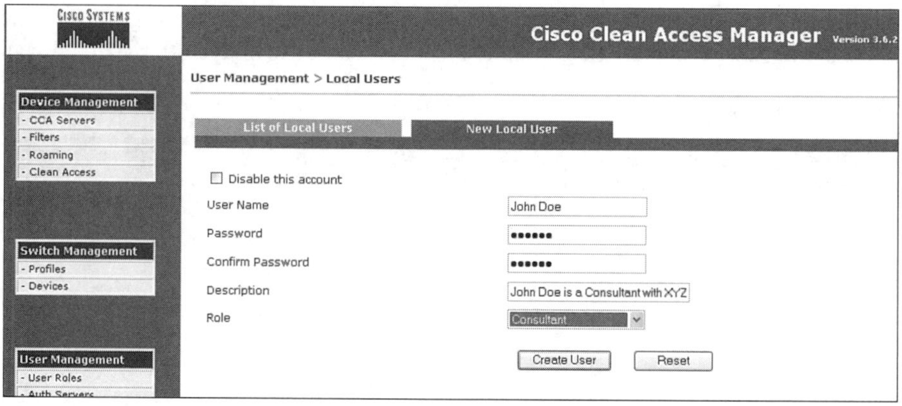

Leveraging of an external authentication server offers several advantages over using the local user database on the NAC appliance. The benefits of the external authentication server include scalability and the ability to deploy the NAC appliance without having to manually redefine each user. The NAC appliance manager allows mapping rules to be defined to determine which role a user is assigned to after authentication and certification by the NAC appliance. Figure 7-15 displays how you can use an external LDAP database for authentication and mapping rules of user roles, based upon VLAN ID and group name.

Figure 7-15 *Mapping Rules with External User Authentication Server*

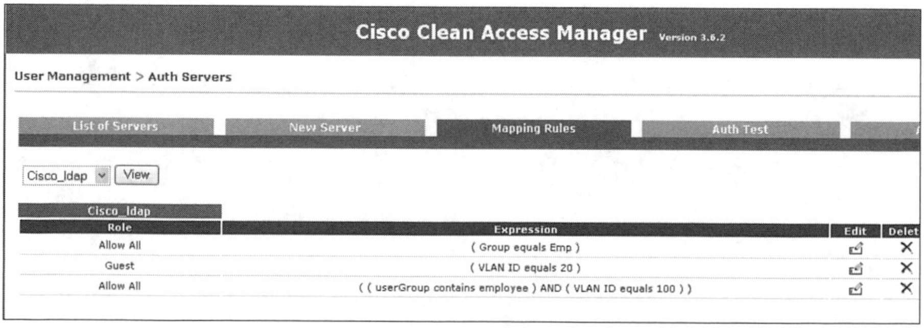

Monitoring

The NAC appliance manager provides excellent monitoring capabilities that can be used to identify what is going on in the network. With the Monitoring feature of the manager, you can display all online users with specific details, including the following:

- user's IP address
- MAC address
- VLAN
- logon time
- user role

Figure 7-16 displays a summary of the monitoring statistics, and Figure 7-17 shows the specific user characteristics or parameters that can be displayed for each online user.

Figure 7-16 *Monitoring Summary*

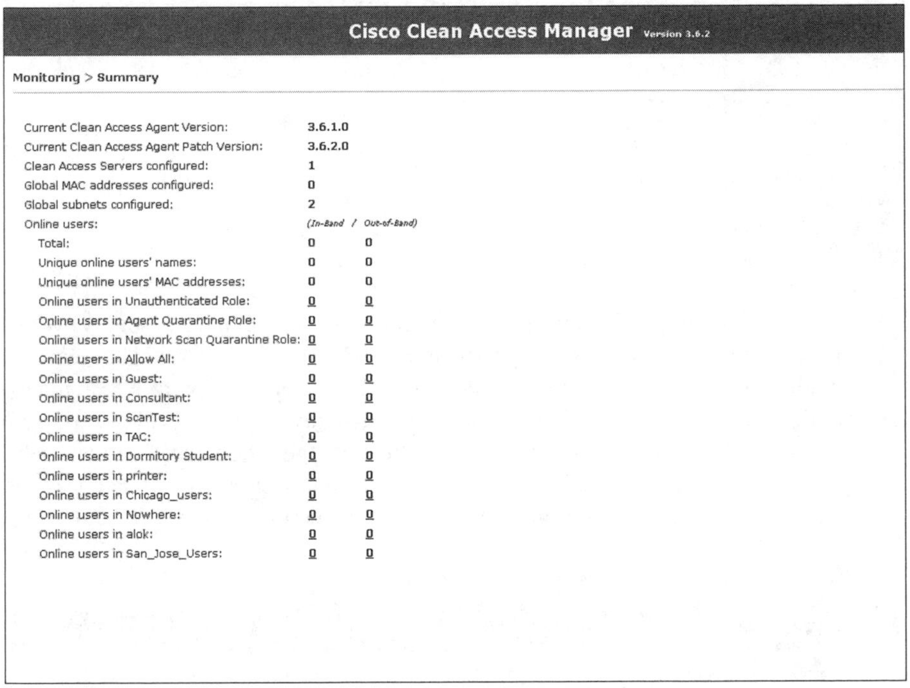

Figure 7-17 *Online User Information*

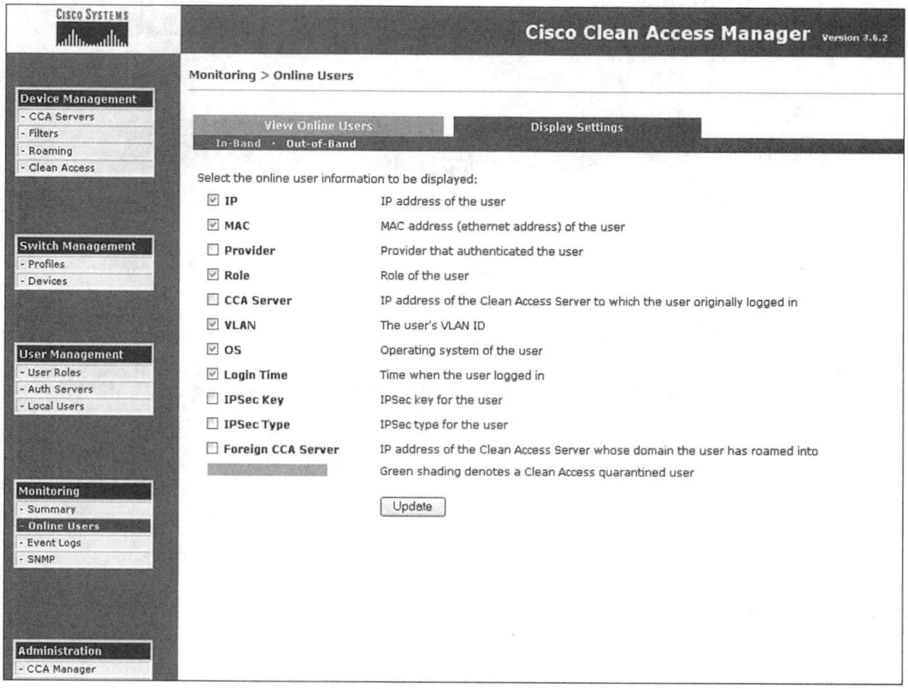

The NAC appliance manager also features the display of event logs as an option under Monitoring. Event logs can contain items including admin logon, rule creation, policy deployment, and antivirus/antispyware updates. Figure 7-18 displays a sample of events in the event log.

Figure 7-18 *Event Log*

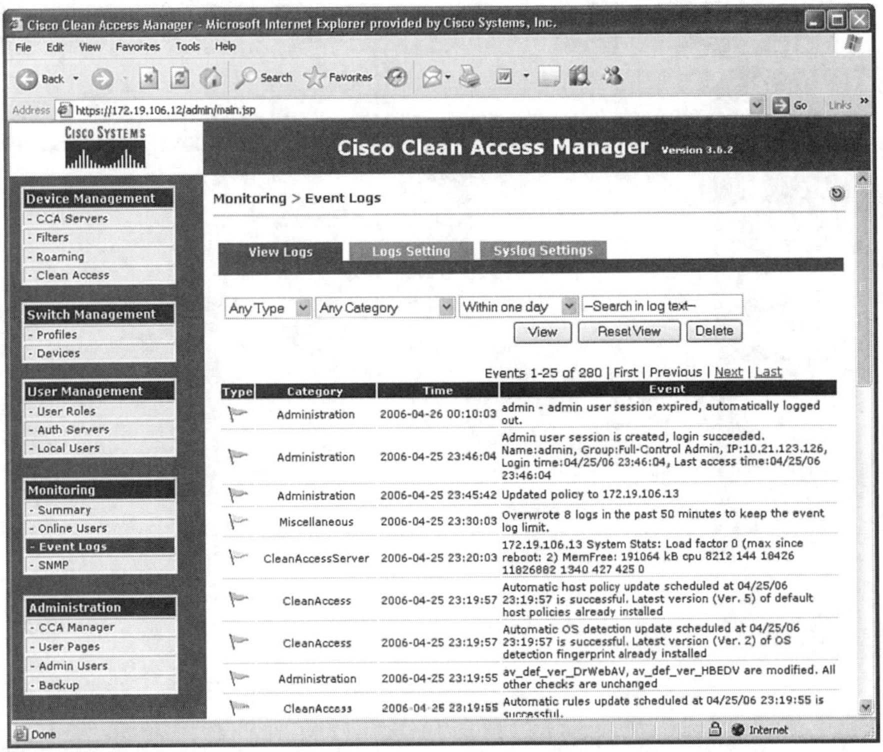

The Monitoring function also provides the ability to configure SNMP parameters. SNMP parameters that you can configure under Monitoring include community strings and threshold values. The SNMP area under Monitoring also provides the ability to download updated SNMP MIBs for the NAC appliance. Figure 7-19 displays a sample of the configurable SNMP parameters for Monitoring.

Figure 7-19 *SNMP*

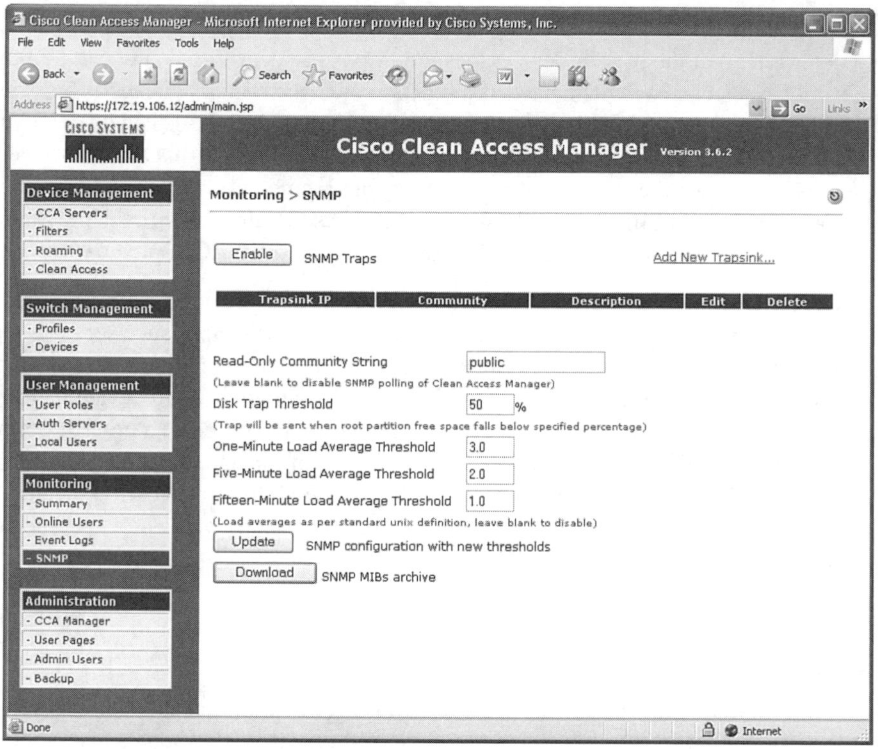

Administration

The NAC appliance manager also contains an Administration option in the manager GUI. The functions contained under the Administrative option include the traditional IP addressing, the manager, SSL certificates, definition of admin users, and the ability to back up the NAC appliance manager. These administrative features are not described in detail because they are conventional and not the focus of this chapter on the security features of the NAC appliance.

Summary

NAC is the process of identifying, authorizing, and verifying the security posture to determine that the user or device does not impose a security risk and can join the network safely. NAC can be implemented as a function of Cisco router/switches as NAC Framework, or NAC, can be implemented as a turn-key NAC appliance. NAC can be deployed in-band, where all data traffic from the user goes through the server, or OOB, where the server is involved only in the authentication, scanning, and remediation process and is removed from the normal data traffic flow of the user. OOB offers higher-scalability deployments because the data throughput is not limited by the capacity of the NAC appliance server.

The NAC appliance is also marketed as CCA. The NAC appliance architecture is composed of a server, manager, and optional access agent. The NAC appliance server is managed by the NAC appliance manager because NAC appliance servers do not have an exposed command-line interface (CLI) for all functions, and there is not a device manager. The optional access agent at the time of this publication is offered as a no-cost option and is designed for Windows end stations. The presence of the agent enables advanced security posture validation on the end station, including the ability to check for specific files, services and applications, and to inspect Windows registry values for specific values or vulnerabilities.

References

Cisco Systems, Inc. Cisco Clean Access Manager Installation and Administration Guide, Release 3.4. http://www.cisco.com/en/US/products/ps6128/products_user_guide_list.html

Cisco Systems, Inc. Cisco Clean Access Manager Installation and Administration Guide, Release 3.6. http://www.cisco.com/en/US/products/ps6128/products_user_guide_list.html

Cisco Systems, Inc. Cisco Clean Access Server Installation and Administration Guide, Release 3.4. http://cisco.com/application/pdf/en/us/guest/products/ps6128/c1626/ccmigration_09186a00803d26d8.pdf

Cisco Systems, Inc. Cisco Clean Access Manager Installation and Administration Guide, Release 3.5. http://www.cisco.com/application/pdf/en/us/guest/products/ps6128/c1626/ccmigration_09186a00804ce7c3.pdf

Cisco Systems, Inc. Cisco Clean Access Manager Installation and Administration Guide, Release 3.6. http://www.cisco.com/en/US/products/ps6128/products_user_guide_list.html

Cisco Systems, Inc. Cisco Clean Access Server Installation and Administration Guide, Release 3.5. http://www.cisco.com/application/pdf/en/us/guest/products/ps6128/c1626/ccmigration_09186a00804ce39d.pdf

CHAPTER 8

Managing the Cisco Security Agent

The Cisco Security Agent represents the last line of defense in a layered self-defending network. The Cisco Security Agent operates directly on the end station by monitoring the OS kernel and requests to the file system, network resources, and registry keys. The Cisco Security Agent can reside directly on the PC, laptop, or server in the network. Cisco Security Agent is supported on Windows, Solaris, and Linux machines.

Cisco Security Agent can provide a day-zero defense against new network attacks since the Cisco Security Agent is looking for malicious behavior directly on a workstation instead of known worms and viruses that can participate in a network attack. *Day-zero* is a fancy way of saying that an attack can be stopped by looking at the symptoms of an attack, rather than a unique identifier or signature of the attack. For example, a virus may delete a specific system file, but day-zero protection would notify the user that something was trying to delete any system file rather than looking for a specific virus. Day-zero protection does not require any host signatures and is a good complement to other signature-based defenses, such as network IPS.

The Cisco Security Agents are centrally managed by the Management Center. The Management Center features an easy-to-use web GUI and uses HTTPS between the Management Center and the Cisco Security Agent on the end station to ensure security during the configuration process. The Cisco Security Agent Management Center includes support for the following features:

- Day-zero protection against certain attacks
- Host intrusion prevention
- Protection against buffer overflows
- Port scan detection
- Distributed personal firewall protection
- Protection against spyware/adware
- Application inventory
- Location-based polices depending upon whether the machine is on a home network or the corporate network
- Policies to restrict access to removable media, including USB devices

- Support for International Windows
- Native end-station Cisco Security Agent Panel support for French, German, Japanese (Kanji), Chinese, Italian, Spanish, and Korean
- Application inventory and use-tracking
- Hot fix and Service Pack (SP) checking
- File and directory protection
- Enforcing security policies for data on Clipboard
- Antivirus DAT checking
- Windows XP Home Edition support
- Embedded Cisco Trust Agent in Cisco Security Agent
- Auto-enrollment group for Windows, Solaris, and Linux
- QoS marking of applications from Cisco Security Agent
- VMWare qualification
- Tablet PC qualification
- Solaris 9

Cisco Security Agent also contains an optional component known as the network shim. The network shim provides additional protection on end stations, including protection against attacks by detecting SYN floods, port scans, and malformed packets at shim layer on the OS at the end station.

Management Center for Cisco Security Agents

Cisco Security Agents are configured and deployed from the Management Center to the end-station desktop. The Cisco Security Agent Management Center can manage up to 100,000 Cisco Security Agents. The Management Center for Cisco Security Agents is a standalone management product and, like Cisco Incident Control Server (Cisco ICS), is not included in the Cisco Security Manager.

A web browser is used as the GUI to the Management Center. Configuration between the Management Center and the Cisco Security Agent is secured with HTTPS/SSL. The homepage for the Management Center for Cisco Security Agents is displayed in Figure 8-1.

Figure 8-1 *Management Center for Cisco Security Agent Homepage*

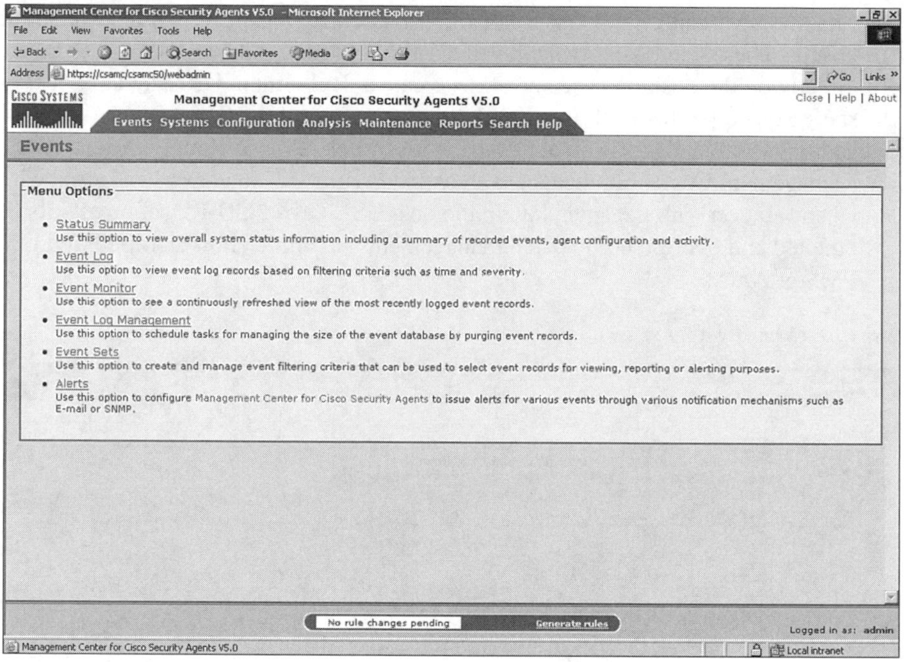

The Management Center allows the configuration of security policy rules for device groups. The Management Center provides default device groups, such as Linux servers. Hosts or end stations that contain a Cisco Security Agent are included in at least one device group. Security policies are composed of individual rules and are applied to hosts in a device group. Managing the security policies on the Cisco Security Agents can involve the following processes, which are discussed in the following sections:

- Deploying the Cisco Security Agent kit to the end station
- Displaying the end-station hostname in the device group
- Reviewing the security policy for a device group
- Attaching rules to the security policy
- Generating rules and deploying to device groups
- Using event monitor and viewing the event log
- Running application analysis

Deploying Cisco Secure Agent Kits

The Management Center can create a Cisco Security Agent Kit for a device or device groups. These agent kits are deployed onto end stations and install the Cisco Security Agent directly on the desktop. The agent kits create a deployment URL, and a user at the end station can type this URL into a web browser to install the Cisco Secure Agent on the end-station desktop. You can create an agent kit by selecting **Systems > Agent Kits** from the Management Center homepage, as shown in Figure 8-2. Agent kits can also be installed on an end station with the agent kit zip file on a USB key or CD-ROM. Agent kits can also be bundled and distributed by patch management and application distribution products like SMS or Altiris.

Figure 8-2 *Cisco Security Agent Kits*

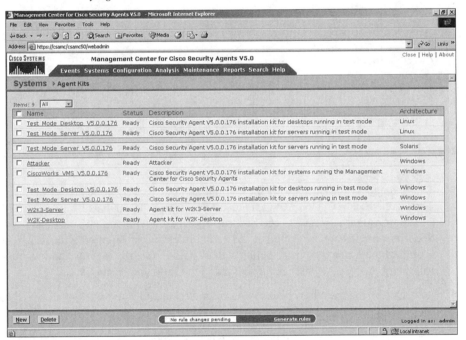

Displaying the End-Station Hostname in the Device Groups

The hostname of the end station must be associated with a device group. A hostname is automatically associated with a device group as indicated in the Cisco Security Agent kit. A hostname can also be added to additional device groups. The ability to associate a hostname, such as a Windows workstation name, with a device group enables common security policies to be deployed to different end stations, including Solaris Web Server, SAP Servers, teleworkers, and so on. For example, a Linux web server in New York City

for business-to-business (B2B) can be part of the Linux device group, Web Server device group, New York City data center device group, and the B2B server device group.

The ability to include a host in a device group and apply a security policy to a device group enables common configurations to multiple end stations to be deployed with a common security policy for the device group. A device group can have multiple security policies applied to the device group. The same security policy can also be applied to multiple device groups. Figure 8-3 displays an example of several of the device groups including the auto-enrollment group for Linux and the default group for systems that install the Desktop agent kit.

Figure 8-3   *Device Groups*

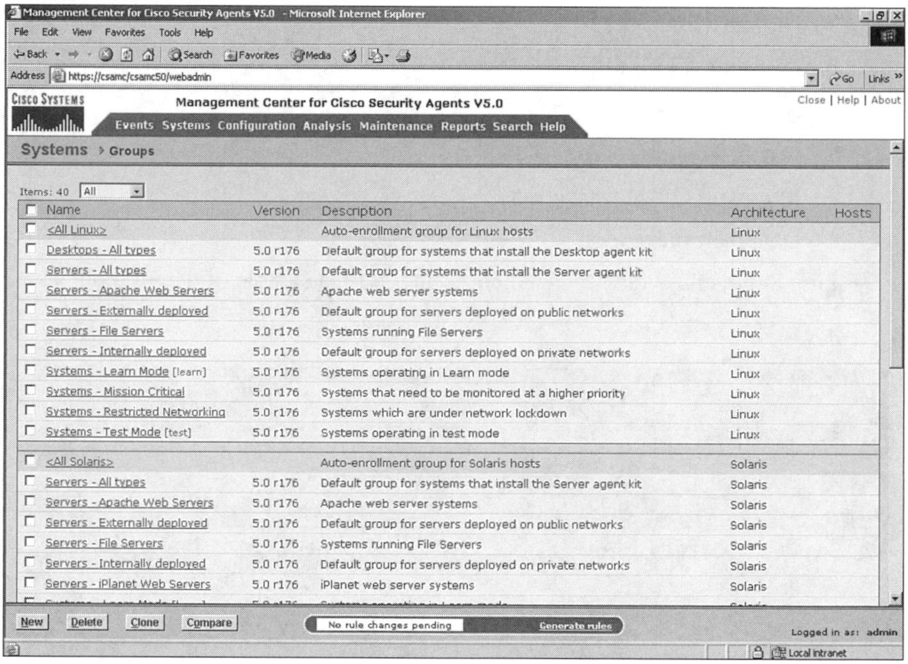

Reviewing Policies

Policies contain the set of security rules that will be attached to a device group. Several default policies are provided to help get users started. These default policies contain a baseline that protects end stations against many day-zero attacks. You can copy and modify default policies or customize your own. Examples of these default policies include a Common Security Module and the Cisco VPN Client Module. The Management Center for Cisco Security Agent also includes support for the following default policy groups:

- Generic Server
- Generic Desktop

- Microsoft IIS v4.0 and v5.0
- Apache v1.3
- Microsoft SQL Server
- Microsoft Exchange
- Sendmail
- Domain Name Server (DNS) servers
- DHCP servers
- Network Time Protocol (NTP) servers
- Domain Controllers
- Distributed Firewall
- Browser protection
- Instant Messenger control
- Microsoft Office protection
- Data theft prevention

Figure 8-4 displays the Management Center with a sample of default policies.

Figure 8-4 *Policies*

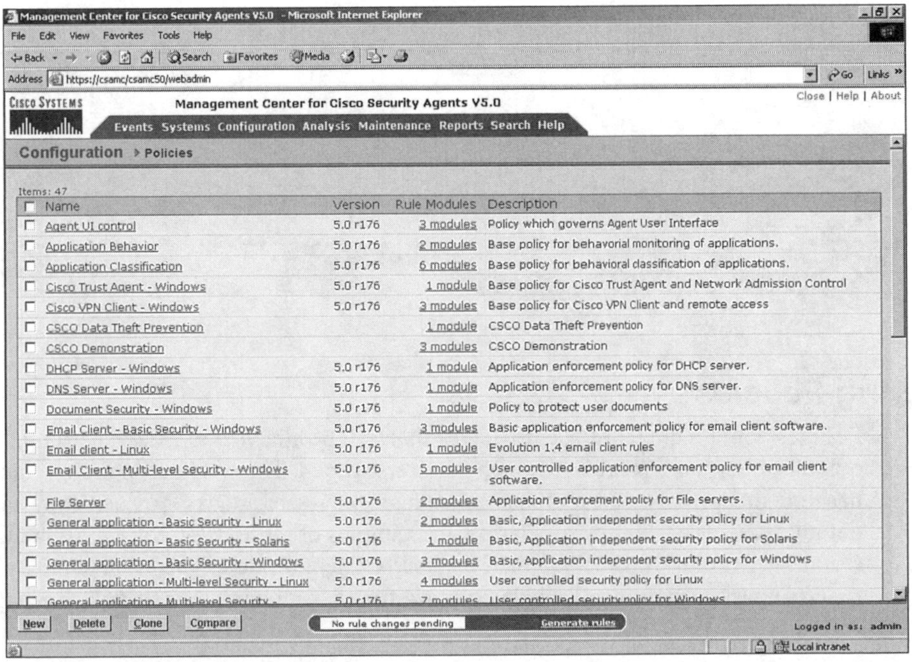

Attaching Rules to a Policy

A policy is composed of individual rules. A collection of rules is named a rule module. Rule modules are generally specific to a particular OS. Rules define each component of the specific security posture in the rule module, which can be attached to a security policy. Rules can also refer to an application class to indicate which applications or processes are policed by the rule. Rules can also be composed with variables, so common information between rules can be defined once and referenced multiple times. Example of variables in rules includes event sets, query settings, file sets, network address sets, network services, registry sets, COM component sets, and data sets. Figure 8-5 displays some the rules that compose the Common Web Server Security Module default policy.

Figure 8-5 *Rules of the Common Web Server Security Module Policy*

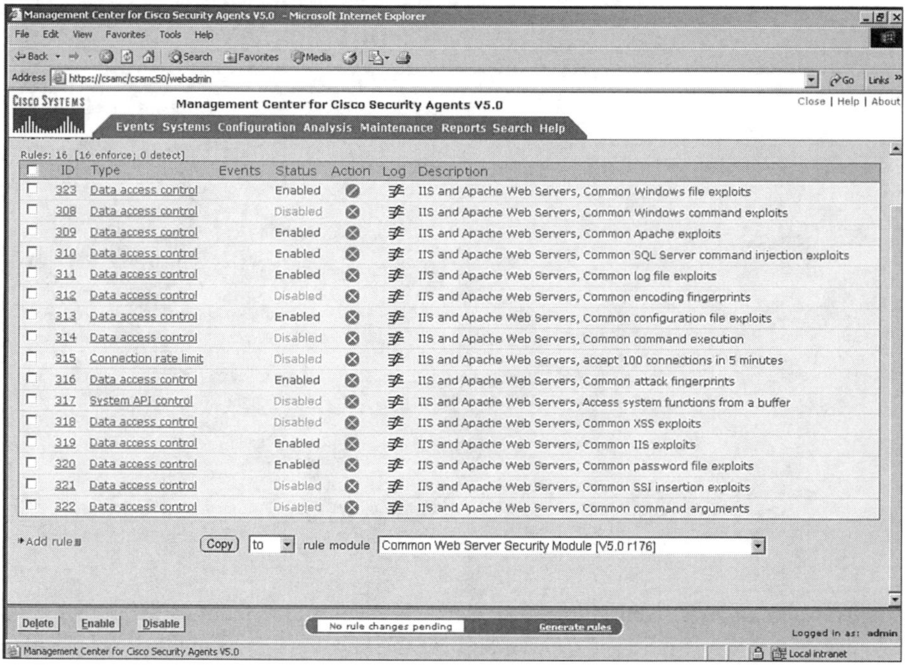

Generating and Deploying Rules

Updating the security policy on an end station requires that the new rules be generated and distributed to the end station. The Management Center for Cisco Security Agents GUI displays the option to Generate Rules at the bottom of the screen and informs the user of the number of new rules that have been configured, but have not yet been generated into a deployable security policy. The Generate Rules process also informs the user of any policies that have been configured but are not associated or attached to any device group.

The Cisco Security Agent on the end station will automatically receive the new security policy from the Generate Rules process during the next automated or manual update cycle. An example of how to initiate the Generate Rules process is provided in Figure 8-6. The end station can elect to poll the Management Center to manually receive the new security policy by selecting the update option directly from the Cisco Security Agent icon on the end-station desktop.

Figure 8-6   *Generate Rules*

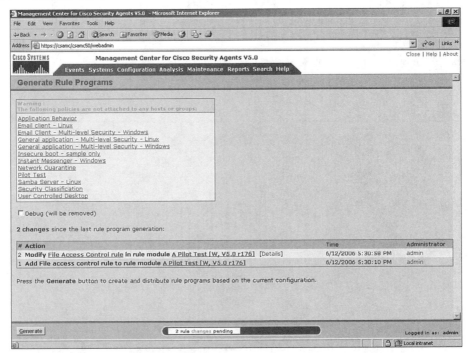

The Management Center for Cisco Security Agents also features the ability to force connected workstations to poll in and get the latest policy using the "send polling hint" capability. If the user configures the send polling hint on the Management Center for Cisco Security Agents, a User Datagram Protocol (UDP) message can be sent from the Management Center to the host when there is a change in the policy for the host. This UDP message instructs the Cisco Security Agent on the host to download the new security policy prior to the next scheduled polling period.

Using Event Monitor

The Management Center provides an event monitor and event log to view and record significant events that occur at the end-station Cisco Security Agents. It is often advantageous to filter out some of these event logs to reduce false positives and provide a quick mechanism to view a specific event log of interest. Figure 8-7 displays the event monitor in the Management Center, and Figure 8-8 displays the window to configure an event filter to restrict the number of Event Logs that are viewed in the Event Monitor and Event Log.

Figure 8-7 *Event Monitor*

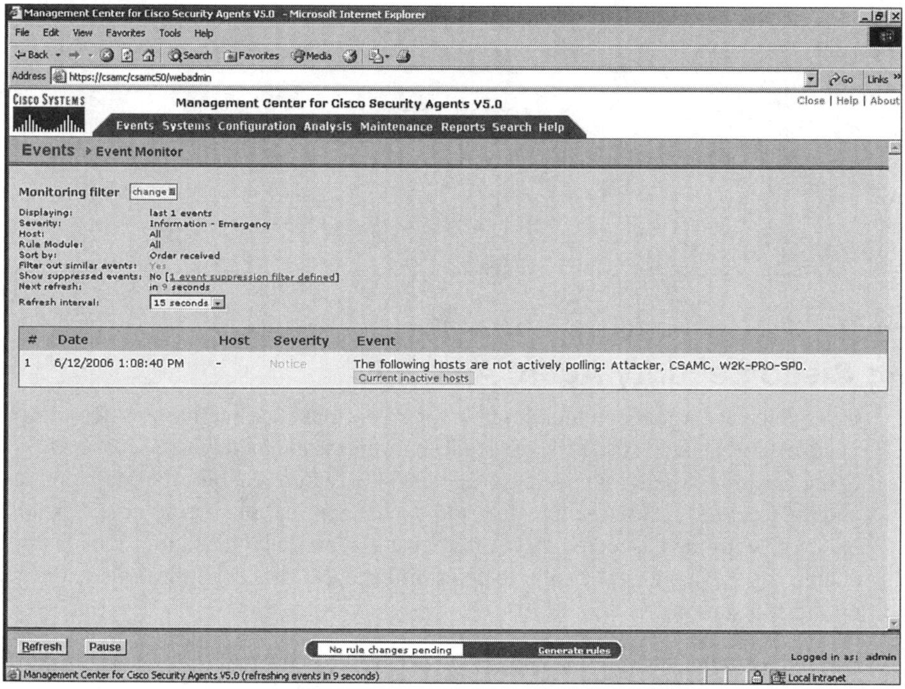

Figure 8-8 *Event Filter*

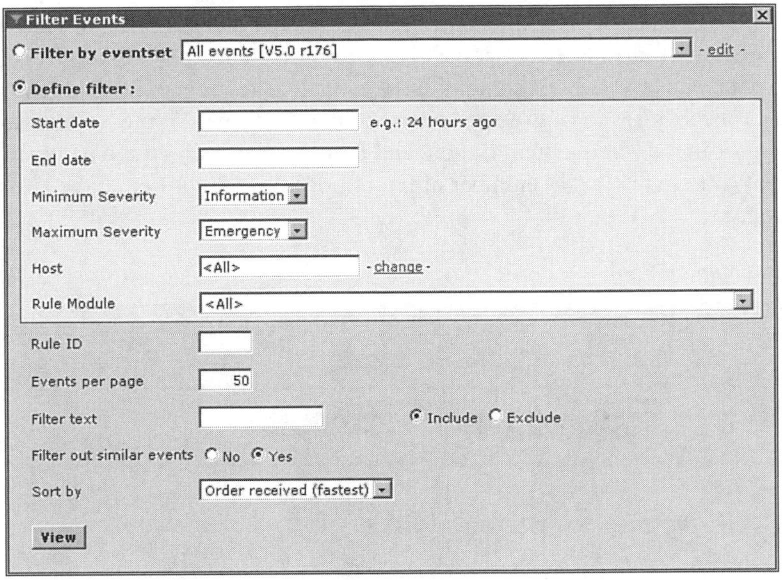

Running Cisco Security Agent Analysis

Cisco Security Agent contains support for an optional application profiler known as Cisco Security Agent Analysis. This application profiler is enabled with a separate license for the Cisco Security Agent Management Center. This feature enables the Management Center and the Cisco Security Agent to determine what applications are deployed on a PC, laptop, or server with the Cisco Security Agent installed on that end station. This feature also enables the Management Center to determine the use pattern of these detected applications on the end stations.

Application analysis is enabled on a per-device group basis and will analyze all hosts in that device group. Application analysis is initiated by selecting the Application Deployment Investigation option under Analysis in the Management Center. Application Deployment Investigation includes a list of reports to display information gained from the application profiling process. The information in the reports that are generated by the Profiler contains statistics about how often an application is used. The reports generated from the analysis also contain network data statistics, including network source, destination, and service traffic patterns. Information in the reports about how applications are used on an end system can provide valuable input into the construction of effective rules and security policies for device groups. Reports that are generated by the application analysis include the following:

- Anti-Virus Installations Report (Norton and McAfee)
- Installed Products Report

- Unprotected Hosts Report (No associated Policy Groups)
- Unprotected Products Report (No Policy to protect that Product)
- Product Usage Report
- Network Data Flows Report, which includes the following information:
  — Number of unique source/destination combinations
  — Number of client hosts
  — Number of server hosts
  — Filter report by source, destination, protocol
- Network Server Application Report, which includes the following information:
  — Associates the application with open service ports
  — Identifies which service ports are not used or are lightly used

Application Deployment Investigation is an optional feature of the Management Center for Cisco Security Agents. The Management Center also contains a feature called Learn Mode. Learn Mode is used as a mechanism to eliminate query-responses for common application and service use on the desktop with the Cisco Security Agent. The Cisco Security Agent will often query the user when a new application is running and ask the user if this is the expected behavior. Learn Mode enables the Cisco Security Agent to learn the normal application and service use on a desktop without having a query-response pop up to the user for each application or service. The Cisco Security Agent is placed in Learn Mode during the first 72 hours of deployment of the Cisco Security Agent on the desktop.

In addition to Learn Mode, there is also an optional Test Mode for a security policy. Test Mode is designed for policies and will log any activity from the policy but will not query or deny network activity, based upon a policy in Test Mode. Test Mode is designed to inform what the effect of a new security policy would be on a host before actually enforcing the new security policy on the end station.

The Analysis module also contains an Application Behavior Investigation feature in addition to Application Deployment Investigation. The user must select the specific application, the time to end the analysis, the application, and the specific host in the Management Center to investigate the behavior of that application. The Management Center will allow the selection of an application class for analysis on a particular host. However, it is recommended that analysis only occur for one specific application at a time on a particular host. The Application Behavior Investigation feature can create a recommended rule module to increase security, based upon the analyzed application behavior on the end station. This rule module generation feature of Application Behavior Investigation will create a new application class in the created rule module for the analyzed application.

Cisco Security Agent

The Cisco Security Agent sits directly on the end station. The Cisco Security Agent is often identified by an icon of a red flag at the bottom of the desktop. A waving red flag notifies the user of suspicious behavior that could be indicative of an attack.

The Cisco Security Agent Panel is composed of the following categories:

- Status
- System Security

Figure 8-9 provides an example of the Cisco Security Agent Panel.

Figure 8-9   *Cisco Security Agent Panel*

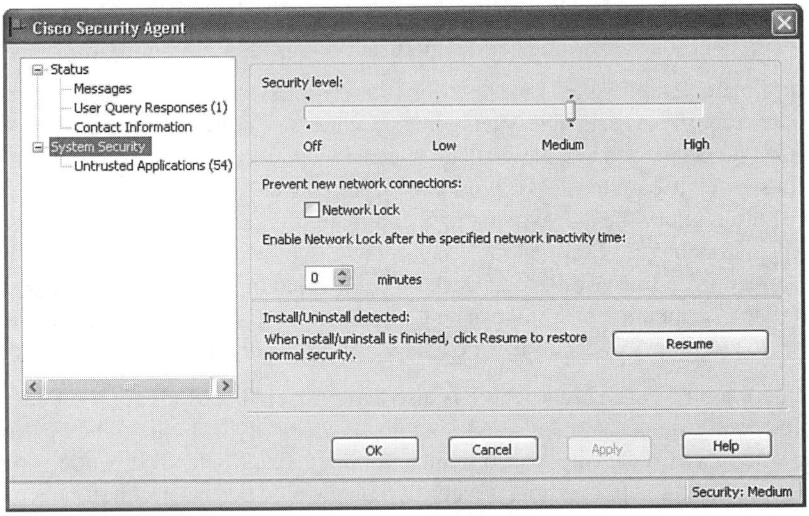

Status

The Status area of the Cisco Security Agent panel provides information to the end user on what the Cisco Security Agent is doing. This status feedback on the Cisco Security Agent Panel is important because the end user typically does not have any direct access to the Management Center for Cisco Security Agents.

The main Status area provides several items of important information about the Cisco Security Agent including the following:

- Host name
- Management Center
- Registration date
- Last poll time (to check for a new policy configuration)
- Last download time (to download a new policy configuration)
- Software update
- Network Admission Control posture results
- Poll button (to poll Management Center to download a new policy configuration)

The following subcategories are available in the Status category:

- **Messages**—The Messages subcategory provides information to the user about what important events have been detected by the Cisco Security Agent.
- **User Query Response**—The User Query Response subpanel provides details on what permissions were asked to the user (for example, application *x* attempted to modify memory in process *y*; the user was queried and the response was "Yes").
- **Contact Information**—Optional information, including name, phone number, location, and e-mail address to contact the end user on the desktop with the Cisco Security Agent.

System Security

The System Security area provides a mechanism where certain users can specify a default security policy (high, medium, low) if this option is allowed by the Management Center. The System Security area also provides an option to restrict new network connections after a certain network inactivity timeout.

The System Security area also provides a vehicle to display to the user which applications are natively untrusted by the Cisco Security Agent. These untrusted applications can result in the user being queried about permission to use the application if the application attempts to modify critical system resources. The Cisco Security Agent panel also provides an option to remove applications for the untrusted list, if this option is enabled by the Management Center. Figure 8-10 displays a sample of the display of a few of the untrusted applications on the Cisco Security Agent Panel.

Figure 8-10 *Untrusted Applications*

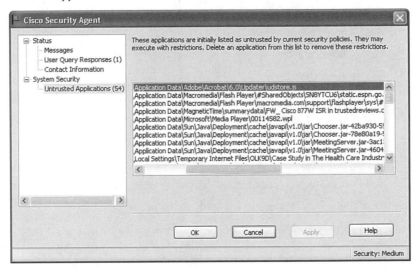

Summary

The Cisco Security Agent is often the last line of defense in a self-defending network. The Cisco Security Agent sits on the user's desktop and monitors OS kernel activity for suspicious behavior. The Cisco Security Agent can be self-defending, as the Cisco Security Agent can ask user permission or block suspicious activity on the desktop and defend against a network attack. The Cisco Security Agent can prevent "day-zero" attacks because it looks for symptoms of an attack rather than a unique signature of the attack. Cisco Security Agents are a good complement to other signature-based defenses, such as IPS, in a layered self-defending network. The Cisco Security Agent is considered to be a Host IPS (HIPS) product that complements Network IPS and other self-defending components within the network fabric.

The Management Center for Cisco Security Agents is the centralized management product to manage the agents. A Management Center can manage up to 100,000 agents. A host that contains a Cisco Security Agent is placed into a device group in the Management Center. A host can belong to more than one device group. Security policies are attached to device groups and contain a definition of the security policy that is monitored or enforced on the end station. Multiple security policies can be attached to a single device group, and a single security policy can be attached to multiple device groups. Security policies or policy groups are composed of rule modules. A rule module can be applied to multiple security policies. A rule module is fundamentally a named collection or container of individual rules.

References

Cisco Systems, Inc. Cisco Security Agent 4.5 Data Sheet. http://www.cisco.com/en/US/products/sw/secursw/ps5057/products_data_sheet09186a008033a40f.html

Cisco Systems, Inc. Using Management Center for Cisco Security Agents Version 4.5.1. http://www.cisco.com/en/US/products/sw/secursw/ps5057/products_configuration_guide_book09186a0080422f08.html

Cisco Systems, Inc. Using Management Center for Cisco Security Agents Version 5.0. http://www.cisco.com/en/US/products/sw/secursw/ps5057/products_configuration_guide_book09186a00805ae89c.html

Sullivan, Chad. Cisco Security Agent. Cisco Press 2005.

Sullivan, Chad, Jeff Asher, and Paul Mauvais. Advanced Host Intrusion Prevention with CSA. Cisco Press 2006.

Cisco Security Manager

This book details how a layered defense is the best defense to protect a network against attacks. A layered defense as part of a self-defending network is similar to layered defenses in sports such as football and soccer. These sports have an initial defense against the opposition followed by additional layers of defense closer to the critical resource of the team. In a soccer or football analogy, the critical resource is the goal, and in a network environment, the critical resource is often a server or remote PC. In the sports analogy, a layered defense is only effective if the different layers are implementing a consistent strategy and are on the same page as to what they are trying to accomplish. For example, a football defense in which the cornerbacks are playing zone defense while the safeties think that everyone is playing man defense is probably not going to be very effective because the layered defense is not coordinated and is inconsistent.

In the network environment, centralized management is an effective way to ensure that the layered defenses are all executing the same plan. Centralized management is also an effective tool to let the security operations manager know when part of the layered defense is behaving incorrectly or is being ineffective.

Centralized management is composed of two main functional areas:

- Configuration
- Monitoring/mitigation

Cisco offers a centralized management product line called the Cisco Security Management Suite. The Cisco Security Management Suite is composed of the Cisco Security Manager and Cisco Security MARS. Cisco Security Manager and Cisco Security MARS are the follow-on products to the CiscoWorks VPN and Security Management Solution (VMS) product.

Getting Started

Cisco Security Manager can centrally manage many of the individual components of the Cisco Self-Defending Network. Examples of devices that can be managed by the Cisco Security Manager include IOS routers, Adaptive Security Appliances (ASA), Intrusion Prevention Systems (IPS), PIX Firewalls, and Catalyst 6500/7600 LAN switches.

The Cisco Security Manager has three main views to manage a :

- Device view
- Map view
- Policy view

Cisco Security Manager is an integrated application because all supported device platforms are managed together. For example, the process to configure an access control list (ACL) is the same for a Cisco IOS router as an ASA security appliance. The process to configure a VPN is also independent of platform type and allows a single VPN with multiple platform types. For example, a single VPN can be created with IOS routers as the hub devices and PIX Firewalls as the spoke devices.

The integrated approach based upon service or function like firewall or VPN is a contrast to the previous product, CiscoWorks VMS. CiscoWorks VMS was platform-based, with a separate Management Center for each platform like IOS routers or PIX firewalls. CiscoWorks VMS also used a separate GUI or web browser for each Management Center or platform while the Cisco Security Manager features a single, integrated GUI. New features in the Cisco Security Manager that were not present in the CiscoWorks VMS product include the following:

- Single client GUI to manage multiple platforms
- Single access control list (ACLs) rule table for PIX, FWSM, IOS CBAC, and IOS ACL
- Catalyst 6500/7600 chassis management
- Topology map view to graphically manage the network
- Ability to import command-line interface (CLI) that has been modified by telnet/ Device Managers
- Coexist with multiple Java Runtime Environments (JREs) on a server
- Mine or filter audit reports based upon admin, date, string
- Flex-config template for nonsecurity IOS features
- Multithreaded backend server for performance increase
- Support up to 5000 devices with a single server
- Manage ASA 7.x
- Import device list from CiscoWorks Resource Management Essentials (RME)
- Hierarchical virtual private network (VPN)
- Apply access control lists (ACLs) to a group of interfaces
- Define access control lists (ACLs) for a specific time-range
- access control list (ACLs) hit count information

- Scheduled configuration deployment at specific date and time
- ASA device status
- Dynamic Multiple VPN (DMVPN)
- Aswan 2.0 (MPLS to IP Security (IPSec) VPN)

Cisco Security Manager provides a JumpStart menu so that new security operations users can quickly learn how to import, configure, and deploy configuration to security devices.

Figure 9-1 displays the JumpStart menu of the Cisco Security Manager.

Figure 9-1   *JumpStart*

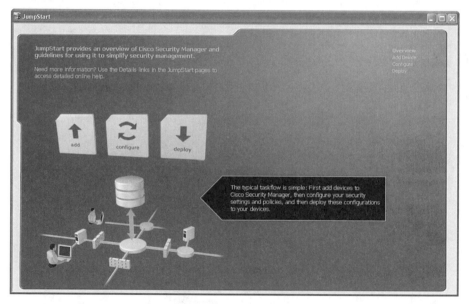

Cisco Security Manager includes several features to enable the integrated management of 5000 devices of separate platform types. One of these features is the ability to filter a list of devices by platform type. Another integrated feature is the ability to create a single device group with mixed device platforms. These device groups can be used to apply security and VPN configuration settings to a group of devices. Device groups can be based upon categories such as data center locations (for example, Los Angeles, San Francisco) or functional groups (for example, Engineering, Finance, ACME Corp, and so on).

Device View

This section describes how to add a device in Device View. You also learn how to configure access control lists (ACLs) from Device View.

Add Device

Cisco Security Manager can add a new device in several ways. The most common way is to import a device and its existing configuration from a live device on a network. Cisco Security Manager can also import a list of devices from other CiscoWorks applications through a Device Credentials Repository (DCR). Cisco Security Manager can also "hot-stage" a new device and then deploy the configuration for that new device once the device in activated and placed in the network with its bootstrap configuration.

Figure 9-2 displays an example of initiating the process to create a new ASA device, and Figure 9-3 indicates how to place this new device into a device group. It is common practice to place a device into a device group based upon device location or functional group. However, any type of device group based upon function, asset cost, and so on can be created and used.

Figure 9-2   *Add New ASA Device*

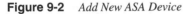

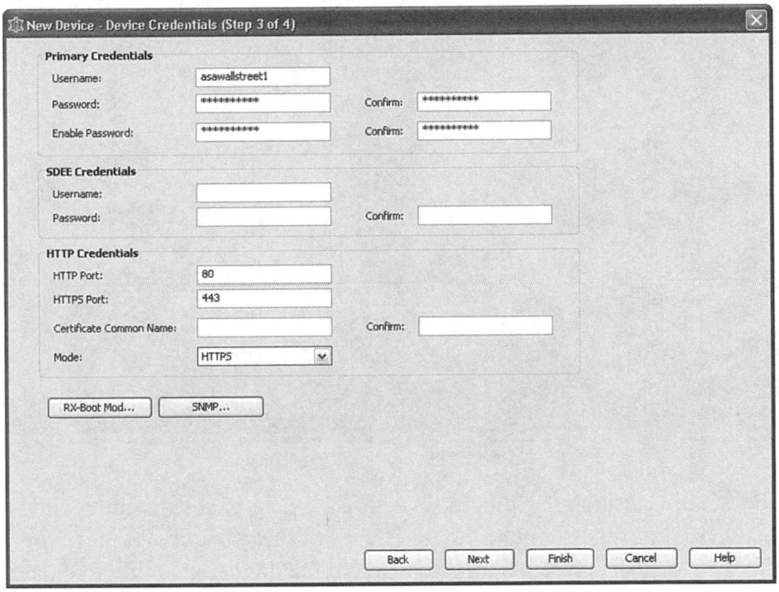

Each device in the Cisco Security Manager contains the set of management credentials shown in Figure 9-4. Some of the most used primary credentials include the username, password, and enable password. These primary device credentials can also be stored in a separate device identity server like Cisco ACS. Cisco Security Manager can natively store primary credentials for a device or retrieve these primary credentials from an external Cisco ACS server.

Figure 9-3   *Place New Device in Device Group*

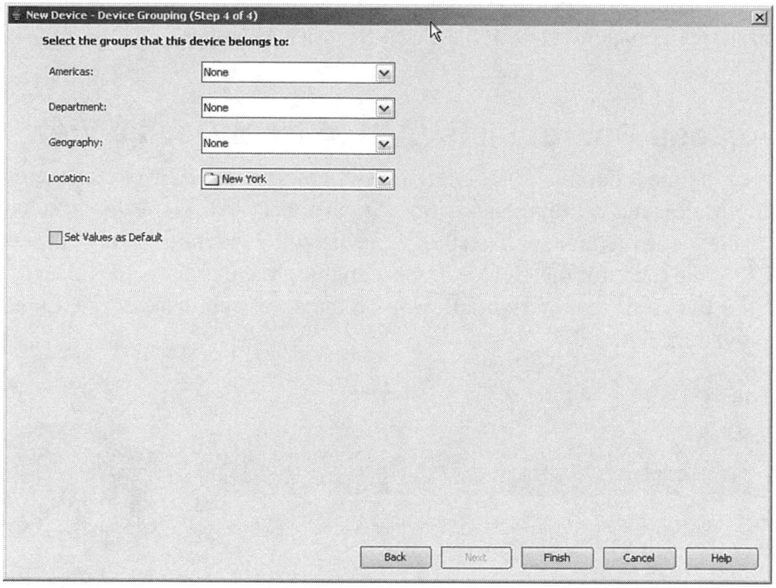

Figure 9-4   *Device Credentials*

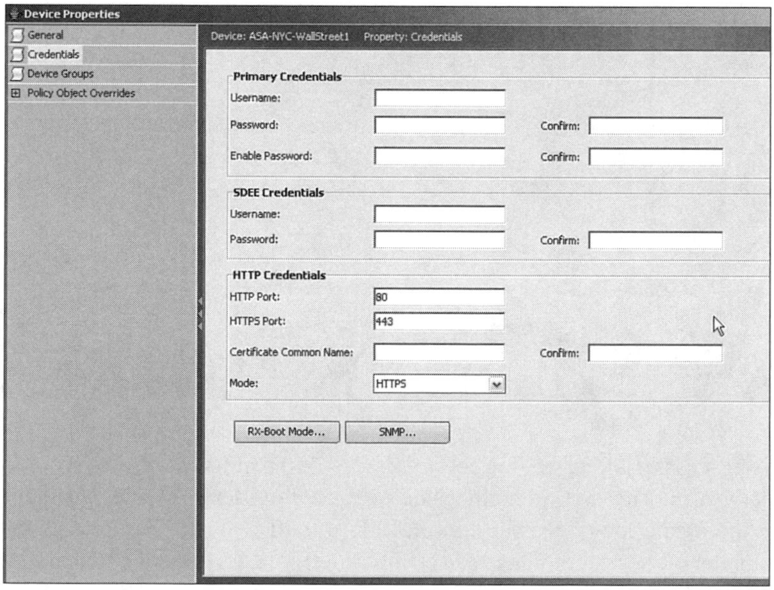

Device credentials are required for the Cisco Security Manager to communicate with the device. Many Cisco security products that use device managers also use HTTPS for centralized management with the Cisco Security Manager.

Configure Access Conrol Lists (ACLs) from Device View

One of the most popular tasks in security operations or security management is configuration and deployment of access control list (ACLs) rules. The selection of a device in Cisco Security Manager from the device list will by default display the access control list (ACLs) rule table for that device. Users can initiate the process to add an access control list (ACLs) to that device by right-clicking on the access control list (ACLs) rule table as displayed in Figure 9-5.

Figure 9-5   *Add an Access Control List (ACLs) to a Device*

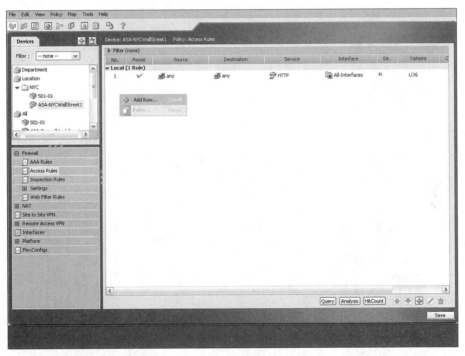

This process to add an access control list (ACLs) results in the display of the Add Firewall Rule wizard. This wizard includes fields for permit/deny, source, destination, service, interfaces, and logging. The Firewall Rule wizard also supplies default values for these parameters. These parameters can be modified, deleted, or added directly in the wizard. You also have the option to select the OK button to create the access control list (ACLs) with the default values.

Cisco Security Manager enables the user to right-click and edit a specific column in the access control list (ACLs) to create the new access control list (ACLs), as shown in Figure 9-6. This figure shows a modification to the destination field in the access control list (ACLs) rule.

Figure 9-6   *Right-Click and Edit a Column in the Rule Table*

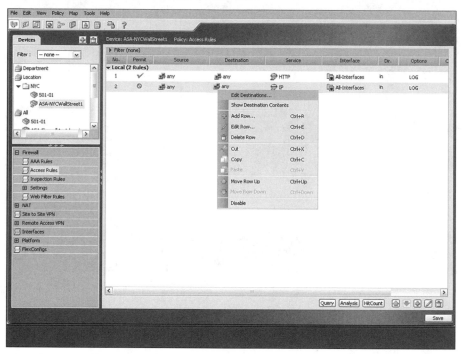

Alternately, you can also select the rule number and then edit the fields of the access control list (ACLs) rule with the Edit Firewall Rule wizard shown in Figure 9-7. The Edit Firewall Rule wizard contains the same fields as the Add Firewall Rule wizard. The Edit Firewall Rule wizard enables the user to manually edit the fields or to add predefined objects for source, destination, and service fields in the access control list (ACLs) rule.

Figure 9-7 *Edit Firewall Rule Wizard*

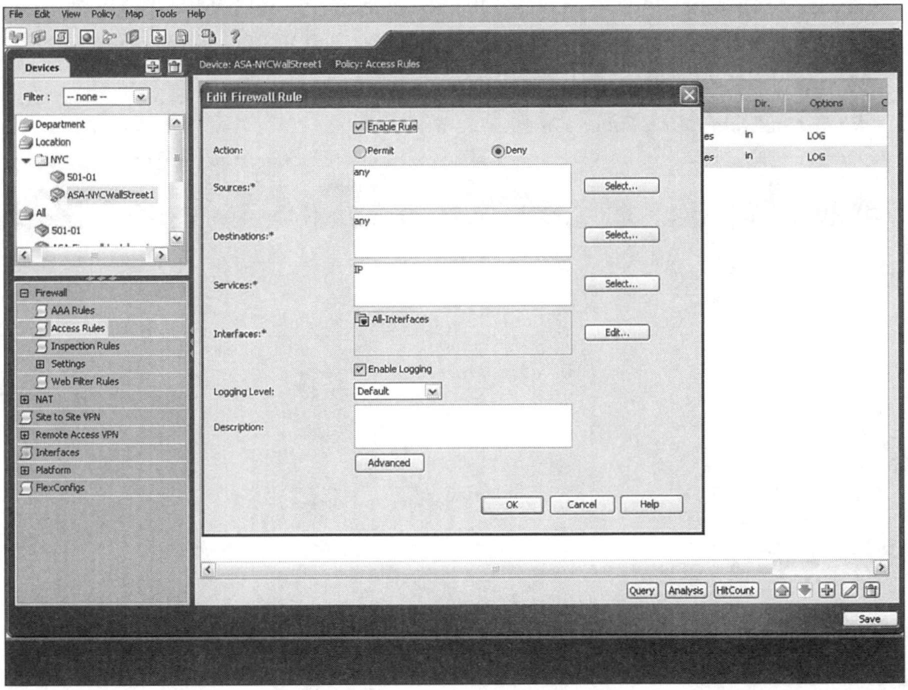

Configuring Interface Roles

Cisco Security Manager introduces a feature that enables you to configure an access control list (ACLs) rule for multiple interfaces. The ability to configure an access control list (ACLs) rule for multiple interfaces reduces the administrative burden on security groups and increases security because rules can now be defined for a group of interfaces rather than a single interface. Interface groups or roles are created by matching a name pattern in the interface name. For example, the External interface group or role includes any interface that contains the name "Outside."

Cisco Security Manager creates many default interface groups or roles. In addition to the default roles, users can also manually create any customized interface role. An example of the interface roles that are provided by default includes the following:

- All Interfaces
- External
- Internal

Figure 9-8 provides an example of how to select the External interfaces in the definition of an access control list (ACL) rule. Be sure to examine all the name patterns that are included in any default interface role prior to deploying access control list (ACLs) rules that reference a default interface role. For example, the External interface role group may include Ethernet1 by default, while the Internal interface role may include Ethernet0. Any customized interface role can be created in the Interface Role object in the Policy Object Manager. Interface roles that are created in the Policy Object Manager can be selected in the access control list (ACL) rule table.

Figure 9-8 *Apply an Access Control List (ACL) Rule to External Interfaces*

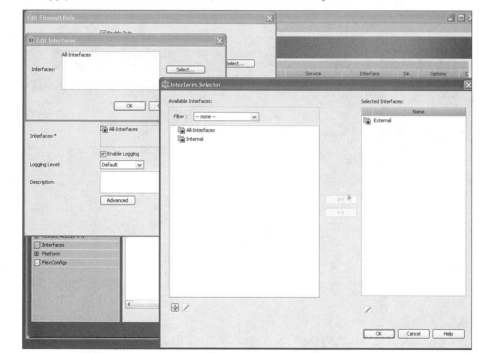

Apply Access Control List (ACL) Rules to Multiple Devices

Cisco Security Manager offers several mechanisms to apply a list of access rules to a group of devices. Once you are satisfied with the access control lists (ACLs) that are configured for one device, you can share and copy the access control lists (ACLs) to multiple devices from the Device View. The ability to share policy between multiple devices types is a powerful feature because you can apply this firewall access-rule table policy to a wide variety of devices, including a Cisco IOS router without the IOS firewall feature set. The IOS firewall feature set is also known as Context-Based Access-Control (CBAC). The security policy contained in the access control list (ACL) rule table will be configured with

plain access control lists (ACLs) (TCP state information is not maintained for the connection) if the CBAC firewall feature set is not installed on the IOS router.

To share or apply firewall rules to multiple devices from the Device View, you can select a rule table and then initiate the share policy process. The process to share an access control list (ACL) rule policy from one device in the device view to multiple devices is initiated by right-clicking on the access-rule tab for the device and selecting the share policy option. Figure 9-9 displays an example of how to define a policy to be shared or applied to multiple devices. The shared policy must be given a name in order to be referenced and applied to multiple devices.

Figure 9-9   *Mark an Access Control List (ACLs) Rule Table to Be Shared*

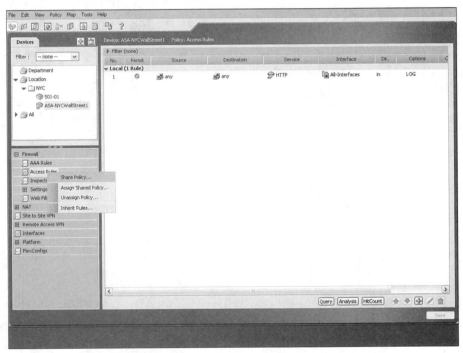

The shared policy in the example shown in Figure 9-10 is named NYCWeb Policy and is composed of all access control list (ACL) rules in the rule table for a particular device. To apply NYCWeb Policy to multiple devices, select the policy assignment option and select the devices, group of devices, or all device options.

Figure 9-10 *Assign Shared Access Control List (ACLs) Rule Policy to Multiple Devices*

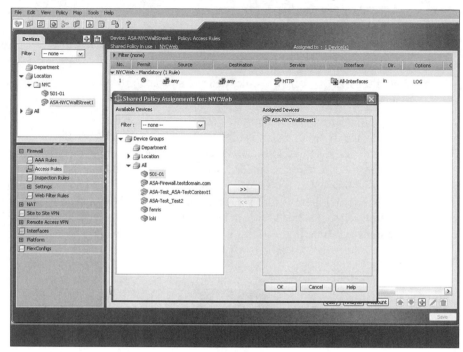

Invoking the Policy Query

As you have learned in this chapter, the Cisco Security Manager product provides the flexibility to apply a policy from one device to a group of devices. The end configuration of a device can be the result of several applied security polices. The access control list (ACLs) rule table for a device will display all the applied policies to that device. Cisco Security Manager contains a policy query function to indicate what specific policies have been applied to a device. The policy query function is invoked from the bottom of the firewall access control list (ACLs) rule table. Invocation of the policy query function enables the user to interactively display any particular rule combinations that have been configured for the device. Examples of the rule types that can be used in a policy query include the following:

- **AAA rules**—The AAA rules determine what traffic will be sent to the AAA server for authentication.

- **Access rules**—access control list (ACLs) rules have been discussed in this chapter and previously in this book.

- **Inspection rules**—Inspection rules are protocol or application inspection rules like the kind you learned about in Chapter 3, "Cisco Adaptive Security Appliance Overview," for HTTP protocol inspection.

- **Web filter rules**—Web filter rules determine what traffic will be sent from the device to an external web filter URL server.

Figure 9-11 provides an example of the type of information that can be used in a policy query for a device. A policy query is initiated by selecting the Query button at the bottom of the rule table for a device. This example is for a policy query of the access control lists (ACLs) that match a particular source, destination, service, and interface query. Wildcards can also be used for the fields in a policy query. Both full-matches and partial matches of a query are displayed. Figure 9-12 displays the result of the policy query and the matching access control list (ACL). In addition to Policy Query, there is also the rule analysis and hit count functions available in the access control list (ACL) rule table for a device.

Figure 9-11 *Policy Query Definition*

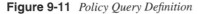

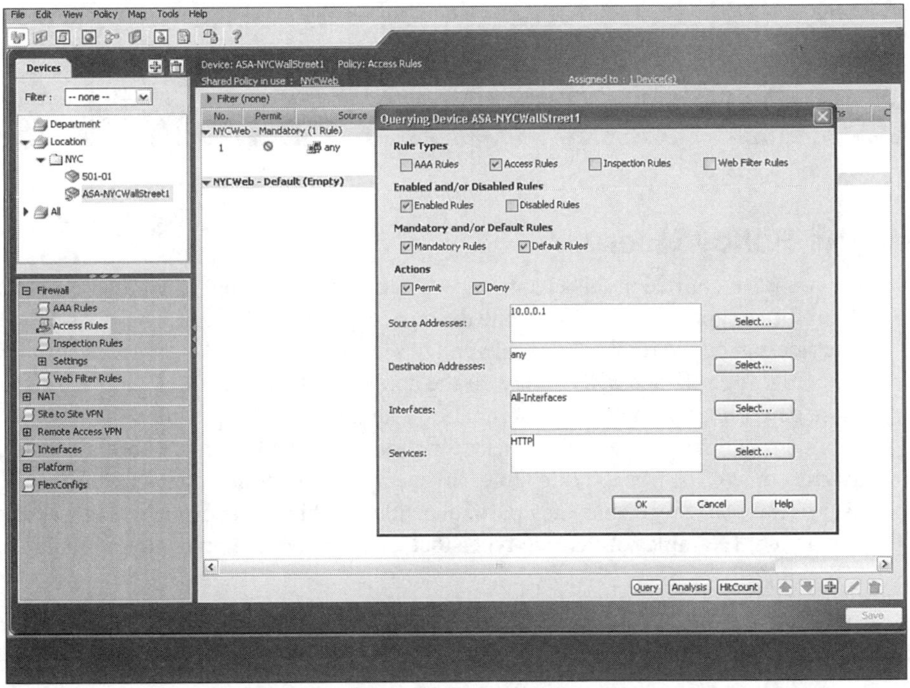

Figure 9-12 *Policy Query Results*

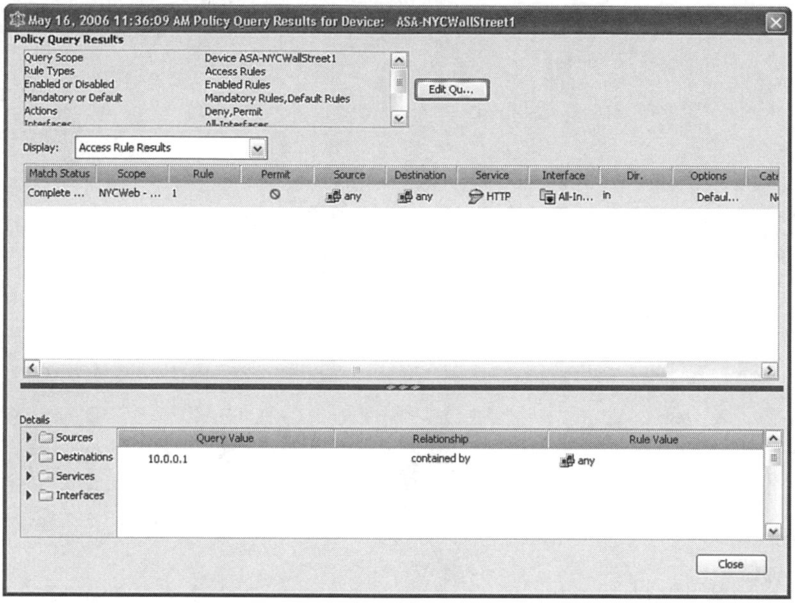

Using Analysis and Hit Count Functions

The Analysis and Hit Count buttons are located next to the Query button at the bottom of the access control list (ACL) rule table for a device. The Analysis function performs an analysis on the access control list (ACL) rules in the rule table for the device. The rule Analysis function will display access control list (ACL) rules that conflict or overlap. For example, say that someone has configured a rule to permit any traffic to the web server destination object for web service (in other words, permit source of any destination of "web server" object for service of HTTP). Let's also say that several weeks later another admin added a rule to deny any traffic to the web server destination object for web service further down in the rule table. The Analysis function would display that these rules are in mutual conflict. An example of how Analysis would display a conflict for these access control list (ACLs) rules is provided in Figure 9-13.

Figure 9-13 *Analysis*

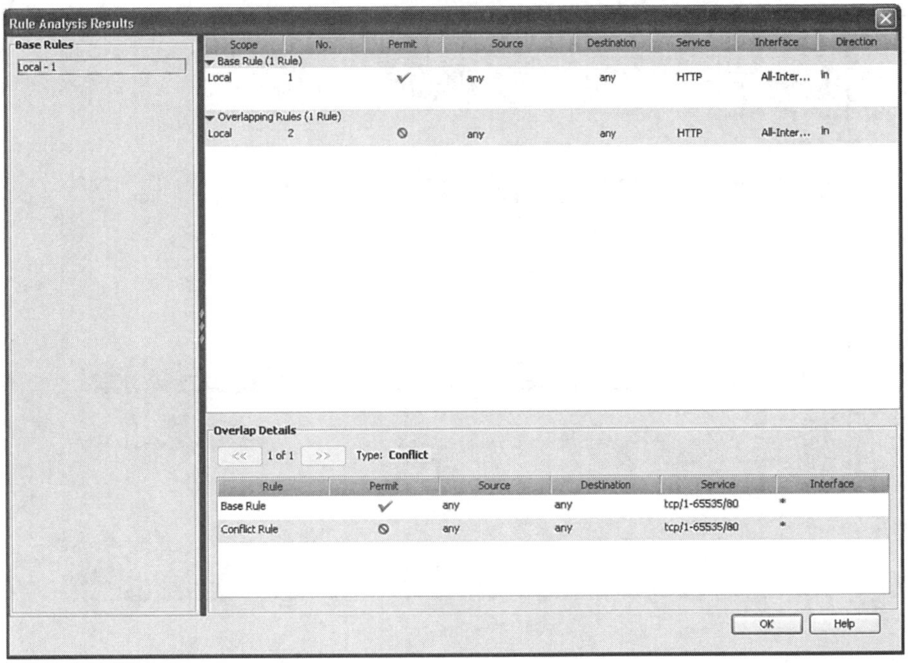

The Hit Count function displays how many times the access control list (ACLs) has been "hit" or triggered on the device. Hit Count statistics are very valuable in debugging scenarios because the user can see which access control list (ACLs) rules are being used on the device to determine which access control list (ACLs) rule is affecting network traffic. The Hit Count functionality is reset to zero when the device is rebooted. The Hit Count utility in the Cisco Security Manager also displays a delta or the number of times that the access control list (ACLs) rule has been triggered on the device since the last time the Hit Count utility was used for that device. In the previous example of the analysis of an access control list (ACLs) rule conflict, one rule would never receive any hits or be triggered on the device because it would be in conflict or superseded by the other conflicting and higher-priority rule.

Map View

Cisco Security Manager features an easy-to-use topology map to manage a network, including networks that are self-defending. Several default background maps are provided, and a customization feature enables users to create their own background map on the topology by importing a JPG, BMP, or GIF file. To access a topology map, click the Map View icon, which is the second icon on the left and next to the Device View icon on the main homepage. Figure 9-14 displays an example of how to launch the map view.

Figure 9-14 *Launch Map View*

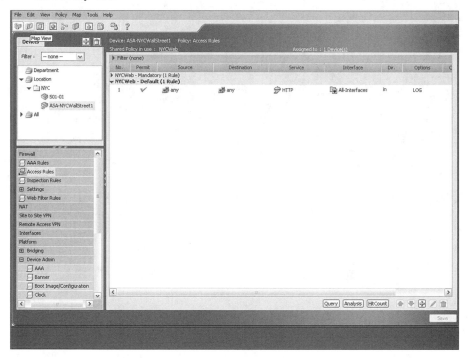

Figure 9-15 displays a sample topology map background. Cisco Security Manager uses a right-click methodology like many other Windows applications. The drop-down list that appears by right-clicking directly on the topology map enables you to add a device or change the background map.

Figure 9-15 *Topology Map Background*

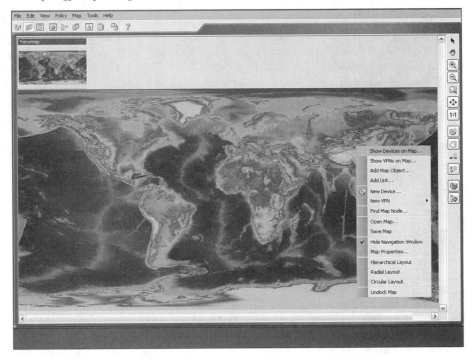

As you learn in the next sections, devices and other nodes like networks and hosts can be added to the topology map. You also learn how to configure a firewall from the topology map.

Showing Devices on the Topology Map

Cisco Security Manager provides a mechanism to easily add devices from device groups to the topology map. Users can right-click on the topology map to show a device to the topology map by using the Device Selector option from the drop-down menu after the right-click select. The show device feature for a topology map involves displaying a device that is already imported into the Cisco Security Manager. The New Device option is designed to add or import a new device into Cisco Security Manager directly through a topology map.

Figure 9-16 displays an example of showing a device on the topology map by selecting the Show Devices on Map option. The user may manually place the device at the desired location on the map, for example a security appliance at the Wall Street office may be placed in the NYC region on the map. The show device option will also add the networks that are directly connected to each interface on the device to the topology map.

Figure 9-16 *Show Device on the Topology Map*

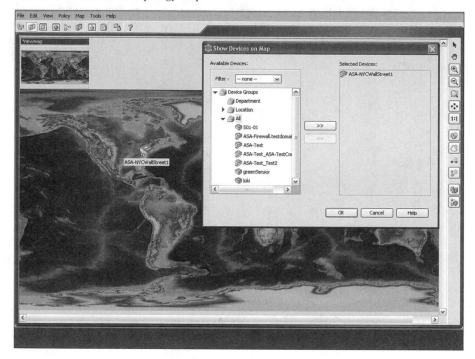

Adding Cloud Networks and Hosts to the Topology Map

The Cisco Security Manager examines the interface IP addresses to determine if devices are located on the same subnet. As shown in Figure 9-17, the Cisco Security Manager features the Add Link icon on the right side of the map to draw the connections between devices on the map. If the user tries to add a link between two managed devices on the map that are not on the same subnet, the Cisco Security Manager will create a cloud network between the devices to indicate that the devices are not on the same subnet.

Figure 9-17 *Create a Link Between Devices on the Topology Map*

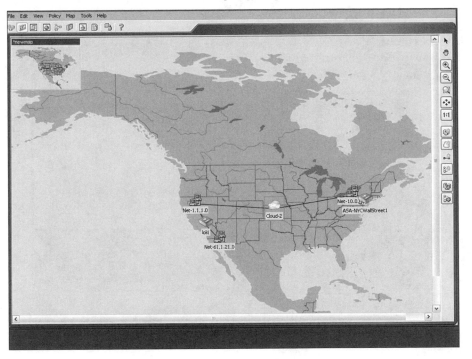

The process to manually add additional networks and hosts to the topology map is initiated by selecting the Add Map Objects to Map icon on the right-hand side of the topology map. Networks and hosts can be manually defined, or they can be selected from existing network objects. Network objects can be used in the access control list (ACLs) rule table and in other configuration options in the Cisco Security Manager. Hosts are typically nonmanaged devices to the Cisco Security Manager and can be added to a topology map to help create a visual picture of the management and critical resources in the self-defending network.

Configuring Firewall Access Control List (ACLs) Rules from Topology Map

The "Device View" section of this chapter detailed how to add an access control list (ACLs) to a device from the device view. You can also configure access control list (ACLs) rules on a firewall device from a topology map in the map view. The topology map view is a good fit for smaller networks or for security or network operators who prefer to view their network graphically with a topology map. In addition to smaller networks, topology maps can also be a good fit for the commercial or small–medium business customers.

From the topology map, a user can select a firewall by right-clicking it and then select the firewall access control list (ACLs) option for it. Figure 9-18 provides an example of how right-clicking the ASA-NYC-WallStreet1 firewall icon enables the user to select the access-rules configuration option for that device. Figure 9-19 displays an example of the rule table for that firewall. The access control list (ACLs) rule table for the device that is launched from the topology map is identical to the access control list (ACLs) rule table that is displayed for the device in the device view, as discussed previously in this chapter. Users can display, add, edit, or delete access control list (ACLs) rules for a device directly from the topology map. Users can also access the advanced functions of the access control list (ACLs) rule table, including policy query, rule analysis, and access control list (ACLs) hit count.

Figure 9-18 *Configure Access Control List (ACLs) Rules from the Topology Map*

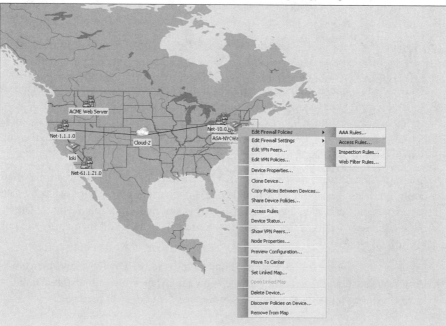

Figure 9-19 *Access Control List (ACL) Rule Table for Device from the Topology Map*

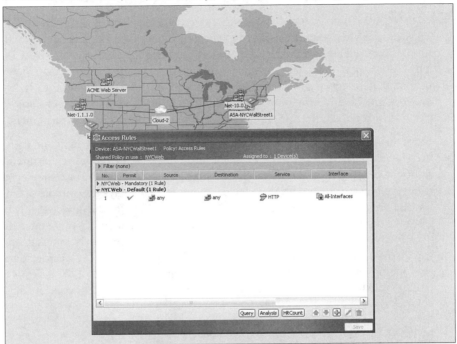

Policy View

The Policy View, the Map View, and the Device View are the three main areas in the Cisco Security Manager to define and enforce the security configuration of a device in a Cisco Self-Defending Network. The previous example in the Device View detailed how a security policy or access control list (ACL) to permit HTTP or web traffic could be copied, or shared between multiple devices. Any shared policies that are created in the device view are also displayed in the Policy View.

Some users will want to select a device from either the device view or map view and configure a security policy for that device. Other users may want to start by selecting a security policy and then applying this security policy to multiple devices. The Policy View allows the user to first select or create the security policy and then apply the policy to the multiple devices.

The icon to launch the Policy View is located next to the Device View and Map View icons. Policy View, in addition to the Device View and Map View, can also be launched from the view drop-down tab on the main Cisco Security Manager homepage.

Figure 9-20 displays the policy types that can be configured in the Policy View. Policy types include Firewall (access rules, inspection rules, and so on), Network Address Translation (NAT), remote-access VPN, PIX/ASA/FWSM platform (bridging, routing, and so on), site-to-site VPN, router platform (802.1x, NAC, QoS, and so on), and FlexConfigs. FlexConfigs is a CLI template that enables a user to manually define CLI to be deployed to a device or group of devices. There are also predefined FlexConfig templates for common deployments that involve nonsecurity features, including how to configure voice over IP (VoIP) on IOS routers. FlexConfig also supports network and service objects, which can also use the Cisco Security Manager rule tables and VPN components.

Access Control List (ACL) Rules Security Policy

Let's say that a security operator wants to define a security policy to block the nasty Sasser virus on all devices in the . This operator can simply create a firewall access control list (ACL) rules policy from the Policy View to block Sasser and apply this policy to all interfaces of all devices with a single rule. Figure 9-21 displays how a rule to block the Sasser virus can be configured from the Policy View.

Figure 9-20 *Policy View Feature Set*

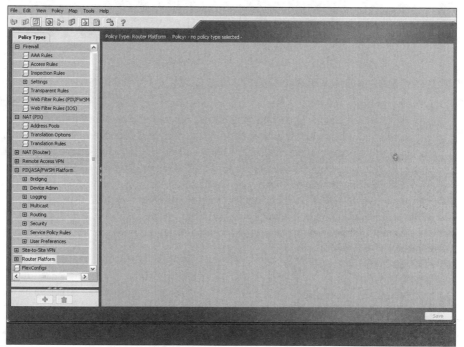

Figure 9-21 *Policy Rule to Block the Sasser Virus*

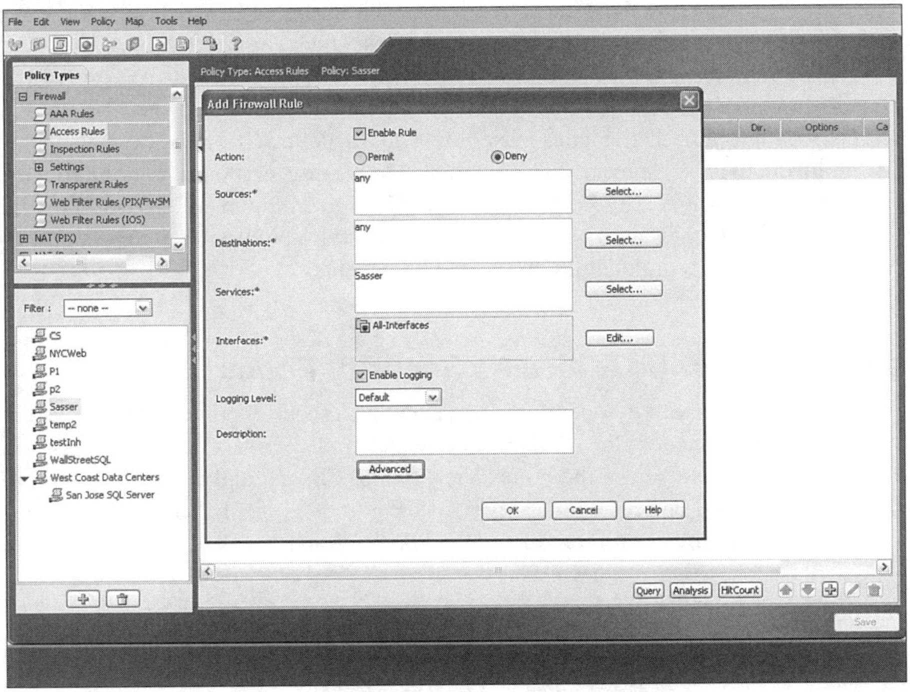

Policy Inheritance and Mandatory Security Policies

Security policies can be applied to all devices, a group of devices, or a single device. Security policies can also be implemented in a hierarchy. For example, say that a user wants to define a security policy to protect an SQL server in a data center in San Jose. The user may want to construct a common high-level security policy and then have the security policy for the San Jose SQL server inherit all the access control list (ACLs) rules defined for the common high-level security policy. The advantage of a policy hierarchy is that the common, course-grained security policy can be defined once and leveraged many times while being maintained or managed in a single, common policy. An example of how to create a policy hierarchy by allowing a policy type to inherit the security policy from a parent policy type is displayed in Figure 9-22.

Figure 9-22 *Policy Inheritance*

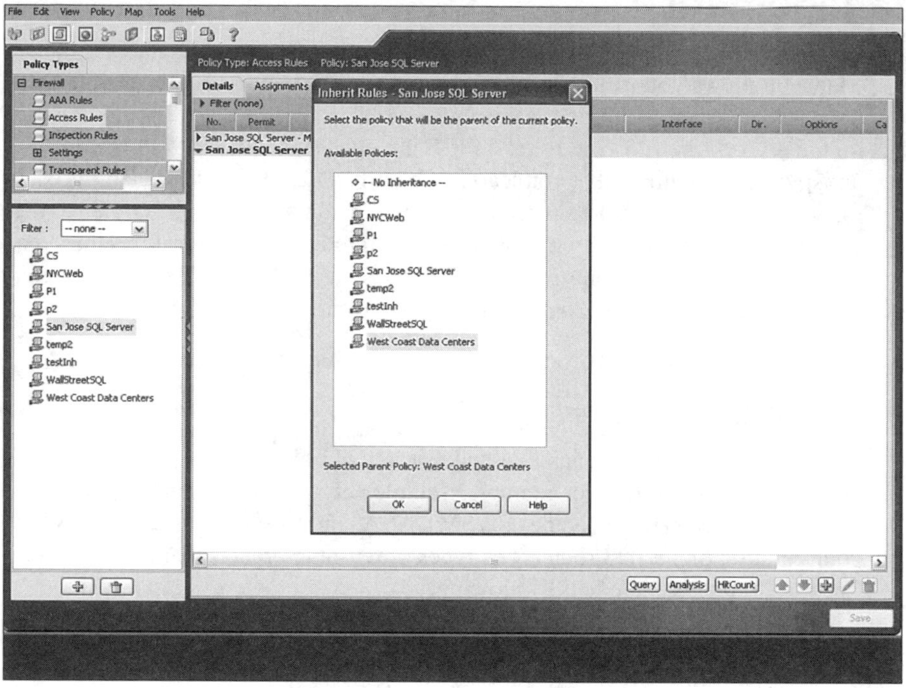

A security policy created from the Policy View can be either mandatory or default. Mandatory security policies take precedence over default security policies. Mandatory security policies can also be applied to specific administrative privileges. The ability to have mandatory security policies allows for multiple security operations and the network operations group to view and configure the same set of devices. For example, a senior security operator may define the security policy to deny IPSec VPN traffic received on an inside interface as mandatory because it may be required by corporate policy. Another security operator may have the ability to add default security policies to that device but cannot delete or modify the mandatory security policy.

IPS Management

Cisco Security Manager also provides centralized IPS management. Cisco Security Manager allows you to add an IPS System device to the centralized device list. Cisco Security Manager also supports the ability to select an IPS device, including the AIP-SSM on the ASA or the IPS feature set on IOS and then select the IPS signatures, like the IPS antispyware signatures that you learned about in Chapter 3. IPS signatures can be applied to a device as demonstrated in Chapter 3, or IPS signatures can be copied to a group of devices. The Cisco Security Manager can also import the IPS signatures that were deployed by the Cisco Incident Control Service (Cisco ICS) product discussed in Chapter 4, "Cisco Incident Control Service," on worm mitigation.

Object Manager

Cisco Security Manager enables a wide variety of objects to be created and configured for any supported platform. For example, a single network object can be used in the rule table for a Firewall Services Module (FWSM), ASA, and for the remote-access VPN configuration on an IOS router. The types of reusable objects that are supported in Cisco Security Manager include the following:

- **Networks/hosts**—Objects for source/destination fields
- **Service objects**—Objects for service fields
- **Service groups**—Combination of service objects (for example, IPSec)
- **Interface roles (groups)**—Combine interfaces from a device into a group
- **Authentication, authorization, and accounting (AAA) server groups**—List of AAA servers for failover, and so on
- **AAA server objects**—AAA server details including RADIUS/ TACACS+, and IP
- **Access control lists (ACLs)**—Reuse ACL between components including quality of service (QoS)
- **ASA group policy**—Define system policy/preferences for ASA
- **Certificate authority (CA) servers**—CA configuration
- **Dynamic Host Configuration Protocol (DHCP) servers**—DHCP parameters including IP address, timeout, and so on
- **FTP Map**—Deep packet protocol inspection of FTP parameters
- **HTTP Map**—Deep packet protocol inspection of HTTP parameters (for example, GET)
- **IPSec transform sets**—Define AES/3DES, SHA, and so on, for IPSec VPN
- **TCP Map**—Deep packet inspection of TCP, including Checksum

- **GPRS Tunneling Protocol (GTP) map**—Deep packet inspection of tunneled network packets over 3G phone networks
- **Time range objects**—Define ACLs for a specific time range
- **Domain name rules matching**—Configuration domain name matching for digital certificates
- **User group**—Group configuration for remote-access VPN
- **Traffic flow objects**—Define packet matching for deep packet inspection
- **User templates**—Templates for CLI tokens
- **Categories**—Apply colors to rules and objects to find/filter

Figure 9-23 provides an example of launching the object manager, and Figure 9-24 shows the resulting object management homepage it is displayed in. Note the object manager supports the ability to find and filter objects based upon fields including name, group, and description.

Figure 9-23 *Manage Objects*

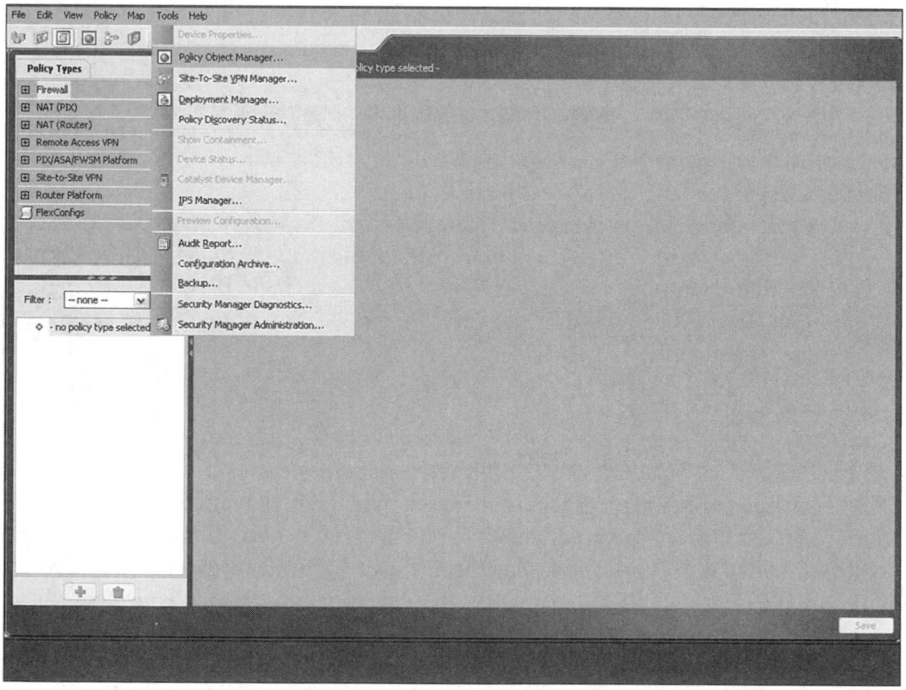

Figure 9-24 *Object Homepage*

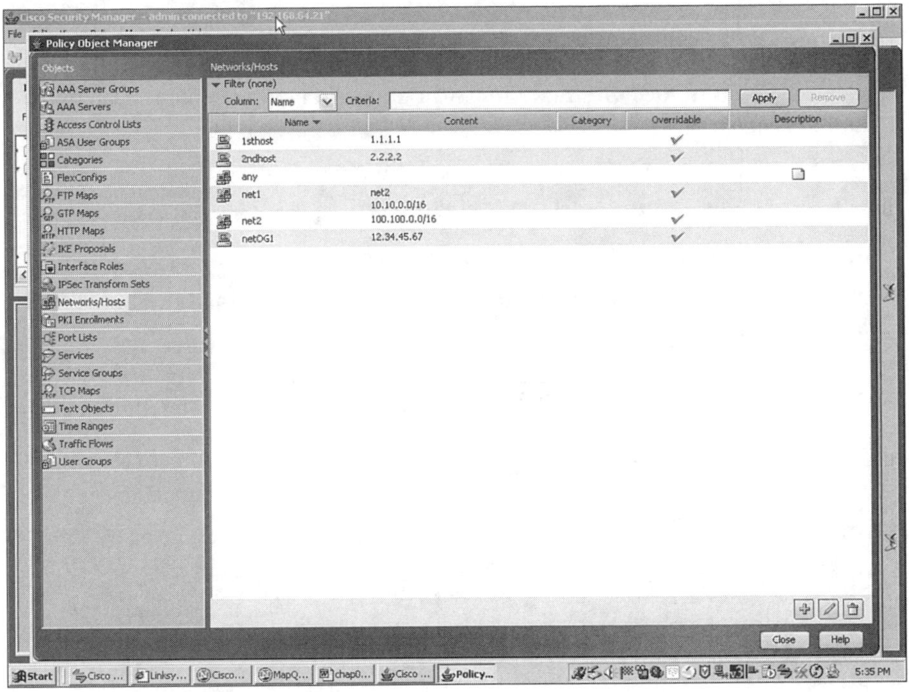

Network and service objects can be created directly from the access control list (ACLs) rule table, or they can be created directly from the Policy Object Manager. Objects can be nested and contain other objects. Network objects can be a single IP address, a single network, multiple IP addresses, multiple networks, or a collection of objects, or a combination of IP addresses, networks, and objects.

Value Override Per Device

Cisco Security Manager contains an object management feature called value override per device. Value override allows the same object name to have different values or contents for different devices. For example, say that the user wants to have a common security policy to allow HTTP from all inside networks to all destinations. A single network object with the entire list of inside networks could be a very large object. A more attractive and more secure approach would be to have a single security policy with a source object named "inside networks" and then have the contents of "inside networks" be a variable that contains only the inside networks that are protected by each device. The per-device object override features allow a single access control list (ACLs) rule with a network object to be defined for multiple devices, but with the contents or value of the network object, such as the

"inside network" example, to be defined uniquely for each device. A display of the value override per device check box is displayed in Figure 9-25.

Figure 9-25 *Value Override Per Device*

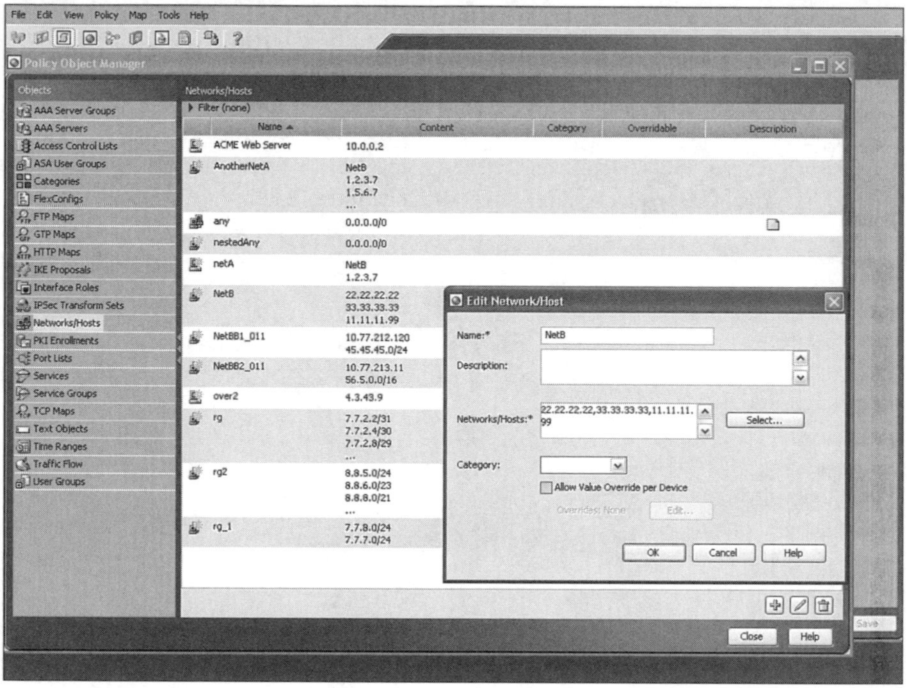

Summary

The Cisco Security Management Suite provides configuration and monitoring of a . The Cisco Security Manager product is the configuration component of the Cisco Security Management Suite, and the Cisco Security MARS product is the monitoring component of the security management suite. Cisco Security Manager is a centralized management product that can configure up to 5000 security devices. Cisco Security Manager supports many of the products previously discussed in this book, including the ASA, IOS routers, and IPS sensors. Cisco Security Manager also supports Catalyst 6500/7600 chassis configuration and security linecard modules, including the FWSM, VPN SPA, and the IPS services linecard module (IPSM).

Cisco Security Manager features three main views: Device View, Map View, and Policy View. The Device View is similar in ease-of-use and scope to that of a device manager, such as the ASA Device Manager (ASDM). The Device View also features the ability to share or copy policies from one device to another. The Map View allows users to place devices and hosts on to a topology map and graphically configure their . The Map View enables a

user to select a device from the topology map and configure the device directly from the topology map. The Map View can be advantageous for smaller networks. The Policy View enables the user to select or configure the policy first and then apply the policy to multiple devices. The Policy View is designed to enable the user to configure and apply a single security policy to hundreds or thousands of security devices.

References

Cisco Systems, Inc. Cisco Security Manager 3.0 Data Sheet. http://www.cisco.com/en/US/products/ps6498/products_data_sheet0900aecd803ffd5c.html

Cisco Security Monitoring, Analysis, and Response System

Chapter 9 discussed Cisco Security Manager in detail. Cisco Security Manager is the centralized configuration management product for a self-defending network. The Cisco Security Monitoring, Analysis, and Response System (Cisco Security MARS) product is the monitoring and mitigation platform for a self-defending network. Cisco Security Manager creates and deploys configurations to self-defending network devices including Cisco IOS routers, Catalyst 6500/7600 Firewall Services Modules, and Adaptive Security Appliances. Cisco Security MARS complements the Cisco Security Manager by providing best-of-breed monitoring of the self-defending network.

This chapter provides an overview of Cisco Security MARS. You learn about Cisco Security MARS features, the dashboard, how Cisco Security MARS displays a security incident, and how Cisco Security MARS can mitigate an attack or allow a network to be self-defending. This chapter also provides details on Cisco Security MARS integration with Cisco Security Manager, including how to select a syslog from an incident in Cisco Security MARS and receive a display of the access control list (ACL) rule in Cisco Security Manager that created the syslog.

Understanding Cisco Security MARS Features

Cisco Security MARS is different from the conventional Security Information Management Solution (SIMS) or other traditional security monitoring products. Cisco Security MARS offers several advantages based upon the following features:

- Import Netflow data
- Create baseline of normal network traffic
- Import configurations of monitored devices
- Understand traffic flow across Network Address Translation (NAT) boundaries
- Integrated Nessus Vulnerability Scanner input
- Display topology map of network and attack vectors
- Reduce false positives by reporting incidents
- Provide mitigation by deploying configuration to shut specific ports to stop an attack

- Provide mitigation by displaying an access list to stop an attack close the source of the attack

Cisco Security MARS is offered as a turnkey appliance. Cisco Security MARS includes an integrated Oracle database and can handle up to 10,000 events per second. The Cisco Security MARS product line also features different appliance form-factors including a low-end model that supports 500 events per second, excluding Netflow data. A turnkey appliance allows the Cisco Security MARS product to be up-and-running quickly without an extensive installation or tuning process. Cisco Security MARS displays a security incident during an attack, based upon input and events from devices within the self-defending network. A partial list of the sources from which Cisco Security MARS can accept input and events includes the following:

- Cisco IOS routers
- Cisco Catalyst LAN Switches (Catalyst OS 6.x)
- Cisco PIX Firewalls
- Checkpoint Firewalls
- Cisco VPN Concentrators
- Netscreen Firewalls
- Cisco IPS Sensors
- Enterasys Dragon IPS Sensors
- Snort IPS Sensors
- ISS IPS Sensors
- eEye REM
- Foundstone
- Cisco Security Agent
- Symantec Anti-Virus
- Cisco ACS
- Windows Host Log
- Solaris Host Log
- Linux Host Log
- IIS Web Server Log
- Apache Web Server Log
- Oracle Audit Logs
- NetApp Logs

Cisco Security MARS has the ability to see the entire self-defending network based upon input and events from the preceding sources. This diverse selection of input, combined with the network configurations and baseline traffic, allows Cisco Security MARS to report on specific, high-level, actionable security incidents rather than displaying and reporting based upon individual and voluminous firewall syslog and IPS Sensor events. Cisco Security MARS

also supports a global controller functionality. The global controller provides a centralized management station for multiple Cisco Security MARS local controllers.

Summary Dashboard

Cisco Security MARS uses a web browser for the client GUI. Cisco Security MARS also facilitates the download of Adobe SVG to display the topology graphs. Cisco Security MARS requires Internet Explorer for the web browser and uses HTTPS to ensure secure monitoring. After a successful logon to Cisco Security MARS, you are presented with the dashboard under the Summary tab. Figure 10-1 displays an example of the top of the Cisco Security MARS dashboard.

Figure 10-1 *Cisco Security MARS Dashboard*

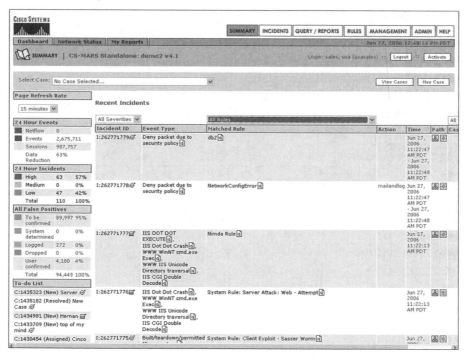

The dashboard includes a summary of security incidents, or a high-level indication of a possible network attack or vulnerability based upon input from devices and hosts in the self-defending network. In addition to incidents, the dashboard also includes information on events within the last 24 hours, false positives that are detected, a hotspot, and an attack diagram including source and destination of the attack.

Incidents

The focal point of the Cisco Security MARS dashboard is a list of recent incidents. In addition to the dashboard, incident information is also available by selecting the Incident tab at the top of the Cisco Security MARS GUI. All incidents are supplied with an incident ID, event type, matched rule, time, and path information. Figure 10-2 provides an example of an incident ID selected from the dashboard (highlighted). In addition to selecting an incident from the Summary Dashboard, incidents can also be selected from the Incident tab at the top of the Cisco Security MARS GUI. Figure 10-3 displays the resulting information from the incident selection in Figure 10-2. Figure 10-3 also provides an example of how an incident is displayed with the matching rule that triggered the incident and the subcomponents of the incident. Subcomponents of the incident include the following fields:

- Event Type
- Source IP/Port
- Destination IP/Port
- Protocol
- Time
- Reporting Device
- Reported User
- Path/Mitigate
- False Positive

Figure 10-2 *Select Incident from Dashboard*

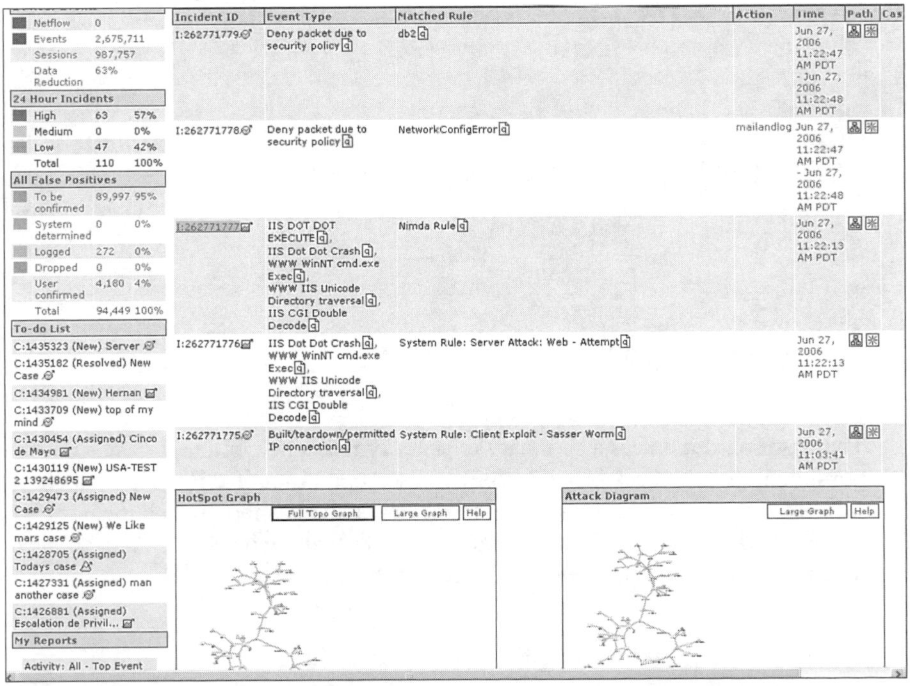

Figure 10-3 *Incident Details*

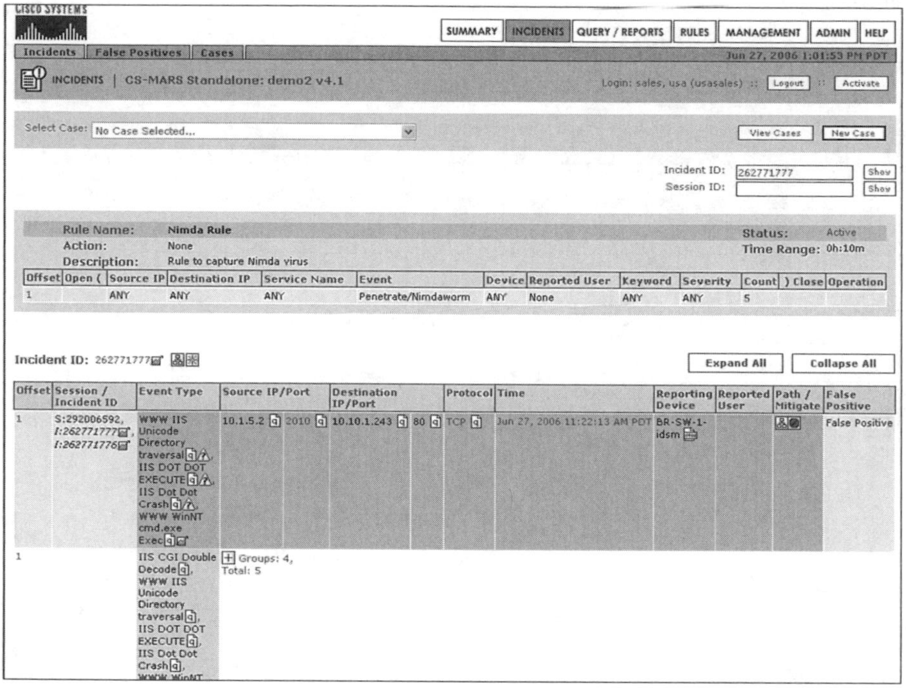

Cisco Security MARS displays security incidents to the user that may require action as opposed to simply providing a real-time viewer of IDS and firewall events. In addition to providing high-level security incidents to the user, another powerful feature of Cisco Security MARS is the ability to recommend or apply a mitigation action to stop the incident or attack.

Displaying Path of Incident and Mitigating the Attack

Figure 10-3 displayed details of the security incident for a Nimda worm. Selecting the red icon in the Path/Mitigate field for this incident results in the display of the path of the network attack. Figure 10-4 provides the resulting display of the path of the security incident through the network.

Figure 10-4 *Path of Incident*

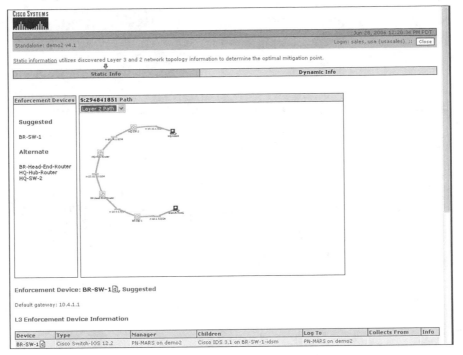

In addition to displaying the path of the network attack, Cisco Security MARS can also generate the command-line interface (CLI) commands to mitigate or stop the network attack. The CLI commands used to mitigate an attack are displayed with the path by selecting the path/mitigate option in the incident. Cisco Security MARS has the ability to automatically shut a LAN port to mitigate the attack. Cisco Security MARS will generate the CLI for an access control list (ACL) rule to stop an attack, but will not deploy the CLI. The suggested CLI recommendation is typically based upon the device closest to the source of the attack. This choice may not be the optimal mitigation point based upon the user's point of view. Cisco Security MARS allows the selection of alternate devices within the path of the network attack in case the user does not wish to mitigate the attack at the device that is closest to the source of the network attack. Figure 10-5 displays the suggested CLI to configure an access list to stop the Nimda attack.

Figure 10-5 *Suggested CLI to Mitigate the Attack*

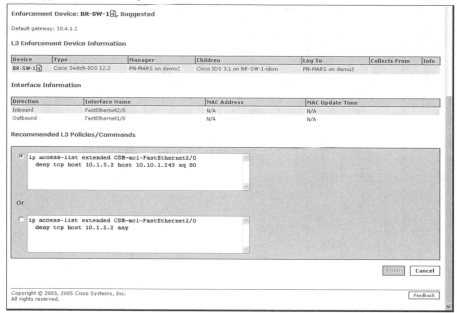

Hotspot Graph and Attack Diagram

Cisco Security MARS relies heavily on SNMP to gain topological awareness of the network. Cisco Security MARS requires SNMP read access to construct a Layer 3 and Layer 2 topological map of the network. Cisco Security MARS uses Simple Network Management Protocol (SNMP) to gather information about the device. Cisco Security MARS also uses SNMP and a seed device to discover the neighboring devices for each known device in the network. A seed device is a starting device to discover the network by attempting to discover every device known by the seed device and then attempting to discover every device known by each newly discovered device.

SNMP allows Cisco Security MARS to create the hotspot graph and the attack diagrams. Use of SNMP by Cisco Security MARS is complemented by the integrated network scanner. The integrated network scanner is used to gain information about the hosts and applications that exist on the network. Cisco Security MARS combines the device discovery of SNMP with the scanning information about the hosts and applications to construct the hotspot graph. Cisco Security MARS uses the host scanning for OS and application fingerprinting. OS and application fingerprinting is used to assist in ensuring that an incident is relative to the target and valid. For example, a detected Windows exploit attack against a Linux server is not a valid incident. Both the hotspot graph and the attack diagram can be displayed on the main Cisco Security MARS dashboard. Figure 10-6 provides a sample of a hotspot topology graph. In our example, the hotspot diagram displays the network for the Nimda incident on the dashboard.

Figure 10-6 *Hotspot Graph*

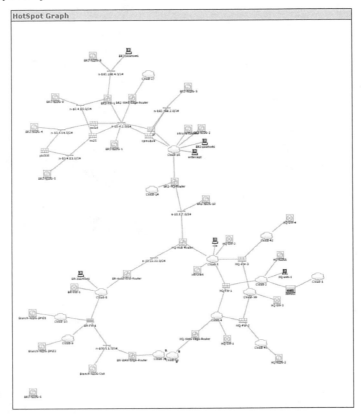

The hotspot graph displays the path of the incident or attack across the network. An attack diagram allows the user to highlight a vulnerable path between two points in the network and receive a display of the session IDs of the events that are incorporated into the security incident. Figure 10-7 provides an example of an attack diagram for the Nimda incident. Both the hotspot graph and the attack diagram are launched from the icons next to the incident ID from the details on the incident. The hotspot graph and attack diagram on the dashboard typically correspond with the latest incident listed on the dashboard.

Figure 10-7 *Attack Diagram*

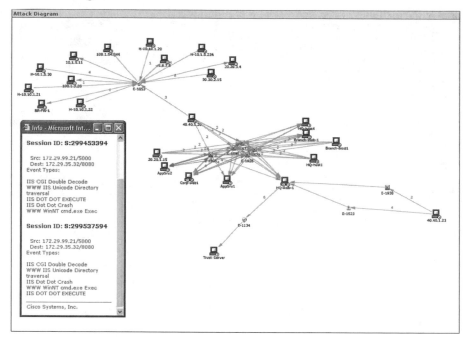

Rules

To display an incident, a matching rule was used to trigger that a possible security incident or attack was in progress. Cisco Security MARS includes a set of system rules that are automatically configured and applied to detect security incidents or attacks. Figure 10-8 displays a system rule to detect an active backdoor connection. An active backdoor connection typically signifies that a host has been attacked and that a connection is open for someone to remotely access and control this host, perhaps for use in a botnet.

Figure 10-8 *System Inspection Rule to Detect an Active Backdoor Connection*

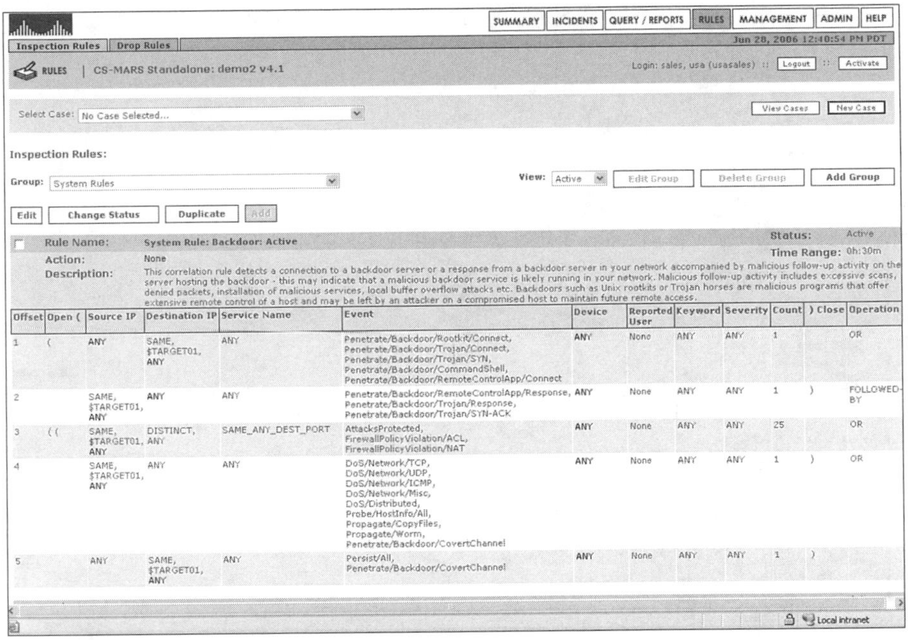

In addition to the active backdoor system rule, some of the automatic or system inspection rules include detection of client exploits, firewall configuration issues, password attacks, scans, viruses found, viruses cleaned, worm propagation, and sudden traffic increases to a port.

In addition to the canned or predefined system inspection rules, Cisco Security MARS also features the ability to create customized or user inspection rules. User inspection rules can be ideal for homegrown or custom applications. These customized rules are created with the following parameters or fields:

- Source IP
- Destination IP
- Service
- Event
- Device
- User
- Keyword
- Count
- Operation

Rule information for a specific incident is available by selecting the incident details from the dashboard. General rule information is also available by selecting the Rules tab from the top of the Cisco Security MARS GUI. Cisco Security MARS was one of the first security monitoring products on the market to incorporate Netflow data. Netflow is a feature of Cisco IOS routers and Catalyst LAN switches. Netflow is essentially a record of a traffic flow between a particular source and destination through the IOS router. Netflow contains a high-level record of the source IP address, destination IP address, the time of the connection, and the duration of the connection.

Cisco IOS routers and Catalyst LAN switches running IOS periodically send a Netflow record to a Netflow collector such as Cisco Security MARS. This Netflow record is sent over User Datagram Protocol (UDP) and is highly efficient because it is merely a record of a traffic flow as opposed to a packet-by-packet dump of the traffic flow. Netflow contains the following information:

- Source IP address
- Destination IP address
- Ports/protocol
- Total packets
- Total bytes

Netflow is used by Cisco Security MARS to create a baseline of normal network traffic. This baseline is used to identify anomalous network behavior that can be indicative of several types of network attacks, including distributed denial-of-service (DDoS) attacks and worms that are sending large amounts of network traffic. Cisco Security MARS also contains integrated system inspection rules for IPS (Intrusion Prevention Service) that leverage Netflow information to signify a security incident or network attack, thus reducing the false positives that are sometimes associated with IPS. Netflow information, including the number of Netflow events received in the last 24 hours, is available on the dashboard.

Query/Reports

Cisco Security MARS features a collection of predefined reports in addition to the ability to create a custom report. Reports are generated from the event data in Cisco Security MARS that is collected from the devices in the self-defending network, including routers, LAN switches, firewalls, IPS sensors, and hosts. Cisco Security MARS also features groups of reports. Figure 10-9 displays a sample of the report groups in Cisco Security MARS.

Figure 10-9   *Report Groups*

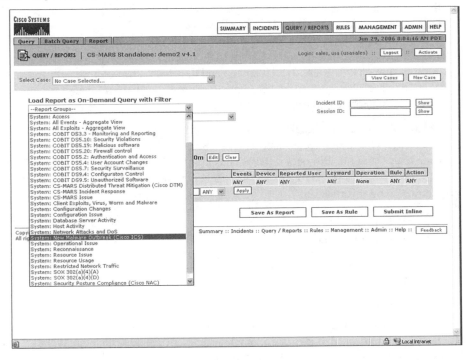

There are several report groups in Cisco Security MARS for topics that you have previously learned about in this book. For example, there are report groups for attacks and DoS, firewall control, malware outbreak (Cisco ICS), and security posture compliance (Cisco NAC). In addition to the topics previously discussed in this book, Cisco Security MARS also features a report group for Distributed Threat Mitigation (DTM).

DTM is designed to enable branch IOS routers, specifically Integrated Services Routers (ISRs), to dynamically configure themselves with the necessary IPS signatures to reduce the risk of an attack at the branch office in an automated, self-defending fashion. DTM is an emerging technology, and it is strongly recommended that DTM be tested in a small pilot network to verify scalability prior to any deployments in production networks.

In addition to the DTM report group, Cisco Security MARS also includes the option to be a DTM controller. The DTM controller is essentially the brains behind the DTM battlefield. The DTM controller in Cisco Security MARS receives input in the form of IPS Security Device Event Exchange (SDEE) events and syslogs to help to determine what specific attack is occurring in the branch network. Cisco Security MARS can then automatically enable the identified and necessary IPS signature on the branch IOS ISR. Figure 10-10 provides an example of the reports that are available as part of the DTM report group.

Figure 10-10 *DTM Reports*

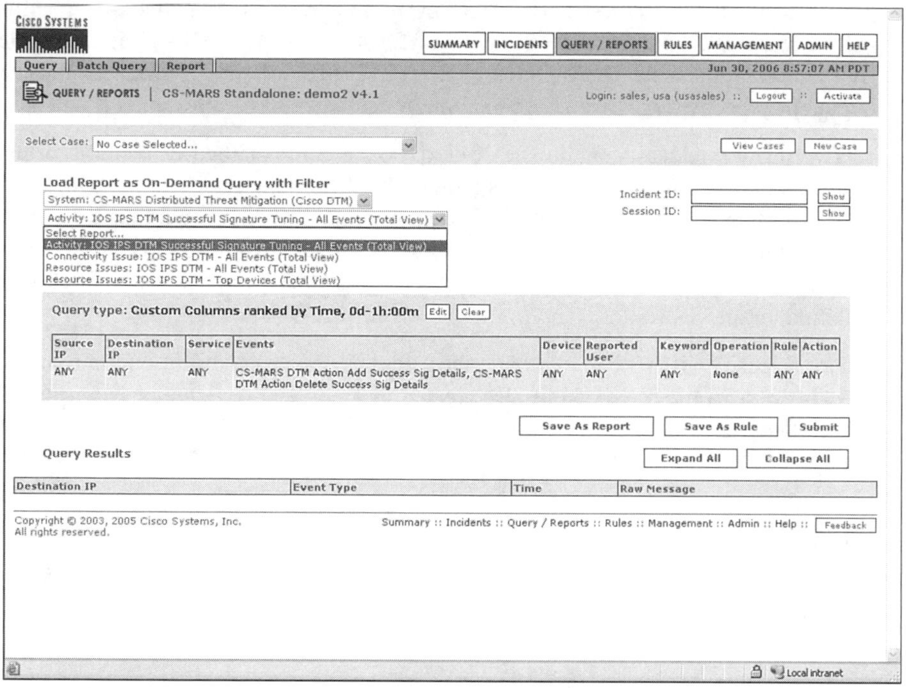

Cisco IOS ISRs can implement many features, including voice, routing, and security in a single device at a very cost-effective price point. The combination of feature-richness and low price point enables ISR routers to be deployed in remote branch offices in environments where an organization may have thousands of remote branches. To keep the price point of the ISRs attractive, their memory footprint, or capacity, is often substantially less than that of a dedicated security appliance such as an ASA (Advanced Security Appliance). The reduced memory footprint of the ISR creates a situation in which the entire IPS signature set cannot be simultaneously enabled on the ISR. The branch environment is often remote, and there may be no security or IT professionals resident at the remote branch to manage these devices. The combination of the remoteness of the branch and the limited memory capacity of the ISR can be addressed in certain, small-scale situations by managing the IPS signatures on the ISR with a DTM in Cisco Security MARS. DTM is currently not scalable to large networks, and DTM should be implemented only on select remote ISRs with Cisco Security MARS.

ISRs contain a file called named attack-drop.sdf. This attack-drop.sdf file lists all the IPS signatures that are enabled on that ISR device. In addition to the attack-drop.sdf file, some of the larger ISR routers may also run the 128MB.sdf or 256MB.sdf signature files if they have enough memory. These attack-drop.sdf, 128MB.sdf, and 256MB.sdf files are frequently updated on Cisco.com to contain the latest, most relevant IPS signatures.

DTM can automatically enable the desired IPS signature on the ISR by monitoring network events that originate from networks around the ISR and updating the attack.sdf file on the ISR with the desired IPS signature. The monitored network events that are used by Cisco Security MARS to apply dynamically apply IPS signatures to ISR to mitigate a threat can originate from an IPS appliance, ASA IPS (AIP-SSM), a Catalyst 6500/7600 IPS service module, or an ISR router.

Cisco Security MARS cannot create the initial attack-drop.sdf file on the router. This attack-drop.sdf file must be initially created by CLI, Security Device Manager (SDM), or Cisco Security Manager.

Management

The Management tab in the Cisco Security MARS graphical user interface (GUI) enables the user to view events and create IP addresses, services (ports or protocols), and admin accounts in Cisco Security MARS through the following tabs:

- Event Management displays the network events that are seen by Cisco Security MARS that can be used to trigger an incident. The event management tab is one of the more commonly used management tabs in Cisco Security MARS. An example of the event display in event management is provided in Figure 10-11.

- IP Management displays what IP addresses or networks are known by Cisco Security MARS.

- Service Management displays what ports or protocols can be used in rules.

- User Management tab enables the creation or modification of a user account in Cisco Security MARS.

Figure 10-11 *Event Management*

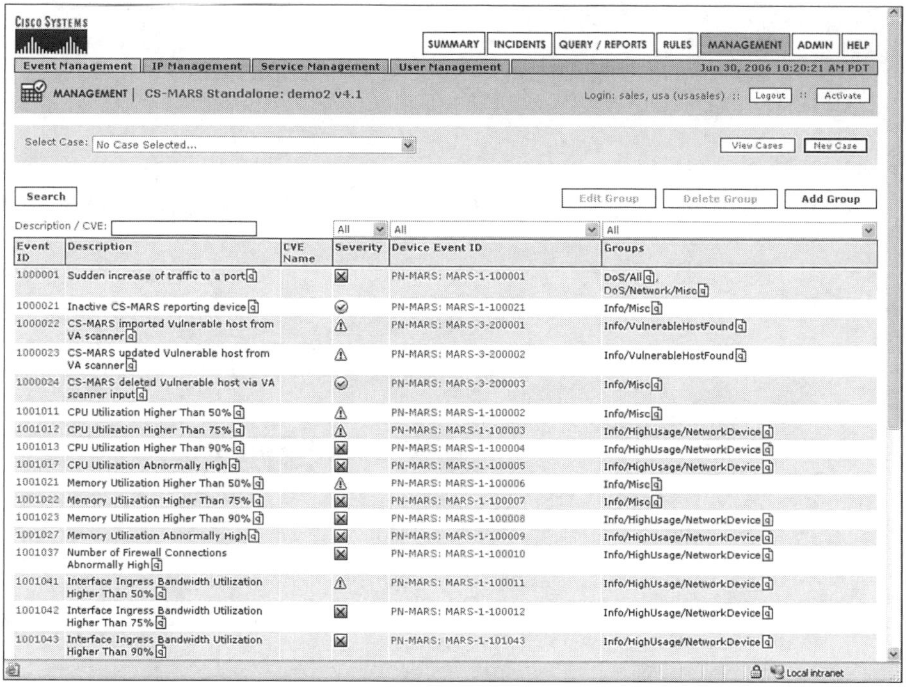

Admin

The Admin tab of the Cisco Security MARS GUI enables the configuration of administrative functions like system setup, maintenance, user management, system parameters, and custom setup. System setup is a critical step because system setup controls how devices are discovered or imported into Cisco Security MARS. Figure 10-12 provides a display of the system setup options.

Figure 10-12 *System Setup*

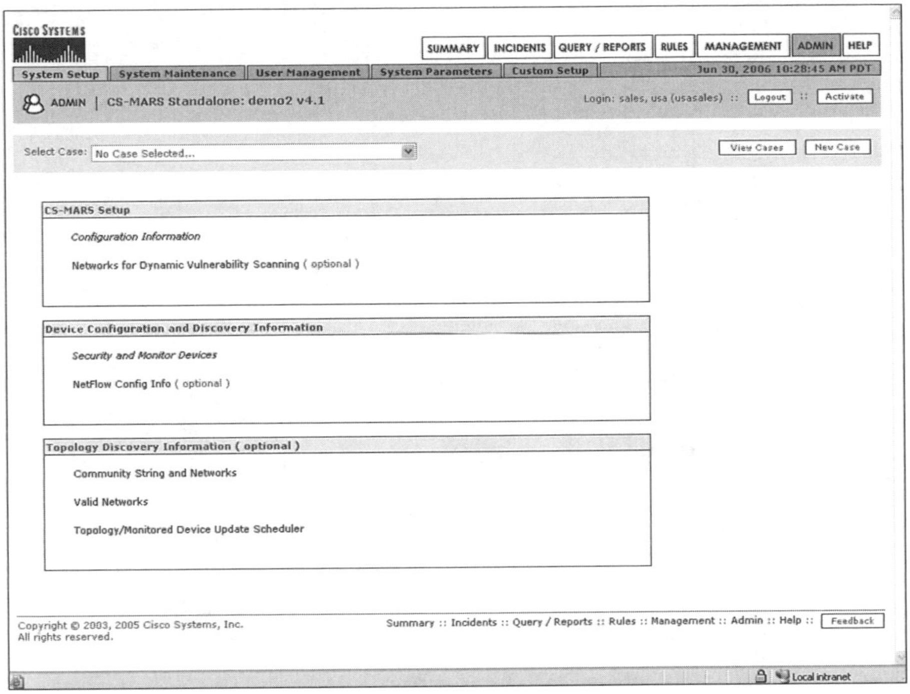

Cisco Security Manager Linkages

Cisco Security MARS supports integration or "linkages" with Cisco Security Manager. The ability to directly integrate between Cisco Security MARS and Cisco Security Manager enables security operators to cross-launch between the monitoring and configuration components. The ability to correlate or cross-launch between monitoring and configuration components can be especially useful in debugging or trouble-ticket situations.

Cisco Security MARS contains a feature that directly links an incident with a security policy in Cisco Security Manager. Specifically, Cisco Security MARS enables the user to select a syslog from a security incident and display the access control list (ACL) rule in Cisco Security Manager that generated the syslog.

Cisco Security MARS provides an incident to signify to the security operator that something of significance is occurring within the network. The incident is composed of various events that are reported by the devices within the self-defending network. Cisco Security MARS contains an entry under Reporting Devices in the Event entries for the incident. Figure 10-13 displays an example of how an incident can indicate that a reporting device has a policy link to Cisco Security Manager.

Figure 10-13   *Incident with Cisco Security Manager Policy Entry*

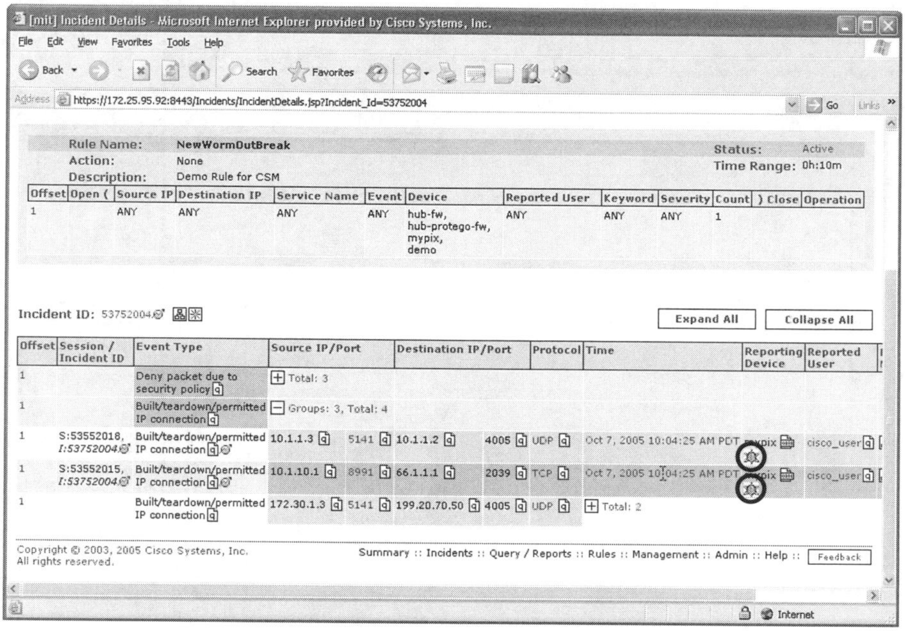

This policy entry is supported only for Cisco devices that are configured by Cisco Security Manager to deploy access list rules to these devices. Selecting this policy entry displays the access list configured by the Cisco Security Manager that generated the syslog in the security event. The ability to display the access list rules from the security event in Cisco Security MARS allows for quick debugging of many security situations and can allow the user to quickly address and rectify the security event that is reported by Cisco Security MARS.

The policy link in Cisco Security MARS displays a copy of the desired access list rules configured in Cisco Security Manager. Figure 10-14 displays an example of how to launch the policy link from the reporting device in Cisco Security MARS, and Figure 10-15 displays the resulting access control list (ACL) rule table from Cisco Security Manager.

Figure 10-14 *Launch Policy Link from Cisco Security MARS*

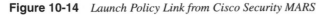

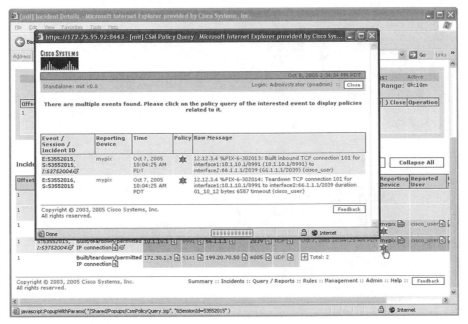

Figure 10-15 *Access Control List (ACL) Rule Table Display*

The linkages between Cisco Security MARS and Cisco Security Manager provide another example of how centralized management is the "coach" that allows the self-defending network to be deployed and managed in an integrated and holistic fashion.

Summary

Cisco Security MARS is a monitoring and reporting component of a self-defending network. Cisco Security MARS can also mitigate or generate configurations that can stop certain attacks and can allow the network to be self-defending. Some of the configurations that can be generated by Cisco Security MARS include the CLI to shut a LAN port, enable an IPS signature on an IOS ISR or an access control list (ACL) rule. Cisco Security MARS can automatically generate CLI to reduce the risk of an attack, or Cisco Security MARS can recommend the CLI to be manually deployed by SSH (Secure Shell) or the Cisco Security Manager. Cisco Security MARS will only recommend and will not deploy the CLI to configure an access control list (ACL) rule.

Cisco Security MARS contains a high-level summary dashboard that includes incidents, hotspot graphs, and attack diagrams. An incident can be an indication that a high-level security attack, such as a Nimda attack, has been detected on the network. An incident is composed of security events and monitoring data that is received from known devices in the self-defending network, including routers, LAN switches, firewalls, IPS devices, hosts, databases, and storage appliances. Netflow data can be used to establish a baseline of normal traffic on a network. Netflow can be used to identify and filter false positives from valid security incidents. Rules are used to trigger a security incident. Cisco Security MARS contains many default or system inspection rules. Cisco Security MARS also features the ability to create custom or user-defined rules.

The dashboard lists actionable, high-level security incidents. A hotspot graph and attack diagram are also created for a significant security incident. A hotspot graph contains the path of the network attack, including the source, destination, and known devices within the attack path. The attack diagram displays the session IDs reported by devices for the incident. Cisco Security MARS and Cisco Security Manager are components of the Cisco Security Management suite. Cisco Security MARS contains linkages with Cisco Security Manager. For example, a user can select a syslog from an incident and see the access control list (ACL) rule policy in Cisco Security Manager that generated the syslog.

References

Cisco Systems, Inc. Cisco Security Monitoring, Analysis and Response System 4.2 Data Sheet. http://www.cisco.com/en/US/products/ps6241/products_data_sheet0900aecd80272e64.html

Cisco Systems, Inc. *Cisco Security Monitoring, Analysis and Response System Q&A*. http://www.cisco.com/en/US/products/ps6241/products_qanda_item0900aecd8027a051.shtml

Cisco Systems, Inc. Cisco Router and Security Device Manager. http://www.cisco.com/en/US/products/sw/secursw/ps5318/index.html

Cisco Systems, Inc. Technology Preview: Configuring Distributed Threat Mitigation in Cisco Security MARS. http://www.cisco.com/en/US/products/ps6241/products_configuration_example09186a008067a2b0.shtml

INDEX

NUMERICS

E–F

G–H

I–J–K

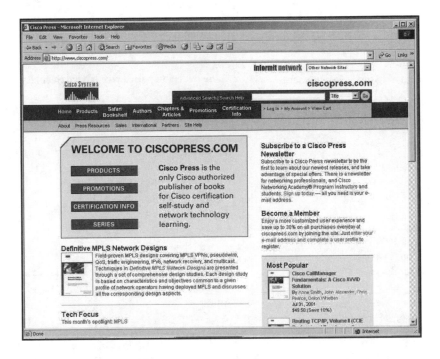